"*Growing Up Feeling Good* is a book no child sho[...] will be richer for reading it and learn that they are [...] *Growing Up Feeling Good* is also a fantastic resource for parents & teachers." **- June Pihl, Former State President, Oregon State PTA**

"It is the desire of all parents that their children grow up with positive feelings about themselves. I have found Ellen Rosenberg's book, *Growing Up Feeling Good*, to be an excellent resource for parents and caring adults to share with their adolescents. A comprehensive life handbook, *Growing Up Feeling Good* helps young people value themselves, and provides a wealth of information that helps prepare them for the many physical and emotional changes they will face. *Growing Up Feeling Good* is open, honest and right on target." **- Guy W. Sims, Superintendent of Education, Muscogee County School District, Columbus, GA**

"*Growing Up Feeling Good* fills an ever-widening gap between pre-adolescents and their families. It offers a marvelous venue for both pre-adolescent and parent to look into each other's mind and soul. *Growing Up Feeling Good* offers crucial information to help youngsters navigate the very complicated waters of late childhood and early adolescence. It's honest, clear, thoughtful, non-threatening and laced with good will and humor. *Growing Up Feeling Good* is a wonderful foundation for the kinds [...] the bedrock for healthy [...] **t Zeller, Ed.D., Director, [...] Elliot-Pearson Departm[...]**

"I rea[...] great! It's the longes[...] how to have livelie[...]

"*Grou*[...] the personal anecd[...] ny daughters expres[...] t or other adoles[...] erg's book." - Sand[...]

"*Grou*[...] randchildren. The d[...] . I wish I had this b[...] ndmother of 7

"Few books come along that impact children, parents and teachers. *Growing Up Feeling Good* allows children to find out answers to questions that sometimes they are not comfortable talking about with their parents or guardians. *Growing Up Feeling Good* is also an excellent reference for parents and teachers. My wife and I are both educators who have background in child development and *Growing Up Feeling Good* was a very valuable resource for us when our two children were growing up all the way through their graduation from high school. I highly recommend *Growing Up Feeling Good* as a "must" for all parents/guardians to share with their children." **- Dr. Darrel Lang, Program Consultant, Health, Human Sexuality and Physical Education, Kansas State Department of Education**

"I received *Growing Up Feeling Good* early in my adolescence, and it has helped me through many of the growing pains associated with my teenage years. It taught me that no 'crisis' was unique to me. Ellen's straightforward and honest delivery helped me feel more grounded, more clear about what was real, and more comfortable dealing with any problem I may have had." **- Ryan Abrams, Age 18**

"Ellen's book is great! It's really helped me to understand a lot of things. It's also made it easier for me to discuss sensitive issues with my parents and friends." **- Case Bodamer, Age 13**

"*Growing Up Feeling Good* is a wonderful tool to help every student with the roller coaster ride of adolescence. I was given the book when I was twelve and it helped me through some difficult times. It made me feel that I was normal and boosted my self-confidence. It gave me the strength to be myself, to be who I am and not be afraid." **- Christina Fitzpatrick, Elementary School Teacher**

"Rosenberg deals sensitively and supportively with the questions and quandaries faced by pre and young teens. [book] provides an unusually complete compilation of up-to-date and accurate information about growing up female and male, drugs, popularity, divorce, step families, and much more." **- *School Library Journal***

GROWING UP
FEELING GOOD

—

by Ellen Rosenberg

REVISED EDITION

LIMA BEAN PRESS, INC.
630 Shore Road, Suite 505, Long Beach, New York 11561

First published in the United States of America by Beaufort Books, 1983
Revised edition published by Beaufort Books, 1987
Published in Puffin Books, 1989
Second revised edition published in Puffin Books, a division
of Penguin Books, USA Inc., 1995
This third revised edition published by Lima Bean Press, Inc., 2002

Illustrations by Judy Golden
Cover design by Foster & Foster

ISBN 0-9711349-0-1
Library of Congress Control Number: 2001118372

Printed in South Korea.

DEDICATION

To my husband, Roger, and our children, Andy and Hillary:
The love we have for each other—and all that we continue to share is something I will treasure for the rest of my life.

To all children:
May you be blessed with a lifetime of love, good health, and inner peace.
May you have the wisdom and sensitivity to be able to respect not only yourself, but those around you.
May you have the strength and confidence to be who you are and the courage to become all that you dream to be.

ACKNOWLEDGMENTS

There are so many people to thank:

George Greenfield, my literary agent, who believed in this book from the very start. Thank you for your creative energy, support, and all you have done to make *Growing Up Feeling Good* a reality.

Helene Sloan, Professor Emerita, Chairman, Department of Health & Nutrition Sciences, City University of New York, Brooklyn College, my mentor and dear friend—You "planted the seed" which led to my concentration on developing programs for and related to children. Thank you for your wisdom, sensitivity, and encouragement. Knowing you has so positively influenced my growth and has enriched my life.

Dr. Michael Carerra, Director, Adolescent Sexuality and Pregnancy Prevention Program, The Childrens' Aid Society, New York—you were the catalyst that inspired my decision to specialize in the area of human sexuality. Your personal advice and encouragement made an immeasurable difference.

I am very grateful to those who carefully reviewed chapters and sections of my book. "Thank you" seems inadequate for giving of your time, insight, and expertise. Your contribution was invaluable:

David Friedli, Principal, Omaha Nation Public School, Macy, Nebraska (review of drug chapter);

JoAnn Owens-Nauslar, Ed. D., Health Educator, President of "Fitness is Living," Lincoln, Nebraska, the Director of Professional Development for the American School Health Association (review of AIDS section and entire sex chapter);

Valerie Pinhas, Ph.D., Professor of Health Education, Nassau Community College, Garden City, New York, psychoanalyst, certified substance abuse and alcoholism counselor, New York State (review of entire book, with special concentration on the drug chapter);

Andy Rosenberg, my son—for your invaluable reviewing and consultation. Your input made a significant difference, especially in drug chapter revisions;

Mindell Seidlin, M.D., Assistant Professor of Clinical Medicine at NYU School of Medicine, former director, Bellevue Hospital AIDS program (review of the AIDS section);

Ron Sylvester, Educational Consultant (review of drug chapter);

Sally Sylvester, Health Educator and HIV Prevention Specialist, Scottsbluff, Nebraska (review of AIDS section and entire sex chapter).

Hillary Sussman, my daughter—for your insightful critiques/evaluations and consultation. Your input and support continue to mean so much.

Marion London, Director, Project Charlie—for your consultation, insight, accessibility, support, and your wonderful friendship.

I will always be grateful to all others, too numerous to name, who shared their professional knowledge and experience with me. Thank you for your time, resources, and information, as well as your enthusiastic response to what this book represents. While people have offered specific input I take full responsibility for the accuracy of the text.

Growing Up Feeling Good is much richer because of all the people in schools and communities across the United States who let me into their lives and trusted me with their personal feelings and concerns. I remain deeply touched and thankful for all you shared.

To all the children and parents who participated in my RAP sessions-special thanks for your trust and all that you shared with me. The more that we shared, the more I learned that such sharing (talking about feelings) was so needed. My *Growing Up Feeling Good* programs and book are an outgrowth of our beginning experiences together.

Special, special thanks to my parents-for all you have given of yourselves, for always caring enough to listen, and for all you continue to teach me about expressing and sharing love. Largely because of you, I have wonderful memories of "growing up feeling good."

To Emma—Love, hugs and gratitude for all your assistance and support.

I will always be grateful to my husband, Roger, for understanding and respecting what this book represents, and for helping to keep our family in balance when I was in "hibernation," passionately working to meet my deadlines.

And I will always smile at the memory of all the supportive extra hugs from my children, Andy and Hillary, all the calls from upstairs to my little writing room in the basement to see how I was doing when I first wrote this book. Thank you for never running the other way when you knew I was approaching with papers in hand, to ask you to read "just one more section and tell me what you think!" Your responses continue to be so helpful and your support continues to mean so much.

Susan Suffes, my editor for the first edition. Working with you meant so much. Thank you for your openness, for being so accessible, for your time, excellent advice, and commitment to *Growing Up Feeling Good*.

Deborah Brodie, my editor at Viking Children's Books for the previous revised edition. Working with you was inspiring and always, wonderful. Your wisdom, clarity, and sensitive suggestions made such a difference. Beyond all you gave to *Growing Up Feeling Good* professionally, thank you for your personal support and for your friendship, which I treasure.

To Jennie Chun—Thank you for all the time and hard work you put into incorporating and helping to finalize the revisions for this new edition; and for your patience, expertise, and enthusiasm for all that *Growing Up Feeling Good* represents. Working with you has been such a pleasure.

Contents

PREFACE

Growing up is an adventure. It's exciting and fun, but also can be difficult. Some things that may happen with friends, family or at school will be easy to deal with. Other experiences will be more challenging. *Growing Up Feeling Good* is filled with life lessons and tools to help you live the day-to-day changes, feelings, relationships, pressures and choices that you'll face while growing up.

Since starting my school programs in 1976, I have spoken with and especially, listened to, more than a million students, staff and parents in forty-six states. Through anonymous sharing cards and open discussions, students continue to tell me what's really going on in their lives, what they want and need to know, what they often tell me they haven't told anyone else.

The first edition of *Growing Up Feeling Good* was published in 1983. As kids' lives have changed, *Growing Up Feeling Good* has been updated and revised. I'm so glad to be able to share this newest edition with you.

I hope that *Growing Up Feeling Good* will help you feel even more positive about yourself and your relationships, and help to enrich your life while growing up – and beyond.

You may decide to read *Growing Up Feeling Good* with friends and family, and discuss it in school. You might even want to leave it open at a certain page on your parent's pillow with a note saying. "Please read – so we can talk about this later!" And especially, you can curl up in a private place and read it all to yourself.

Part I

GROWING UP FEELING GOOD ABOUT YOUR BODY

Before I explain what the changes are, it's important for you to understand why they happen in the first place.

You may have been told about the pituitary gland (pi-too-i-terry) which is located at the base of your brain and is in charge of when and how your body will grow. Development will begin when the pituitary gland signals the release of hormones or chemicals which travel around your body in your bloodstream.

Estrogen (es-tro-jen) in girls and testosterone (tes-tos-ter-own) in boys, are the main hormones which are responsible for causing the changes in you that take place during puberty (pew-ber-tee: the period of growth when you develop and mature).

Perhaps it would be easier to imagine that inside each person is a "growth clock" with an alarm set to go off when their body is ready to begin to mature. Some time, it may be as early as age nine or not until age sixteen or seventeen, your body will start to change. If you start in your late teens, you may not finish developing until you are in your early twenties.

The alarm or signal from your pituitary gland is "set" at a special time for you. It has nothing to do with when your friends start to develop. And you cannot change the timing of the "clock".

This means that boys and girls who are the same age will be at different stages of development throughout the growing years. Some of your friends will be first to mature and some will be last. There's no telling exactly where you will fit in.

How do you think you would feel if you were among the first to develop? The last? In the middle? Maybe some of the feelings you think you would have will help you understand how other kids might feel if that's what happened to them.

Physical development doesn't always match feelings or maturity. Some kids who feel very grown up and mature inside might find that they will have to wait for their bodies to develop and catch-up to those feelings. Others might be physically developed at an early age but not yet mature inside.

If kids thought aloud, you might hear someone say, "How come I'm the tallest?" Or perhaps they might be thinking, "I'm thirteen, I'm supposed to have started to develop by now. Why do I have to be the one to wait? I hope there's nothing wrong with me." Lots of kids wonder whether they are growing as they should. I asked myself those same questions.

If you're very concerned about waiting too long to start developing, speak with your parents or guardian and together with them you can check with your doctor. Chances are it's your old friend, the pituitary gland, that's taking its time with your "signal". Hang in there. Just keep telling yourself that your turn will come too!

Though you can't do anything about your size or how quickly you will grow, it's important to accept your own time schedule for development. Hard as it may seem, try to be patient. It's also important to respect differences in others.

How does your size compare to that of your friends right now? If you are more or less developed, does it add to or take away from how good you feel about yourself? Maybe this is the first time you've thought about this.

Please note: I purposely wrote Chapters 1, 2 and 3 as if to girl readers and Chapters 4, 5 and 6 as if to boy readers. It seemed more personal to write it that way. But I want you to know that even though I write "you", all chapters are for both boys and girls. I feel it's not only important to understand your own development, but also what happens to the other sex.

If you become aware of the many feelings and concerns which might relate to each other's growth, hopefully there will be greater understanding, more respect, and less teasing.

Well, let's begin – we've got a lot to talk about!

GROWING UP FEMALE
FEELING GOOD

CHAPTER 1

BREASTS

What Are Breasts?

When a girl's body begins to mature, she will notice two bumps in her chest area. These bumps will grow into soft, sensitive, round organs known as breasts. People also call them mammaries, bosoms, and boobs. Lots of kids refer to them as "tits."

You may be interested to know that it is also normal for boys to experience some breast swelling during puberty. This is caused by hormones and has nothing to do with being like a girl. In time, this swelling will go away. Both girls and boys may feel some tenderness in their breasts as development takes place.

Breasts are composed mainly of soft tissue (not Kleenex!) and mammary glands. These glands produce milk when a woman gives birth to a baby.

The openings of the mammary glands are in the nipples. A nipple can be found in the center of the darkened area, called the *areola* (air-EE-o-la), in the middle of each breast. Nipples may stand out a lot or a little. Sometimes they may even point inward (which is called inverted nipples).

You may find that a few hairs will grow around your nipples and breasts. Many girls and women have such hairs. It is important not to pull them out, as you might cause an infection, but you can trim them carefully with scissors if you wish.

Both boys' and girls' breasts can be sensitive when touched. The nipple is usually the most sensitive part of the breast and may become erect (stiffened and pointy) from time to time, such as when brushed over by a bed sheet, if the temperature is cold, or when touched directly.

Breasts help to round out a girl's shape and add nicely to her appearance. The shape and size of the breasts is mostly due to the amount of soft tissue that is present around the mammary glands. Though the amount of soft tissue may vary from woman to woman, all women have about the same supply of mammary glands. So, whether larger or smaller, no matter how different breasts appear on the outside, they all "work" the same on the inside (yes, even if you're flat!).

What Size Will You Be?

If you just look around your classroom, in department stores, on street corners, especially at the beach, or anywhere, you will notice that breasts develop in many shapes and sizes (check this out if you haven't noticed already).

When I was younger, we used to call smaller breasts lemons, oranges, or even tangerines. Medium-sized breasts were grapefruits, cantaloupes, or just plain melons, and big boobs were called watermelons. We were sure that women with "watermelons" didn't need a life preserver when swimming because "the bigger they were, the better they would float!" We would say things like, "Oh, can you believe how big Debby got this summer? Hers are almost like watermelons! It's amazing she doesn't fall over when she walks!"

Even though we laughed and giggled and whispered about her breasts (which appeared "humongous" compared to our flat chests!), Debby seemed to be very proud of her development. She never toppled over and even played soccer as well as she did before she grew. We soon stopped whispering and got used to Debby's new shape. I think we were secretly jealous because most of us didn't even have a hint of a bump on our chests and were beginning to worry that we would be flat-chested forever.

Girls today continue to wonder what size they will be. The fact is, you may be as large as, larger than, or smaller than your mother, sister, or grandmother. Breast size can be very different in the same family (my sister is larger than I am and she's younger).

When your breasts start to grow, usually it will take several years for them to reach their full size. Only then will you have an exact answer about your size. I'd have to be a wizard to be able to figure it out for you ahead of time. You may develop like other women in your family. Or you may not.

It's also important to know that like feet, breasts can be different sizes even on the same body. Though some girls worry that they will be lopsided, especially when one breast begins to develop earlier than the other, this difference is quite normal (and won't make you lopsided). In time, they usually grow to be about the same size.

Some people think large breasts are terrific. Others prefer smaller breasts. Ten-year-old Amy said, "I don't want those big things hanging on my body." Jennifer, age eleven, told me she wears three sweatshirts just to make it seem like she is very developed.

There are girls who want to make themselves appear larger and those who are so glad their body has not yet begun to change. Still others are very happy just the way they are, developed or not.

How do you feel about breast size? Have you already started to develop? It really is so hard to imagine how it will feel to have breasts. It might help to realize that it is not better or worse to be larger or smaller. Everyone is different.

Karen's breasts were small when she was growing up. She remembers comparing herself with friends who were very developed and thinking that maybe the boys would be more interested in them because they were bigger. Girls still compare and wonder about this. Boys still look! But there's a difference between liking to look at breasts and liking a person because they have breasts.

I think you'll find, as Karen did, that people will like you because you're you, not because of how developed you are. If someone cares more about your size than about you as a person, they're not much of a friend anyway.

The size of your breasts has nothing to do with the kind of person you are or whether people will think you are more womanly. That depends upon how you feel and who you are inside. You can't control your size but you can always control who you are as a woman.

When Will Your Breasts Develop?

Another concern about breast development is when? How quickly will breasts appear and when can you expect them to arrive?

Just as you cannot know for sure what size you will be, you also can't know exactly when your body will start to change . . . until it does.

Maybe that's very frustrating to you. I know it was to me. I was impatient. I was tired of looking like a child, especially when many of my friends were beginning to look more and more like women. I wanted to know when and no one could tell me. Have you had any of these feelings?

The plain truth is that your breasts will grow when they're ready to. It all depends upon when your pituitary gland gives the signal to start the release of your hormones. It's up to your body, not you! No amount of watering will make your breasts develop faster or sooner. Praying won't help. Neither will exercises.

Well, at least you don't have to study for breasts! They will simply start to swell, possibly when you least expect them to grow. You do not have to worry about going to sleep flat and waking up with fully grown breasts. (I can remember getting out of bed in the middle of the night just to check if my breasts had appeared!)

Since growth is a process that takes place over a period of time, your body will have time to get used to having breasts. When you're an older teenager (say around seventeen or eighteen), it will be important to learn to do breast self-examinations. Doing this examination regularly will help you know your own breast tissue so that if there is ever a change, you would notice it as early as possible. It's important to be as aware as you can about the health of your breasts.

Feeling Good about Breast Development Is Not Always Easy

Some girls do not seem to be able to feel good about their breast development. They may curve their shoulders forward in order to make their breasts seem smaller or less noticeable. They may also curve their shoulders to try to hide breasts that seem too tiny.

Judy, now thirty-two, remembers carrying her school books in front to try to hide her growing chest. I, of course, carried my books in front to try to hide the fact that I didn't have a growing chest!

Susan, a thirteen-year-old with larger breasts, shared, "Every time the teacher is ready to call on someone to come up to the board, I wish I could hide under my desk. I'm afraid to walk up to the front of the room because people tease and make fun of me when I'm up there. The teacher can't hear them, but I know they do it."

It may not always be easy to be more developed than most other girls, just as it can be hard to be much less developed. Being right in the middle seems the easiest. But, as I mentioned before, certain girls will be larger and others will be smaller. That's just the way things are.

I suppose there will always be people who like to tease. Breasts seem to be a target for teasing. Some kids tease because they are embarrassed about their own lack of development. If they call attention to others, maybe they think less attention will be on them. Still others might tease because development is so new and a bit strange. They may be jealous or uncomfortable about the changing bodies all around them.

Accepting these changes may take time. I wonder what would happen if Susan stood tall, walked proudly to the front of the room, completed her work at the board, and walked proudly back to her desk—smiling at everyone as she moved!

Do you think Susan's classmates would still feel like teasing if she seemed so confident and ignored any remarks? What else do you think she could do?

Dawn, age fourteen, shared the same kinds of feelings that Susan had. But Dawn was embarrassed about going up to the front of the classroom because she hadn't yet started to develop breasts!

I wonder if anyone really grows to the exact size they hope to be, when they hope to be. Dawn and Susan might feel better about themselves if they could accept where they are in their development. It would also help if other kids would realize that development cannot be controlled, and teasing can be very hurtful.

It would really help if people would try to be strong and happy about who they are and worry less about what size they are.

Wearing a Bra

Jodi, an eighth-grader now, so clearly remembers coming home one day in the sixth grade and saying to her mother, "I must have a bra *today*! I can't wait until tomorrow. . . ."

Said Jodi, "If size was considered, I probably could have waited a few years. But Mom took me for a bra that afternoon." Jodi's mom must have understood that the bra was important to Jodi more because of Jodi's friends (many of them wore bras) than her tiny breasts. Jodi told me she got a training bra and felt terrific, like she really belonged.

Did you ever wonder why it's called a "training" bra? It really doesn't do any training. I can't imagine what breasts could be taught to do!

Marge, now in her forties, remembers, "I was so excited to get a bra before my close friend. But I never grew out of that first bra into a bigger size. The bra that I wear now is the same as when I was twelve (not the same bra—new bra, same size!). When my friend finally did get her bra, she bulged out of it really soon, then kept bulging and bulging and needing new sizes. I was so jealous!"

It might be fun to ask your mom, grandma, aunt, or older sister about their first bras. Though it may have been many years ago, you might be surprised to find they will smile and talk about special, often funny experiences that will be wonderful to remember and even better to share with you.

Girls often ask me, "What if I don't want to wear a bra? Do I have to?" Wearing a bra is a matter of your own choice and comfort, even if you are playing a sport. Whether you are larger or smaller breasted, you may prefer to wear a bra for support if you run and jump for long periods of time. Or you may not.

Many doctors feel you will not harm or stretch the breast tissue if you do not wear a bra during exercise or at all. You may wish to wear a bra, but you don't have to.

Lisa, age eleven, said she plans to wait until her best friend wears a bra so they can start wearing them together. Lisa is very developed and her friend has not yet begun (Lisa could be waiting for years!).

Jessica, age twelve, said she refused to wear a bra at home but made sure to take one away with her when she went to summer camp in case the other girls in her cabin wore bras. Sure enough, they did and she was glad she brought one. Much to the surprise of her parents, she even sent home for more bras.

Debra, age ten, said, "I think I would feel uncomfortable about wearing a bra because if I wear light-colored shirts, boys might see my bra and make fun of me." Jill, age eleven, said, "It makes me feel very grown-up to wear a bra. Sometimes I wear shirts that you can see through a little, just so other people can know I'm wearing one!"

Lisa did not want to be the only one wearing a bra. Jessica did not want to be the only girl without a bra. Debra thought she would feel funny and be teased if anyone noticed she was wearing one. Jill sometimes wore clothes that would make sure other people know she was wearing a bra. As you can see, there are so many different ways girls may feel about wearing a bra. How about you? What are your feelings?

As far as I know, "Bra Laws" just do not exist! I have never seen a sign anywhere which states, "Girls with breasts will not be allowed in without wearing a bra." The choice is up to you.

Take a good look in the mirror. If you can say to yourself, "I feel really great about the way I look," then you'll be able to feel more confident and proud about your appearance, bra or no bra (no matter what anyone else is doing).

Talking About Bras

Many girls have told me they find it hard to share their feelings about such things as wearing a bra or not. They feel kind of funny or embarrassed. They're not sure what to say and are sometimes worried about what parents or friends will say back.

If you have ever had those funny feelings, at least you know you are not alone. Lots of girls have them (grown-ups, too!). Since parents or friends can't know exactly how you feel unless you tell them your feelings, it is important to get your courage up to try.

Once you begin, you'll probably be surprised and relieved to find it will be easier and easier to talk. And it usually feels a lot better if you get your feelings out rather than keeping them inside you.

The first words are often the hardest to get out. Here are some ideas about how you might begin to talk about your feelings (you can add your own ideas to this list):

What you might say to your parents if you want a bra

- "Mom, Dad . . . I really want to wear a bra!"
- "Most of my friends are wearing bras. I'd feel better if I could wear one, too."
- "This is kind of funny to talk about, but I want to get a bra (or go shopping for a bra)."
- "I don't know if you've noticed or not, but I think I'm ready to wear a bra."
- "I want to talk with you about wearing a bra."
- "Mom, what age were you when you started to wear a bra?"

Did you notice that I suggested you can say, "Mom" or "Dad"? I'll never forget the thirteen-year-old girl who ran after me in the hall after I presented a program to her class. She said, "Can you tell me how I can help my friend? She lives with her dad and she doesn't know what she's going to do when she needs to talk with him about periods or bras and those kinds of girl things. How can I help her?"

We talked for a while and when I left her, I felt relieved that she seemed to understand that even though dads don't have breasts, they know about them. They also know about bras and even about periods. So, even if it feels kind of funny or embarrassing, that friend could say to her dad (turning feelings into words), "Dad, I feel kind of funny saying this to you. I didn't know if I could talk with you about getting a bra. But I thought I'd try."

One dad told me how relieved he was that he was able to talk to his daughter about bras. He said, "It was great that she felt we could talk about it. But we both decided that she'd probably be more comfortable shopping with her grandmother."

It would be great for both boys and girls to understand that you can talk with both moms and dads—and other important male or female adults you trust—about personal things. If you've never tried talking with a parent or other adult of the other sex before, you can decide to start now. It's never too late to start.

You might be happily surprised to find yourself feeling even closer to that person once you see how special it is to be able to talk about things like this that are important to you. You can learn more, too.

What you might say to your parents if they insist on getting you a bra and you don't want to wear one

- "Mom, Dad . . . I really don't want to wear a bra!"
- "Please don't make me wear a bra. I don't want to wear one."
- "I want to talk with you about not wearing a bra."
- "I don't even want to talk about bras."
- "Most of my friends don't wear bras and I think I'd feel better if I waited a little longer before I got one."
- "It's hard for me to say this to you, but I hate bras. Please don't make me wear one."

What you might say to your friend if you think she needs a bra

- "Did you ever think about how great you might look if you wore a bra?"
- "This is not easy for me to say, but I really think you need a bra."
- "Wouldn't it be fun to go shopping for a bra?"
- "____, you need a bra!!"
- "I really think you would look great (or even better) if you wore a bra."

Many girls feel it would be better to say such things privately, when you're alone with that friend. If you consider the other person's feelings and try to be nice, you'll find it easier to be honest. (Keep in mind that what your friend decides to do is her own choice. This is a *personal* decision.)

How to Figure Your Bra Size

In case you are thinking about getting a bra, you might be interested in knowing how to figure out what size bra you can wear or if you are ready to wear one.

If you place a tape measure around your body right under your breasts and add five to that number, you will determine your bra size.

For example, if right under your breasts measures 29 inches, you would add 5 to 29. This equals 34, so your bra size would be 34.

Cup size can be measured by placing the tape around your body at the fullest part of the bust (at the nipples). The difference between this measurement and your bra size gives you the cup size. If the numbers are equal, the cup size would be AA. If the difference is 1 inch, the cup size equals A, 2 inches would equal a B cup, and so on up to D and DD.

A first bra usually has no specific cup size (usually it's "one size fits all") and can start at size 28. During the years when your body is growing and changing, it's a good idea to check your measurements every six months, as you might find your size will change.

There are many different styles of bras from which to choose. Most stores carry bras up to size 42 or 44. Larger sizes can be bought at specialty stores.

Just as there are salespeople who are trained to fit your shoe size properly, there are women who are trained to fit bras. My sister and I called these women "bra ladies." It is their job to help you find a bra that is comfortable and the right size.

You may be thinking, "Oh gross! I'm not going to let anyone measure me!" Well, it might help to realize that these women fit bras all day long for girls and women of all ages, shapes, and sizes. They are used to seeing lots of breasts. They'll probably understand that this experience is new for you and will be sensitive to your feelings.

If you do not feel comfortable, it may help if you tell your feelings to the saleswoman (or at least to the person who might be shopping with you). You might say, "This is the first time I'm getting a bra. I feel funny (or embarrassed or uncomfortable)."

These feelings are very natural. And if you really object to having someone you don't know measure you, you can do what my mom and I did when I got my first bra. We had the "bra lady" explain to us what we needed to do and then did all the figuring ourselves. The saleswoman was able to check if we were right once I tried on the bra. After a while I didn't mind letting her help me. I just had to get used to the idea; so will you.

You can also simply help yourself to one of the many bras hanging on racks in the teen sections of many clothing stores and see how it feels to try it on.

It's nice to know there are several ways to feel even better about shopping for a bra.

Bra Giggles

My friends and I used to call bras "over-the-shoulder-boulder-holders" and laughed at bras and underwear in store windows and magazines.

We laughed even harder when we tried on our mothers' bras and stuffed them with socks and stockings. How amazing it was to imagine that we would fill our own bras some day. We were excited, scared, and impatient at the same time.

Once, while playing volleyball in gym class in the eighth grade, I was positioned in the back row and noticed something fall onto the floor right in front of the net. It was round and white.

I remember thinking it was a strange looking volleyball. Did the ball lose all its air? When we realized what had happened, we dropped to the floor and doubled up with laughter.

The one girl who remained standing in the front row (who was definitely not laughing) appeared very red—no, purple in the face. She had stuffed her bra with a good-sized piece of cotton and it flew out while she was jumping for the ball.

If it were me, I think I would have run into the locker room, crawled into the nearest locker, and thrown away the combination, never again to appear on the gym floor. But she really took it very well. After a few minutes, she just started laughing with the rest of us.

Funny and embarrassing things just seem to happen while a person is growing up. In fact they never stop happening. It's wonderful to have a good sense of humor and be able to laugh at yourself.

When the laughter quieted down, we all continued the volleyball game (I still smile when I see balls of cotton).

We would have liked her—and did—even without what appeared to be breasts. All she had to be was herself.

I Hope by Now You Realize . . .

Though there may not be anything you can do about how and when you develop, I hope by now you realize there are many things you can do to try to feel as good about yourself as possible. You can understand what is happening to your body and why. You can wear clothes that are flattering to your size, whatever it may be.

You can let yourself be the special person you are inside and accept yourself, whether you have "watermelons," "grapefruits," or "lemons," or have not yet begun to grow. You may be very happily surprised that your friends will respect and appreciate you as you respect and appreciate yourself.

REMEMBER: *People do not make friends with breasts;*
they make friends with people!

CHAPTER 2

PRIVATE PARTS

Did you ever wonder what is inside the different parts of your body? Though each part is important, I think the sex organs, also called *genitals* (JEN-i-tulls), are especially interesting because they are involved with *reproduction*, being able to create babies.

There are lots of slang names for these organs, probably because kids and even some adults feel embarrassed or don't know their real names.

No matter what you call them, it's important to at least know the correct names and learn as much as you can about how these organs work. The more you understand about your body and yourself, the more confident and comfortable you will be.

Internal Genitals

First, let's take a look at the inside (internal) parts.

If you make a paper circle that measures four inches from side to side, then put the top of the circle about one inch below your belly button, you'll have a better idea of about how much room your internal reproductive organs take up. Such a small area for such important organs!

UTERUS (YOU-ter-us), also called the womb (rhymes with *room*), is shaped like an upside-down pear. This is the special place where an unborn baby grows when a woman is pregnant. The unborn baby is referred to as an *embryo* (EM-bree-yo) in the beginning months of development and after that a *fetus* (FEE-tus) until born. It's almost like magic that the uterine walls are able to stretch and stretch as the unborn baby gets larger and larger (sort of like a balloon that slowly gets filled with more air).

The uterus gives the unborn baby a place to grow and develop. Since the lining of the uterus has many blood vessels, it helps the baby develop by supplying nourishment (food) and oxygen. The uterus also has strong muscles that help move the baby out when it is ready to be born.

CERVIX (SIR-vicks) is the "neck" of the uterus. Since the uterus sticks its "neck" out into the back of the vagina, the cervix is between the back of the vagina and the uterus. The glands in the lining of the cervix secrete a sticky fluid called mucus (MEW-kuss). When a woman is pregnant, the cervix is usually closed by a plug of mucus that prevents bacteria from entering the uterus.

OVARIES (O-va-reez) are about the size of a walnut and can be found on either side of the uterus. When a girl is born, her ovaries contain from tens to hundreds of thousands of follicles. Each follicle is a small sac that contains an immature or unripe egg cell (not the kind you find in the supermarket!).

The ovaries are responsible for releasing female hormones or chemicals that help to make a girl's body develop and mature. They also have the important job of releasing one ripened egg cell each month, usually beginning when a girl gets her period.

A single egg cell is called an *ovum*; many eggs are called *ova*. These are the egg cells that can be *fertilized* (FER-ti-lized) or entered by a sperm cell from a male in order to develop into a baby. Because the ovum is so tiny (much smaller than the head of a straight pin), the only way you can see it is under a microscope.

More about egg cells and what happens when they ripen is included in the next chapter, on menstruation (getting your period).

You can get an idea of what your *Fallopian* (fa-LO-pee-an) *tubes* look like if you put your arms out at your sides, shoulder height, and point

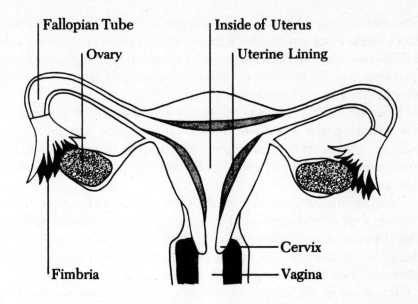

Fallopian Tube

Ovary

Inside of Uterus

Uterine Lining

Cervix

Vagina

Fimbria

your fingers to the floor. (Try it! It's really fun to imitate Fallopian tubes.) Each tube is about 4 inches long, and it extends down from either the left or right side of the uterus toward the ovary.

Each Fallopian tube is like a roadway that transports the ovum from an ovary to the uterus. If fertilization (sperm meets egg) is going to take place, it will happen in one of the tubes.

The outside ends of the tubes look like fingers and are called *fimbria* (FIM-bree-a). They flare toward each ovary but do not connect with the ovaries. That's why when an egg ripens in an ovary, it has to burst through the surface of the ovary in order to get out and be drawn into the Fallopian tube to start its journey toward the uterus. When the egg cell bursts through the surface, that's called *ovulation* (ah-vue-LAY-shun).

So now you know it's one of the Fallopian tubes that receives the egg cell that is released by the ovary. The tubes have tiny, wavy hairs called *cilia* (SILLY-uh) that help move the egg along since it can't move by itself.

VAGINA (va-JIE-na). The *vagina*, if you spread your legs apart, is the second opening from the front down between your legs. The *urethra* (you-REE-thra), through which liquid waste, or urine, passes, is the first; and the *anus* (AY-nuss), the passageway for solid wastes, is third. Since solid waste passed through the anus contains bacteria (back-TEER-ee-a) that can cause infections if spread to your vaginal and urethral openings, it's healthier for you to wipe yourself from front to rear after having a bowel movement.

Since the vagina connects the uterus with the outside genitals, it's not surprising that it is the birth canal. It's fantastic how the vaginal walls are able to stretch and allow a baby to pass through. If a girl or woman uses tampons when she has her period, this is the place where they are inserted.

Most of the time, the walls of the vagina are close together. If you imagine a glove without a hand in it, that's what the vaginal walls are like. Then imagine putting a hand in it and watch, in your mind, how the glove expands and allows your hand to enter it. Like the empty glove, the walls of the vagina are able to expand when necessary.

The walls of the vagina form a tube that measures about 3 to 5 inches long. The opening of the vagina can be seen if the *labia* (LAY-be-a), or lips, are parted. Sometimes the walls of the vagina will feel moist, as if they were sweating.

There are vaginal muscles which you can tighten, relax, and even exercise. You can locate them when you go to the bathroom by trying to stop your urination in the middle. The outer part of the vagina (including the opening) is sensitive to touch. The innermost part is not.

HYMEN (HI-mun). This is a flexible fold of tissue that surrounds and partly covers the opening of the vagina. It looks slightly different on each girl. Some girls are born without one (they can get along fine without it).

The appearance of the hymen changes when it becomes stretched. Some parents are concerned that using tampons (inserted through the opening of the vagina) will cause the hymen to be pushed back, but it's flexible enough to prevent this from happening in most cases.

The usual way for the hymen to become pushed back is the first time a woman has *sexual intercourse* (SEX-you-al IN-ter-corse) with a man. (See special note below.)

SPECIAL NOTE: Even though I'm going to talk about sexual intercourse later, here's an explanation (just to make sure we're both talking about the same thing). When a man and woman have sexual intercourse, they hug and get very close, then they move together in a special way that allows the man's penis (I'll explain more about male bodies in Chapter 4) to be placed inside the opening of the woman's vagina. They just fit snugly together. Remember, the walls of the vagina are able to stretch to allow this to happen in a comfortable way.

There are lots of feelings that go along with having sexual intercourse. The penis and vagina are only parts of people. Penises and vaginas don't love each other; people do! Most parents have very strong feelings about what they want to teach their kids about sexual intercourse and when they feel it is appropriate to make the decision to share so closely—especially since this kind of sharing can sometimes lead to pregnancy and can possibly result in serious infections and diseases, including AIDS.

If you haven't already talked with your parents about this, it will be important for you to give them a chance to share their feelings and ideas with you. This is a very personal topic. Besides sharing any feelings about religious beliefs and values, you might also find that your parent—or other important adult in your life—will talk about such concerns as marriage, love, respect, responsibility, and the importance of understanding what the possible results of sharing so closely can mean.

P.S.: Since people don't usually talk openly about these kinds of things, it may surprise you to learn what sexual intercourse really is. You might find it hard to imagine being so close to someone and might even be saying to yourself, "Yich!" That's very natural.

Lots of kids can't relate to the idea of sexual intercourse. That's because it's not for kids. It's an adult sharing that is hard for most kids to understand. But, as you continue to read about how each sexual organ works and learn more about the feelings that can go along with such closeness, you'll have a better understanding of what intercourse means, and why a man and a woman fit together in this way.

External Genitals

Now for a look at the outside (external) genitals.

The *vulva* (VULL-va) refers to the entire outside genital area of a girl or woman. (Lots of people mistakenly call the outside area the vagina.) Many girls find it confusing to look at their vulva. There are so many overlapping folds of skin that it is often hard to know which part is which. After reading about these parts, it might be very interesting to see if you can identify them on yourself.

If you hold a small mirror up to your genitals, I think you'll agree that the many soft folds look a lot like the petals of a flower. Each girl's vulva has a slightly different pattern or design, even though all the parts are the same.

MONS PUBIS (monz PEW-bis). This is the area of soft tissue that forms the shape of a triangle pointing down between your legs. This soft, moundlike area is the place that becomes covered with pubic (PEW-bick) hair when your body develops.

MAJOR LIPS or **LABIA MAJORA** (LAY-be-uh muh-JOR-uh). These are two folds of skin that divide the mons pubis in half from top to bottom. They usually appear closed together and don't have hair on them until a girl reaches puberty.

MINOR LIPS or **LABIA MINORA** (my-NOR-uh). These are two hairless folds of skin found inside the major lips. Sometimes these lips are very small and sometimes they're larger and flappy. Girls and women can have different sizes, just like with breasts.

The space between the minor lips is called the *vestibule* (VES-ti-bewl). It is rich in nerve endings and blood vessels. Located inside this vestibule are the urethra (first opening from the top) and the vaginal opening (second).

CLITORIS (CLIT-uh-russ). The clitoris is located where the top folds of the minor lips come together, and it looks like a little button peeking out from under a "hood" that gives it protection. Be sure to wash regularly under this hood. It's very important to wash your entire vulva often as it is an area where bacteria (germs that cause infections) can grow if you don't keep yourself clean.

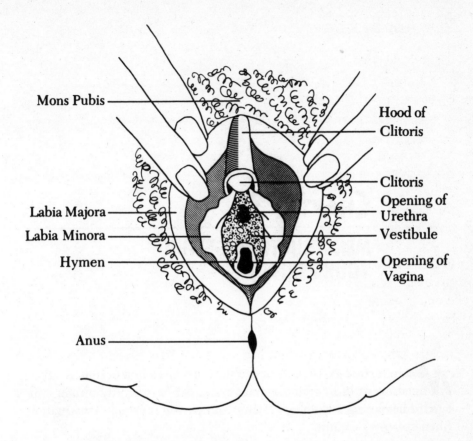

Mons Pubis

Hood of Clitoris

Clitoris

Labia Majora

Opening of Urethra

Labia Minora

Vestibule

Hymen

Opening of Vagina

Anus

As a general guide, it's best not to use any kind of powder with perfume in it in the genital area. Also, if you tend to get urinary tract infections, it's best not to use bubble bath.

The clitoris has many nerve endings that make it very sensitive and sometimes tingly when touched. (More about these feelings later.) Some people say the clitoris looks like a tear drop. What do you think yours looks like?

I hope this chapter was able to clear up any questions that you might have had about which part is which and what does what. I also hope you have a greater appreciation of how magical some of these organs are.

Let's go on to Chapter 3. I think you'll find menstruation to be fascinating, and much easier to understand now that you know so much more about how the organs of reproduction work.

CHAPTER 3

MENSTRUATION (GETTING YOUR PERIOD)

Menarche (me-NAR-kee) or the start of a girl's first period, is a special event in her life. It means that she is officially on her way toward becoming a woman. Having your period is called menstruation (men-stroo-AY-shun).

If you've already gotten your period, congratulations! You can review this information so you're sure you understand exactly what's happening inside. You can also check out any concerns you still might have about getting it.

If you haven't gotten yours yet, you may be waiting another month, a few years, or just a few more days (tomorrow at 2 o'clock?). Once again, there's no way to predict *exactly* when it will arrive, except to tell you some time between about ages nine and seventeen, when your body is ready.

Whether you want it or not, your period will be a regular part of your life. I hope this chapter will help you feel as good as possible about getting it. Most important is that you get your facts straight, understand how you feel, and have a good idea about what you need to do when you get it.

What's a Period and Why Do You Get It?

Your body will begin to get ready to menstruate when your ovaries get a chemical signal from your pituitary gland. This signal will tell an ovary, "Hey, give this kid a break. She's been waiting for her period long enough!"

The pituitary gland actually signals many changes at once. It tells an ovary to pick one of those thousands of unripened eggs so it can begin to mature. It also signals the ovaries to release the special female hormone called estrogen so that the development of your body and genital organs can take place. And it tells the uterus to make its lining thicker, kind of spongy and cozy, in case the egg is fertilized.

Since there's a right and a left ovary, they usually take turns getting an egg ready.

Let's turn to the ovaries themselves.

Though many eggs start to ripen, usually only one egg at a time gets to develop fully with the help of those hormones signaled by the pituitary gland. It takes about two weeks for the unripe egg to mature. Then it's ready to leave the ovary. You know from chapter two that the egg has to break through the surface of the ovary since there is no tube or passageway leading out of it.

Let's say it's "break out" time. The ripened egg is ready to go, and it's out! When the egg is released, we say that *ovulation* (ov-you-LAY-shun) has taken place, or a girl has ovulated.

With the help of the fingerlike ends of the Fallopian tube (fimbria) and the wavy hairs called cilia, the egg can now be drawn into the tube, where it might be fertilized (entered by a sperm from a male).

If a woman's egg is fertilized, she has become pregnant. In fact, the reason that a girl is born with eggs in the first place is so it will be possible for her to choose to try and have a baby when she's an adult.

The egg will live only about forty-eight hours. If it is not fertilized during that time, it will simply disintegrate or break down.

Meanwhile in the uterus...

After ovulation, another special female hormone called *progesterone* (pro-JES-ter-own) joins with the estrogen to help the uterus build up its lining. The lining will continue to become thicker and richer with blood and nutrients. It will be thickest about one week after ovulation. If an egg is fertilized, a chemical signal will let the uterus know that the lining is needed to supply food and oxygen. When that happens, the hormones stay at a high level so the lining will remain thick.

If no signal is sent, the uterus will know that no egg was fertilized and the lining will not be needed. The hormone level will then start to get lower. Blood vessels and tissues from the lining, along with the discarded egg, mix together and then start to pass from the uterus, through the cervix, into the vagina and to the outside. It takes several days for the lining to completely pass out of a girl's (or woman's) body.

The passing out of this lining or "special blood" is called *menstruation* or getting your period. The same thing happens all over again about every four weeks.

Whew! Are you still with me? I hope so. How about a quick review?

Each month, an egg will develop in and be released from an ovary. The lining of the uterus becomes thick and snuggly in case the egg is fertilized. If it is, the lining stays to nourish and supply oxygen to the growing embryo. If the egg is not fertilized, the lining is not needed and passes out of the body slowly through the opening of the vagina. After the lining flows out, another egg is signaled to mature and the whole cycle starts all over again.

It's possible for a girl to get her period before she begins to ovulate or release an egg. That may come a bit later. It's also possible for a girl to start ovulating before she begins her first period.

Sometimes Periods "Skip"—Keeping a Calendar

In the first years when you get your period, you might find that it will skip a month or more until your body gets used to menstruating. Changes in your life can also affect menstruation. A change of climate, very heavy physical activity (like training for a marathon, running many hours a day), losing a lot of weight, or emotional changes like those brought on when parents divorce or you move to a new town—any of these events might have an effect on your hormones and could alter the schedule of your period.

Stephanie, age fourteen, shared, "When I was thirteen, I spent the summer at a camp which was in another state from where I lived. Even though I seemed to be on a regular schedule, I remember not getting my period for the whole summer. I was really nervous that something was wrong with me and wrote my mother about it. She told me it was normal and not to worry (I worried anyway). Sure enough, about a month after I got home again, my period came back."

It's a great idea to keep a record of when you get your period. You can put a big dot or circle on your calendar around the day your period starts. You can also make marks for when it finishes. That way you'll have a pretty good idea of when you can expect it to come again and you can be prepared. (For example, if you think your period might be starting soon, you can wear jeans or other dark-colored clothing instead of light colors. You can also be sure to have some form of sanitary protection with you.)

Keeping a record also lets you check how often your period comes. Remember not to be surprised if it's not on a regular schedule, at least in the beginning months, and possibly even beyond that time. If you're concerned about this, be sure to let your parent know; you can also call your doctor.

If you count getting your period as day 1 of the month, you'll probably find it will start again a few days before or after day 30. Each person's schedule will be slightly different. Even your own schedule will change from time to time. For example, you might get your period on day 29 one month and not until day 32 another month. Once they start, periods can last 3 to 7 days or maybe more.

Days means days and nights. Periods don't stop at night and start again in the morning. Once they begin, they'll keep going until they end.

Is It Scary to Get Your Period?

Jill, age eleven, said, "I have a cousin who didn't know what was happening when she got her period. She was scared stiff that something was wrong with her when it started."

My mother told me she first heard about periods from her older sister, who said, "All of a sudden you just bleed." My mother answered, "What do you *mean* you bleed? I never heard of anything so stupid!"

I suppose it really can be scary to get your period if you don't know anything about it. But it also can be scary if you don't know enough about it. Periods aren't scary! In fact it's very exciting to get your period. It means you're developing and on your way to being a woman. Kids think periods are scary mainly because nothing like that ever happened to them before and they can't imagine what it is like. Also, the word "blood" makes some people squirm and think that they're going to be hurt.

Now you know that when you get your period and it seems like you are "bleeding," it's only the lining of the uterus that wasn't needed. Because it includes blood, mucus, and tissue, it will appear reddish, like you know blood to be. The color can be slightly different each time you get your period. It might be bright red, darker red, or even brownish.

Though most of the time the fluid or flow will be smooth, it will sometimes appear "clumpy" because of thickened, tiny clots of blood, tissue, and mucus.

Since you know what to expect, I hope you will not be scared when you notice reddish stains on your clothing. It will simply mean that your period has begun. And that's great!

Another reason that some kids are scared is because they think all of a sudden blood is going to gush down their legs for everyone to see. Not so! Periods don't gush, they trickle.

The lining drips out bit by bit over several days. (Remember, that means nights, too.) It's not like turning on a faucet! It's more like when you don't completely shut off a faucet and it drips out steadily, but only a tiny bit at a time.

You can take a measuring spoon and put four to six tablespoons of water in a cup, and that's about how much fluid will slowly flow out during your period. Not so much, eh? It seems like much more than it really is.

Ten-year-old Jennifer said, "I don't want it. Do I have to get it? Please, no." Well, Jen, periods are just a part of life for us women. Want it or not, your period will come. Wouldn't it be terrific if you could look forward to getting it and know that whenever it begins, you'll be ready!

How Will You Know When You Have It?

Periods don't seem to care about tests, bus trips, baby-sitting jobs, summer vacations, soccer games, swimming, white pants, or anything. They just begin when your body is ready, no matter where you are or what you are doing or what you're wearing. Time of day doesn't matter. You don't even have to be awake.

Periods often start about a year or two after your breasts begin to develop or a year or so after those somewhat curly pubic hairs start to appear. But even if you have breasts and lots of pubic hair, there's no guarantee that your period will start right away. You may still have some waiting to do. Menarche may also have to do with when your growth spurt starts.

If you are awake and get your period, you might notice a dampness on your underpants or between your legs. Sort of as if you had urinated and hadn't quite wiped yourself completely.

You might also feel damp if you have a *discharge*. This is a clear, odorless fluid that also passes out of the vagina. It is not a period and having a discharge doesn't mean for sure that your period is about to arrive. Rather, it means that your hormones are working. If you find that the slight amount of dampness is a bother to you, you might find it helpful to wear a pantyliner to keep your underpants dry.

Although discharges are normal, if they cause itching, change color, increase in amount, have an unpleasant odor, or seem to have changed in any way, this can mean that you might have a type of infection in your vaginal area. It is important to speak with your parent(s) about any changes so that you can be properly treated, by your doctor, if necessary. Lots of girls have talked with me about having discharges and have been relieved to know they aren't the only ones to have them. Be sure to let your parent(s) know if you have any concerns at all about your discharge (or anything else).

You might not even feel any dampness when you start your period. In fact, you might not feel anything different. You might simply go to the bathroom one day and notice that you have started your period. You'll know this if your underpants have reddish or brownish "stains." (My children didn't want me to use the word *stains*. They thought it sounded "yucky." But it's a very good way to describe what will probably happen. Don't worry about the stains. They'll wash out with a little soap and cold water.)

Another signal of your period could be if you feel cramps in your lower abdomen or belly. Since the uterus has to get rid of the lining it doesn't need, the uterine walls contract (draw together, squeeze) so that the lining can be passed out. This contraction is sometimes felt as a cramp.

Because hormones can also affect feelings and moods, some girls and women can sense that their periods will soon begin because of changes in their emotions. You may have heard people talk about P.M.S. That stands for *pre-menstrual syndrome* and has to do with emotional changes related to hormones before a period begins. Lots of people joke about P.M.S. and perhaps don't realize that these changes in the emotions actually have to do with changes in the body. Some girls and women describe the changes as quite strong and noticeable. Others don't notice any change in their emotions. Even if your mom or other women in your family have noticeable changes, that doesn't mean you will. Each girl or woman will experience the changes related to hormones in her own way.

What If Anyone Sees?

Still another way you'd know is if someone else told you they think they noticed a stain on your clothing. You're probably thinking that you'd "die" of embarrassment if anyone ever told you that. Or that you could never imagine saying to someone that you think they might have gotten their period. This has happened to me a few times. I guess I was a little (maybe a lot!) embarrassed, but I was more thankful that the person was nice enough to realize I would want to know. And the times I've told other people that they better go to the bathroom to "check," they've really appreciated my telling them.

Several years ago, during one of my school programs, a fifth-grade boy raised his hand and said, "No way would I ever walk up to a girl and tell her." The boys and girls in that classroom talked together about how they felt and what they would do—and what girls wished friends would do—if ever they noticed those reddish "trickles" on someone's clothing. Everyone seemed to agree that it was important for girls to be told so they could take care of their needs and know to get a sanitary pad.

That same boy who had said, "No way," raised his hand again at the end of the program and said, "I don't think I would be comfortable saying anything. But I can understand that it's important for the girl to know her period has started." It helps to realize that periods are a natural part of life and it's just not possible to always know when they begin.

Maybe the more boys and girls understand about periods, the easier it will be for them to try to help one another. For example, if you let someone else know that she might have gotten her period, you could also ask if there is anything you can do to help . . . like going to her locker to get an extra change of clothes for her or going to the nurse's office and getting her a sanitary pad.

If you don't feel comfortable telling a girl yourself, you can ask a friend of hers to tell her or you might tell a teacher. Since this is very personal, it's important to respect privacy and not tell anyone else.

What would you do? Would you tell someone else or keep quiet? Would you want someone else to tell you?

Parents and First Periods

A first period means different things to parents as well as to the girl who gets it.

My mom was so excited! She gave me a long, hard hug that I'll always remember. I think we both couldn't believe it. Only later did I understand why there were tears in her eyes.

Stacey, age fourteen, was really surprised when her parents told her to pick her favorite restaurant so they could take her out for dinner to celebrate getting her period.

Martha, age seventy-two, remembers getting her period when she was "ten years and ten months." She had never even thought about periods because she believed they were for when you were older. Her older sister helped her get set with clean pieces of cloth (pads and tampons weren't invented until later), and then they went to tell their mother. Her mother smiled, turned around, and gave her a really hard slap in the face. She has never forgotten that slap!

If a mother slaps her daughter today, you can probably guess that her mother slapped her, and she's carrying on the tradition. Consider it for luck. The old reason was to knock the devil or evil spirit out of you because people didn't understand periods and thought the blood meant something evil. (I just met a girl who hasn't gotten her period yet. She said the only thing she's worried about is being slapped when her mother finds out it started. If you're wondering if your mom is planning to do that to you, why not talk with her about it.)

Seanne, age twelve, said her mom invited her to join her women friends for coffee or tea in the afternoons whenever she wanted because now she's "one of them." It made her feel so grown-up.

Bernice, now in her fifties, also remembers getting her period when she was ten years old. She said her mother did a terrible thing when she took away her dolls and carriage because she was now a woman. She was very upset because she loved playing with her dolls and she "really didn't feel like a woman yet, anyway." Even though her father and mother argued about this, her mother wouldn't give in. Bernice had to sneak to her older sister's house to play with her niece's dolls. Her father felt so bad about it that he secretly made her a carriage out of old bicycle wheels.

Dean, now in her forties, remembers having sad feelings and crying when she got her period at the age of thirteen. Said Dean, "On top of this [sadness], my mother gave me a lecture! She never had much discussion with me about sex or reproduction, but now that I had my period, I guess she felt it was time. She told me, 'Now you can get pregnant!' Rules about boys became stricter and I had the feeling from my mother that bad things could happen now that I had it.

"Because I had such a sad beginning to my period, I wanted to make sure my daughters felt very good about theirs when the time came. My oldest daughter got hers a few months ago and our family celebrated by having a special toast with some punch."

When Kelly got her period at age twelve, she and her mom went to tell her dad. (Yes, dads know about periods, too.) He gave her a huge hug, told her he was proud to have such a grown-up daughter, and handed her a cigar. (Not to smoke, of course. Just to be funny.)

While different parents have different reactions to a daughter's first period, most daughters seem to feel relieved. They no longer have to wonder about when and where it will happen. They no longer have to go to the bathroom all day long to keep "checking" if they "got it." And now they can say, "Me too," to their friends who already started to menstruate.

Will Getting Your Period Hurt? What About Cramps?

You may have heard your mom or sister complain about being uncomfortable during her period. That doesn't mean you will be uncomfortable. Once again, each body is different.

Yes, you could get cramps in your lower belly or even in your lower back. This is normal. You could also get headaches, feel depressed (those mood changes I spoke about), feel kind of "swollen" or bloated (because your body might hold in fluids), and find that a few pimples appear on your face.

Remember, the uterus is working very hard to contract so the lining will flow out. The contractions, along with changes in hormones, may cause any one or many of these reactions. Most cramps are mild; some are pretty strong.

It might sound like periods are a real bother to have. I admit that I have felt that way many times. But menstruation is just one of those things that you're going to have to try to accept as part of you.

Not everyone gets cramps. And if you do, there are things you can do to help you feel better. You can use a heating pad, rub your lower belly, lie down and take it easy, curl up with your knees to your chest. Getting exercise and eating nutritious foods—no junk!—can really be helpful, too.

If you are still uncomfortable, it's important to let your parent(s) know so they can help you. If necessary, you can speak with your family doctor. He or she may recommend one of the medications that are specially made to relieve cramps or aches from periods. Remember never to take any medication before speaking to your parents. And never use a friend's medication.

You see, you've got lots of choices to help you feel good. It would be impossible for me to tell you if your own period will be more or less comfortable. There have been times when I had my period and I actually forgot that I had it. Every once in a while, I've had slight cramps.

But they were often a signal that my period was coming. Once I had it and the first day or so was over, the cramps seemed to go away and I wasn't uncomfortable at all.

I supposed the best thing is to realize that there may be some cramps to deal with. They probably won't last too long. And, if they bother you, you can do some of the things I've suggested, as well as get advice from your parents and doctor. You can also ask your friends who have their periods what they do.

What About Baths and Showers?

Yes, yes, yes. Go right ahead and wash! (You know, the thing you do with soap and water?)

The water won't bother your period (it's okay to shower without a pad). Your period won't even bother the water! But body odor will bother your friends and family and make it unpleasant even to be with yourself. So do yourself, and everyone, a favor and keep clean. Not only during your period but all the time.

Can You Still Play Sports?

Yes, yes, yes. You can do everything you usually do. Just because you have your period doesn't mean "stop everything." Exercise is great, with or without your period.

If you have cramps and don't feel like playing, do what you feel is most comfortable. But remember that exercise is one of the things that can help cramps. So you might push yourself a little and try to play.

What About Swimming?

So many girls have asked me, "What if you get your period in the pool?" "If you get your period when you're in the pool, what should you do?" or "If you're in the pool, would you know it or feel it?"

It will be harder to tell if you get your period while swimming because you'll already be damp between your legs (and all over). So probably you'd notice it if you got out of the pool and went to the bathroom. Or if someone you're swimming with notices a slight "spot" on your bathing suit and tells you about it so you can go to the nearest bathroom and check.

Though I'll talk about sanitary pads and tampons later, if you have your period and want to swim, you need to wear a tampon—or not go in the water for the few days that you have your period. (Going in the water without protection when you have your period is not sanitary.) So, if you find out your period has begun after starting to swim, it is important not to go back in unless you have tampon protection.

Sanitary pads were not made to be used while swimming. I learned about not wearing pads in the water from an experience that still makes me smile. When I was younger, I tried swimming in a lake with a pad on. All of a sudden I felt it float away from me (horrors!) and I swam as fast as I could to shore. I prayed that it would sink before anyone noticed and didn't stay around to find out.

It's also not very sanitary to wear a pad instead of a tampon in the water.

What If You Get Your Period in School (or Anywhere Else)?

If you haven't got your period yet, or even if you have, this seems to be one of the biggest concerns about periods. After reading this section, I hope you'll feel more comfortable about getting your period in school, as you realize there are many different ways you can take care of your needs. You have more choices than you probably think you have.

Let's imagine you are in math class, in the middle of taking a test. And you're not quite sure, but you think you've got your period. What should you do?

Would you tell your teacher? Would you ask to be excused so you could go to the bathroom? Would you wait until you finished your test before doing anything? Would you do nothing and pray that it's really not your period? Think about this before reading further.

Well, do you have an answer? Maybe you'd tell your English or social studies teacher but not your math teacher. Maybe you'd feel differently if you weren't taking a test. Maybe if your math teacher was a woman instead of a man, you'd ask for help. If you are fourteen, you might give one answer, eleven, another.

It's so hard to know exactly what you would do and how you would feel if this happened to you. Since you're going to have your period many times, chances are you'll have at least a few periods that start in school.

Perhaps the most helpful thing is to realize that you do have several choices. Whether you're in English, gym, lunch, math, library, or any class, only you will be able to decide what choice will make you feel the most comfortable and which will be easiest for you at the time.

There are many things that might make a difference in what you choose to do. You might talk about your period with a teacher with whom you feel close and probably won't go near one that you don't like. You may really want to talk to your teacher about this, but you may be too embarrassed or just not know what words to use.

While I was first writing this, my own daughter, Hillary, age eleven, said to me, "No way would I go up to any one of my teachers. Come on, Mom, you know kids won't do that!"

Well, maybe they wouldn't. Maybe you wouldn't. And since there are several choices, you certainly don't have to, unless you want to. But if you realize you can, you might take a chance and be happily surprised at how helpful some of your teachers really can be.

Here are some questions that have been asked over and over again. I think you'll find that my answers and suggestions will help you think about which choices seem right for you.

"What if I have a man teacher?" or "What if the nurse is a man?" Though men don't get a period, you can be sure that they know about periods. Knowing that a man teacher as well as a woman teacher will be able to understand may make it easier for you to talk about getting your period with them.

Both men and women teachers also know that it's not so easy for you to just come up to them and blurt out, "Hi, I think I got my period. . . ." They'll probably try to be as helpful to you as possible. But they can't help you unless you let them know you need help.

Many teachers have told me they keep a box of sanitary pads in their back closet or in a special drawer so that anyone who needs one can just take it. If your teacher hasn't mentioned a "pad supply," it's a good thing to suggest even if you haven't got your period yet. (Are you thinking that you'll have to sneak over to the pads so your classmates don't see? Keep reminding yourself that periods are natural—expected. If anyone makes fun of you, he or she probably doesn't really understand what periods are all about. That person might even be jealous!)

You may have to get up your courage to speak with your teacher and ask for help. Sometimes the thing that can help you the most won't always be the most comfortable thing to do. It's okay to realize you're not comfortable, then go ahead and do what you have to do anyway.

I'm not saying you must speak with your teacher, just that you can if you want to.

"What should I tell my teacher?" What you say will depend upon whether or not you've decided to tell your teacher about your period.

If you want to talk with your teacher about it, you might say privately: "Mr. or Ms. So-and-so, I think I got my period. May I please go to the nurse's office or to the main office?" Or simply, "May I go to the bathroom?"

If you don't want to tell your teacher about your period, you might say: "Mr. or Ms. So-and-so, may I please go to the bathroom or the nurse's office?" If need be, you can even say, "I don't feel well and would like to go down to the nurse."

Sometimes teachers won't let you go to the nurse unless you say you don't feel well. It's usually best to tell the truth. But if you must say that you don't feel well in order to get out of the classroom, do so.

Some teachers have told me that they have a special signal in case a girl needs to leave the room because of her period. With that signal, she can just leave, no questions asked. Perhaps the best thing would be for your class, or at least the girls in your class, to get together and speak with your teacher about being able to leave the classroom, to take care of your needs, even if it's in the middle of a test!

"What if your teacher won't let you leave the classroom?" While most teachers are understanding, I suppose there may be a few who will make it really tough to leave the room. They may have certain times that you're allowed to go to the bathroom during the day, and that's it!

You may have to say, "It's an emergency." If that doesn't work and they still won't let you leave, *don't stay!* Just say something like, "I'm very sorry, but it really is an emergency, and I have to go." Then keep walking out. Just remember to be respectful. Don't talk back or be fresh.

If your teacher follows you into the hall, you can explain privately. If not, you can explain later. The worst thing would be to stay in your class worrying about your period. It's not fair for you to have to do that. It's your right to leave the classroom to take care of your own needs. No teacher should make it embarrassing or difficult to leave so that you're forced to stay.

I know this is easier for me to say and may be much harder for you to do, but imagine how you would feel if you couldn't go to the bathroom when you thought you had your period, and you'll understand why I feel so strongly about this. (You can tell your parents what made you walk out without permission and they can talk to your teacher with you, if need be.)

"What if you're too embarrassed to tell the nurse?" Here again, you have a choice. A nurse knows a lot about periods and is a good person to go to, especially since nurses usually have sanitary pads. They won't laugh or tease and will be happy to help you.

But if you're much too embarrassed and just can't push yourself to talk with the nurse about your period, then you don't have to. The choice is up to you. (Sometimes it helps to say things quickly so you'll be less embarrassed. It can also help to write what you need on a piece of paper and hand it to the nurse instead of saying the words aloud.)

While many girls have a nice relationship with their school nurse and can talk easily with her (usually the nurse is a woman), some girls don't wish to speak with the nurse because they don't like her. Just a reminder—you don't have to like someone to let them help you. You don't need to be the nurse's friend, you just need her pads and her advice. (It's one of the reasons she's there.)

If you decide not to tell her, then you'd better have another choice so that you can take care of yourself. The first thing you might do, if you don't want to talk with the nurse or your teacher, is go to the bathroom. The bathroom is a good *first* stop, no matter what you choose to do. You can put a fairly thick pile of toilet paper or tissues in your underpants, so you know you're protected until you get a pad.

If you don't have any sanitary pads in your classroom, locker, or pocketbook, many girls' bathrooms have sanitary napkin dispensers. If you put a dime, or whatever the sign on the machine says, you will be able to buy a pad, put it in place, and then go back to your classroom.

"What if the nurse isn't there?" Even if you want to talk with the nurse, she could be out for lunch, or just not in your school on that day. What to do?

Many nurses have told me they keep a supply of sanitary napkins in a certain place so that even if they are out of the office, any girl can come in and get what she needs.

If you do not know where your school nurse keeps the supply, it would be a good idea to talk with her now, even if you haven't got your period yet (so you'll be prepared).

If the nurse's door is locked or she doesn't keep an open supply, you can also go to the main office. The secretaries often keep sanitary pads in the office closet just in case someone like you comes in for help. They, too, will understand your needs.

If you don't want to talk with the office secretaries about your period, you can ask to use the telephone (with a first period, you might want to call home, share the good news, and get any help from your mom, dad, or someone else who is close).

Or you can keep your own supply of sanitary pads so you can always count on yourself to be prepared. You can put one in a glasses case, a pencil case (one that's not see-through), your pocketbook, locker, or in the special mini-pad case that some of the companies make.

If you don't want to keep a mini pad around, there's no excuse for not keeping a supply of tissues in your desk, zippered pencil case, pocketbook, locker, or jacket pocket.

From this minute on, you know that you can always be prepared (by putting a pile of tissues in your underpants to absorb the menstrual flow until you get a pad). Remember, it's not a gush, so with tissues in place, you'll have time to figure out what to do next. You may walk a little funny so the tissues won't fall out, but you'll be protected, at least for a while.

"What if you get your period in school and you have white pants on?" or "What if the blood gets on your clothes?" If you've already got your period, you can keep that calendar and know to wear jeans or something dark around the time you expect your period. You can even wear a panty liner or mini pad so your clothes won't get stained. But if you never had it before, you can't know when it will begin.

Even a calendar can't always exactly predict when it will start. So getting the special blood on your clothes is not only possible—but almost guaranteed. Not guaranteed all the time, but often enough for you to be prepared to know what to do.

If your clothes are stained, you can do one of several things. You can call home and ask someone to bring you a change of clothes. In case no one is home, it would be smart to have a key. Then someone in the office or even a teacher, an aide, the nurse, or anyone who is free can drive you to your home so you can change. In case no one is home, schools usually require you to put several names on an Emergency Information form. Perhaps a relative, your parent's friend, one of your friend's parents, or a neighbor you trust can pick you up and take you home.

It's a better idea to keep an extra pair of jeans or sweatpants, and extra underpants plus a plastic bag or two in your locker or in the back closet of your classroom, just in case. You can go to the girls' bathroom, nurse's office, or even gym locker room, and rinse your clothing in cold water (the blood stains usually come out easily), place anything damp in the plastic bag, and keep it in your locker or back closet until it's time to go home.

"What if I think my clothes are stained and I'm afraid to get up from my desk chair?" If you're pretty sure that your dress, pants, or skirt might be stained in a way that could be noticed if you stand up from your desk—here again you've got another choice.

Call your teacher over to your desk and either write a note so they can read it as if looking at your work or whisper that you need their help. Ask your teacher to ask you to leave the room, stand behind you as you get up, and to keep on walking closely behind you as you walk out of the room.

That way, no one will see and you can get to the bathroom quickly. Have the teacher send a friend in to help you. If you're right about the stains, your friend can go to your locker, closet, or wherever you keep your extra change of clothes. She can try to get a sanitary pad for you from the bathroom dispenser, your locker, the teacher, the nurse, or the school office. She or he can also make a phone call for you if necessary.

A teacher at one of my programs told me her student took my advice and did this—and it worked great! You see, school can be a friendly place to get your period. You've got lots of choices. All of them will help you take care of yourself. Think about what might feel best to you and know that you can always try something else the next time. Maybe you can even add to my list of choices.

"What if you get your period on the bus, on vacation, at camp, at your grandparents' home, while baby-sitting, on a date, when you're sleeping at a friend's home, on a plane, in the backseat of your family's car with your brother sitting next to you, or anywhere else?" Okay, imagine yourself in any one of those situations. Go down the list. Do you have an answer for each? Which one(s) do you think would be the hardest for you to deal with? Do you know why?

Believe it or not, you are already prepared for most of these cases, possibly all. After I share a few more thoughts with you, I think you'll be able to feel more confident about getting your period, no matter where.

There's really no magic. All you have to do is be *prepared*. Not so much with sanitary napkins as with an understanding of how to figure out what your choices might be.

For example, if you're on a bus, simply wait until you get off in order to go to the nearest bathroom, put the tissues in place, and arrange to get a sanitary pad. If you're on a bus trip with schoolmates and you're not scheduled to stop anywhere, you can speak with the teacher or parent in charge and she or he will instruct the bus driver to pull into the nearest gas station so you can go to the bathroom.

Always have your own supply of tissues. Put them in the glove compartment of your family car, bring them with you when you baby-sit or go on a date or anywhere else. You can also keep one or two pads in the trunk or glove compartment of your car and bring them on vacation or to camp with you, just in case.

If you anticipate (think ahead about what your needs might be), then you can prepare yourself for most situations.

Even a plane has a bathroom. If you have to wait until you land before getting a sanitary pad, you can keep putting new tissues (or napkins or folded paper towels) in your underpants to continue to absorb the flow.

If you go away to summer camp or go on a vacation, you can always pack away a small box of sanitary pads. (Keep them in a drawer, your cubby or shelf, or your suitcase in case you need them, but always have tissues with you.)

If you're on a date with a boy and think you have your period, find the nearest bathroom. If you do have it, and your clothes are okay, and you happen to have a pad with you or can get one from a bathroom dispenser, then fine. Put the pad in place and go back to your date (just as you would if you had gone to the bathroom for regular reasons).

If your clothes are stained and you need to change, or if you need to get a pad, ask to stop back home or ask a parent, neighbor, or friend's parent to meet you with whatever you need. (It may seem awkward to you, but probably the easiest thing would be to straight out tell your date that you got your period and have to take care of things. Probably, you're not the first girl he knows who has got her period. If the person you're going out with doesn't know about periods, it's time he learned!)

If you're in the backseat of your car, with your good old brother right next to you, you can ask your parent to pull over or drive to the nearest bathroom. If that's too far away for you to wait, ask your brother to turn around and close his eyes (no cheating!) until you tell him you're ready. Then you can easily slip some tissues (or even a pad that you've kept in the glove compartment) into your underpants and know that you'll be fine.

If you're baby-sitting, at your grandparents', at your friend's home, or anywhere, you can follow these same ideas. Bathroom first. If there's none around, use the tissues that you now know to have with you. If you don't have a sanitary pad or tissues, you can also use napkins, paper towels, or anything like that to absorb the flow. Then take it from there. Change if you need to change; get a pad as soon as possible, and try to realize that you're not alone . . . there are lots of people who care and will help you.

"How should you act if you're having your period, and it's all around school that you have it?" If it's all around your school that you've got your period, you've got a few things you can do. You can ignore anyone who bothers you or tell the person(s) it's none of their business. Or you can give them an answer they'll probably never expect. If someone says something to you about your period, you can just say, "Yes, it's true. Isn't that great? I feel so good that I got it!" The main thing is to be calm. Don't let anyone rattle you. (If they do, don't let them know it!)

They may be expecting you to be really embarrassed. Instead, if you act proud, smile, thank them for mentioning it, and tell them how much you wanted it, what more can they say? You'll have taken all the joy out of it for them if you don't react as they hoped.

"What if you don't have your period and people are saying you do?" You've got some more choices. You can go along with it as if you really got it and say, "Thanks, it's true." Though this answer isn't really honest, it would take people by surprise and maybe stop their talk.

Some girls feel the need to say they have their period when they don't, or that they don't have it when they really do. The more girls (and boys) understand and accept that each person is different and that's okay, the less they will have to lie just to feel like they belong.

You can also say, "It's a rumor. If you want to go on talking about it, be my guest. But it's a little silly because I haven't even got it yet. I wish I did already, but I didn't. Maybe if you keep talking, I'll get it and we'll all be happy." If you give them the idea that they're not driving you crazy with their teases and talk, they'll probably stop.

The message that needs to come through for either situation is that getting your period is really okay, and you're happy to have it or wish you did. If their talking about your period doesn't seem to bother you, my guess is it won't be much fun for them to talk about it anymore. Just try to keep your cool and outwit them.

Sanitary Pads and Tampons

It's time to talk about just what those pads and tampons are made of, how and why they work, when you need to wear them, and how often they should be changed. . . .

First, let's deal with sanitary pads.

Sanitary pads are made up of soft fibers that can absorb the menstrual flow. They are worn inside your underpants. When the lining trickles out the vaginal opening, it will be absorbed by the pad waiting for it on the outside.

Pads are very easy to use. Most pads have a long sticker on the back that is protected by a strip. Once you peel that strip off, you can stick the pad into your underpants and wear it until you need to change it again. They're very comfortable. Unless you're wearing super-super-super tight pants, they're not noticeable.

When I was growing up, we had only the kind of sanitary pads that you had to hook onto elastic sanitary belts (for sanitary napkins). My friends and I called them Mickey Mouse pads. Even though most of us used them, we thought it was more mature to use tampons. I now know that it's simply a matter of choice. Anyone can use either pads or tampons, depending upon how she and her parents feel.

It's a great idea to get some pads even before you have your period. Put one on just to feel what it's like and learn how to use it. If you've never worn one before, it's likely you'll be relieved to realize that they really don't make you look like you're walking with a volleyball between your legs. As I've said before, they're soft, comfortable, and no one need know you have one on.

Pads (and tampons) absorb the flow of a period much the way a sponge takes in water. They can take in just so much and then can't take in any more. When a pad or tampon is "full" (has taken in all the flow it can), you simply wrap it up, throw it out, and put a new one in place. No big deal, eh?

A word about "wrapping it up": Sometimes bathrooms have a special little bag for throwing away sanitary pads. Most of the time, they don't. So you can easily put layers of toilet paper or tissues around your pad and then throw it *in the garbage—not the toilet!* (You can't imagine how many people don't think about the poor old plumbing and clog up the toilet by tossing in their pad and trying to flush.)

When it's all wrapped up, you don't have to be concerned about anyone ever bothering with it. I used to wrap mine many times, just to make sure no one would know what was underneath. One of the first few times I got my period, I wrapped my pad up very well (with tons of layers of toilet paper) and tried to bury it in the trash basket in the bathroom at school. I remember being so surprised to find there were five or six other "wrapped treasures" already buried. I wasn't the only one.

You may be wondering which to choose, pads or tampons. I'll talk about that after I discuss what tampons are.

Okay, let's think about tampons. You already know what they're made of—soft, absorbent fibers. But how are they different from sanitary pads? For those of you who aren't sure, tampons offer protection by absorbing the flow of your period from the inside, while sanitary pads protect you by absorbing from outside your body.

Since the lining of the uterus leaves the body through the vagina, tampons are inserted (gently guided in) through the opening of the vagina so that the lining trickles right onto the tampon fibers and never reaches the outside. You can find your vaginal opening by parting your inner lips (minor lips or labia). Remember, the vagina is the second opening as you move down from your belly button!

Some girls have asked what would happen if they accidentally tried to place the tampon in the wrong opening. They'd realize it was wrong because only the vagina will let the tampon in comfortably (if they're relaxed).

When a tampon is in place correctly, you shouldn't even feel it inside. In fact, you just might have to remind yourself that you're wearing one so you can take it out before putting another in. It's so comfortable, you could forget all about your period! Pay attention to the time you put it in. That will help you know about what time is right to change it for a new one.

Placing a tampon in your vagina may seem a little strange at first. But it becomes easier with each try. (It helps to know which is the right opening.) Some tampons come in an applicator that makes it simple to insert. A removal cord (like a string) is attached to the end of the tampon, so you can take it out when you wish. Remember, if for some reason it doesn't feel right when you put it in, you can just take it out and insert a new one.

Are you ready to learn? Here's what you would do if you decide to use a tampon. Wash your hands before opening the tampon wrapper. They all come wrapped so they remain sanitary. Hands clean? Now open and take off the wrapper and you're ready to insert it (or at least to learn about how).

Notice that the applicator is made up of an outer tube and an inner tube. To insert it, part the soft folds of skin at the opening of your vagina with one hand. It's easier if you do this in a sitting or squatting position with your knees apart. With your other hand, place the outer tube end into the opening and tilt it toward your back as you move it just inside. (Yes, inside the vagina.)

Hold onto the string with your finger and gently guide the tampon inside. Push it back and in a slightly upward direction. Keep holding on to the removal string and the outer tube you just put in.

The next step is to push the inner tube all the way into the outer tube. Then let go of the removal cord and take both the outer and inner tubes out. The tampon is now left snugly in place in your vagina. Remember, the walls of the vagina are amazing in the way they can stretch. They'll know just how to make your tampon feel right at home.

If you are having difficulty inserting the tampon, it may be due to a tightening of the muscles around the opening of your vagina (like when you make a fist if you're a little nervous or concerned about something). It might help to use some water-based lubricating (LOO-bri-kay-ting) jelly (it can be bought at most drugstores) on the tip of the tampon so that it slides in easier. Do not use oil-based Vaseline because it's not healthy for the vaginal canal. It can also help to keep telling yourself, "Relax, relax . . . ," so that the muscles at the vaginal opening loosen up and make it easier to insert the tampon. (Can you just hear a chorus of "Relax, relax" coming from each stall of the girls' bathrooms at school?)

To take the tampon out, just pull gently on the removal cord in a slightly downward but forward angle (don't yank!). Since the tampon is now moist, it will slip out easily through the entrance of your vagina.

If you choose to use tampons, you'll be happy to know that tampon manufacturers include instructions along with diagrams (pictures that show you how to insert the tampon) in just about every new package. It's a good idea to keep these with the package in case you need an extra review of the steps I've just described.

A reminder about the hymen (the tissue or "membrane" that surrounds the opening of your vagina): It's very flexible and won't be pushed back if you use tampons according to proper directions.

Remember in Chapter 2 when I explained that the usual way to push the hymen back is by having sexual intercourse? Now you can understand that parents who are concerned about the hymen and tampons usually are not so much concerned about the hymen itself, as more concerned about what they believe pushing the hymen back means.

If your mom or dad has questions about this, ask them to read this information with you.

Important note: Wearing a tampon will not prevent you from urinating, since the tampon is placed in the vaginal opening and urine passes through your urethra (first opening).

It's Very Important to Change Your Pads and Tampons Regularly

You need to change pads or tampons often so that harmful bacteria does not build up. Such bacteria can lead to infections.

A good guide is to change whatever you use every few hours during the heavier flow days in the beginning of your period. Toward the end, you can make fewer changes because the flow is less and less and your pad won't "fill up" as quickly. But even if the pad is not filled, don't leave it on more than those few hours. Put a new one in its place. (Whether you decide to use tampons or not, more details about nighttime changing are covered in the section "Are Tampons Safe?")

While it's easy to tell whether a sanitary pad is ready to be changed (all you have to do is look), you might be wondering how you'll know when to change your tampon. Well, you really don't know for sure. Unless, of course, you discover a few spots on your underpants. That's one way to find out that your tampon can't absorb any more fluid.

A helpful idea with tampons is just to remember when you last put one in. As you learn more about how your body gets its period, you'll get to know how heavily you will trickle out that menstrual blood. That will help you decide how often you need to change.

Start by changing every couple of hours and see if that's often enough. If you find your tampons are just about full after two hours, you may want to change them after one and a half hours. Experiment. It's really the only way to find out. If you guess wrong about when to change, the worst that could happen is that you'll leave the tampon in even after it has absorbed all that it can and you might get a few spots on your clothing that can easily be washed out with soap and water.

Even when you know what to expect during your period (how heavy or light your usual flow is, how often you usually need to change your sanitary protection), it's possible for you to forget or just not figure your changing schedule right.

Another thought about spots: If your pad is ready to be changed while you're still asleep, you might notice period stains on your pajamas, nightshirt or nightgown, and sheets. This, too, is *normal.* You can't help it unless you feel like setting your alarm every few hours so you can change. If it concerns you, change your own sheets. If not, at least know that whoever changes them will probably know about periods, too.

What About Toxic Shock Syndrome?

Well, for one thing, Toxic Shock Syndrome, or TSS, is an illness that is quite rare. Doctors feel that it is caused by a certain kind of bacteria. It's not caused by tampons, but of interest is that several of the cases of TSS have been women who happened to have their period and were wearing tampons at the time.

TSS has also been found in lesser numbers in men, children, and women who no longer get their periods. (Yes, getting your period does come to an end. You can read about this in the section on menopause at the end of this chapter.)

Some of the symptoms (signs that a person might have it) of TSS are violent, sudden vomiting and/or diarrhea along with fever that may reach 102 degrees or higher; a rash (like a sunburn); feeling as if you're going to faint; and dizziness.

Since these symptoms could also signal other illnesses, you don't need to panic if you have them. Just know to check them out with your doctor right away.

Also be aware that since TSS can be serious (it can even cause death), it's very important for anyone who has one or more of these signs to contact a doctor. If, at the time, a tampon is in place, she should take it out until the doctor checks what the symptoms mean.

Are Tampons Safe?

Yes, if you remember to change your tampon every few hours. A good hygenic practice is to change your tampon every two to four hours. Another good practice is to wear junior or regular—rather than super—tampons, especially when you first start using tampons and need to develop the habit of changing them regularly. This will make you have to change them sooner rather than later (because they're less absorbant than super tampons). Also, it's better to use tampons and sanitary pads that do not have deodorant in them.

It's a smart idea not to wear tampons when you go to sleep at night. Wear a sanitary pad instead. That way the tampon won't be left in place for too many hours. You might also want to use tampons and sanitary pads in turns once in a while during daily use.

Tampons may not be safe if you often forget about your tampon and leave it in for too many hours at a time. Wearing it too long can cause bacteria to grow and may produce an infection such as TSS. It's just as important to change your pads regularly.

Which Should You Use?

This is a very personal decision. It wouldn't even be fair if I tried to tell you what would be better for you. You've got to decide that for yourself.

It depends on how you feel. You may think that one is easier or more comfortable to use than the other. You may just like one more than the other. It may also depend on what your friends are using (or not using).

Parents may have definite feelings about which to use, so be sure to talk with your mom or dad (or both) about this. If your parents feel one way and you feel another, make sure you understand their feelings. And let them know how you feel, even if you don't agree. They can't know or act on your feelings unless you tell them.

I think by now you have enough information to make your decision. The nice thing is that you can always change your mind!

Buying Sanitary Pads and Tampons

Sharon, age twelve, asked, "What happens if you go to the store and ask for sanitary pads? I would be ashamed." Jeannie, age thirteen, said, "Everyone will know!" There are so many girls who have told me they feel kind of funny about buying sanitary pads and tampons. Others have thought it was no big deal.

A fifty-year-old friend recalls feeling very shy when she had to buy her first pads. After walking around the store for almost twenty minutes, she finally went over to the person behind the counter. She had such trouble getting the words out. She managed only to ask for "Ko—" and finished with "—dak" instead of saying the brand of pads that she really wanted. After all that time, she walked out with film instead of her pads.

Most drugstores place their stock of sanitary pads or tampons right out on shelves where they're easy to see (and easy to reach). So, most of the time, you won't even need to ask for help. You can just take what you want, bring it up to the cash register, pay, and leave.

Just in case you still feel really funny about buying pads or tampons yourself or if you can't find them on the shelves, here are some choices to think about.

You can ask your parent, sister, brother, or friend to do it for you. You can also walk up to the counter and say, "I'm buying this for a friend!" (No, not honest, but if you must, you must.)

You can practice saying, "I'd like to buy these, thanks very much." The less you stand around the store waiting to be helped, the quicker you'll make your purchase.

Another choice is to very calmly approach the salesperson and ask, "Where do you keep the tampons or sanitary pads?" Then bring one to the counter, say "thank you," smile, and walk slowly out the door. (Try it. You might be very surprised how that can work.)

If you're concerned or shy about buying pads or tampons, it might help to remember that the first time you buy them may be a bit awkward. The second time will probably be easier, and so on, until you feel you can order anything you want!

Menopause

Just as your period has a beginning, it will have an end. The ending of menstruation is called *menopause* (MEN-o-paws). Some people also refer to this as the "change of life." When your period finally stops, your ovaries will no longer release eggs, and you won't be able to become pregnant.

It's impossible to predict when you will reach menopause (just as you can't tell exactly when menstruation will start), but you can figure somewhere around age fifty (it could be a few years earlier or later). When this happens, hormone amounts get lower and your period gradually lessens until it stops completely.

Besides changing your period schedule, the lowered amount of hormones may also cause a woman to have symptoms such as headaches and hot flashes. (It sounds like it could be a new rock group, but it really means short, sudden feelings or rushes of heat.) Your grandma or mom might have talked about them. Each woman will get symptoms in her own special way. They're signals that menopause is taking place, although not all women get such symptoms.

Just as a girl can start releasing eggs before she actually has her period, a woman can continue releasing eggs after her period seems to have stopped. It's not a case of stopping your period one month and that's it. Even after your period has changed, you still could be ovulating (OV-you-lay-ting: releasing an egg). Ovulation will stop when menopause is complete, a year or two after it started.

It's important to remember that menopause takes place over time.

A Few More Thoughts

Lots of girls are confused about periods and getting pregnant. Just because you have your period doesn't mean you're going to be pregnant. To cause a pregnancy, sperm from a man's body must be introduced in or around a woman's vagina so they can move through the vagina toward the Fallopian tubes, where they might find an egg. Only if a man's sperm fertilizes or enters an egg cell will a woman become pregnant.

So sperm do *not live* in your closet or under your bedsheets, and they do not hide in swimming pools or hang out in book bags. You don't have to be concerned about sperm or becoming pregnant until later in your life, at a time when you feel you're ready for sexual intercourse.

One more time: Having your period allows you the *choice* to try to become pregnant. But even though your *body* might be ready to become pregnant, as a young girl *you* are not ready! That decision is best saved until you are much older . . . when you're an adult.

GROWING UP MALE
FEELING GOOD

Chapter 4

PRIVATE PARTS

The Penis

A four-year-old boy came up to my son in a store and said, "I'll bet if I said *penis* real loud, people would laugh!"

Talk about boys' or girls' sex organs often brings with it giggles and red faces. I hear those giggles at the beginning of many of my programs. But as I talk about these organs and tell kids things about them that they have always wondered, they forget about their blushes and want to know as much as they can.

Just as for girls' sex or reproductive organs, there are many slang names that people use in place of the real names for boys' sex organs. You can probably make a list of them. While some of them might make you laugh, others are strong. These are sometimes used in a way that has little or nothing to do with the genitals and much more to do with being angry and trying to get at someone.

Even if you have a favorite slang name that you use, it's a good idea to at least know what the real names are. So I'll use the real names to help you learn them.

Boys, too, have outside (external) and inside (internal) genitals. The genitals mature during puberty because of the release and influence of the male hormones (the old "growth clock" does it again!). We'll start with the outside (external) genitals.

A boy's outside sex organs include his penis and *scrotum* (SKRO-tum), the sac with two pouches that is located behind the penis.

The *penis* (PEE-nis) is a boy's main sex organ. The longer part is called the shaft, and its smooth, round head is called the *glans* (glanz). The glans is very sensitive to touch because it has lots of nerve endings. The underside of the penis just below the glans is also sensitive, and the rest is much less so.

At the very tip of the penis is the tiny opening of the *urethra* (you-REE-thra). In a boy, the urethra carries urine from the bladder through the penis to the outside. It also carries a special fluid called *semen* (SEE-men), which I'll talk about later. Urine and semen are never carried at the same time, so they can't get mixed together. (In a girl, the urethra carries only urine from the bladder to the outside.)

You'll find that the skin of your penis is hairless and "loose." Imagine that the skin fits over the shaft as if it's a glove that's a slightly larger size. When the penis is soft, the skin seems like it's kind of wrinkled because it's a bit "roomy."

So many boys have asked me, "What's inside my penis?" Have you ever wondered about that? Just in case you're not sure, let's take a good look together.

Inside the penis are nerves, blood vessels, and different kinds of tissues. Some are called "spongy" tissues because when blood flows into the penis, these tissues fill up the way a sponge fills up with water. As the tissues are filled, the penis expands and gets stiffer or hard. This is called having an *erection* (ee-RECK-shun).

During an erection, the "loose" skin is filled in and allows the penis to have enough stretching space to become longer and slightly wider. It stays this way for a short while because the blood vessels tighten and keep the blood in the spongy tissues. Very soon, the blood vessels slowly let the blood flow out of the spongy tissues and the penis returns to being soft.

I'll talk more about erections (how often, when, feelings about having them) in the next chapter.

What does *circumcised* mean? A boy is born with a flap of skin attached to and almost covering the glans of his penis. Many parents

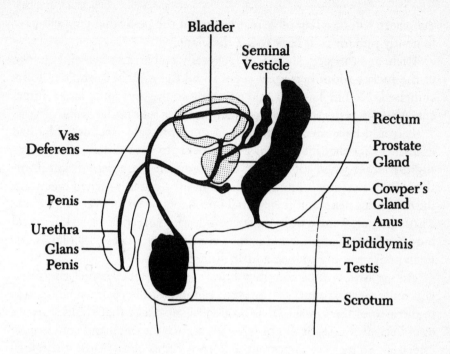

Bladder

Seminal
Vesticle

Vas
Deferens

Penis

Urethra

Glans
Penis

Rectum

Prostate
Gland

Cowper's
Gland

Anus

Epididymis

Testis

Scrotum

decide to have this flap, or *foreskin* (FOUR-skin), surgically removed shortly after birth. Depending upon your religion, removing the foreskin might be done at a special ceremony or by a doctor.

If your foreskin is removed, it's called being *circumcised* (SIR-come-sized), or having a *circumcision* (sir-come-SIZZ-zhun). If it is not removed, you're said to be *uncircumcised*. Most boys in the United States are circumcised. (This means not everybody is.) It's a decision that parents make.

One twelve-year-old boy asked, "If I'm not circumcised, does that mean that my penis won't grow normally?" No! Circumcision will not affect how your penis grows, how sensitive it is, or how it works. Your penis will grow because the male hormone, *testosterone* (tess-TOS-ter-own), is released inside your body. The foreskin is on the outside and has nothing to do with growth.

On a circumcised penis, the glans is showing all the time because there's no flap of skin covering it. Not being circumcised simply means that there will be a flap of skin at the tip of the penis that you will have to gently pull (or roll) back to see the glans.

Rich, age thirteen, shared, "I feel really embarrassed when I change in the locker room because I seem to be the only one who's not circumcised. No one has ever said anything to me. But mine looks different. Also my penis seems larger than that of a lot of other kids."

It would have saved Rich a lot of uncomfortable feelings if he had known earlier that it's natural for his penis to look different as well as slightly larger when soft. That's because of the extra flap of skin (foreskin). Rich also didn't know that if he and the other boys had erections, the size of his penis and theirs would probably be about even, with some a little longer, some a little shorter. And, when erect, his foreskin would move back all by itself, making his penis look almost exactly like theirs. Each penis is going to look a little different anyway.

An important thing to remember, if you are not circumcised, is that you must clean around the foreskin regularly. There are small glands in the area of the foreskin that produce a substance that could store up or collect. If it does, it might have an unpleasant smell and could cause infection. So it's very important to keep the area clean. Most uncircumcised boys and men have to move the foreskin back in order to wash, but not to urinate (pee).

If you wash your penis often, especially in and around the foreskin, then things should be fine. Of course you also have to wash your penis (and the rest of your body), even if you are circumcised!

If you're uncircumcised and find (at any time as you're growing up) that your foreskin is feeling a bit tight, and this makes you uncomfortable around the head of your penis, or if you're having trouble moving back your foreskin, be sure to tell your parents and have them take you to your doctor.

What about penis size? If you really wanted to measure your penis, you'd need to take two different measurements: one when your penis is soft or nonerect, and one when it's hard or erect. Your penis is larger when erect, smaller when nonerect.

More important is to know that the size just doesn't matter, at least not to the penis and how it works. Those boys and men who are concerned about penis size seem to believe that a larger penis means you're more manly, a smaller one, less. Not so! Once again, being a man has much less to do with size than it does with how you feel about yourself inside.

If you looked up at your dad when you were little, you might have wondered if your penis would ever be like his (or like that of other grown-up males you might have seen). Maybe. Maybe not. Your penis might grow to be smaller than your dad's—or larger. All you can do is guess. Since it's all up to your hormones (and I've never heard a hormone speak), there's no way to predict.

You can't look at someone and guess how large his penis is. Just because someone plays football and is bigger than anyone else in your grade, doesn't mean that his penis is probably bigger than that of the smallest boy in your grade. It might even be smaller!

Though other books may tell you an average penis size in centimeters or inches, I refuse! There's no point sitting around waiting with a ruler, hoping you'll be a certain size. Nothing you do can change the size your body will be. Your size will be your size. Whatever it happens to be, you'll still be the special person that you are.

Remember if you can:
Penis size is not the measure of a man!

The Scrotum and Testicles

The **SCROTUM** (SKRO-tum) is a pouch that hangs behind and slightly below the penis. It's a bit darker in color than the rest of the body and becomes slightly covered with hair when a boy reaches puberty.

The scrotum has the very important job of holding and protecting the two **TESTICLES** (TES-tic-kulls) or **TESTES** (TESS-teez) that are inside. Most of you probably know the testicles as "balls" or "nuts."

Sometimes, one or both testicles do not "drop," or move down into their section in the scrotal sac, as they are expected to do shortly before birth. Instead they remain in the abdomen, where the temperature would be too high for sperm to live. This condition is known as having **UNDESCENDED** (un-dee-SEN-ded) or **UNDROPPED** testicles and can be discovered by your doctor during a regular check-up (if you haven't already realized it yourself).

Doctors have several methods to try to bring the testicles into place. If you have this condition (or think you do), be sure to talk with your parent(s) about any question or concern. Also, make sure that your doctor fully explains anything he or she needs to do.

Temperature in the scrotal sac is important because sperm (male sex cells) are produced in the testicles when a boy reaches puberty. Females have egg cells (female sex cells) and males have sperm cells. A girl's ovaries develop so that they can release egg cells that can be fertilized, and a boy's testes develop so they can produce sperm cells. It's the sperm cells that can fertilize the egg cells.

Sperm cells are produced only in the testicles. In order for the sperm to stay healthy, they have to be kept at a temperature that is about three degrees lower than the regular body temperature. That's why the scrotum is outside a male's body.

The muscles of the scrotum respond to heat and cold so that the temperature inside can be right. For example, if the weather is freezing and you're standing outside waiting for your school bus, the muscles will contract (squeeze together) so that the testicles will be pulled closer to your body and can be warmer. If you're sitting in a hot bath, the muscles will expand (relax) so that your testicles will be farther away from your body and will not get too warm.

Internal Organs

Let's look at the inside (internal) organs.

TESTES (TES-teez) or **TESTICLES.** Most males have two. They're delicate and very important. That's why many boys and men wear a "cup" or "jock strap" (a supporter or pouch that holds the genitals in place) when they exercise or play sports. Even though some boys wear it to be macho, cool, or to seem more grown-up, this protection is important because it helps support the scrotum and prevents the genitals from flopping around. Football players, baseball catchers, and other athletes even wear protection cups inside special jock straps, called cup supporters, to be extra safe. Your testicles need extra protection even when you're not playing sports, so don't let anyone kick or hurt you there—and be careful not to hurt anyone else.

If you looked inside the testicles, you'd see hundreds of tubes and compartments. Each testicle is suspended by a spermatic cord (sort of like a puppet on a strong string) in its own section, one on the right and one on the left side of the scrotal sac.

Most boys and men find that their left testicle hangs slightly lower than their right one. Go ahead and check this out in a mirror. Do you see what I'm talking about?

Don't be concerned if one testicle is (or isn't) a little lower; I mainly wanted you to understand that if it is, it's natural for it to be that way! I've had many boys come up to me after my programs to tell me they were very relieved to learn that it's "okay to be lopsided" and that nothing is wrong with them. Even dads have told me they didn't realize this is true. You may want to make sure your older brother and dad know this is normal.

In Chapter 2, you learned that girls have two ovaries that produce female hormones and release egg cells. The testes have similar responsibilities in boys and men. They release the male hormones (most important is testosterone) and produce sperm.

Sometimes it happens that a boy may be born with only one testicle, or an older male may need to have a testicle removed because it's unhealthy. As long as a male has at least one healthy testicle, it's still possible for male hormones to be released and for sperm cells to be produced that will be able to fertilize a female egg cell. (If a boy has one testicle, his scrotum may appear slightly different. That's fine.)

Just as it's important for girls to learn about how to examine their breasts for any changes, when you're in your late teens, it will be important for you to learn about self-examination of your testicles. Doing so will help you understand how to be more aware of any changes that might need to be checked out by your doctor.

A word about *testoterone:* A boy's testicles may start to release testosterone as early as age eleven or not until later. When this happens, his body will begin to develop and change. Testosterone controls growth of hair on the body and face, genital growth, voice deepening, muscle and body development, and sexual interest. (Let's hear it for testosterone!)

SPERM are the male sex cells. They're made in the **SEMINIFEROUS TUBULES** (sem-i-NIFF-er-us TOO-byewls) of the testicles. This is the only place in the body where sperm are made. Sperm have a head, neck, and tail and look like teeny, cute tadpoles. The only way you can see them is under a microscope.

While girls are born with all the egg cells they will ever need already in their ovaries, sperm will not be present in a boy's testicles until they start to develop during puberty. Once a boy starts to produce sperm, he continues for the rest of his life.

Once sperm cells develop and mature, they will be capable of fertilizing a female egg cell. (Reminder: Just because your body is ready to fertilize a female egg, it doesn't mean that *you* are ready. That's something you are better off saving for when you're an adult. More about that later on.)

Both testicles are able to produce millions of sperm each day. Several things can lessen sperm production. Some examples are wearing very tight pants or underwear, sitting in the same position every day for long hours at a time (as truck drivers or bomber pilots do), altitude, or being sick for a while. Sperm production usually goes back to normal when the conditions change (for example, if you're feeling better).

The inside organs work together so that the sperm can be produced, transported, and passed to the outside of a boy's or man's body. Join me as I follow the path that sperm take once they're produced in the testicles.

You already know that the sperm are produced in the seminiferous tubules in the testicles.

The **EPIDIDYMIS** (ep-i-DID-uh-miss—looks harder to say than it is!) is like a storage and ripening chamber that is attached to each testicle. After the sperm are produced, they are moved into the epididymis, where they receive nourishment and stay for several weeks until they fully ripen or mature.

The epididymis also helps to pick out the stronger, healthier sperm so that they're the ones to move on. Many of the weaker or damaged ones simply get absorbed by the tubes in the epididymis and are passed out of the body as waste.

The mature sperm move from the epididymis into the **VAS DEFERENS** (vas DEAF-er-enz) by contractions and the sweeping motion of **CILIA**

(SILL-i-uh), tiny, wavy hairs. They won't be able to swim by themselves (they have cute little tails!) until they mix with fluids from other internal (inside) organs. We're almost up to that part.

The vas deferens is like a long, thin roadway that transports sperm and also helps store them at its wider, upper end. Once in the vas deferens, the sperm are moved up and away from the testicles and around the back of the bladder, and are passed on to mix with the fluid in the *seminal vesicles* (SEM-i-nal VES-i-kulls).

The two seminal vesicles are small saclike glands that contribute an important part of the special fluid called SEMEN. Once the sperm mix with this fluid, they can whip their tails and move along by themselves.

Besides giving the sperm their first chance to become active, this seminal fluid provides them with nourishment (seminal fluid from the seminal vesicles, get it?).

From here, the fluid that now contains sperm flows into the two **EJACULATORY DUCTS** (ee-JACK-u-la-tory). These two ducts connect the seminal vesicles with the opening of the urethra in the prostate gland (hang in there, we're almost through!).

There is only one **PROSTATE GLAND**. It's found at the base of the bladder and is about the size of a walnut. The prostate gland contributes a thin, milky fluid that makes up the largest part of the semen.

The prostate gland has valves that control whether a man will ejaculate semen or urinate. Both urine and semen pass through the urethra but never at the same time.

The prostate gland is supposed to shrink when a man gets older. But sometimes it doesn't. Your dad, uncle, or grandpa might even have complained about an enlarged prostate gland. Because it's so close to the bladder, you can imagine that a larger prostate would cause pressure on the bladder and have an uncomfortable effect on urination. This is a condition that must be treated by a doctor.

The **COWPER'S GLANDS** are two tiny, pea-like glands that are found on either side of the urethra, at the base of the penis, just under the prostate gland.

Just before semen is about to be released through the urethra, these glands give off an *alkaline* or *basic* fluid that helps the semen pass through more easily and safely. The fluid moistens the path of the urethra and offsets the acid of the urine that passed before it. That means that it offsets or balances out the acid so the sperm can pass through more quickly and easily. (Your science teacher will be proud if you know that when bases and acids are mixed together, they balance or neutralize each other.) It might also interest you to know that the vagina is acidy, too.

A word about semen: As you now know, semen is made up of fluid from the seminal vesicles and prostate gland, and a smaller amount from the Cowper's glands. It also contains millions of sperm that make up a very small part of the fluid.

The amount of fluid (usually about one or two teaspoons) can be slightly different from man to man and even different for the same man from time to time. It has to do with such things as a man's health, when he last released semen, or his age. Semen can be thick and almost like gelatin one time and be thin and more watery another.

Semen is passed out of a boy's or man's body through the opening at the tip of the penis. When this happens, it is called an *ejaculation* (ee-jack-cue-LAY-shun). Or we can say that a boy has ejaculated.

If this is the very first time you're learning about ejaculations, you may be surprised, very curious, or possibly a bit nervous. Maybe you're thinking, "Hey, that's great!" Or maybe you're scrunching up your nose and saying to yourself, "Yuck! Does this really have to happen to me?" All those feelings are natural, especially if you can't imagine what it would be like to ejaculate semen. But as you understand what ejaculations can mean and how natural they are to have, you'll probably look forward to the time when you will have them.

I'll talk more about ejaculations and wet dreams (that's when a boy ejaculates in his sleep) in Chapter 6.

Now that you've read this chapter, I think you'll find that the rest of the changes that boys go through in puberty will be easier to understand.

CHAPTER 5

ERECTIONS

How Often Do Boys Have Erections? And When Might They Happen?

Erections are just a natural part of being a boy. Boys can start having erections as soon as they're born. As I explained in Chapter 4, when a boy has an erection, his penis becomes stiffened, slightly longer and wider.

Erections can happen on and off throughout the day and night. Even though there's no special schedule for erections during the day (you'll probably get one sometimes but you may not), there seems to be an erection pattern that's connected with when you dream during sleep. If you wake up close to when you've just had a dream, you might wake up with an erection. An erection from dreams or pressure on the bladder is common for boys and men when they wake up. Erections during sleep can also relate to what you dream.

It wouldn't work for a boy to think to himself, "I want to have an erection now," wait three seconds, and expect to magically, instantly become erect. An erection may happen, but only if the body is willing. It's interesting that erections happen because of a reflex. That means that a message from a boy's brain or his body lets the nerves in charge of erection know that "it's time for another one."

These erection nerves are located in the lower part of the spinal cord. After getting an "erection message," they then send signals that cause an extra supply of blood to flow into the spongy tissues of the penis. More blood flows in than is able to flow out. The penis gets larger, bit by bit, as the blood fills up and stays in these tissues. While this is happening, the color of the penis becomes slightly deeper, as if it's blushing.

The erection lasts as long as the messages continue sending in the extra blood supply. This keeps the spongy tissues filled. When the "erection messages" stop, blood flow gradually returns to normal and the penis once again becomes soft.

Lots of different things can cause an "erection message" to be sent: seeing or talking with someone you like; touching the sensitive parts of your penis, scrotum, or other areas around the penis; certain sounds, smells, or dreams; sexual feelings; physical activity.

A boy could get an erection while he's standing up in front of the class giving a book report, while he's playing a sport, when he's talking with the new girl in his class, or while he's looking at pictures in certain magazines.

Because erection is a reflex, a boy can have an erection when he doesn't even expect it or want it. Once he has it, he just has to wait until it becomes soft again. He can't prevent it from happening, and he can't force his penis to bulge if it's not in the mood!

Kids sometimes call an erection a "boner." But the penis doesn't have a bone in it. A dog's penis does. So does the penis of a male fox (just in case you were wondering about foxes!). And those of some other animals, too—but not humans. "Boner" probably started because of how hard the penis can get.

It's possible that influences such as taking certain medications, being very tired, or drinking a lot of alcohol can have an effect on a person's being able to have an erection. Difficulty in having an erection at those times doesn't have to mean that a male will continue to have difficulty getting an erection. It may only seem like a problem at that moment, and the next time, he'll probably have an erection as he always did before. If you ever have any question or concern about having erections, it would be important to let your parent or family doctor know.

———

Some erections end in ejaculation. That's when that milky whitish fluid called semen spurts out of the tip of the penis. You can read more about ejaculation and wet dreams in the next chapter.

Erection Feelings, Concerns, and Confusions

Susan, age twelve, wanted to know what happens if a boy has an erection when he's swimming. She asked, "Would he have to get out of the water?"

If anything, Susan, a boy would probably keep right on swimming. No matter what sport a boy is playing, erections won't prevent him from continuing. They usually don't last that long anyway.

Sometimes boys have erections in the water because the pressure and wetness can send a message to the erection control center. Just as nipples often become erect when it's cold or when they're brushed lightly by clothing, so the penis can become erect in response to friction or pressure.

Another factor has to do with what a boy is wearing while he swims. Depending on how tight and what style a boy's bathing suit is, he might purposely stay under water until his erection becomes soft. Or his erection may be just the reason to come out of the water—boys have many different feelings about when and where they have erections.

Kevin, age twelve, told me, "I started wearing looser bathing suits so it wouldn't be so easy to notice when I get an erection. I used to be really embarrassed 'cause I thought everyone would know."

Jeff, age eleven, said his older brother likes to wear "bikini, skinny, tight bathing suits and just kind of parades around, showing off, when he gets hard."

Thirteen-year-old Josh described how he "takes care of" his erections when he's in school and doesn't really want people to notice. "I just fix it so it's flat against my stomach. I stick my hand in my pocket and adjust myself. If anyone sees me with my hand there, I make like I'm looking for something and then put my hands in my back pockets and search around. I can usually come up with a piece of paper or pen or something. It only takes a second to move my penis against my body. Then I don't think about it."

Kenny, age twelve, said, "I used to worry about blushing when I got an erection. They never bothered me when I was by myself, but I always thought other people would know. I don't know why, but it doesn't bother me anymore. I guess I just got used to having them."

It's usually a relief to learn that you're not the only person in the whole world to feel a certain way or have a particular concern. So much of what these boys said was similar. Maybe you have felt the same way.

Now that you know more about your sex organs, semen, and how you get an erection, it's time to talk about wet dreams and ejaculation.

Chapter 6

EJACULATIONS AND WET DREAMS

What Is an Ejaculation?

Ejaculation is a special part of growing up for a boy. It means he's officially on his way to becoming a man. You now know that when ejaculation takes place, semen spurts out through the opening at the tip of a boy's penis. (You can read about semen in Chapter 4).

Ejaculation is the only way that semen can get outside a boy's or a man's body. Since semen is the fluid that transports sperm, this means that ejaculation is the way for sperm to move from the inside to the outside of the body, so it might fertilize a female egg cell (when a man and woman decide they're ready to try to have that happen—more about this later).

REMINDER: Sperm contained in the drops of fluid released from the Cowper's glands before ejaculation can also cause a female egg to be fertilized. This is often called *pre-ejaculatory fluid*.

Sperm may not be part of a boy's beginning ejaculations (just as ovulation may not occur when a girl first gets her period). In time, each ejaculation will contain millions of sperm. Since sperm are very, very tiny, you can't just look at your semen and tell if sperm are present. They can be seen only under a microscope.

Many kids confuse a boy's ejaculations with a girl's periods. An ejaculation is *not* like a period, but both are the surest signs of puberty for boys and girls. That's probably the only thing they have in common. An ejaculation is nothing like a period except for the fact that a special fluid is passed out of the body through the genitals.

A girl can't control when she gets her period. It could start anytime, anywhere. An ejaculation is different. It doesn't spurt without advanced notice when a boy is awake. A boy will be able to feel an ejaculation coming on.

So a boy doesn't have to be concerned that an ejaculation will take him by surprise, at least not while he's awake. It's a different story when he's asleep. His thoughts and dreams might excite the nerves that signal ejaculation, without his even realizing it. If a boy has an ejaculation when he's sleeping, it's called having a *wet dream*. (I'll talk more about this in a little while.) If he has an ejaculation when he's awake, it's just called an ejaculation.

Boys don't need pads for ejaculations the way girls do for periods. The little spurt of semen simply comes out (some people call semen *come*) and will soon dry up. Periods are reddish in color; semen is whitish. While periods occur about every four weeks and flow out over several days, it takes only a few seconds for semen to be passed out during ejaculations, and these may happen a few times a day—one, two, or more days in a row—or not for several days or weeks. There are no schedules for ejaculations as there are for periods.

Finally, a period is the specially built-up lining of the uterus that is no longer needed. Semen is the important fluid that contains living sperm. Girls can't "get" semen and boys can't "get" a period.

How Does a Boy's Body Know When to Ejaculate?

Like erections, ejaculations happen because of a reflex. Once again, signals are sent to the lower spinal cord. This time the message is in two parts.

First an "ejaculation alert" message is signalled to the internal organs that help to make semen. This tells them to contract and force their fluids along with sperm into the passageway that will lead them into the urethra and out of the penis—sort of like getting ready in the "starting gate."

While the fluids are gathering together, other contractions shut off the bladder from the urethra so that urine does not mix with semen. (All you kids who were concerned about this can breathe a big sigh of relief!)

Now all is ready for the second message, which will signal certain muscles in the penis to contract and squeeze semen through the urethra so it can spurt out of the penis. The contractions usually have a rhythm to them and last for several seconds. How strong these contractions are can differ from man to man and can also vary in the same man from time to time.

Many people make the mistake of calling semen sperm. The fluid is called semen. Sperm are found in semen.

How about a review? A reflex causes a signal to be sent to the "ejaculation control area" in the lower part of the spinal cord. Two messages are sent. The first message tells the inside organs, "ejaculatory alert, get your fluids together, be sure to shut off the bladder so that no urine mixes with the semen, and get ready to go." The second message says, "Fire away. . . ."

An interesting thing is that, once that first message is sent, ejaculation can't be interrupted. That's because the reflex has already set everything in motion and it's too late to stop it. A boy will be able to feel that ejaculation is coming, but he can't prevent it from happening once it has started.

An erection is usually the first step leading to ejaculation, though *not all* erections end in ejaculation. At certain times, a boy may wish to allow the sensations that caused an erection reflex (see Chapter 5, page 64) to continue so that stronger feelings of pleasure are felt in and around the area of the penis. These are usually sexual feelings.

If these feelings build up high enough—such as can happen when a boy's penis is touched—the ejaculation reflex will be touched off, messages sent, and you know what happens from there. At the point where these pleasurable feelings are the strongest, a boy may or may not have what's known as an *orgasm* (OR-ga-zum) along with his ejaculation. An ejaculation is often accompanied by an orgasm but doesn't have to be.

An orgasm can be felt as nice, kind of tingly feelings of warmth as well as several short contractions—or flutterings—in the genital area. This is a very personal experience and may be slightly different for each person. Both the orgasm and the ejaculation represent a release from the strong pleasurable feelings that were built up. After erection and ejaculation, the penis returns to being soft again.

Girls as well as boys can experience orgasms. Even though girls don't have ejaculations as they are described for boys, similar feelings of warmth and pleasure can build up in their clitoris and in and around their vaginal opening, reach a high point, and then be released through orgasm. This can happen to girls when their vulvas or other sensitive areas are touched. More is said about "tingly-when-touched" feelings in Chapter 9.

When Can You Expect to Start Ejaculating?

Your first ejaculation will usually come after your genitals have begun to grow and after you have grown some pubic hair. But, once again, there aren't any rules. You could start ejaculating as early as age eleven or not until later in your teens. It's up to your hormone schedule.

I can't tell you that you'll ejaculate only when you have a hundred new pubic hairs or more . . . I can't promise that you'll have started to ejaculate by the time you're fifteen.

All I can hope to do is let you know what to expect, so that if you wake up one morning and find that your sheets have a "funny" spot on them, just pat yourself on the back, pinch your cheek in the mirror, and say, "Congratulations, you old thing, you!" And then go about your day with a special smile because you know that something important has changed in you that will never be the same again. With this change come new feelings, new responsibilities. . . .

What About Wet Dreams?

As I told you, a boy is said to have a wet dream if he ejaculates semen while he's sleeping. Another name for wet dreams is *nocturnal emissions* (nock-TER-nal ee-MISH-unz). *Nocturnal* refers to night—you might have learned about nocturnal animals such as the owl or bat. *Emission* refers to a discharge or flow of fluid.

A boy's first ejaculation most often happens as a wet dream and goes along with pleasurable thoughts. Michael, age seventeen, said that he remembers that his first wet dream happened when he was twelve years old. He was dreaming of kissing his favorite female movie star while they were together on a faraway private beach. When he woke up, his dream lady had vanished, and only the semen remained to remind him she had been there.

Other boys may have only slight memories of what went on in their dream. Still others who have wet dreams don't remember dreaming at all. All of these boys are normal.

If you've already had a wet dream, do you remember how you felt the first time you realized you did? If you haven't had one yet, think about what feelings you have about wet dreams. What questions would you like answered? What are your concerns? (You might want to write these down to make sure that you get all the information you need.)

Joel, age fourteen, learned about wet dreams before having them, so he wasn't surprised when he discovered a wetness on his sheets. He told me, "When I had my first wet dream, it just proved to me what I had thought all along . . . that I was normal!"

Hoorah for whomever it was who made sure Joel knew that wet dreams are normal and expected. Many boys at my school programs who didn't know about wet dreams before having them told me they thought they peed in their bed or thought something was wrong. They would have been so relieved to understand what was happening to them and to know there's nothing a boy can do to control them while he's asleep. Wet dreams can't be prevented, just accepted and understood as a natural thing for a boy's or man's body to do.

There are some boys and men who have told me they haven't noticed ever having a wet dream. It's possible that they haven't had one. I know of no rules that say you *must* have a wet dream. But since a boy might not have realized his body has become able to ejaculate, he might notice it for the first time after he has been sleeping (a time when he was not controlling his thoughts, dreams, and actions).

How Will You Know If You've Had a Wet Dream?

You may or may not wake up after having a wet dream. If you wake up, you might feel that your pajamas or underwear or sheets are slightly damp or even a little sticky. That's how semen might be right after you ejaculate. Then it becomes more liquid and just dries up.

Many boys are very concerned about being able to tell the difference between urine and semen. Well, if you wanted to make sure just for yourself, you could check the color of the fluid and see how it feels. Semen can be a little bit sticky and has a milky whitish coloring. Urine looks like yellowish water and is not sticky.

If you don't wake up after having a wet dream, you might feel a slight dampness in the morning, depending on how much time has passed since your wet dream. Or you may be able to find a spot or two on your sheets, or on whatever you're wearing, that seems to be slightly off-white where the semen might have dried up.

The amount of semen is usually around one or two teaspoons of fluid. If you check out how much this is by putting water in a measuring spoon, I think you'll agree that it's not very much fluid. So you might not even notice anything!

Just as it doesn't hurt to urinate (pee), it doesn't hurt to pass semen out of your body. Most men and boys say it feels good.

Is It Scary to Have a Wet Dream?

Perhaps by now you realize that wet dreams are like all the other changes that I've mentioned so far. They're a natural, important part of growing up. Changes become scary when we don't understand what's happening or why.

A good example of how scary the unknown can be is the story told to me by Ralph, who is now nineteen years old. He has a twin brother, who was sick on and off when they were younger. Ralph had already had a wet dream and had never really discussed it with his twin brother.

One day Ralph walked into his brother's room and saw him hurrying to smear tomato sauce all over his sheets. Ralph said, "Are you crazy? What are you doing that for?" His brother answered in a whisper, "A terrible thing happened and I don't want to have to go to the doctor again. I'll just tell Mom that I was eating in bed and accidentally dropped my spaghetti on my sheets. You better not tell!"

Ralph asked, "Well, what happened that was so terrible?" His brother replied, "This stuff came out of my penis and it never happened to me before. It must mean I'm sick again." Ralph said, "That happens to everybody; it's supposed to happen." And then he went on to explain what it was.

Those of you who are still laughing because of the tomato sauce, stop for a moment and think about how scared Ralph's brother must have felt even before he decided that tomato sauce would be a great "cover-up." He had been sick for too long—too many doctors, too much time in bed—and he didn't want to be sick anymore. If only someone had told him that ejaculations were just a natural part of growing up.

What Can You Do with Your Sheets?

Well, you've got a few choices. Only you can decide which one you feel is best. (I'm sure you can add your own ideas to my list.)

The first choice is to simply do nothing! Since having a wet dream is so natural—and most boys have them, even dads, since wet dreams don't stop just because you get older—just let the semen dry, leave your sheets on your bed, and forget about it.

If you're embarrassed or concerned that anyone might see, then change your own sheets. Some boys think they need an excuse to have to change them. So they spill milk, chocolate milk, just something wet (yes, tomato sauce, too), and that seems to make it okay to have to put them in the hamper or whatever. That's really not truthful, but if you need to do that, that's up to you.

Who Should You Tell If You Have a Wet Dream?

This is a special, personal experience. It's possible that if you told your parents about having a wet dream, they'd be happy that you're developing as you should and feel great that you could tell them. It's not the kind of experience where you need help in making a decision—the decision has already been made for you by your body. So it's more a matter of choosing to share because you want to, not because you need to.

One mother told me that she realized she hadn't discussed wet dreams with her thirteen-year-old son. So she went through a whole explanation, and when she was through, her son said, "Gee thanks, Mom, I've been having them for two years!"

Ron, age twelve, said, "None of my friends ever discuss wet dreams." Bill, now in his fifties, shared, "If we said anything at all about wet dreams it was just because we were trying to act like part of the crowd—and no one would ask questions, since we really didn't know what we were saying, anyway."

I supposed there will be some kids who'll want to discuss them and many others who won't. Use your judgment. It's your experience, so you decide. It might be fun to ask your dad, grandfather, older brother, or uncles about when and how they learned about wet dreams. Maybe they used spaghetti sauce, too.

Ejaculations Will Continue Throughout a Man's Life

When a man gets older—it's hard to say exactly when, though some men find this to be true around the age of sixty or beyond—the force of his ejaculations and the amount of semen may lessen slightly. But a healthy man will be able to ejaculate for the rest of his life. This is another difference from periods, which end during menopause (see page 49).

Since a man's testicles will continue to produce sperm, semen will always contain sperm, even though as he gets older, the number of sperm might be less.

Chapter 7

VOICE CHANGE

What Does It Mean for Your Voice to Change?

This is one change that you don't have to check out at the beach. All you have to do is listen. Pay attention to the voices of your father, older brother, uncle, grandpa, male teachers, or men on TV and in the movies. Like everything else, each person's voice sounds a little different. Some voices are higher, some lower, others soft; still others are deep and booming.

If you sing with your school or religious choir, you might have already noticed that every once in a while, another boy or two will need to move from the higher-note to the lower-note section. You, too, may have found that the notes you used to sing easily are beginning to be too high. When you strain to reach them, you might even sound squeaky.

A change in the sound of your voice is another natural part of growing up. When a boy's voice changes, his voice gradually becomes deeper, fuller, and richer.

When Will Your Voice Start to Change?

Voice change usually takes place around the middle of puberty, after your pubic and body hairs have started to grow and often after genital growth and your first ejaculation.

I guess by now you may be tired of having to thank testosterone for your development, but I think it's only fair. After all, it's amazing how your hormones keep track of all the changes they have to make. Imagine if your hormones didn't remember to change your voice or if a girl's hormones just plain forgot to give her breasts. (I know, you're probably thinking that you know some girls with forgetful hormones. Give them time!)

Deepening of your voice will start to happen when testosterone causes your vocal cords and voice box or *larynx* (LAR-inks) to grow larger. Some people also call the voice box the Adam's apple.

You can find it if you move your hand down along your neck from the tip of your chin. At about the middle of the front of your neck, you'll be able to feel a slight bump or ridge. Some people's bumps are easier to notice than others. That's normal.

Voice change is a good example of how testosterone is really responsible for important development all over the body, not just in your genital area.

How Will Your Voice Sound?

Matt, age twelve, said, "I love it when I answer the telephone and people think I'm my father!" Jason, age twelve, said, "I *don't* love it when I answer the phone and people think I'm my mother!"

Though some boys may end up sounding like their parents or other relatives, there's no way to predict that you will, too. The best thing is to wait and see. Let your larynx surprise you!

Matt's voice doesn't make him any more manly, and Jason's voice doesn't make him any less manly. There are plenty of grown men with softer, higher voices. It's not what a person sounds like; it's who he is.

How Long Will It Take for Your Voice to Change and What Might It Be Like?

As with many changes in puberty, voice change often takes place over a period of time. While it's changing, you might not be able to trust your voice not to crack when you're talking or singing.

Billy, now fourteen, told me, "It took about two years for my voice to finish changing. It really didn't bother me that much. There were a few embarrassing times when I was reading aloud in class and my voice cracked. Otherwise, it was no big thing."

John, age thirteen, said, "I really didn't notice it was happening to me. Other people started saying how different I sounded and then I heard it, too. Some of my friends' voices have been cracking a lot, but mine never did."

Bruce, age seventeen, said, "I got used to my mother's friends calling me Lisa (my younger sister) when I answered the telephone. I just politely told them it was me. What I couldn't get used to was when my friends at school cracked up when my voice squeaked. My squeaky voice and their laughter went on for about a year. I stopped talking a lot in public. It was and sometimes still is very embarrassing to talk around girls."

As you can see, each person will grow and change in his own way. Since some boys feel a bit embarrassed that they can't stop their voice from cracking, it would be helpful if you wouldn't laugh or make fun when this happens. They're trying very hard to accept and deal with their own changes, just as you're trying to accept yours.

A Word About Girls' Voices

Though voice change is not considered an official puberty change for girls, their voices also become richer, fuller, and more mature.

Hal, age ten, wanted to know if girls' voices cracked the way boys' voices do. Not that I know of, Hal. They may crack because a girl is hoarse from a sore throat or screaming, but not because of her development.

Listening to the sounds of men's and women's voices around you can be an interesting way to prove that each person is unique.

Don't judge or make fun of anyone's voice,
Since voice boxes never give kids a choice.

GROWING UP MALE AND FEMALE FEELING GOOD

——

Chapter 8

PUBIC AND OTHER BODY HAIR

Remember the growth clock idea? That's when your body signals the release of your hormones so you'll begin to experience the changes of puberty. Growing new hair is one of those changes.

Pubic Hairs: Where Can You Find Them, Where Do They Grow, What Are They Like?

Pubic (PEW-bick) *hairs* are those little hairs that grow a few inches below the belly button. On a girl, they cover the mons pubis (Chapter 2, page 20) and continue down between the legs. On boys, they grow around the base of the penis.

As with all the changes of puberty, pubic hairs will appear when your own body is ready. Your genitals can thank your pubic hairs for the extra protection. A girl's pubic hair usually starts growing after her breasts swell and before her period. A boy's pubic hair often appears after his penis and testicles show signs of growth, and before his first ejaculation. These are only guidelines—not rules—as sometimes the timing of pubic hair growth doesn't work out exactly that way.

You can start looking for them when you're about ten or eleven. But don't be surprised if they don't show up until later.

Since pubic hairs sprout a few at a time, you don't have to be concerned about going to sleep without them and waking up with hundreds. You'll start with two or three (my son Andy named his first three, "Harry, Sam, and Fred"!), then grow more and more until your pubic area appears "filled in."

Your body is very clever and knows just how much hair your pubic area should grow. I have never heard of anybody tripping over their pubic hair because it was too long.

Pubic hairs feel and are different from the hairs on your head. They're not as soft to touch. People with dark hair on top usually have dark pubic hair. Light-haired people often have light pubic hair. The pubic hairs probably won't match exactly and will usually be a bit darker than the hair on your head.

It's normal to find funny little pubic hairs in your bathtub, on your underwear, and on bathing suits or sheets, just as it's common to find head hairs on your coats, jackets, and sweaters. All you have to do is look at your hairbrush to know that hairs often come out. New hairs grow in to take their place. The same thing happens with pubic and other body hairs.

When Pubic Hair First Grows In

Jodi, age thirteen, wished that it would all grow in at once. Said Jodi, "It's really funny-looking to just have half."

Bobby, age thirteen, said he was the first one of his friends to really have a lot of pubic hair. He loved to show it off in gym class by taking an extra long time to get out of the shower.

Thirteen-year-old David told me, "When I was at camp last summer, I was more developed than any other kid in my group. No one else had pubic hair and I had a ton. I was very self-conscious 'cause I remembered what they did to the guy that had them last year—they teased him to death. So I changed in the bathroom most of the time."

Fourteen-year-old Michael changed in the bathroom because he was the only one without pubic hair. The feelings work both ways.

Since pubic hairs are controlled by your hormones, they can't be forced to appear before their own schedule. They also can't be pushed back in once they come out. So the best thing you can do is try to accept yourself for who you are and trust that your body will develop when it's ready.

Underarm Hair

Hair will also begin to grow under your arms. It will probably grow sometime after your pubic hairs and will be softer. Once again, you'll notice a few hairs at first, then more and more. And your body will know how much hair to grow.

An eleven-year-old boy at one of my programs asked, "Does pubic hair grow under your arms?" Underarm hair is *not* pubic hair. Pubic hair is pubic hair.

Shaving the hair under your arms seems to depend on the customs or habits of the people where you live. In the United States, most girls and women shave under their arms. They usually wait a few years until they have enough hairs to bother to shave. Shaving can sometimes irritate tender skin such as that under your arms or on your face. So, if you feel you want to start shaving, it's important to talk about this with your mom or dad so they can help choose the best type of shaver for you and also show you how. In other countries, it's common for women not to shave under their arms. Boys and men usually do not shave their underarms in any country. It's a very personal decision.

I often get the question, "If you don't have hair under your arms, should you use deodorant?" The answer is *yes!* Using deodorant doesn't depend on the amount of hair you have. It has to do with how much you sweat! Whether or not you have underarm hair, it can help to use deodorant if you find you're sweating a lot. (More about taking care of your body in Chapter 10.)

Peter, age ten, said, "My big brother wanted hair under his arms so badly. When he finally got it, he stretched out the arm holes of his short-sleeved shirts so people could see his hair through the sleeve when he raised his hand in class." Peter went on to tell me that this was really important to his brother because he was shorter than many of his friends. Growing hair made him feel bigger.

Diane, age twenty-three, remembers developing very early. She had a lot of pubic and underarm hair by the time she was eleven, and most of her friends had very little or none. She shared, "Whenever I had to change in front of them, I tried to keep my arms in close to my body so no one would notice how much hair I had. My mother thought eleven was too young to shave."

As with other hair that starts to grow during puberty, there can be many feelings that go along with getting underarm hair. So often these feelings are tied up with whether you're first or last among your friends to develop.

Hair on Your Chest

Before I talk about hair on a boy's or man's chest, I want to remind you that girls might also grow a few hairs. As I told you in Chapter 1, these hairs might be around the nipples or the breasts. This is very normal.

A friend of mine told me that when he was growing up, his father always used to tease that he had a "basketball team of hair on his chest . . . five on each side" (that was supposed to make you smile). The interesting thing is, now that he's all grown up, there still aren't that many more "players."

Some men will be very hairy, with hairs all over their upper and lower chest, shoulders, and even upper back. Others, like my friend with the "basketball team," have only a few. Still others have medium amounts. Also, people from different races or ethnic groups may have more or less body hair than others.

Chest hair usually appears late in puberty. If puberty starts late for you, chest hairs may not show up until you're twenty or older. The important thing to remember is that each boy is going to develop in his own way and the way of his race or ethnic group.

You may grow a lot of hairs on your chest or just a few. The amount of hair has nothing to do with being manly. That depends upon who you are on the inside.

Mustaches and Other Facial Hair—Shaving

Both boys and girls grow new hairs on their face during puberty. One of the first things to show up is a darkening of the hair around the sideburn area and over the upper lip. Depending on how dark the hair is over the lip, it may seem like a mustache. (And sometimes it is!)

I was in the supermarket a few weeks ago and on the checkout line saw a boy who used to be in one of my programs. When I went over to say hi, the first thing his mother said to me was "Look at him! Can you believe his mustache?" He turned away from me and never looked back. I had the feeling he was very embarrassed.

Some kids are proud of this new growth of hair. Others wish it wasn't there. If anyone (including moms, dads, and kids who tease) talks about this or any other part of your development in a way that makes you feel funny, embarrassed, or angry—let them know how you feel. I hope that boy told his mother what he was feeling when he turned away. That's the only way she'll understand and learn he doesn't want her to do it again.

If the hairs over your lip seem very dark and you have strong feelings about not wanting them there, at least you know you're not the only one who's got those hairs. And you do have a few choices as to what you might do about them.

If you're a boy Try speaking with your parents about shaving. Most parents I've spoken with want their sons to wait as long as possible before starting to shave. As one parent said, "You shave because the hairs are dark and you don't want them there. But once you shave, they come in even darker and are sort of prickly. The longer you wait to shave again, the more prickly they get. So once you start to shave, you have to keep shaving. I want my son to start as late as possible 'cause he's going to be shaving for a long time!"

Boys usually do not need to shave until their middle or late teens. As that father said, once you start, that's it. You'll be shaving forever (unless you grow a beard). Some boys will grow hair early, others later. Again, you can be manly with or without hairs on your face. If you don't feel very manly, probably you won't be. If you do, then whether or not you have hairs won't matter as much.

When I was in high school, there was one boy in my class who had very dark hair on his face. We called him Shadow. Even if he shaved in the morning, he looked like he had "shadows" on his face before school was over. Though lots of boys were jealous because he needed to shave, Shadow told me secretly (he was a good friend of mine) that he wished he didn't always have to shave so often.

I guess the best thing is not to compare. What may seem really terrific on someone else might not even be terrific for them and might not work out the best for you.

Do you remember watching and imitating your father shaving when you were a little boy? (I even imitated my father, and I was a little girl! I guess shaving seemed like it would be a lot of fun.) Did you look up and wonder, "When will it be my turn?" Well, your turn will come. If not this year, maybe next. But once you start, you'll do it forever, so think about whether or not you really want to rush it.

Each parent will probably feel a bit differently about shaving. If you're not sure how your parents feel, ask them. If you feel you're ready to shave, make sure you speak with your mom or dad to make sure you know what steps to follow.

Very important note about shaving (for both boys and girls)
Whether you use an electric shaver or one with a blade (there are many types to choose from, including disposables—ones you can throw away after using), make sure you clean your shaver properly after each use. You can run the blade shaver under hot water; electric razors are usually cleaned with a special kit. Ask your parents to help you if you're not sure what to do.

Be careful how you shave, since even the shavers that are considered to have safety blades can cut you if you don't know what you're doing (and sometimes even when you do). So remember to get your parents (or someone older you trust) to teach you about shaving before doing it yourself.

If you're a girl I strongly suggest you speak with your parents about any of these methods before using them. You would be wise not to use them without permission and proper adult guidance.

Here are a few things you might want to know about if you have unwanted hair on your face or other parts of your body (boys and men might also choose some of these methods).

Tweezing is fine for eyebrows (and even chin hairs) but it's a good idea not to tweeze your mustache. This method can be a bit uncomfortable and has to be done fairly often. Tweezing is not permanent. So if you tweeze, just expect the hairs to grow in again and plan to keep on tweezing them out.

One caution—although tweezed hairs do grow back, I know someone who tweezed her eyebrows when she was a teenager and didn't really know what she was doing. She tweezed so much of the part that she felt was "too bushy" and didn't realize she was tweezing out a lot of her eyebrows. That part never quite fully filled in again. If you're not sure about what you're doing, ask first.

Waxing is another way to take care of unwanted hair (this can be used for eyebrows, legs, or mustaches). Wax is spread over the unwanted hair in the direction of the hair growth. A special cloth is used to remove the wax and with it comes the unwanted hairs. Properly done, waxing usually lasts several weeks and is best handled by someone who is professionally trained and licensed to do this.

Bleaching unwanted hairs is another choice. Instead of removing hair, it's like using a cover-up to lighten the hair that is still there. Bleaches that are prepared for *facial* (FAY-shul) hair (hair on the face) can be bought in a drugstore. Sometimes bleaches will result in a difference in color, causing the area above the lip to look yellowish or orangy. Be sure to watch out for redness or irritation if you have sensitive skin.

You also might want to know about a procedure called *electrolysis* (ee-leck-TROL-li-siss). This is a way to permanently remove unwanted hair from the face, legs, or other areas of the body. After several treatments (some people need many, others less), this method can remove hair permanently. It must be done by a trained and licensed electrologist.

If you use any of the creams for removing unwanted hair (often called superficial hair) that can be bought in a drugstore, be aware that the chemicals in them might cause irritation if your skin is sensitive. Along with the unwanted hair, it's also possible for fine, baby hair to be removed that would probably disappear by itself.

Even more desirable would be not to do anything. It may not make you feel completely better—but perhaps at least a bit better—to know that lots of kids have those same hairs to deal with, just like you. If you think you can live with them until the more permanent hairs take form, then just leave the hairs alone and wait (if it's really excessive, you and your parents might want to talk to your family doctor).

Important message for boys and girls If you tamper with your facial hair in a way that harms your hair, it might never lighten up. Every time you tamper with your hair, you cause something to happen to it. Be careful not to take advice from someone who doesn't know the facts. Never use a chemical, cream, or anything on your hair that you have not first discussed with your parents, doctor, or at least a trusted and informed adult.

If you are concerned about mustaches or other hairs on your face, let your parents know how you feel. They may not be in favor of any correction method. I'm not suggesting any one in particular, but I hope it will be helpful for you to know what choices you have to consider. What you do is up to you and your parents to decide.

Hair on Your Legs—Shaving

Shaving legs seems to be done mostly by girls and women. As with underarm hair, whether you shave your legs may depend on the customs and habits of the people in your culture. It's another personal decision.

Cathy, now thirty-two, told me, "I used to be very embarrassed about having so much hair on my legs, even though it was very light. I used to hide my legs under my desk in school, putting them as far under as they could go. My mother finally gave me permission to shave them during the summer when I was sixteen. I was going to be in a talent show at camp and I begged for permission to shave because I was planning to wear shorts and didn't want all the hair on my legs to show up on stage. My mom figured it was time and let me do it. I was so relieved and have been shaving my legs ever since."

Robin, now age twenty-eight, told me her "hairy-legs story." Picture this. Robin couldn't stand having such dark, hairy legs when she was growing up. At fourteen, she refused to go to her aunt's wedding unless her mother let her shave. She claims that her legs would have looked awful with tiny black hairs showing through the nylon stockings. Even though she pouted and sulked for a week before the wedding, her mother wouldn't give in. So Robin started a big fight and never went.

As with everything else, each parent will probably feel differently about if and when you should start shaving your legs. Once you start, you need to continue, because the hairs get prickly and slightly darker. But if you decided to stop shaving and let your hairs grow long again, they would eventually get softer.

Once, my daughter brushed up against my legs and I hadn't shaved that day. All she said was, "yuck!" Those little hairs become prickly if you wait too long to shave. If your hair is light, you probably can wait a few days or longer between shaves. Each girl who makes the decision to shave has to decide for herself how often she needs to shave in order to feel good.

Talk with your parents if the hair on your legs concerns you. It might help to remember that what you feel is so noticeable, may be noticeable only to *you*. I don't know if anyone really paid attention to Cathy's legs before she hid them under her desk. She was the one who felt so self-conscious. (She told me no one ever said anything to her.) But she had to deal with her feelings and try to make herself feel as comfortable as possible. You owe it to yourself to be honest with yourself and your parents. (They can help!)

Even if your parents are set against your shaving or doing anything about hair that is bothering you, let them know how upset you are. They may not realize how strongly you feel.

Very important note about shaving your legs If you're concerned about the hair above your knees, you should know that this hair will probably not be very noticeable by the time you're in your twenties. If you shave or bleach it, the hair will likely become more coarse or rough feeling and will not be as soft as it was.

CHAPTER 9

WHAT ABOUT MASTURBATION?

"Tingly When Touched Feelings"—What Kind of Feelings Are They and Where Can They Be Felt?

Gently stroking your fingertips will probably make them feel nice and tingly. This is because there are lots of nerve endings at the tips of your fingers, which make them extra sensitive to touch. The more nerve endings, the more tingly you can feel.

If you read Chapters 2 and 4 on girls' and boys' "private parts," you'll probably remember that I spoke about certain areas in and around your genitals that also have many nerve endings. Like your fingertips, they can be sensitive or "tingly when touched."

Because your genitals are special, very personal, private areas of your body, the "tingly when touched" feelings that can be felt in the genitals are also thought of as personal, private feelings.

Sometimes these tingly feelings can be felt when you're not even expecting them, like when tight clothing rubs against your genitals, when you're bicycle riding, taking a shower or a bath, soaping your genitals, sleeping on your stomach, or pressing your thighs together.

Other times these "tinglies" can be felt because a person decides to make them happen. Girls or boys (adults, too) may purposely touch the sensitive areas of their genitals just so they can feel those feelings. This kind of touching often results in having an orgasm (Chapter 6, page 69).

When this is done on purpose, it is said that the person is *masturbating* (MASS-ter-bay-ting). Masturbating or *masturbation* (mass-ter-BAY-shun) is a word that really perks up people's ears because it is a private behavior and few people talk openly about it. So when someone takes the chance and decides to bring up this topic, people's faces may get flushed and they may giggle out of embarrassment.

Why People Can't Talk About Masturbation

Feelings about masturbation have a very interesting history. False beliefs were passed down from generation to generation that made people think something bad would happen if they masturbated. For years and years, people really believed masturbation would cause hair to grow out of the palms of their hands; make their genitals dry up and fall off; make them have a swaggering walk; make them have cold, clammy hands; give them shifty eyes, weak shoulders, hunchbacks, and warts. The list goes on and on.

While I can promise you these are false ideas and won't happen, I know there are still many people who aren't sure. Somewhere in the back of your mind, even you may be wondering if masturbation is really okay.

When most little kids begin to discover their genitals, they usually touch them because they're curious and probably have no idea what their parents think about what they're doing. They often continue to touch because it makes them feel good and hardly ever know this is called masturbation.

As girls and boys reach puberty, they may start to masturbate if they haven't already. Those who do often seem to sense that this should be done alone and not talked about. A remark, look, or scowl made by someone either now or years ago may have given them the message to keep masturbation private or even not to do it at all.

Some kids who touch themselves privately would never say so in public because they'd expect the other kids would laugh or spread the word around. (Chances are, they would!)

If kids learn that genital touching is to remain private, and no one knows what anyone else is doing, then they never seem to be able to get the straight truth about it without someone joking, laughing, rolling his or her eyes around, or walking away. As a result, kids can feel awfully guilty, and they surely won't talk about it. Kids who masturbate may feel they are doing something that no one else in the world is doing or has done. Now you know that's not true.

There Are Lots of Different Feelings about Masturbation

Though many boys and girls masturbate, the number of boys who do is greater than the number of girls. Perhaps this has something to do with the fact that a boy's penis is "out there" and a girl has to explore the many folds of her vulva in order to find her clitoris and other sensitive parts.

Of the boys and girls who don't masturbate, some don't realize they can touch themselves in order to get tingly feelings. Others know they can if they wish but have made a decision not to. That's okay!

Kevin, age eleven, said, "Sometimes when I touch myself, I feel guilty because it feels so good and I don't think I'm supposed to have such feelings."

Lori, age twelve, said, "I don't think I'd ever want to do that!"

Thirteen-year-old JoAnn told me, "Yes, I do it. It feels really good. But I've never talked about it with anyone. I think if my parents found out, they'd kill me."

Sharon, age forty-five, shared, "My mother caught me touching myself when I was about eleven. She walked into my bedroom and asked me what I was doing. I was so glad the lights were dark because I was blushing horribly. I was so embarrassed and didn't know what to say. I didn't even know there was a name for what I was doing! She told me that she hoped never to catch me doing something like that again. Girls don't do that sort of thing!"

Ten-year-old Bobby said, "My Sunday School teacher told me it's a sin. Now I don't know what to do because how could something that feels so good be a sin?"

Fourteen-year-old Sari said, "Masturbating is the last thing I'd think of doing. I don't understand why anyone would want to touch their genitals on purpose. It just seems strange."

Tom, age eighteen, shared that when he was in the seventh grade, he tried to talk about masturbation with a friend, just to see if his friend would say that he did it, too. Instead his friend said, "Only weirdos do that." Tom never discussed it with his friends again until he was much older.

Twelve-year-old Todd told me, "I talked about this with my parents and they think it's a real healthy thing to do. They're glad it feels so good."

As you can see, there are so many different kinds of feelings about masturbation. Some kids feel guilty and confused about having such tingly-type feelings, especially if they're caught. Others feel "tinglies" are great, still others don't feel they're right for them at all. Lots of times these feelings come from how we are raised and what our parents, teachers, friends, brothers, sisters, and religious leaders tell us.

How Parents Feel about Masturbation

Most kids have told me they have not talked about this kind of touching with their parents. Most parents never discussed it with their parents, either! Some parents would probably think it's great if their child felt good about these feelings. Many other parents, often due to religious teachings and values, feel masturbation is wrong and would probably be upset if they learned their child enjoyed such feelings.

So many parents still feel uncomfortable and confused about masturbation. They want the best for their children as they grow up, but they are still not sure whether such touching is healthy or not. And it's hard to talk about it.

Often, when parents don't have positive feelings toward masturbation and are concerned that their children might masturbate too much, they will give them a mean stare and ask them in their most parental tone of voice, "What are you doing?" Or they will try to discourage their children from touching themselves. This especially happens when children are young and don't realize that if they touch themselves, they should do this privately. Do you remember any stares from your parents? Did they bring a new toy over to you in the middle of when you were touching just to take your attention away? Think back. . . .

Other parents feel that masturbation is a healthy, normal part of their son's or daughter's development. They want their child(ren) to understand that touching themselves can be a very pleasurable experience. But they also want them to understand that certain behaviors are private and are to be done alone (say, in one's bedroom), not in public.

Learning about your body and especially your genitals starts very young. It might give you a better understanding of how you feel today if you try to think back to when you were little. What messages about your body and touching did your parents give you? Did they make you feel good, bad, or guilty about interest in your own body? Did you feel you could ask them anything about yourself and your development? What do you wish you could have asked them but never did? Can you ask them now?

Touching Yourself Is a Very Personal Choice

Touching yourself is a *choice.*

If you choose to touch, it's healthy. Lots of people of all ages do (yes, even senior citizens!). You won't grow warts or hair on your palms, or need special glasses if touching makes you tingle and feel good. Touching doesn't have anything to do with who you like or what type of person you are.

If you don't choose to touch, that's healthy, too. Lots of people of all ages don't.

Wanting to touch your genitals is a natural part of growing up and developing sexual feelings. (In fact, your hormones even help to bring out these new feelings.) What you do about these feelings has to do with what you feel and what you've been taught. If you've never discussed this or haven't been taught anything one way or another, then do what makes you feel comfortable and good.

If you find that touching your genitals feels good, but you know your parents or religious teachings say it's not right, then you'll have to try to balance your own feelings with respect for your parents and your religion. This is a very personal decision. If your feelings confuse you, I encourage you to talk about them with your parents or religious leaders.

Also, many kids feel less confused when they discuss masturbation with their older sister(s) or brother(s). They can really help you to make up your mind about what's right for you. Sometimes a special friend (one you know would never laugh at you or make you feel foolish for bringing up the subject) can help clear up the mystery. Often your friend can be relieved to know that you have the same feelings that he or she does.

Sometimes it's difficult to know how your friend(s), sister(s), or brother(s) might respond to the topic of masturbation. But if you feel close to them, it's worth taking the risk.

CHAPTER 10

TAKING CARE OF YOUR BODY AND APPEARANCE

Keeping Your Body Clean

Along with all the other physical changes of puberty, your sweat glands will cause you to perspire (sweat!) more and your oil glands will cause your skin to become more oily. All the more reason to shower or bathe regularly.

Even if you don't sweat a lot, make yourself a bathing or shower schedule. If you're old enough to be reading this book, you're old enough to really try to stick to that schedule.

If you take a shower in the morning, then play hard at a sport during the day, take an extra shower at night or at least take one the next morning. That way you'll keep your body fresh, feeling good, and clean. You'll also prevent unpleasant odors (phew!) from building up.

Regular washing habits are also important because your skin is constantly replacing old cells with new ones. It's healthy to wash the old ones from your skin surface. You can't really see the teeny cells sliding off your body, so don't bother to look for them. Just wash!

All parts of your body need washing . . . every little crack and fold.

What You Can Do If Someone You Know Smells Awful

One of the hardest things to tell someone is that they smell. Did you ever sit next to someone in class who had body odor (B.O.)?

There was a girl who sat next to me in my seventh-grade math class who I remember smelled awful! I was too embarrassed to tell her. I thought of leaving a note on her desk or in her locker saying, "Please wash." Or possibly leaving a bar of soap on her desk with a note saying, "Hint, hint!" Finally I spoke with my teacher and asked to change my seat. I also asked the teacher to speak to that person about her washing habits and to tell her that maybe people would like to be with her more if they could stand being close to her. She really seemed nice. It was only that she smelled.

I guess if I were the one who smelled, it would be a bit (a lot?) embarrassing for someone to just come up and tell me that. But it would be more embarrassing if I just went on smelling with everyone gasping and whispering about it behind my back, trying to stay as far away as possible.

I feel—if you're bothered by someone's smell—that the kindest thing you can do is to speak with him or her in private. If it's hard for you to talk with the person about this, you can start with, "This is not easy for me to say. . . ." You might go on saying, "I figured you probably would want to know that kids are being bothered by your smell. I think more kids would want to be with you if you washed more. I hope you don't mind me telling you this, but I really like you and I know other kids do, too. But it's just that it's hard to be near you."

Of course I suppose you could just go right up to someone and say, "You smell gross!" but that wouldn't be very sensitive. Honest, yes. Kind, no! Just keep in mind that it will help to let them know and that you are saying whatever you say because you care about them. And you'd rather tell them straight out (honestly) than whisper about it to other kids. If you respect the person's privacy and are as nice as possible when you speak, that can also help to make what you say easier for that person to hear.

I don't pretend that it's easy to say those kinds of things. But think for yourself. Would you rather know than not know if kids were bothered by your smell? Most kids tell me they'd rather know than have people talk about them behind their back and stay away.

Sometimes it's the teacher who smells. That can be tougher to deal with. At least if you tell a classmate about smelling, he or she won't give you a bad grade! (I'm only kidding that a teacher would change your grade. I would like to think that teachers, too, would appreciate knowing that something about them is unpleasant to other people, especially when they can easily do something about it.)

Jessica, age ten, told me, "I liked my piano lessons but my piano teacher's perfume was horrible. She was a very good teacher but I hated being near her because her perfume smelled too much." Jess asked her mom to ask the teacher if she would mind not wearing perfume on lesson days. The teacher was happy to know about Jess's feelings and Jess liked her lessons much better without her teacher's smell.

Unless someone is told about body odor, he or she may not be able to guess. It's a very caring thing to do to let them know. Just imagine how you would feel if someone didn't tell you.

Keeping Your Clothes Clean

Even if you shower very often, you can "blow it" by wearing dirty or unfresh clothing over your clean body.

Kids and adults need to change their underwear daily and change their jeans, shirts, or anything else every few days at the most. Kids notice when teachers wear the same thing every day. Kids also notice when other kids don't change their clothes.

Some people don't have much money to spend on clothes and may only have a few changes. But no matter how many clothes you own, there's no excuse for those clothes to be smelly and unclean. Even if they have a few holes in them, your holes can be clean, too!

Deodorants and Antiperspirants

If you find you're beginning to perspire a lot, it's time to consider using a *deodorant* (dee-OH-dor-ant) or *antiperspirant* (AN-tee-PER-sper-ant). A deodorant helps to control the odor that can result from sweating, while an antiperspirant helps to reduce wetness and control how much you perspire. (I'm beginning to feel like a commercial!)

Most brands give you a choice of sprays, roll-ons, sticks, and powders. You put them on under your arms (on your armpits) before putting on clothing. Some feel dry when you first apply them; others feel sort of wet. (It's a good idea to let your armpits dry before getting dressed). Some are just deodorants, some are antiperspirants, and others are both in one.

You may have to test out a few until you find one that works for you. You can also choose if you want them scented (with fragrance) or unscented (without fragrance). You might want to try one that a parent is using, ask your friends what they use, or just make a decision on your own.

Be careful not to apply a deodorant or antiperspirant on broken skin or if you have a rash under your arms. If you have a rash that takes a long time to clear up, speak to your parents and they may need to check with your doctor.

Reminder: Even if you don't have hair under your arms, you can use deodorant or antiperspirant if you are perspiring more and more.

Keeping Your Face Clean

Keeping your face clean goes deeper than just washing chocolate off the corner of your mouth after finishing an ice cream cone. Here again you need to develop healthy washing habits. Your skin will probably look and feel better if you do.

Washing your face daily with good, mild soap and water will help open up the pores of your skin and keep them clean.

If your skin is sensitive or allergic and breaks out in a rash or pimples from your regular soap, let your parents know. There are soaps that your druggist or doctor can suggest that are specially made for allergic skin.

If you're wearing any kind of makeup—I'll talk about this soon—it's very important to wash it off each day. *Don't* leave it on for the next morning.

Keeping Your Teeth and Breath Clean

I don't need to say much more than brush regularly—in the morning, after meals (if possible), and before going to bed—but you know that already. I used to say that people who didn't brush in the morning had "flannel mouth." Yuck!

It's also important that you learn how to floss your teeth with dental floss. You can ask your dentist or dental hygienist (hi-JEEN-ist) to instruct you in moving the thin string through your teeth to prevent decay and the buildup of dental *plaque* (plack).

Dental plaque is made up of germs and food bits and is held on the teeth by the sticky substance in saliva (sa-LIE-va), the fluid given off by the mouth, like when your mouth waters. Right after it forms, it is soft enough to be removed by brushing your teeth and flossing. If you leave it on the surface of your teeth for too long, it can harden and become difficult to get rid of. The hardened dental plaque has to be removed by a dentist or dental hygienist.

It's important to keep in mind that dental plaque forms about every twenty-four hours and therefore should be removed each day.

You can use a mouthwash after you brush to make your breath feel that much more fresh. (Some kids don't need to take anything to have a fresh mouth!)

Even nice people can have bad breath. Keep in mind the kind of things you eat. They can give you a clue as to times your breath might be stronger than others. For example, if you eat onion rings for lunch and don't get a chance to brush, you might want to stay a little farther away from your friends when you talk with them. Onions can be yummy but can really affect your breath. Or you can simply say, "Watch out, don't come too close. I have onion breath!" And then it won't matter as much because they'll know that you know.

Since we eat different things all the time, some stronger than others, it's hard to completely keep unpleasant odors away. Besides cleaning your teeth and trying to prevent cavities, regular brushing (along with mouthwash, if you wish) will help to get rid of the old smells and make way for the new ones.

If someone has bad breath most of the time, the same things I suggested for body odor apply here. As uncomfortable as it might be for you to say it and for them to hear it, usually people would rather know than not know. Only then will they realize they've got to do something about it.

Once again, a teacher with bad breath can be a bit tougher to deal with than a friend. Steve, now twenty, told me, "When I was in high school, my friends and I left a gift-wrapped bottle of mouthwash on one teacher's desk. We were thankful he took the hint. I guess we just didn't realize we could have spoken to him about it."

Braces

If you're one of the thousands of kids who must wear braces, just keep telling yourself, "I'm going to look great when the braces come off!"

You may feel they're a big pain and probably wish you never had to deal with them, but this is one of those times when a few years of "bother" can be worth the happiness and good feelings about how you look when you don't have to wear them anymore.

Be sure to get lots of information from your dentist (who takes regular care of your teeth) and orthodontist (who puts on braces and cares for your teeth when they are not lined up properly) about what kinds of food are right for you to eat with your braces. Gooey, gummy, hard, chewy food is usually a "no-no." Fresh vegetables and fruit are easier to manage when cut into smaller pieces.

It's very important to clean your braces after meals (so you don't walk around with your lunch stuck in between the wires—gross!). Make sure to ask your orthodontist or dentist how to do that properly.

Keeping Your Hair Clean

More washing habits—shampoo your hair regularly. If you don't, it can start to smell and will probably look like spaghetti that should have been thrown out last week! Try not to wait more than a few days, unless, of course, you're sick. It's important to use a shampoo that will not dry out your hair. If your shampoo label says "acid balanced" or "low pH," you'll know it will nourish your hair properly.

Some conditioners, such as creme rinses, work on the top layer of your hair to help to reduce tangles so you can comb it more easily and not break the hair strands (that's when you get split ends).

Other conditioners work on the deeper layers in your hair and add ingredients that help prevent hair damage. They help to give hair the ability to stretch and return to normal (so it won't break), add moisture (moisturizers do this), and make it softer to touch.

Someday you might find little flaky, white flecks, called dandruff, appearing around your shoulder. They especially show up on dark sweaters, shirts, or coats. Not to worry! This simply means that your scalp is dry and it's a helpful signal for you to try to do something about it by using moisturizers. Also check the shampoo you're using. It may be irritating your scalp and causing this problem. You may want to try a different shampoo, or even a special anti-dandruff shampoo.

If you can't clear up your dandruff by using a quality shampoo, speak to your parents. Advice from your doctor may be necessary.

Hairstyles

I guess one of the most important things about your hairstyle is whether you can look in the mirror, pinch your cheeks, and say, "You great-looking thing!" Your hairstyle should be attractive for you and make you feel good about yourself.

This means that even if all of your friends have decided to wear their hair a certain way, you can decide for yourself if you even want to think about that style for you. Their hairstyle may not make you feel good. Each person has a right to his or her own style.

If the only way you'll be accepted is to wear your hair like everyone else, then I suggest you may need to start finding other friends who realize that hairstyles don't make the person. People can have beautiful hair and be not-so-nice type people inside—or they can be wonderful. (Beautiful hair people can even smell from body odor!) People without the latest hairstyle can really be nice—or not. Being nice usually has nothing to do with hairstyles.

Tammy, age fourteen, told me, "I got a new haircut and really liked it. Then I went to school and the kids teased me and made me feel awful." Rachel, age twelve, said, "It took me three weeks before I tried wearing my hair in a ponytail to school. I loved it at home but was afraid people wouldn't like it because it was different from my other style."

Billy, now age forty, had lots of hair until his infamous very, very short haircut in the seventh grade. He refused to take his hat off in school for three weeks until some new hair grew in. Says Billy, "I felt like a freak. Everyone would have made more fun of me if I took off my hat. It was bad enough with it on because everyone knew why I was wearing it!"

It's natural for kids to care what other people say. Adults do the same. But it's one thing to let other people tell you what's right for you and quite another to listen to people you respect, think about what they say, and then make your own decision based on your own feelings.

Sometimes it will be tough to stand up to everyone and be who you are. So many people try to tell others what to do, what to wear, what to say, how their hair looks best, and so on. The day you believe that it's your body, your clothes, your hair, and your right to make your appearance feel good to you is the day you'll not let other people rule your feelings.

You want a perm really badly? If your parents say okay, then why not try it; that's the only way you'll find out if it's right for you. You want to let your hair grow to see what a different style looks like? Why not!

It was interesting talking with Jeannie, age thirteen, who had a new hairstyle that all her friends hated. Three weeks after they teased her, one, then two, then more, decided they wanted to try that style, too.

When choosing a hairstyle, consider what you feel is comfortable, easy to manage, and flattering for you.

More about perms If you want this kind of a curly look, it's a good idea to find a beauty salon that will take the time to explain to you and your parents exactly what they plan to do to your hair. Perms should last about two to four months, depending on how long your hair is and how fast it grows.

Combs and brushes They're those things with handles on one end and teeth or bristles on the other. The idea is to pull them through your hair regularly. Even a great hairstyle can look like a mop if you don't. Be sure to clean your combs and brushes regularly. If they're dirty, they can help create unhealthy scalp conditions. Besides, dirty combs and brushes look gross.

A personal word about taking care of your own hairstyle It's helpful for you to learn how to do your own hair. If you depend on your mom, dad, sister, or brother to do your hair for you, one day they won't be home and you'll be left wondering how you will ever face people if you have to do it yourself.

My doing-your-own-hair story is this. My mom always used to do my hair for me. One night, she decided that it was time that I learn how to do it myself. She refused to help me and said I should try my best.

I cried and yelled and blamed her for the fact that I would be ugly in school the next day. But none of my begging helped. She was sticking to it and I was forced to try.

To my surprise, I was able to do it. And from that night on, I've done my hair myself. It didn't take very long for me to feel that I was the only one able to do my hair the way I really liked it.

It's interesting how we sometimes have to be forced to learn. I encourage you to at least try to do your hair on your own. Try on the weekends, for starters—if you wish. But start. That way you'll soon be able to be responsible for your own hair care.

My mom told me afterward that it was such a hard thing for her to do. It would have been so simple to just come out of her room and set my hair for me. But that wouldn't have helped me learn.

Taking Care of Your Nails

First of all, never cut, pick at, or bite your *cuticles* (KYEW-ti-kulls). These are the areas of thin, sometimes hard skin that peek out from around the back of each nail. It's good to push your cuticles back, but this should only be done when they are wet, after a bath or shower. This can be done with a soft Q-tip or towel. You can injure the cuticle or the nail bed, which is right behind each cuticle, if you push them back when they are dry.

Your nails will grow faster if you regularly move your cuticles back off your nail. They will look nicer if you keep them clean and try to let them grow as long as is comfortable for you. Keep your hands clean, too. Of course, no nail biting, please!

Nails should be filed straight across. Don't file into the corners. Both boys and girls should keep their hands and nails groomed. A good hand cream will help keep your hands softer, especially after you've been in windy, cold weather, in the sun, or in the water. Using a moisturizing cream on your face is also a good idea to help prevent dryness.

It wouldn't be fair not to mention your toenails. Please cut them straight across, too. Are you one of those people who cuts his or her toenails or one who lets them grow so long that they're about to cut through your socks or maybe even your shoes? Well, I know I've given you a lot to think about, but see if you can remember your toes, too.

Athlete's Foot

It's a good idea to dry in between your toes so the area doesn't stay moist. This will help prevent an infection called athlete's foot, which is caused by an organism called a *fungus*. I've already told you that some infections are caused by bacteria. This is another type of infection.

Fungi (FUN-jie, many funguses) love moisture and darkness and may try to grow there. Lots of kids and adults get this. (You don't have to be an athlete to have it!)

Athlete's foot causes the area in between your toes to itch and sometimes peel. Because this infection can be spread, it's wise to use your own towel and make sure it's cleaned. Even if you don't have athlete's foot, other kids might, and they may not know to cover the infected area (by keeping their socks on or by wearing shoes). They may not even know they have it. Or they may be embarrassed to let anyone know they have it (by protecting their feet) and will still go around barefoot. To lessen your chance of getting athlete's foot, you might consider wearing thongs any time you're in a public shower area or locker room.

There are special creams, powders, and sprays to treat athlete's foot. So tell your parents if you even think you might have it and they'll help you to take care of it as soon as possible.

Acne (Pimples)

Hillary, age ten, looked in the mirror one morning and said, "Is that a pimple? It better not be. I don't deserve it!"

Well, Hillary, even nice people have acne (AK-nee). In fact it's probably safe to say that pimples visit most people at one time or another. Acne is an expected part of puberty, not one of the best parts, but at least kids who have one, a few, or tons of pimples can know they've got lots of company.

Pimples show up because pores of the skin get plugged up with waxyish oil. So, often pimples result because the oil and sweat glands in your skin are changing. They can also result from unclean washing habits. But just because someone has pimples doesn't mean he or she doesn't wash. They may have very clean habits but still get pimples. Some girls get pimples around the time of their periods.

Besides appearing on your face, sometimes pimples cluster on your neck, back, and even your buttocks (rear end or behind). This can possibly happen due to irritation from underwear, tight jeans, or the laundry detergent that is used to clean your clothes. Sometimes it happens in the summer when you sit around in wet bathing suits.

Usually acne will show up as whiteheads or blackheads. Blackheads appear as blackish pimples on the surface of the skin. Whiteheads happen when the waxy oil shows under the surface of the skin, and appear whitish when they come to a head and open up on the surface.

Neither whiteheads nor blackheads should be squeezed. If you apply a hot washcloth to the pimple (as hot as you can stand it), this will help to bring all the pus to the surface. Then put on some alcohol and let it dry itself out, being careful not to puncture it.

If you squeeze your pimple, part may be squeezed out, but there probably will be another half or so that can squeeze inward (back into the surface of the skin) and cause a hard knot underneath. Sometimes squeezing a pimple can cause an infection in your entire body (because the pus can cause bacteria to travel through the body).

Medicated acne creams can be used at night. Antibacterial soaps and pore cleansers can help prevent and treat pimples. If pimples are bothering you, make sure you speak with your parents. You can also get advice from the pharmacist or your doctor.

All you have to do is look at the faces of kids whose bodies have started to develop and change. Keep looking from day to day. Only a few of the kids who don't have pimples will get away with not having them at all. Most kids will have at least a few. Pimples are kind of sneaky. They'll appear one day, disappear in a few days, only to appear again—maybe in the same spot, maybe in a different spot. You really can't count on a pimple to do what you want it to do.

Thirteen-year-old Janie said, "As soon as you think your face has cleared up, they can come back to haunt you again. I hate the way they make me look."

Rodney, age twelve, said, "I don't mind a couple of pimples. They're just a part of adolescence." (Ad-ul-ESS-ense, the period of years between childhood and adulthood.)

Rodney, Janie, and so many kids that I've spoken with have different attitudes and feelings about pimples. Some accept them and treat them and don't get hung up about having them. Others really are embarrassed, feeling that their friends are looking at their pimples all the time and thinking how awful their face looks.

If you also have been embarrassed by your pimples, it's very natural to feel that way. Maybe you, Janie, and any other kids who might get pimples in the growing-up years would be less embarrassed if you realized there are loads of other kids who have acne, too. Hardly any kids are completely pimpleproof.

If you *don't* squeeze and *don't* pick at them, they'll have a better chance of healing quickly without leaving any marks on your skin. Remember to use lots of hot water to open up your pores.

Pimples will go away on their own time and have little to do with what food you eat (even chocolate and french fries can't be blamed for pimples). Some will stay longer, others will seem to disappear very quickly. For each person, pimples will be slightly different.

If your pimples continue to be a concern, your parents and family doctor may suggest that you seek advice from a dermatologist—a doctor specially trained to treat acne.

So much for pimples! Let's move on.

Using Makeup

Fourteen-year-old Jennifer told me, "I was allowed to have my own lipstick in the seventh grade. After all those years of watching my mom use hers, it felt great to have my own. But I'm still not allowed to use eye makeup. Some of my friends have started to, but my parents are really strict about it."

Laurie, age twenty-five, talked with me about her mom's "wet test." Her mom wouldn't give her permission to wear eye makeup. Said Laurie, "Most of my friends wore makeup and I didn't want to feel left out. So I had to sneak putting it on after leaving my house in the morning. When my mom asked me if I was wearing it, I said no. Most of the time I got away with it, except when she gave me the wet test. She'd put water on my eyes and if makeup came off, she'd know I was wearing it and wasn't telling the truth. Then she'd give me some kind of punishment and get upset with me. It was really hard, though. I didn't want to lie to her but I didn't want to feel left out either."

Danny, age eleven, said, "I think some girls look stupid the way they put on so much makeup. I don't think it's right until about the eighth grade." Erin, age eleven, agrees with Danny about eye makeup but thinks it's okay to use a little lipstick at "special times."

Beth, age thirteen, said her mom lets her wear eye makeup if she wants to, as long as it's not too heavy. Debra, age twelve, said, "Even if my mom or dad gave me permission, I wouldn't want to wear it anyway. None of my friends do and I think it's silly for kids my age to start."

So many different feelings. The decision to wear makeup is very personal. Using it seems to depend on three main things: when you are ready, when your friends are ready, and when your parents give you permission to use it.

How much is too much? I guess if kids start mistaking you for someone who should be in the circus, you'll know you look more like a clown than the regular old kid that you are. If you look in the mirror and wonder who it is staring back at you, that would be another clue that you might have used too much. But it's also possible that the "new" face in the mirror may take a little getting used to. So give yourself a little time to think about your feelings. The nice thing is that you can change your mind.

How much is enough? Only you can answer that for yourself (with the guidance of your parents). I feel that enough means using as much as you need to make you feel that bit more attractive—an accent, a touch, so that it shows in a very soft, flattering way. More than that really makes me question what you're trying to say about yourself.

Many kids use heavy makeup to try to get others to pay attention to them. Many use too much because they think it makes them look tough, cool, and maybe even older.

It's very important for you to realize that your clothes, whether or not you comb your hair, how neat you are, how clean you are, how much makeup you use, all make a statement about who you are as a person. Even when you don't say a word, people will look at you and get a certain *impression* (im-PRESH-un), a feeling about you. Not that you're dressing or acting the way you do for everyone else, it's just that you need to look yourself straight in the eye and be happy with what you see, no matter what your friends think or do. If you're honest with yourself, then probably you'll be able to know if you feel good looking that way or if you think it's just not for you.

Really important: Make sure whatever makeup you do use is quality makeup. Your skin is soft and sensitive. If you're using eye makeup, be careful not to go too close to the inside of your eye. And don't go to sleep at night with your makeup on. Cleanse or cold cream it off each day, then put it on again in the morning, if you wish.

Also important: To guard against illness, eye diseases, and other infections, it's healthier not to borrow or share your own makeup—such as lipstick, mascara, or other kinds of eye makeup.

It's Important to Exercise

It's very important to make time for physical activity. Whether you run, swim, dance, skate, or play sports with other kids, try to fit some kind of exercising into your schedule a few times a week. This is a great goal to have all throughout your life.

It's healthy to balance school or any other kind of work—and also TV—with exercise. It's great for your body, great for how you feel, can be very relaxing, and can be lots of fun! You don't have to be a super athlete to be able to enjoy activities that feel good to you. Go at your own rate with what you like to do. If you're not sure about what you like, try a few activities until you find one that's fun.

Some people make the mistake of thinking that if they have only fifteen minutes or half an hour, it's not enough time to bother trying to exercise. After all, what could be done in such a short period of time? The answer is, "More than you think!"

Even if you jump rope (a good one to get has ball bearings in the handles), do sit-ups, walk or run around your block a few times, you'll be surprised at what a difference it can make in how you feel. When you return to your studying, or whatever, you'll be refreshed and probably much more able to concentrate.

If you already exercise, terrific! If you don't, how about taking the first step? At least think about what you'd like to do and when you might fit that activity into your schedule—then you're on your way.

Eating Properly, Getting Enough Sleep

Eating right is not only very important for how you look and how your body grows, but also for how you feel and how much energy you have.

Not taking in enough food, or the right kinds of food, is like trying to run a car without supplying it with enough gas. It would be unfair to expect your body to do all that you'd like it to do without giving it the necessary fuel. Food is fuel!

Did you ever fall asleep in your morning classes at school? If you didn't fall fast asleep, were there ever any times that you had to fight to keep awake? Did you or didn't you have breakfast on those mornings? My guess is, "Probably not." Of course, the other question to check out is what time you went to bed the night before.

Starting the day off with a good breakfast (not only one that tastes good, but one that's good for you) is most important. A healthy breakfast might include a citrus fruit, like an orange or orange juice, some whole grains, like bread or cereals (if you want to sweeten your breakfast cereals, you might try adding fruit instead of sugar), and milk. You might also consider having eggs a few times a week. All it takes is a decision to care about yourself enough to get up a few minutes earlier so you can have time to eat before going to school. Try it!

Scott, age ten, told me he loves to cook. He really wanted to make himself french toast in the mornings, but his mom said he couldn't cook while she was sleeping and she didn't want to get up. I suggested to him that he ask his mom to let him show her how he cooks later in the day when she's up. Then he could prove to her that he's responsible and can handle cooking in a safe way on his own. You guessed it! He now has permission to cook breakfast and he feels great about it.

As far as the rest of the day goes, people seem to eat for lots of different reasons. Some people are actually hungry, but many others are bored, nervous, eat because the food is in front of them, don't know what else to do. . . .

It would help to begin to take notice of exactly what you're eating, when, and why. It can be interesting to write down everything that you eat for several days. Even tiny bites of things. Then you can see what kind of eating habits you have, what's in your diet, and whether you are getting enough of the important fuels.

Healthy eating means including lots of different types of foods in your meals (be sure to include whole grains and vegetables). You can also cut down on drinks that have caffeine, foods that have high fat content (less crunching on the fat of your lamb chops, eating chicken without the skin) and limit how much extra sugar you add. Your family doctor can also recommend what vitamins might be good for you to take.

Some kids mainly or only eat foods that don't contain meat. You may have heard the term *vegetarian* (vej-eh-TAIR-ee-an). Others don't eat meat but feel it's okay to eat fish and chicken. And lots of kids eat everything! If you have decided to limit your diet to only certain foods, it's especially important to speak with your family doctor to make sure that what you are allowing yourself to eat is as balanced as it needs to be.

Are you eating the same exact thing each day or are you eating lots of different things? Do you have heaping portions or smaller ones? How many seconds and thirds of dessert do you have?

Have you looked in the mirror lately? Do you consider yourself overweight, skinny, sort of in the middle? Just right? Does the way you look make you feel good about yourself?

If you're heavier than you'd like to be, it may be that your body will thin out as you begin to develop. It also may mean that you've got to change some poor eating habits and start to exercise.

If you're honest with yourself and decide you wish to try to change, talk with your parents so they can cooperate with your new eating plan. Perhaps you can help them make up a new menu for family meals. You can also talk about what kinds of snacks are good for you.

You'll find that you've got to combine good eating with exercise and the right amount of sleep. Sleep adds to your strength and is very important.

A good way to tell if you're sleeping enough is to be aware of how tired you are during the day. Some kids find they can stay up later; others find they need to go to sleep very early. Not sleeping enough can run down your strength and make it easier for you to get sick.

Only you can answer how you feel, how much energy you have, if you seem to get very tired by late afternoon or can't seem to keep your eyes open all morning. Since each person's sleep needs are different, it would be impossible for me to tell you how many hours of sleep are right for you.

It's up to your parents to help guide you about what bedtime might be right for you. It's up to you to be honest with them and with yourself about how tired you are.

Believe it or not, the health habits you have now will have an effect on your health as an adult. So it's very important to think about what you do and what you don't do about your own personal care.

Just remember that your habits took time to form and will probably take time to break. Even if you understand what and why you should change, it can be hard to change right away. So be patient with yourself, but be strong about what you now know is good for you.

CHAPTER 11

DIFFERENT SHAPES AND SIZES, DIFFERENT MOODS AND FEELINGS

Does Your Size Make a Difference in How You Feel?

Are you skinnier, fatter, taller, shorter, more developed, or less developed than your friends? How does this make you feel?

If you're happy with your weight, size, and stage of development, you'll probably feel really good about that. If you're not happy about some of those things, you might not feel as good. You might even feel miserable!

I know that I've told you over and over again that you can't help what size you are and you can't speed up or slow down your development. But I also know that no matter how much you understand that, it still can be pretty hard to accept your size and feel good. Kids always seem to compare themselves with each other, forgetting that a person can't help how developed he or she is.

Cari, age eleven, grew taller than her friends at an early age. She told me, "At first, I was embarrassed when everyone started calling me 'too tall' and making fun of me. I felt comfortable with my size, but their teasing made me uncomfortable. I just started calling them names back and then I told them to stop. They listened and I didn't have any more embarrassment."

Heather, age twelve, said, "When we had to do pull-ups on the rings in gym class, my gym teacher always used to say things like, 'We'll have to make this one lower for the shorter people. Some short people can't reach this.' And she'd always look straight at me. I was so mad and embarrassed because there were a lot of people in my class who were much smaller than me and she just picked on me and my shortness. Also, whenever I answered her, she always mimicked my voice in a high tone as if I was a Munchkin. And my voice really wasn't that high!"

Jimmy, age ten, wanted to know, "How can I help my friend from being teased about his height?" Peter, age eleven, wanted to understand why his friend was so short.

Eddie, age fourteen, is still quite small. He finds that when kids choose up sides for baseball, unless they know him and how he plays, they'll usually pick him last because he's so much smaller. They figure that small means "not as good." But he shows them how wrong they are when he starts to play. Then they're sorry they didn't pick him first! It's very frustrating to him because he seems to always have to prove himself to kids who are bigger.

Marion, now thirty-five, remembers how great she felt because she was so much taller and more developed than all of her friends. It made her feel very grown up. Said Marion, "No one dared to tease me! The only problem sometimes was when my parents expected more from me because I looked older."

Stephanie, age fourteen, talked with me about how bad she feels when kids tease her about her weight. They call her "fatso" and "hippo" and that really hurts her feelings. She told me that there are times when she wants to go to school events, like to a sports game, but she's afraid if she goes, kids will be mean and talk behind her back. She feels that kids only look at her weight and don't give her a chance.

So many shapes and sizes! Kids have so many different feelings about how they look and how other people seem to see them.

If you have feelings about your size and development, it might help to write them down. Make a list of what about yourself makes you feel good and what doesn't. Then try to decide if the things that disturb you can be changed. Or do they have to do with development that you cannot control?

If you can change something, then begin to think about how. For example, if you feel that losing a few pounds would make a difference, then you can try to eat more wisely. Have a salad instead of mounds of potatoes with gravy. Have a piece of fruit for a snack instead of three cupcakes. Try eating one piece of bread instead of two. *Exercise regularly!* With a new attitude and better understanding of how your habits can affect you, you'll begin to see results.

You can help control your weight, how clean you are, the way you wear your hair—but how tall or short, how developed or undeveloped, that's not up to you! So try to keep the teasing down and the understanding up.

If your parents (or those around you) seem to expect too much of you because your development makes you appear older, or if you feel you're being treated as if you're younger because your size is small, remind them of your age. They may not realize they're doing this.

If you hear anyone making comments or fun of anyone, maybe you can spread this understanding to help others feel good about themselves, too.

Eating Disorders—A Word of Caution

Certain kids who feel they're too heavy really have a distorted (not the way things really are) view of themselves. They think they're too heavy but they're really quite thin. Because they don't want to gain any weight, they try to starve themselves or eat very little. People who feel and behave this way are called *anorexics* (an-or-EKS-iks). The condition they have is known as *anorexia nervosa* (an-or-EKS-ee-a ner-VOE-sa).

Some people make themselves vomit their food up after meals (they often eat a lot, or binge, then vomit) just to make sure they won't gain any weight. This condition is called *bulimia* (buh-LEE-mee-a).

Both anorexia nervosa and bulimia can be very dangerous. Even though people with these problems lose more and more weight, they still think they're not thin enough. If they lose too much weight, they will not allow their bodies to get the nourishment needed to stay healthy. Sometimes it is necessary for them to be put in the hospital so that doctors and nurses can make sure they eat or are fed what their bodies need. Depending on how undernourished they are, they may need to be fed through a tube that's placed down their nose, or *intravenously* (in-tra-VEE-nus-lee), which is done by placing a needle underneath the skin, usually on the inside of the person's arm; the needle is connected to a long tube through which liquid nourishment flows. (This needle way of feeding is used a lot in hospitals when people have operations or when they're too ill to be able to eat on their own.)

Beth, age thirteen, told me, "I'm really worried about my friend. She always talks about how fat she is and how all our friends are thinner and that she has to lose weight. I don't understand why she feels that way because she's not fat at all. Most of the time, she throws away what her mom made her for lunch. She always tells me that she feels horrible."

Some kids feel that their weight—and how good they think they look—has to do with how special or important they are. They think their weight will influence whether or not someone will want them as a friend or whether someone will want to go out with them. They often walk around school (or anywhere) comparing themselves to others, thinking constantly about how everyone else is thinner. It's hard for them to think of anything else but their weight.

No matter what size or weight you are, you deserve to feel good about who you are because who you are has nothing to do with what you weigh or what you look like on the outside. I realize that this is a hard message for kids who are very frustrated and want so badly to lose weight, especially when they see themselves as heavier than they really are.

If you know you're walking around school and all you think about is your weight—or if you're thinking about or actually eating less and less or throwing up your food—you deserve to take steps to help yourself so that this problem doesn't go further. You don't have to deal with this alone. You need to ask for help from your parents, a doctor, or a licensed specialist who treats people with eating problems.

Another Caution

Some kids (and adults) who are much heavier than is healthy for them find that they eat more and more. This just makes them even heavier.

Usually, this kind of eating is not because they're hungry. They may think or say they're hungry, but really they eat because they're upset or concerned about something, want attention, or just don't feel good about themselves. There can be many different reasons. The name that is often attached to this kind of eating is "compulsive overeating."

Going for Help—If You Have an Eating Disorder

If you know you have an eating disorder of any kind, or you know that you don't feel good about yourself because of how you feel you look, don't wait. Be good to yourself. Let someone know you need help, now.

Even those who are closest to you may not be able to just look at you and know you need help. That's why it's so important to be sure to tell them, in writing or aloud.

Although parents can often be a great help to kids with these conditions, it's sometimes very important to also speak with doctors, counselors, therapists, or any other professional who is specially trained to offer help and guidance. Getting this kind of help is not a sign of weakness. It takes a lot of strength to admit that you have a problem that you can't seem to handle so well by yourself.

If your mom or dad (or both) suggests that you speak with a professional person trained to help you understand your eating or any other type of problem, try to realize they're saying this because they care about you and are concerned. Also, it takes strength for parents to admit that neither they nor their child can handle the particular problem on their own.

If you can't imagine how to tell your parents that you're vomiting after meals, eating very little, or eating more and more without control, you can start by saying, "This is very hard for me to talk about . . . but I've been doing things that I know are not good for me and I need to talk with you. I need your help." Or you might begin with: "I've been walking around trying to figure out how to tell you this. I know you'll probably be very upset. But I need your help. I'm scared. I've been sneaking in the bathroom after eating and throwing up (or substitute any other behavior that applies to you). And I know that's not good but I can't seem to help it. Will you help me? Please?"

Maybe you've been keeping what you're doing a secret because you're afraid that your parents will get very angry, think you're "crazy," or even love you less. While there are parents who don't care about their children, most do. And, more than anything, they want their kids to feel good. If you push yourself to tell them, they may be upset at first. That's a natural response. But more than likely, you can count on them to get you the kind of help you need. Besides, it's very lonely and scary to try to handle something so dangerous by yourself. You need an adult to help you.

If your parents get very upset and don't help you, it doesn't mean you're not special or worth it; it just means they're having a problem dealing with your situation, too. So you need to speak with someone else, such as a counselor at school, your family doctor, a trusted teacher, your priest or rabbi. You can also call a telephone operator for information about health or counseling services in your area. Another source of help is the emergency room at the local hospital; call and ask them about what services the hospital offers and where to go. You can also check with your librarian for a listing of what health services are in or near your town.

If the first person doesn't seem to be able to help you, go on to the next, and the next, and the next until you find someone who can. You're worth it.

Some kids don't go for help because they're so embarrassed and afraid if they admit what they're doing (for example, if they're vomiting their food), other people will think that's disgusting or horrible. They're ashamed to tell anyone.

Although it may be very hard to be honest about your feelings and about what you may be doing that is not good for you—you deserve to allow yourself to be helped. It's too hard for anyone to handle what you're dealing with alone. If you don't care about yourself, it's all the more reason to go for help so that you can begin to understand why.

You deserve to feel good. And there are people all around you who will be happy to help if you let them know you need them. The first step in going for help is to admit you need it and then decide that you want to feel better about yourself and want to behave in a way that will be healthier for you.

If You're Worried That a Friend Has an Eating Disorder

If you're worried about a friend, you can let your friend know how concerned you are and encourage your friend to go for help. You can talk to your friend about who might be good to talk with and even offer to keep your friend company because you realize that taking the first step for help can be hard to do alone.

If your friend doesn't want to go for help or won't admit there's a problem—and you continue to be concerned or find that the situation is even getting worse—it's very important not to be silent about your concern.

You can go to your own parents, a school counselor, or another adult who would be good to approach and let that person know that you're worried about your friend and why. They will know the importance of respecting privacy and will also know what appropriate next step to take to make sure your friend is helped. You might also consider speaking with your friend's parent(s).

While most kids are afraid their friend will be angry and feel they're violating trust, keep in mind that if your friend does have an eating disorder, that can be very serious. Even if your friend might be angry at first, he or she will probably feel relieved that you took the first step. Your friend might not have been able to do so. In time, your friend will probably thank you.

If you are too uncomfortable about the idea of talking with someone directly about your concern for your friend, you can at the very least leave an anonymous note (without putting your name on it) in a school counselor's mailbox, stating your reason for concern. Counselors (and other professionals) will know what appropriate steps to take in order to start helping your friend. They will also be aware of the importance of respecting privacy.

Staying silent and not letting anyone know of your concern is not a helpful choice.

When It's Your Turn to "Sprout"

Growth may come on suddenly. This is often talked about as a *growth spurt*. You may grow several inches in a very short time (even a few months). In the beginning of puberty, boys will sometimes need a year or more to catch up in height with girls of the same age.

The bottom of your pant legs might move higher and higher above your ankles. You may find yourself feeling a bit awkward, gawky, uncoordinated (almost like you're going to trip over your own feet) for a while, until you get used to your new size. Your nose may seem like it's on the wrong face. (Sometimes the nose does grow before the rest of the face. Then the face catches up and all looks right again.) Try not to worry. This is all very natural.

New Moods, Feelings, and Emotions

You may find there will be times when you will be cranky, irritable, easily excited, sad, edgy, moody, or even feel like crying without being able to figure out why you feel this way. You might also feel fine again without understanding what made you feel better.

These mood changes (changes in your emotions) are influenced by your hormones and the many feelings you might have about yourself, your body, and the people closest to you. Such moods are considered a natural part of the growing up years.

In time, you will learn to be able to handle your emotions in a way that will reflect your growing maturity. Some boys and girls will experience more noticeable changes in their emotions than others do.

Changes in feelings and emotions may also relate to the excitement, confusion, and frustration that often goes along with learning to become independent (no longer depending on your parents for everything, taking on new responsibilities). While you might find it wonderful to feel more grown-up, you also may find there will be moments when you'll wish you could hold on to childhood a little longer.

Each Person Is Special

Puberty is a time of change: New shapes, new curves, new growth, new feelings and moods, even new braces and eyeglasses—you will change in your own special way, on your own time schedule. You'll have your own feelings, your own concerns and frustrations, your own excitement and happiness, your own hopes and dreams.

You're the only *you* that there is in the entire world! Isn't that incredible? You're unique. There's only one of you. You're one of a kind. You're totally and completely special.

No one—not kids at school, not teachers, not your parents or family—has a right to take away from how special you feel you are. And nothing that you do and nothing that happens to you has a right to make you feel less important. (Even if you make a terrible mistake, it doesn't mean you're a terrible person.)

Some kids think that the only way they can be special is if they have a lot of friends, get good grades, and do everything their parents tell them to do. But that's not it. Being special is not measured by things like looks, size, where you're from, clothes, grades, having a boyfriend or girlfriend, being an athlete, or always keeping your room clean. You're special because you're special. You don't have to do anything to be special. You just are.

Other kids think that the only way they can be special is if they're given positive messages from other people. If they don't hear family or friends say things to them like, "We're really proud of you," or "You're great!" or "I really love you," or "You're my best friend," then they may not think they're special. Or at least they may have a hard time believing they are. (Imagine how hard it is for kids to feel special if they're pushed around or teased every day and never hear anything positive.)

If you're one of those kids who never hears positive messages from others, it doesn't mean you're not special or important. You still are. Even though it can feel good to hear nice things, words don't have the power to make you more or less special.

So when you're at home, at school, or anywhere, you can stand up a bit taller and walk around with a bigger smile on your face because now you know the secret of feeling special. The secret is: remembering that specialness has to do with who you are inside. And no one has the right to take away from who you are. Not with their words, their fists, how they look at you, or how they judge you—unless you let them. You never have to let them. You can decide to hold on tightly to feeling good—no matter what anyone else says or does.

I don't pretend that holding on to your good feelings about yourself will always be easy. With all the pressures and changes and confusions of your growing-up years, you may have to work extra hard to remind yourself that you're special, no matter what.

If you're having trouble feeling good, you now know you don't have to deal with tough feelings alone. There's help around you.

PART II

GROWING UP FEELING GOOD ABOUT YOURSELF

CHAPTER 12

FRIENDSHIP

Friendship Is One of the Most Important Parts of Growing Up

Friendship means caring about another person, being able to trust, getting to know them, and learning about them—what makes them laugh, what bothers them, what their favorite ice cream flavor is.

Friendship means understanding. You don't have to pretend with a friend. It's okay to be who you are. A friend will understand when you're sad and be happy with you when you feel good.

True friends tell each other secrets and know that they won't be spread all over. True friends won't make fun of you if you get a lower grade on your test. They won't tease if you're the first to have braces or the last to grow. They'll tell you in a nice way if your fly is open, if they think your hair is too short, or if you need a bra. They'll try to help you with your homework before school if you had trouble doing it the night before. They'll cry with you if your pet dies.

Friendship is special. This chapter will give you a good chance to think about the friends you have, the friends you'd like to have, and the friends you wish you didn't have.

Some kids have many friends, some have just a few, others don't have any. The same is true for adults. It's not that there are any rules about numbers of friends. In fact, even when certain people seem to have many friends, they can be very lonely.

My feeling is that it's much more important to think about *who* your friends are than how many you have. One or two very good friends can mean much more than a bunch of kids who just *act* like they care—but when it comes down to it, they really don't.

The friendships you make while you're growing up are ones that are often kept, or at least remembered, for a lifetime. If you don't have any friends (you're not alone—lots and lots of kids have talked about this) or would like to make another friend, you can start thinking about it right this minute!

Have You Ever . . .

Have you ever looked at someone in your classroom, in your lunchroom, at a club meeting, walking home from school, on the school bus, or somewhere else, who seemed to be nice? Maybe even the kind of person you might want to have as a friend?

What did you do? Did you go over to the person and say, "Hi"? Did you tell the person your name and ask what lunch period he or she has? Did you say, "Let's sit together on the bus"? Or did you do nothing, wishing you could be confident enough to do something?

Many people feel it's not the easiest thing to just go up to someone and start talking. Adults as well as kids get nervous. Boys and girls of all ages have said to me, "I'm shy . . . and I don't know what to do."

Getting started at trying to become less shy, making the decision that you want to find a new friend, or especially a first friend, takes *guts*. Everyone has them inside.

If you're one of the many shy people, even *you* have guts! Your guts may have been taking a rest for all these years, but that will probably just make them stronger as soon as you decide to poke them a little (a lot?) and let them know you need them.

It's time to realize that being shy or scared doesn't have to prevent you from being able to enjoy all the special things that friendship can mean. You deserve to have at least one close friend. It may be hard for you to believe it, but someone out there will be very lucky to have you as their friend.

Here are some steps you can follow to try to find a new friend.

How to Make a Friend

The first step is to realize that you want to make a friend.

The second step is to think about who you might like to have as a friend. This may take a bit of time. That's natural, since it's not such an easy decision. The exciting thing is that you've made up your mind to do something important for yourself. That's great!

Look around carefully. Try not to judge people by their clothing, how they wear their hair, how developed they are, if they're small or very tall, their weight, what street they live on, or whether they almost flunked gym! These things don't tell you what you need to know if you're thinking about becoming someone's friend. You must learn about who that person is on the inside.

It's more important to find out if the person is nice, if you can have fun together, if you feel comfortable together. Are there things you can enjoy doing together? Would you be able to trust this person? Could you be honest with the person? That kind of learning will take some time.

Until you get to know someone, it's really not fair to make any decisions on the type of person he or she is. You'd just be guessing. You might be right. But you could also be very wrong.

Pay attention at the bus stop or walking to and from school, in the lunchroom, and at recess. Take a good look at the kids in your classes. Watch who walks with whom through the halls. Notice who seems to be alone much of the time (they may be shy, too). After-school clubs and religious classes might give you the chance to meet different kids. The more people you're around, the more choices you have. Keep looking. . . .

You'll be ready for the third step when you've picked out one person who you think might be nice to know.

The third step is to let that person know you're alive, if they don't know already. If you pick someone from your school, you'll probably know a little bit about that person. Sometimes, the person or you will be "new," perhaps because you've just moved to a different school or into a new town, new club, or new activity.

If you've never seen or spoken with the person before, a good start would be to ask them their name and tell them yours. You might say, "Hi, I think we take the same bus in the morning. My name is ____." Or, "Hi, I'm ____. What's your name?"

You might also take a chance and say, "A group of my friends are going into town after school, do you want to come?" Or, "How about eating lunch together?" Or, "That's going to be a tough test tomorrow. Do you want to study together this afternoon?" Or, "How about coming over to my house (apartment) this afternoon, or one day this week?" Or, "I see we walk home the same way. Do you want to meet after school and go together?" Or just, "What did you think of the math test?" or "Wasn't that concert great?" You don't always have to ask someone to actually *do* something with you. A beginning can be just talking with the person if you never have before.

By now, you might be thinking, "I can't just walk over to someone and start talking! What if they don't talk back?" (What if they do?)

Well, this is the tough part. You may think that your knees will shake, your face will flush, and you'll "die" of embarrassment. But what's the most awful thing that could happen? Most kids would answer, "That the person says 'no'." Or worse, he or she could make fun or walk away and totally ignore you! This is called "rejection" (ree-JEK-shun) and it can feel rotten. *But...*

An old Ellen Rosenberg belief is that you haven't really lost anything by trying. You may hurt for a little while and be disappointed, but you still have everything that you walked up to the person with. You have *you* and that's very special. If you groan and moan and feel sorry for yourself, that won't help. Besides, it's better to try to feel sorry for that other person. Just think. They're missing out on getting a chance to know you!

Repeat five times: "It's their loss!"

The trick is not to let rejection stop you or cause you to feel bad about yourself. Lots of kids think, "What's wrong with me? I must be a loser!"

if someone doesn't seem to want to get to know them. If the answer is "no," it doesn't mean something is wrong with you. Most of the time, the person who says "no" probably hasn't even spent any time getting to know the person he or she rejects. So, wouldn't it be silly, and even kind of sad, if kids felt bad about themselves just because someone who didn't even know them said "no"?

The truth is that if someone says "no" to you, you probably just didn't go up to the right person yet. Not everyone relates to everyone else. And even if the person you approach says "yes," you might find that you're the one who doesn't want to be with him or her once you start to get to know that person better.

If someone is not interested, what happens next? You move on to the fourth step. Find a new person to approach and start again.

SPECIAL ADVICE: Sometimes it helps to approach that other kid when no one else is around. If you ask in front of the kid's group of friends, he or she may say "no," even while wanting to say "yes." Jennifer, age fourteen, said, "That's especially true when you think your friends don't like that person."

The fifth step and beyond: Keep trying. You may have to try going up to many kids before finding one that says, "Hey! I'll look for you later. Oh, my name is ____, what's yours?"

I'm not pretending that this will be easy. And I'd be lying if I said you'd feel terrific if kids don't seem interested, one after the other. Rejection can be very painful. You might begin to think that the easiest thing would be to give up. But if you stop trying, you're choosing to give up on yourself. And you're worth more than that. So the lesson here is that you shouldn't stop. Go on to the next, and the next, as tough as that may be. (Remember, it's okay to be uncomfortable or nervous when going up to someone. It's *not* okay to let discomfort stop you from trying.)

Someone (maybe your twelfth, maybe your twentieth pick) will be so happy you came over. Someone will be so relieved that you had the guts to say "hi" first.

Take a chance. The hardest will be the first try. You may really have to force yourself to get the words out. But do it. And see what happens. Once you get back a smile, a hello, or a "Yes, I'd love to come to your house or walk into town with you"—you're on your way.

Remember to be patient with yourself. Building confidence can take time. So can building comfort and trust to form a friendship. I believe that there's someone out there for everyone.

NOTE: If you're the person someone picks to approach, whether you wish to say yes or no is your choice. Whatever you choose, at least be nice.

For example, if you don't feel like spending extra time with that person, you might just say, "That's not good for me but thanks for asking. I'll see you later in class . . ." And then when you see that person again, you can at least make sure to say hi. Remember, you don't have to be someone's friend to be nice.

Some Kids Are Hard to Like

Kids tell me it's hard to like people who tease, show off, lie, spread rumors, are bossy, think they're always right, never share, never listen to anyone else, always have to have their own way, or think they're better than anyone else. What else would you add to this list?

If you're having trouble making friends, it might help to think about how you treat other kids and how you behave around them. Really be honest with yourself. If you realize that you haven't been so nice, that might be the reason people don't want to spend time with you.

While you can't change or erase what you have already done, you can decide right now to start treating people in a nicer way. That can begin to make a difference in whether people want to be your friend.

It may take some time for people to realize that you've changed your behavior. Especially when you first decide to make the effort to be nicer, many kids may still see you as a bully (or whatever else might apply). That could be frustrating, since you know you're trying your best to be nice. But don't give up, and just keep on being nicer. In time, you'll find that more and more kids will trust that you really are nice, and they'll begin to give you a new chance.

What About the Friends You Have?

As I talk about the many questions that boys and girls have asked me about friendship, you'll have a good chance to think about your own concerns and situations.

"What if friends act one way when they're alone with you and another way when they're with the group?" So many kids have talked about this. For instance, Scott, age eleven, told me that he had this really good friend. When they were alone, things were easy between them. "He wasn't loud or show-offy or anything like that. But when he was with the whole group, for some reason, he had to show off. He teased, he was loud, he wasn't even nice sometimes."

Thirteen-year-old David told me pretty much the same thing. His friends were great when he was with them one at a time. But as soon as they got together, they acted up and even teased him.

The reasons for this are probably different for each friend. Very often, kids act this way because they're not sure of themselves in a group. They may feel they have to prove themselves, show off, and get extra attention in order to be accepted.

When they're alone, there's usually a trust that doesn't exist in the crowd. They don't have to prove themselves in the same way. They can just be who they are and don't have to put on an act.

Stacey, age ten, said, "When people are in a crowd, they're more nervous about what they're saying. If they say something wrong, they're afraid kids won't like them. When they're alone, they know that just one person will hear it, and they'll speak more freely."

If you find that you're bothered by how much any of your friends change when they're not alone with you anymore, it's important for you to talk about your feelings with them. You might also ask them if they realize how different they act when you're alone together. If they're fooling around too much, teasing you, or ignoring you, let them know it hurts and you don't think it's funny.

They may not have any idea that they're hurting or bothering you. Once you tell them, they'll probably try to stop—if they care about you and the friendship you have. If they don't stop, you may have to tell them a few more times as they may not understand that you're serious.

If they still act in ways that hurt and it continues to bother you, then you may have to do some thinking about whether you want to remain their friend. It may be time for you to make some changes.

"What if you want to be someone's friend, but you don't want to belong to the group they hang around with?" It would be sad to give up the friendship and unfair to be pressured (feel forced) to be with kids you really don't like.

What you can do is talk honestly with your friend. Say that you care about him or her a lot and want to be friends. But say you're not comfortable, or you don't have the same feelings for their crowd. So you hope he or she will understand that you're not going to join them when their group is around. When he or she can be with you alone, great!

If your friend can't or doesn't want to deal with that or doesn't understand, then you may have a choice to make. To be friends, care about each other, but not see each other very much. Or to be friends and hang out with his or her group, even though you don't want to, just so you can still spend time with that person. What else do you think you might do?

It's not completely up to you, though, since the friendship includes both of you. Even if *you* decide you can deal with this situation, they may not be able to. Or they may not want to.

Friendships don't always work out, even if both people want to be friends. There are sometimes other things that one or both of you may have to deal with that can make being together difficult.

"What if your friends are in different crowds?" Tammi, age eleven, told me, "I'm friends with another group of kids and I'm friends with my group. I'm in classes with both and can be with either group when I want to. I don't feel like I'm in the middle. I can be friendly with who I want."

That's great! Sometimes, when friends are in different groups, one can be jealous of the other. Janie, age ten, said, "When I'm with one friend, the other one gets mad at me and thinks I don't want to be with her. They're not in the same crowd and it's not fun to be with them together. I'd rather see them by themselves. I always feel like I have to choose between them. I hate being in the middle."

Have you ever felt this way? Did you do anything about it? One suggestion would be to speak to both friends, privately. Tell them you like them both and want to be good friends with each of them. But you always feel pulled if you spend time with one instead of the other. Ask them to please understand that it's easier for you to be with them alone, separately, and it would help if they didn't make a big deal about it.

It's important to keep in mind that even if you ask your friends to be understanding, it's going to be up to them to decide to be understanding or not. You can only be in charge of what *you* say and do. You can't control your friends or anyone else. So even if you ask for understanding, your friend may keep on making a big deal. If, after letting your friend know once more how you feel, there is still no change, you may need to make some new decisions about who you wish to be with.

"What about when friendship changes?" or When your feelings change about a friend Susie, age fourteen, shared, "Nothing really happened between us. We didn't fight or anything like that. But my friend spent the night at my house last weekend. And I found out things about her that I didn't know. Things I don't like. She uses words that I don't like to hear. She talks about doing things that make me feel uncomfortable, that I'm not ready for. Maybe we shouldn't be such close friends anymore. I thought I knew her, but I guess I don't. It makes me upset."

Andy, age thirteen, feels, "Friendships change over long periods of time. Not seeing the person can cause this to happen. Even best friends can stop being best friends because they fall in with new people, or they try things that you're against. I find this mostly with girls. They seem to change their best friends much more often than boys do."

Sheryl, age thirteen, told me, "Last week, I just found out that one of my best friends smokes [cigarettes]. When I heard this, I cried and cried. I never would have thought that she'd do a thing like that. But I have another close friend who talked with me for hours and helped me see that it really is her choice, not mine. I can only choose for me. She's not trying to pressure me to smoke, too. In fact, she's hidden her smoking from me all this time. Maybe she thought I wouldn't be her friend if I found out. The truth is, the first thing I thought of is that I don't want to be her friend anymore if she smokes! How could a close friend of mine smoke? But I guess maybe this is what she needs to do right now. I'll have to think about it. Maybe it has nothing to do with me."

Sheryl was shocked and very upset. I think a big part of her reaction was that she thought she knew her friend so well. So did Susie. Friends change. Even best friends! Maybe they would have changed anyway. But often the change is because of pressures at home or at school, wanting to be accepted by different people, or new experiences—or that a person simply matures in a different direction.

You can't know when you start being close with someone in kindergarten or first grade that several years later, they could get involved with drugs, smoking, or stealing or anything else that might be uncomfortable or unacceptable to you.

When you find out about changes like these, it can be really tough to deal with. It can be confusing and sometimes painful. Usually you're not prepared; you never thought about your friends in that way. You never expected him or her to be different from when they were with you.

You end up having to make another choice: Do I keep on being friendly with this person, even though he or she has changed? Do I stop the friendship or stop seeing them as often as I have for all these years? I don't know if I can accept what they've become or what they're doing. I don't want to be exposed to it, I don't want to even take the chance of being pressured. I don't want to deal with it. I don't believe in it. Should I stay away? I don't want other people to think I'm that way or I do it, too. Getting involved might even turn out to be dangerous.

Though the affection between you and your friend may not change, the difference in how they act, what they say, and the kinds of things that have become important to them may prevent you from being able to be as close with them as you were before. Staying away from some-one who you care about when both of you really don't want to lose the friendship can be very, very hard to do.

If you want to keep on being friends with that person, you'll have to work at accepting him or her the way they are with their changes. If they continue to choose to do what they've been doing, it doesn't mean you have to do it, too.

When friends hurt your feelings Sometimes friends say things to be funny and don't realize you're going to feel bad about it. But other times, friends can say things on purpose to be mean. I'm not sure what kind of a good friend they are if they want to hurt you, but maybe he or she got mad and that was the only way this person knew how to get you back. Or maybe you're the only person your friend could take his or her anger out on, even if it has nothing to do with you.

More from Stacey, age ten: "If one of my friends said something I knew she really didn't mean, I'd discuss it with her and make her under-stand why she hurt me."

That's a very good way to deal with hurt. It's true, friends (even best friends) don't always know how you feel. So it's up to you to tell them what hurts you and what doesn't. That's how they learn to become more thoughtful and sensitive to your feelings. When your friends are honest with you, that's how you can learn to be more caring with them.

If you don't tell your friends how you feel, then you can't blame them for hurting you again in the same way. You might say, "I really felt hurt when you did that or said that." Or, "You probably didn't mean to hurt me, but I didn't think it was funny. Please don't say that again."

If you find that your friends still put you down or tease after you've told them how bad you feel when they do this (more than once—to make sure they know you're serious), then maybe that means they don't care about you as much as you thought they did. If you find that seems to be true, maybe it would be smart to start looking around for other friends.

"What if something really bothers you about a friend?" Did you ever have a friend who drove you crazy when he or she did something or said something? What did you do? Did you keep quiet about it or did you say something to your friend? Or did you talk to a different friend about how you can't stand what that other friend did?

Lisa, age thirteen, told me about a friend of hers who embarrasses her. Said Lisa, "She tries to act so cool. I hate it when she comes up and kisses me in public, and I get so embarrassed. But if I tell her, she'll only get mad."

Craig, age nine, said, "I have a friend I don't like anymore. But I'm afraid to tell him because he'll probably beat me up."

Keith, age twelve, said, "I used to spend a lot of time with this friend. But I don't want to be with him as much anymore. He tags along and always asks me what I'm doing after school. I don't want to hurt his feelings, but I don't want to play with him either."

The big concern seems to be how to let someone know how you feel without getting the person mad and without hurting them. The problem is that sometimes you can't help hurting the people you care about, even if that's the last thing you want to do.

If you tell your friend or write a note, try to be kind, sensitive, and private. This can help to make whatever you have to say hurt a little less. The person may not like hearing it and may feel bad, but at least he or she will be able to trust that you're saying it because you care, not to be nasty or mean or to blame anyone.

You might begin by saying:
- "It's really hard for me to say this to you."
- "I would never want to hurt you, but I need you to know . . ."
- "I love you, but when you do that, it really drives me crazy. . . ." (Instead of "drives me crazy," you could say: "gets me angry," "embarrasses me," "disappoints me"—whatever you feel.)
- "Please listen before you get mad. I want you to understand something, and it's not easy for me to tell you because I don't want to end up fighting."

If you ask another friend to tell the person about what you feel, he or she is probably still going to feel bad, and may even be more hurt and embarrassed because you weren't able to say what bothered you yourself. If you keep quiet, let things be, and don't let your friend know how you feel, you're taking the chance that you'll get more and more annoyed or angry. That situation, besides being tough to take, can't be good for the friendship.

Being honest about happy things is easy. But dealing with hurt and things that don't feel so good can be an even better test of a friendship. Finding out that you and your friend can talk about the harder, sometimes painful things, as well as the laughs, can often make you closer.

When friends fight Jeremy, age twelve, told me, "If my friends get mad, I just figure they liked me once and they'll like me again. I don't really worry about my friends, or whether they like me or not. I just know they do. Other people don't feel that way with their friends. Like my sister, if her friends say, 'I don't like you,' she gets all upset. If my friends say that, I just say, 'Good!' And the next day we'll all have forgotten about it."

It's a good feeling to be able to trust that your friends will still be there even if something goes wrong for a little while. Maybe Jeremy's sister will feel less upset as she realizes that it's pretty natural for friends to argue sometimes. Fighting doesn't have to mean the end of a friendship. It could mean that, but usually fighting just blows over or is worked out or forgotten about (or at least not made into an issue) until the next thing comes up.

Lynn, age eleven, said, "Three of us are very good friends. Whenever I have a fight with one of them, the other usually sticks by her and stops paying attention to me. When I talk with her privately, she's really different. She says she likes both of us and just wants to stay friendly with both. But why does she takes sides then?"

It's possible that she may be more sure of her friendship with you than she is with the other girl. Since she doesn't have to worry about you, she sticks close to the other girl. It would help if you told her how this makes you feel. Maybe she will stop taking any sides or at least stop making it seem like she is.

Thirteen-year-old Andy feels that his friends seem to fight a lot. He remembers a time recently when an entire social group got into a fight. "That happened mainly because the telephone can be a deadly weapon. Because rumors are spread back and forth, and you end up going to school having a grudge against somebody and they have absolutely no idea what's going on."

Andy continued, "I think more girls get into fights with their friends than boys do. A lot of girls fight with friends about girlfriends and boyfriends and stuff like that. With me, if my friends and I get into a fight, it almost turns into a joke. After it starts out being really serious, even if we insult each other, with us it's only a game. None of the grudges are held over until the next day."

James, age fourteen, said, "I find there's not much fighting between good friends, at least with friends in my grade. When I was younger, there seemed to be a lot more fighting, but I don't even remember what it was about."

There are so many reasons that kids have given me about why friends fight: boyfriends, girlfriends, being jealous, rumors, telling secrets, misunderstandings, forgetting to meet at a certain time, not calling back, leaving someone out, hurt feelings, being embarrassed, buying the same exact sweater . . . I'm sure you can add to this list.

Since no two people are exactly alike, each friendship is different. Each fight will be a little different—even between the same people. But the one very important thing that can help all friends, no matter what the fight is about, is if they try very hard to talk things out. Some kids have told me they're afraid to do this because what if the friend won't listen?

As I said before, the only way you can be sure someone knows how you feel is to tell them. It's best not to try to talk things out when you or the other person is very upset. Wait for a private, calmer moment.

You can then explain why you did what you did. If you hurt the person and didn't mean to, say you're sorry. If your friend embarrassed you, let him or her know about it and learn you don't want that to happen again. If a rumor was spread, make sure your friend realizes it wasn't you who started it. If you were left out, ask why your friend forgot about or ignored you, or at least let your friend know you felt left out. Try to clear up any kind of misunderstandings, the sooner the better.

You can say, "I don't blame you for being angry with me. That was a stupid thing I did." Or, "I'm so sorry, I didn't realize it would bother you so much." Or, "I can't believe you would have done that to me if you knew how I felt. Now that you know, please don't do it again."

If it's hard to begin, once again, you can say exactly that: "It's really hard for me to say this." Or, "Please don't say anything until you hear everything I need to say." Or, "I hope I don't start crying in the middle of this. . . ." Or, whatever you feel! See how you can turn feelings into words?

Sometimes people try to end fights by saying, "Why don't we just forget about it!" I don't believe that we completely forget. But I do believe we can decide to let go of the hurt feelings, put them behind us, learn from them, and move forward in a more positive way.

It can help to keep in mind that we can't go backwards. We can't change what was already said or what we already did. But, we *can* learn not to say it or do it again. And we can learn to appreciate that sometimes painful situations (even horrible fights) can teach us valuable lessons that can make friendships and family relationships grow stronger.

So, if your friendship is important to you, gather up your courage and take another chance. Ask your friend to forgive. Tell them you'll forgive. Say you want to try again (if you do). If it's worth it to both of you, the fight will be over quickly so you can get on with your friendship.

Just remember, if you decide to wait for the other person to say something, you may be waiting for a long time. Silent wars are no fun! So no matter who started the fight, if you want it stopped, you may have to be the one to talk first.

"What if your friend doesn't keep a secret?" Said Katie, age ten, "It really can hurt if you tell a friend something very private and the next day you get to school and everyone is talking about what you said!"

I don't blame anyone for getting upset if a close friend blabs a secret. Most of the time it's either embarrassing or painful to learn that other people know. The hurt part is that you thought you could trust that friend. And you couldn't.

How many times has someone said to you, "You promise not to tell anyone? You better not let anyone find out I told you this 'cause So-and-so will kill me." One person tells the next not to tell; the next tells someone else. And by the time they're all finished, tons of kids know what they shouldn't know.

That happens a lot. The problem is that you can't be completely sure you can trust someone unless you test the trust out a little bit. You may think someone is close to you and find out they can't or won't keep your secret. But you may not be able to find that out until after the secret has been passed around.

Jamie, age fourteen, suggests that you test if kids can keep a secret. "Tell them something that you don't care about so it won't matter if they tell. That way, you can see if they keep their promise not to let it out."

An interesting idea, Jamie! Roz, now age fifty-two, remembers, "There were always certain people we knew would tell everyone everything. My friends and I used to make up rumors just so we could tell them to this girl in our class who never kept her mouth shut about anything. We called her up and said she better promise not to tell anyone about it. Then we used to time how quickly the rumor spread around the school and [we'd] laugh and laugh and laugh."

According to Cori, age thirteen, "Most secrets are not kept. You can't expect them to be. It also depends on the subject. If it was really important and really, really serious, like, 'My parents are getting a divorce, what can I do?' Or, 'My best friend smokes, how can I deal with that?' then probably there'll be less talk. But if it's who likes who or who is breaking up with who, that will always get around."

What can you learn from this? That certain people can be trusted to keep their mouth shut and lots of others are blabbermouths, gossipers, or snitches! It may or may not depend on what the secret is.

So the next time you have a secret, think carefully about whom you want to share it with. Think even more carefully about how you'd feel if it got out. Then make your decision.

If you're wrong about trusting a friend with something private, it may mean that friend didn't realize what you said was to be kept so private. If you did make your wish for privacy clear, the breach of trust will teach you not to share—or at least to be cautious about sharing with that friend next time. It doesn't mean your friendship has to change. Rather, what you choose to share may change. Now that you know that much more about your friend, you can make better decisions as to what you want to share and what you don't.

When you're right about trust, you'll probably feel even closer to that friend. It's a good feeling.

P.S. If a friend tells your secret and breaks the trust between you, it's possible for the two of you to build the trust back up again. Let your friend know how hurt or upset you were and how hard it is now for you to trust him or her again.

This building of trust may take time but it can happen. And you may find that if it does, you may be closer with that friend. As smart as you need to be about whom you can share private feelings with, you also need to be wise about whom to forgive. If it turns out you're wrong again, at least you'll know that you tried to give an important friendship a chance to be better. Not every friendship will work out the way you would wish.

"What if your parents don't like your friends?" It's possible that your mom or dad (or both) won't like one of your friends or even the whole crowd you hang around with. It can be tough to stay friendly when this happens.

It's one thing if parents tell you why they don't like—or are concerned about—your friends, and suggest that maybe that you should watch out for certain things that they don't trust or think are a poor influence. That can make seeing them a bit uncomfortable because now you might have a question in your mind about them. But it's usually the toughest if your parents out-and-out tell you not to see certain friends anymore, and you still really like them.

What would you do if your parents said that to you about one of your friends? Would you listen to your parents and stop seeing the person? Would you tell your parents you'll listen, then sneak and see your friend in classes at school? How guilty do you think you'd feel if you chose to sneak?

Randi, age twelve, told me: "I was very friendly with a boy who lives around the corner from me. We spent a lot of time together since the third grade. All of a sudden, his parents started getting on his back for spending time with me. We did every school project together that we could. We always signed up for the same committees. I really think his parents thought that their son was doing most of the work and I was just getting a free ride, but that was never true. So they forbade him to do any more projects with me. I knew he wanted to, but he didn't because of his parents. I soon stopped going over to his house and felt funny about calling him if I knew his parents were home. Now it's been a while since his parents became so strict about him being with me. Even though we still see each other at school, something has changed. Slowly we've been getting more and more apart. It's sad because we were really close."

Thirteen-year-old Andrea talked about her parents and how they dealt with not liking one of her friends: "My parents don't like my friend but they let me decide if I still want be close with her. I agree that certain things about her are not like me, but other things are. I can't stand it when they say, 'She's not your type!' I don't have to do what she does just to be her friend. It's not what my parents think. It's true that she smokes. But I don't want to and she doesn't make me feel funny about not smoking when she's doing it."

It's important to respect that your parents are probably trying very hard to look out for you. They don't want you to get hurt. They'd like to see you with friends that are, in their opinion, right for you. And they may just see something that you're not able to see.

You can listen to them, think about what they're saying, and then see how you feel. Your parents may allow you to make up your own mind. But of course, if they really think someone will be a danger to you they may not give you a choice; you may have to listen to their cautions—even if you don't see it that way.

Some more thoughts: If you find it's really hard to listen to your parents about not seeing a friend and you don't want to sneak, talk with your parents about how you feel. I would hope they'd rather have you be honest with them than choose to go against their wishes behind their backs. Maybe you can work things out. They may not have any idea that not being with your friend bothers you that much. Remember, they can't know for sure what you're feeling unless you tell them.

It may help for you to suggest that your parent(s) get to know your friend better. Perhaps you can get permission to invite your friend for dinner or for a visit during the weekend at a time when your parent will be around.

How to Deal with Two-Faced Friends

Michelle, age twelve, explains, "Friends are two-faced when to your face they're your friend, but behind your back they go against you."

It has to hurt when you find out that somebody you think is a true friend really isn't. I would tell the person that you know what happened, that you're very upset about the way you feel you've been treated. See what response you get.

Even if he or she apologizes and promises not to go behind your back anymore, it may take a long time for you to trust the person again. The good thing is that at least you'll know that you weren't treated honestly and you can be more careful about what you say or do around that person.

Liking Someone Whom Hardly Anybody Else Likes

Cathy, age ten, asked, "What if my friend and I don't want to play with a girl because nobody likes her and she can ruin our reputations? Then nobody will like us. Sometimes we like her and sometimes we don't like her at all."

Probably Cathy and her friend like the other girl more at times when the other kids aren't around. They're afraid that other kids will find out they like her and maybe won't be their friend anymore.

Their friends may even say, "If you're the kind of person who hangs around with her, then you can't be my friend, too." That can make it harder to stay friendly with her. I think it comes down to making a choice. As with all the other choices, it helps to understand what each one might mean.

If you choose to keep seeing someone whom nobody likes, then you're taking a chance that your usual friends may not want to be with you, if they find out. But who do you think should decide how and with whom you are going to spend your free time? Your friends or you? Do you think you should be able to like whom you want to like?

If you spend time with that other person, your friends may tease you about it. And they may tease the other person, with or without you around. When that happens, you'll have to decide if you want to go along with any teasing or comments or if you're going to stick up for that unpopular friend.

If you stick up for him or her, your friends may stop and respect what you're saying. They may even invite that person to join them, if they know it's that important to you. Or they may not even listen.

You'll have to follow what your brain and especially your heart senses you should do. Think of the other person's feelings. Be as nice as you would want other kids to be to you. Even if you know how wrong it is to tease and make someone else feel bad, it may be hard to go against what your close friends are doing. This is something called peer pressure (when friends pressure you to do something that you really don't want to do), which I talk about in Chapter 15.

If your friends are giving you a hard time because you like that other person, you can let them know how much that bothers you. You might also let your usual friends know how much your friendship with them matters to you. And when you're with them, that means a lot. But you also want to spend some time with that other person. You can say that you know they don't like or don't want to be with him or her—and that's okay. They don't have to be with that person. It's just not okay for them to make it seem that they like you less just because you want to spend time with the person.

You can also say to your friends that you don't tell them whom to like and you don't feel it's right for them to tell you whom to like. If they're really your friends, then it doesn't matter whom else you like. They're not friends with everyone else you like; they're friends with *you*.

When Friends Use You or Try to Buy You

Steve, age twelve, told me that his friend's little brother "always used to call to come over to play with my brother's computer game. He spent lots of time at our house. When the game was broken, he stopped coming over. When it was fixed, he came back. Then he got his own computer game and hasn't come back since."

That's a good example of using. He came over for the game, not for the person. Another example is when someone asks you to come over for lunch or dinner and, instead of saying, "I'd love to," because you want to be with them, you first ask, "What are you having for dinner?" Using would be if you went because you liked the dinner or you said "no" just because you didn't. You'd be making the food much more important than the person, just as the computer game was to Steve's friend's brother.

When you were younger, kids might have wanted to come over to your house because of a toy that you had and they didn't. Or because your mom (or dad) baked great cookies. Or because they weren't allowed to have candy or soda (pop) in their home and you could have all you wanted. So they might have come over to your house to "pig out."

As you get older, you'll probably find that kids still might try to use other kids, but the reasons seem to change. They may be friendly with someone because they like a certain boy or girl and that person is a way they can get close to the person they like. Or if someone understands science and they don't, they may want to copy their homework or have that person spend time explaining theirs to them. Or, they may just want to get an invitation to the party they know someone is going to give in a few weeks.

If someone's mom or dad is always around and is able to take their son or daughter places and pick them up, someone might just be that person's friend to come along for the ride. Later, people might be friendly with someone because their boyfriend or girlfriend has a car and that's cool or easier to them than walking.

Besides kids who are users, there are many kids who try to buy friendships. Bobby, age nine, remembers one boy in his second grade class who used to give him things. He finally understood that the kid just wanted to be his friend and thought he had to do that to make Bobby like him. Bobby said, "I didn't like taking all that stuff from him. It was nice, but it made me feel weird. I knew something was not right about it."

While some kids make these offers because they really want to be nice and feel good about their friendship, it's sad to me that certain kids feel that have to "sell" themselves. That especially happens when they don't have enough confidence in themselves to believe that someone else will like them for who they are, rather than needing to bribe them with swimming pools, rides, food, or other things.

I imagine that some kids don't realize they're using other people. It may be only when the computer game breaks that they find out they really don't have such a good time with that person. But it's different if they know they're taking advantage of someone. Most people feel that's not very nice. It's even sadder when the other person knows they're being used but wants the company badly and lets it happen.

Can you think of any times when other kids tried to use you or your friends? How about buying friendship? Did you ever feel the need to do anything like that yourself?

What If You Don't Like Someone?

You have the right to choose whether or not you even want to give someone a chance to be friends. If you don't like someone or even feel you hate someone, that's also your right—your choice, your feelings. What you do with those feelings is the issue.

Schools are creating more programs to prevent and put an end to violence and help kids be respectful of each other no matter what their differences. Even so, thousands of kids in schools I've visited across the United States still talk with me about being teased or bullied or worse, on the bus, in school, and on the way home.

There are kids who won't raise their hand in class, won't go up to the board even when they know the correct answer, just because they don't want to deal with what other kids will say or do behind their backs. There are kids who are sick (and even throw up) so they don't have to go to school—because they're so afraid and feel so terrible about the way they're being treated. Many have told me about times they were chased home by groups of kids who threatened and called them names, or who actually beat them up because of differences such as skin color, where they were born, or their religious beliefs.

This kind of behavior towards others is unacceptable. Each person has a right to his or her own feelings, even if that includes hate. But no one has a right to be mean or violent to someone else because of that hate.

So, it's okay not to like someone, but it's not okay to make that person feel miserable, afraid, so he or she doesn't even want to come to school. No one deserves to feel like or be treated like dirt. All kids are trying very hard to feel good about themselves. And, no matter how strong and confident any kid might be inside, it's very hard to hold onto those good strong feelings after being pushed around, made fun of, or beaten up.

Think about whether or not there is someone at school or around where you live whom you don't like. Have you left the person alone or made his or her life miserable? Have you ever really spent time with that person, or do you just not like him or her because other kids don't or because of their looks or something about them that is different from you? Is there someone you feel doesn't like you? How has that person treated you and how has that made you feel?

I believe our world would be a better, more peaceful place if people would respect and accept each other, regardless of their differences. It would be such a relief to so many kids if they could trust that other kids would just leave them alone if they didn't like them. No whispering behind their backs or saying rotten things to their face. No taking their books or throwing papers, hats, or other belongings around school grounds. No laughing at or making fun for any reason. No spreading rumors. No comments at all if the comments are not going to be nice. No pushing them around, no bullying, no knives, no guns, no violence.

Leave them alone. Don't be their friend if you don't want to. Have nothing—or as little as possible—to do with them. But, at the very least, respect their right to be, their right to make the most out of their life—as you deserve to make the most of yours.

No one and nothing has the right to chip away at someone's ability to feel important and valuable. Everyone counts. Everyone is equal. Everyone is worth it, no matter what.

The truth is, not everyone connects. Not everyone wants to relate to everyone else. That's fine. That's life. It's not fine for people to tear each other apart and be disrespectful.

Caroline, age fifteen, asked, "What can I do? I'm only one person!" You can do a lot. You can *choose* to make a difference. You can control what you do and what you say and how you respond to everyone and everything around you. You can control *you*.

So, for example, if you're standing around in a group of kids and they all start picking on someone, you can choose not to be part of that. If someone tries to tell you something behind someone else's back, you can choose not to listen and say, "It's really none of my business. I'd rather make up my own mind." If someone tells a joke that is disrespectful of someone else's race or anything else, you don't have to laugh. You can even say, "I don't think it's funny." You can decide for yourself to treat people with respect.

If you're in class together, during those times when you may have to work on the same project or sit with that person on a school trip—you can be respectful, nice, and not make faces or comments to other kids to show that you're mad because you have to sit with the person. Try to give the person a chance and find something positive about them. Lots of kids have admitted to me that when they were forced to spend time with someone they didn't like—for example, on a school project—they ended up feeling the person wasn't so bad. Most of the time, kids who hate other kids haven't spent any real time getting to know them.

Dealing with Rumors or Reputations

Some kids tell me that they can't wait to graduate because that's the only way they feel they can get away from the mistake they made in the ninth grade that nobody ever let them forget. Reputations can be very hard to erase. Rumors can be very cruel and make kids not even want to come to school. Most kids don't know how to deal with being the one who is talked about.

Jennifer, age eighteen, told me that when she was in tenth grade, a lot of kids in her class spread around the idea that she was a lesbian. She said, "I happen not to be a lesbian, but a lot of kids just kept up the rumor and I think people didn't want to be my friend because of it."

If you personally overhear someone talking about you behind your back and spreading bad rumors—or are told about it by other kids— you have a few choices. One, you can go about your life, be true to who you are, and trust that the people who matter the most to you will not judge you by what other people say. Good friends will usually give you the chance to explain whatever it is that is being said and they'll trust that you're telling them the truth.

If people you believe are good friends don't give you that kind of a chance, ask for it. If they still don't, maybe they're not such good friends. It's important to learn whom you can trust and whom you can't—who is there for you and who is not.

Second, you can go directly up to the person you believe is talking about you and say: "Hey, a lot of kids have told me that you're talking about me behind my back. If you've got something to say, at least have the guts to say it to my face."

I can't promise that this direct approach can change what this person is doing. You can only control what *you* say and do. You can't control anyone else. But I *can* promise that if you don't say anything, then you'll have less of a chance to stop the rumors. The only way to let others know how you feel is to tell them—aloud or in writing.

Kids have talked with me about how hard it is to walk into classes or go into the lunchroom if they know that people are talking about them behind their back. That's a tough thing to deal with. If that's happening to you, and you know you didn't do anything wrong, then keep on walking with your head up high and try your best to ignore the rumors (or at least not to let other kids know that they're getting to you).

If you did do something that you know might have been hurtful or wrong, the faster you apologize and let whomever it is know that you're sorry, the better. You can't go backwards and change what you already did; you can only learn from it and go forward differently.

Rumors spread and reputations change so quickly, whether in school, summer camp, or anywhere else. The main thing to remember is to be yourself and not apologize for who you are. The people who really count will care about you no matter what. While it can be painfully hard to wait, you can figure that, eventually, the rumors will quiet down and the rumor spreaders will leave you alone. Probably, they'll go on to talk about someone else besides you. I wish that weren't the case, but it seems that most of the time that's what happens.

Wiping the Slate Clean

Too bad there aren't laws in each school that would make everyone "wipe the slate clean" at the end of each week, even each day. Think about what that could mean. If you make a mistake, do something you're sorry for, act like a jerk—wouldn't it be a relief to be able to trust that the other kids will give you a new, fresh chance?

Somehow, that just doesn't happen, or at least not enough. No matter how kids may make positive changes, others may still view them the way they used to be—as "stuck-up," "class clown," rumor-spreader, boyfriend-stealer, "druggie"—and not give them a new chance. The fact is, none of us can go backwards. Even if we realize that we were wrong and are sorry about what we said or how we behaved, as I've said before, we can't change what we already did. Whether it was this morning or five years ago, it's history. But we can learn from everything and go forward differently. We can become wiser and even stronger because of what we learned. We can decide not to hold grudges, decide to forgive—ourselves or anyone else—and can choose to let go of what didn't feel good. We can choose to make a fresh start and give that chance to others.

I spoke with Danny, now seventeen, who told me: "When I was in the seventh grade, I always used to push other kids around and pick on them. I don't know, maybe I thought it was fun. But mainly I thought they were better than me. So if I could show them I was stronger or make them afraid of me, then I didn't feel as bad. But one of my teachers helped me understand that what I was doing wasn't good—and I figured I wouldn't bother other kids anymore. But they still thought I was going to bother them because I always used to. It took a long time for them to begin to see me as someone who they might want to hang out with."

Are you saying to yourself, "Yeah, you're talking about me; I wish people would give me a new chance!"? Then, the first step is to give *yourself* a new chance. It's a personal choice—a decision you can make. Next, go ahead and make whatever changes you feel would be important. Remember that you'll need to be patient. It may take a while for other kids to realize you've made those positive changes.

What Can You Do for Others Who Always Seem to Be Left Out?

As important as it is to feel good about yourself and your friendships, it's also very special to try to show other people that you care about them.

Now that you have a better understanding of how difficult it can be for some people to try making friends, why not go over to someone that you've noticed is alone a lot, and start a conversation. If you say hello first, it would probably be much easier for that person to talk to you. And your talk might help him or her feel more confident with others. As you already know, taking the first step can be very hard.

It may take practice to be able to do things for other people, not because of what you'll get in return, but just because you care enough to be nice. There are always opportunities to show someone you care, if you look for them. Besides approaching someone who is often left out, you can say hi to a person who is new in your school and doesn't know many people yet. Or pay attention to someone who seems quiet, shy, or sad. You never know, they could end up being your new best friend! You can also do something nice for a friend or classmate (or anyone you know) who is ill.

You can practice caring about people of all ages. Many older people would probably feel very good to have the chance to talk to someone your age. Talk with your parent or the adult you live with in order to learn how you can make a difference to other people in your community. For example, you might consider making regular visits to a nursing home, hospital, or senior citizen center. Try showing different people that you care. It can feel great just knowing you did something special for someone else.

What If You Don't Have Friends and You Feel Left Out?

If you feel this way (lots of kids do), then this would be a great time to start looking around for someone who seems to be nice. Go back to the beginning of this chapter and reread the part that talks about how you might try to make a friend.

Remember, even if it may be a little scary to go up to someone and ask if he or she wants to meet you in the lunchroom, come over to your home after school, or do anything else, it's important to push yourself to do it anyway. Not trying to do anything about those left-out feelings would be worse.

Some kids are willing to do anything just to find a friend. They may feel very left out and unwanted by kids at school and possibly feel unwanted by their families, as well. Those are the kids who might let themselves do drugs—even if they don't really want to—or join gangs, just to be part of a group.

Joining a gang can be a very dangerous way to find people who seem to like you and make you feel like you belong. While some gangs might be peaceful, there are many gangs who just want to rule over other kids and carry out acts of hatred. Be careful whom you decide to approach in order to find friends. Take your time. Consider what a friend really means to you. Think about what you value and what qualities you want to find in others whom you might want to be your friends.

It's great that you don't have to sit around and wait for a friend to "happen" to you. It can also be a relief to know that you don't have to give up what you believe in or act in ways you know are not *you* just to get people to like you. If you feel left out, you don't have to sit around with those feelings. You can begin to make a friendship happen by taking the first step. You can decide to do something about your left-out feelings right now.

It's a good idea to try to make plans ahead of time to sit with the person in the lunchroom together or arrange to meet after school. Don't wait until the very last minute because they might honestly have made other plans.

Maybe this would be a good time to close this book and think some more about what you want in a friend. Think about who you might want to call. Then go ahead and take a chance. Don't wait. Do it now.

If the person you call is busy—call someone else. And keep calling others you might wish to get to know until you find a new person who says yes. Don't give up on yourself. You're worth it!

Chapter 13

BEING POPULAR

What Does Being Popular Mean?

Twelve-year-old Susan thought "Being popular is being liked by just about everyone." Rosey, age thirteen, stated, "Being popular means being massively socially accepted!" Eleven-year-old Steve felt, "Popularity means that a lot of people like you and know you—not just from your own grade, but from the other grades, too."

I agree with Susan, Rosey, and Steve. Being popular usually means being well liked, accepted, having lots of friends. Being popular can be really important to some kids, while others don't seem to care.

What are your feelings about popularity? Do you think you're popular, unpopular, or somewhere in the middle? How does that make you feel about yourself? Be honest. How important is popularity to you?

I asked these questions of kids of all ages and found there are so many different feelings and concerns that can go along with being popular. As we take a look at some of their answers, think about whether you've ever felt the same way.

Feelings About Popularity

Johnny, age nine, shared, "Being popular is great. It makes me feel really good. I don't have to worry about having someone to sit with in the lunchroom or who I'm going to play with after school. There's always someone to walk with; people always say hello to me in the halls. It makes me feel important."

Angela, age fourteen, stated, "Being popular is really important to me. But sometimes I feel more pressured than good. I feel I always have to be on my guard. I watch everything I say. I try sometimes to act in ways that are not even me. I don't understand it. I wonder whether just having a few friends, instead of worrying about the crowd all the time, would be better."

Lysee and Rachel, ten-year-old identical twins, both felt that popularity was not that important to them. They have had friends they cared about and it didn't matter if that meant they're popular or not.

Rosey not only didn't think it's important to be popular, he didn't even believe that popular groups exist in his grade at school (eighth). He said, "There's no such thing because of the way our school is set up. There are at least six or seven groups in my grade. The people in one group don't have much to do with the people in the other groups. If that's true, how could there be a popular group? Each kid is popular within his or her own group. But some people are friends with everybody. They're based in one group but also have friends elsewhere. Not good friends but friends."

Kevin, age thirteen, said, "I'm one of the most popular kids in my unpopular group! It feels great! Like I belong. I know people care about me and I don't feel lonely like I used to. I'm never bored, because I always have someone to do something with."

Mrs. A told me her twelve-year-old daughter wanted very badly to be in the popular group: "She's been trying to get into that group for a long time. They finally accepted her this year. One night, I found her up very late. She was writing down what she was going to say the next day when she was with them. I know how important it is to her to be with those kids. But now that she's 'in,' I think there's more pressure to stay in than there was to get in!"

Another parent, this time the dad of one of the popular boys at a middle school in the Midwest, said, "I guess Peter is just one of those kids who gets along with everyone. Our house has been filled with his friends since he was little." In answer to my question about whether he thought Peter was pressured by his popularity in any way, he answered, "The only pressure I can think of is finding the time to be with his friends. I guess that's a good kind of pressure!"

Andrea, age eleven, said, "I could be with a lot of kids but still feel very lonely. Maybe that's because I'm never sure if I'm really part of them, or if they're just being polite and don't know how to tell me how to get lost."

Jeremy, age twelve, told me, "Sometimes kids don't even like the person who's popular, but because they're popular, they'll just hang around with them. Then other kids will think that *they're* popular, too."

As you can see, being popular has its pressures along with the rewards. Some kids find it very easy to make friends and be liked by just about everyone. They don't have to put on an act to be popular. They can just be themselves and know they'll be accepted.

Others find that wanting to be popular can force them to do things they wouldn't normally do or be with people they might not even like. It can take them a long time to get into a group and be tough for them to keep up with the group once they're in.

Why Are Kids Popular?

Kids are popular for lots of different reasons. Here's a list of whys made by a group of boys and girls in the sixth, seventh, and eighth grades. Think about what you would add to or take off the list, and see if you agree.

- good athlete
- good-looking
- developed
- has a brother or sister who's popular
- has lots of friends
- liked by most people
- has a certain electronic game or other possession

- rich
- has nice clothes
- gets the best grades
- fun to be with
- a nice person
- doesn't lie or cheat
- dependable and reliable
- a good friend
- skinny
- friends with someone who's very popular
- going out with someone who's popular

A Few Thoughts About the Reasons for Being Popular

Take another good look at that list. Think about the things you feel kids have no control over. For example, kids can't be blamed because their parents are (or aren't) able to afford to buy them new clothes. But kids *can* control whether or not they lie or cheat.

It might be interesting and fun to choose someone like a TV or movie star whom most of your friends know, and then to find out how many people think he or she is good-looking and how many do not. (If you pick someone at school, it may be embarrassing.) I think you'll find that some will think he or she is "awesome" or "gorgeous"; others will think, "eh"; still others will think, "yich!" Since good looks are so personal and people can't help how they look, do you think that's a fair reason for some kids to be popular?

I've already taken up many pages talking about how kids can't control their development. They probably have little or nothing to do with how popular their brother or sister is. Toys, electronic games, computers, or anything like that are usually, if not always, bought by parents, not kids. And yet some people think those things are important enough to make someone popular or not.

Think about it. Is a great game or other possession a good reason to like someone better than someone else? If so, would people be liking the computer or the person? Which would be more important to you? If a person is going to be liked only for what he or she owns instead of for who he or she is, maybe the people who feel that way aren't really worth having as friends.

Twelve-year-old Jeremy feels, "Being good at sports is so important for popularity that even a person who is not nice can be popular just because they're a good athlete."

Mrs. M told me that her thirteen-year-old son came home the other day and said, "I don't feel very popular right now." He had been on the football team and just missed making the basketball team. When she asked him why, he said, "All the girls seem to go for the guys who are on the team. Well, I guess I'll just wait until I make the baseball team!"

How do the attitudes among the kids in your school compare to those that Jeremy and Mrs. M's son talked about? Are most of the popular kids you know also good athletes? Do you think they'd be popular even if they weren't good at sports?

The popularity of someone who "gets the best grades" is, in a sense, like that of a "good athlete." That's because good grades are partly in your control and partly not. You can control how hard you study, whether your work is completed on time, how well you pay attention, and anything else that you may *choose* to do in order to try to get higher grades. Some things are not in your control like, for example, having a disability that might change the way you need to learn or limit your learning ability.

Each person's ability to work and get good results is a little different. Some kids seem to get high grades without even working. Others can only do well in school if they study a lot. Some kids work very hard but still get lower grades. But those lower grades may be the highest they are able to get! For some kids, getting 70 is like getting 100. Of course, there are also kids who get lower grades who don't try and don't care.

Do you think kids should have less of a chance to be popular if their grades are lower but they're trying their hardest and are doing the best they can?

Being skinny goes along with looks. Do you think it is right for someone to be more or less popular because they weigh more or fewer pounds? (Do people become friends with pounds?)

If a person is popular because they're going out with someone who's popular, or because they are friendly with a popular person, what do you think might happen when the person stops being friends or going out with that other person?

It might be interesting to think about the personalities of the popular people in your school. Check off which qualities they seem to have that are on the list and add anything that we missed.

What Makes Someone Unpopular?

Here's another list of whys to think about. Once again, a bunch of kids helped me make up these reasons. Someone might be unpopular because the person:

- shows off
- is a spoiled brat
- never does his or her work
- is not athletic
- has raggedy clothes and is poor
- is ugly
- is too fat or too skinny
- is not developed
- gets lower grades
- borrows something and doesn't give it back
- is unreliable or undependable
- lies
- cheats or is dishonest
- is not responsible
- is a pest
- hurts someone whom everyone likes
- is a tease or bully
- agrees to do something and then doesn't
- is crippled or disabled or something like that
- is not nice or considerate

Kids can work at and change some of these things. Kids can decide not to lie, cheat, or tease. They can stop bragging or showing off and can start being nice. They can stop being pesty and stop hurting other people.

They can decide to stop. But—even if they want to change—some people find it really hard. Though some kids do tease and hurt just to be mean, many kids do it because they feel it's the only way they can get attention. That's sad to me, but it surely doesn't make it right. It just might help if you understand. (You might even say to someone, "You know, I like you anyway. You don't have to bother acting or saying something like that.")

A disability, being poor, not having nice clothes, being ugly, getting lower grades—these things often prevent others from even trying to get to know a person. People seem to be so quick to judge. They often see someone with something a little different about and they make a decision that they don't want to know that person—without knowing anything else about him or her.

Besides thinking about how much those reactions can hurt or embarrass someone, it's also important to realize that not being able to catch a ball has nothing to do with whether someone is nice or not, or if they could be a close friend.

Not having the use of an arm or leg, not being able to see or hear, not being able to get higher grades, having to be placed in a separate learning class, not having enough money to get new clothes, not being handsome or beautiful, being too fat or too skinny don't mean that a person can't be a special friend or well liked by a lot of people.

If you've ever stayed away from someone who has a physical disability, my guess is it was because you might have been uncomfortable about it, didn't like the way the disability looked, didn't think you would know what to say, were scared. You may not ever have learned that people with disabilities have the same kinds of needs and feelings that you have. They're not as different as you think! I talk more about this in Chapter 23, Having a Disability.

I've already spoken about how being a good or bad athlete can often make kids more or less popular. Lots of kids have talked about what a horrible feeling it is to be picked last for a team, or for other kids to laugh or get angry when they miss a ball.

It would help if kids would learn that each person is different. Some are better than others at things, but that doesn't necessarily have anything to do with the kind of person they are. It's sad that so many people walk around wishing they were someone else, or wishing they could do something that would make them popular . . . when all they need to do is be themselves.

No matter what a person looks like, what talents he or she has or where he or she comes from, each person is special. If only more people would give one another a chance.

Feelings About Being Unpopular

Twelve-year-old Liz shared, "I watch all the popular kids running around together, doing things, laughing and whispering in the halls. I hear them talking about the parties they're going to on the weekend, where they're meeting after school, not to forget to call tonight. And I feel like crying. I wish, just once, someone would ask me to come along with them into town, or go to one of their houses."

Kenneth, age thirteen, told me, "I know that I'm not very popular. I don't play sports and I don't really like any girl. My grades are good, though. It doesn't seem to be enough. I wish I would have something else about me that would make me popular."

Cary, age nine, told me, "There's someone in my class who has a problem walking normally. She sort of leaps like a frog because she has to raise her leg in a strange way while walking. Everyone calls her Froggy, including kids from other grades. It makes her a laughingstock and she's not popular at all. It makes me sad that people make fun of her, because I had to do a report with her and she really is nice."

Twelve-year-old Stephanie talked about how embarrassed she feels every time her teacher tells the class to pick someone to work with on a project. Said Stephanie, "All the popular kids pick each other and I always have to wait for the teacher to ask us to raise our hands if we don't have a partner. That's the worst part because everyone knows that I'm one of the ones not picked. I feel like shrinking when that happens!"

I suggested to Stephanie that she talk with her teacher about her feelings. Maybe next time, he or she will just assign partners and could even put Stephanie with someone she'd like to get to know better.

Twelve-year-old Debbie stated, "I really don't care that I'm not with the popular group. I'm not going to do what they do just to go around with them!"

Peter, age twelve, said, "In elementary school, I was very popular and I had three best friends. When the kids in all the schools combined into one school, my best friends just left me and went into another group with the popular kids from the other schools. I hardly ever see them anymore. I get very lonely sometimes."

Dana, age thirteen, said, "The thing that really hurts is when everyone is talking about a party and I know that I'll never be invited. In elementary school, kids used to give birthday invitations out in lunch because they weren't allowed to give them in class. My heart would always pound so loud as I watched, hoping I would get one, too. But I didn't . . . except once. And my mother is very friendly with her mother so I know she made her invite me."

For some kids, being thought of as unpopular by classmates is embarrassing and pretty lonely. Others don't really care if they're considered popular or not. They've got their own good friends, and they're very happy. They're also relieved not to have to keep up with anyone.

What Might You Do If You Want to Become More Popular?

More than anything else, I'd have to go back to, "Take a chance and be yourself!" That's the only way you will be liked for who you are, not for the pizza you think you need to buy for the whole group, not for helping with social studies homework, not for the clothes you wear, not for where you live, not for what you look like.

Some kids are afraid to let others know them. They always stay on their guard. They feel they have to put on an act to impress people, to make people like them. They're not confident that people will accept them just the way they are. Sara, age 14, told me, "I'm so busy acting for my friends that I don't know who I really am."

The problem is, when does the act stop? How long do you have to keep it up until you feel you can try to be yourself? How many pizzas do you think kids buy for the crowd until they feel that maybe they'll be accepted without buying anymore? How many times will a boy or girl have to say, "You want to copy off of my paper?" before he or she is confident enough not to need to buy the friendship or popularity anymore?

It might help to think about the many reasons that kids think people are unpopular. Do you spread rumors? Lie? Never shower? Talk behind people's backs? Tease? Bully? Always clown around? Can you be trusted? Do you use deodorant? Are you a snob? Why do you think people might be staying away from you? While certain things like your size or your skin color can't be changed and must be accepted, the way you act and the kind of person you are *can* be developed differently.

The exciting thing is that you can begin right now to try to make some important changes in yourself if that's what you realize would be important. Instead of staying in the background, where it might seem safer, start to let people know you're around. You can smile and say "hi" to more people. Learn some new names and tell others yours. If you're nice, friendly, and start to show others that you care, you're on your way!

Besides approaching kids in the halls, lunchroom, or your classes, you can also join a club. That's a great way to meet kids who have similar interests. You may be worried that kids in the club already know each other, which is a normal worry. But figure if they've been together in that club for a while, it's not surprising that they'd seem to be close. That doesn't mean they won't welcome you to become part of their club group. You don't have to be good friends with people to enjoy being in a club with them. If you like the things that they like, you'll find that you can have fun together. And you might just find a new friend or two.

As I've already said, it can be a little scary and hard to take a chance on yourself. What if people don't like you back? But how much do you feel it's right to try to change yourself in ways that aren't you, just to be accepted and popular with more people? Even if you were popular when you acted in that changed way, would you be happy with yourself inside? And, if you know you're pretending to be who you're not, whom would other kids be liking anyway? A fake you. Also, think about how long you might have to pretend.

You don't deserve to have to pretend to be someone else. If someone doesn't seem to like you or even want to get to know you for who you are, then you haven't gone up to the right person yet. The sooner you begin to believe that you're worth it and special just the way you are, the stronger and more confident you'll become. And if you start letting people know you as you really are, then you've got a great chance to be happy within yourself and happy with your friends, because at least you'll be sure they care about you because you're you—whether you have one friend, two, or twenty.

REMEMBER: Getting people to begin to notice you differently and building friendships take time. Just because you're friendly doesn't mean people will flood your telephone lines and gather at your door right away. As you let others know you and you reach out to more and more people, you'll begin to see that others will start reaching back. Try to be patient. And never give up on yourself.

CHAPTER 14

BOYFRIENDS, GIRLFRIENDS, "GOING OUT"

Depending on where you live, you may use other words than *going out* to describe having a girlfriend or boyfriend. Maybe you and your friends call it "going steady," "going with," "having a boyfriend," "having a girlfriend," or "hanging around with." They all mean pretty much the same thing.

What Does "Going Out" Mean?

Christa, age thirteen, said to her mom, "Mom, I'm going out with Andy!" Her mom replied, "Where?" Christa said, "No, Mom, you don't understand, we're not going anywhere. We're just going with each other, get it?"

Until about eighth or ninth grade, *going out* is just an expression, a saying. It usually means that you're that person's girlfriend or boyfriend. Starting in about the ninth or tenth grade, when someone asks to "go out" with you, it can also mean for one date, not necessarily for keeps. But even if you're older, saying that you're "going out" with someone still can mean you're seeing mainly that person.

Notice that I have written "ninth grade" twice? That's because it's so hard to know exactly when "going out" and "not going anywhere" will stop, and "going out on a date" will start. Since each person is different, it may be earlier or later than the ninth grade.

Fourteen-year-old Jeff raised an interesting point: "It depends where you live. When you ask a girl out here [suburb of a big city], that does not mean you have to go any place. But I could ask out a girl that I know who lives in the city to go to a movie with me. That doesn't mean we're necessarily going out; that means we're on a date. There's a difference between what goes on here and what goes on in the city. Kids seem to start dating earlier in the city than out here."

Besides thinking about what the words *going out* mean, it's interesting to take a closer look at what having a boyfriend or girlfriend can mean. You'll probably find, as I have, that a boyfriend or girlfriend means different things to different people at different times.

In the Beginning . . .

Valery, age thirty-three, remembers when a boy walked her home in the sixth grade. That meant they were going out! Said Valery, "We hid a special rock in the garden and only the two of us knew what that meant."

In the beginning, going out or having a boyfriend or girlfriend is a way of testing or practicing what it might be like to have one special person you care about. It's a way of learning if you would like to *focus* on or give all your attention to just one person instead of several people at once. It's planning what it might be like when you get older.

According to 15-year-old Keri, "If you went out in the fifth or sixth grade, you felt great about yourself. In the seventh and eighth grade, you went out so other kids could think highly of you. It almost didn't even matter who it was. Now, in the tenth grade, not as many people are going out with each other. People seem to go out because they want to, not to impress anyone else."

Glenn, age thirteen, stated: "In the fourth grade it was marrying on the playground. In the fifth grade, more marrying, but really nothing. In the sixth grade, people started going with each other. In the seventh grade, dating was important and exciting. I'm in the eighth grade, and it's just sort of there. Not that many kids are going out with each other. The only people who are excited about it are those who never dated before and are just starting."

Monica, age thirteen, said, "Having a boyfriend or girlfriend in the fourth grade was a joke. The important thing then was getting married, getting divorced, who was having kids first (we made up families). In the fifth grade, people went out with others mostly to impress people. Things changed about in the sixth grade. Now [eighth grade], dating is very important. Not for impressing, but just for me personally."

Joanne, age forty, remembers, "We started having boyfriends in the fifth grade. By sixth, many of us were going steady. I think sixth was even more social than seventh or eighth. Maybe because we went to a new school after sixth and up until then, we all knew each other. In seventh, we had to start all over meeting people."

Jeff, age fourteen, says, "In fourth grade, it was—hey, there's a girl, what do I do? In fifth and sixth grade, it was all sports, no time for girls. In seventh grade, it was, Sports? I don't want to play sports! I'm going out with this girl. In eighth grade, total concentration on girls. So dating got a lot better. A lot more serious, too."

While Keri thought having a boyfriend impressed people in the seventh and eighth grade, Monica thought that happened more in the fifth grade. Joanne was more social in the sixth grade, while Jeff is "really concentrating" on girls in the eighth grade. Glenn said that seventh grade was the time when kids really were excited about going out.

So many different feelings. What does going out with someone mean to you? If you don't have an answer, don't be concerned. You don't have to know how you feel. Maybe you're interested in having a boyfriend or girlfriend, maybe you're not. Maybe you haven't even thought about it and don't care; maybe you've just been thinking about going out with someone but really haven't done anything yet about your new feelings. All of those possibilities are normal.

As with physical development, there's no set time when your feelings about having a special, going-out relationship with someone can be expected to start. For most kids, this will simply happen whenever they feel ready.

When Will "Liking Someone" Start for You?

Keith said to me, "I'm eleven years old; when am I supposed to start liking girls?" Well, Keith, I wish I could give you an answer, but I can't. I'd only be guessing. There is no such thing as "supposed to." You may start liking someone as early as elementary school or perhaps not until after high school. Each person will have their own time schedule for becoming interested.

Being ready depends on how you feel, how your parents feel, what your friends are doing, and even has to do with your hormones.

Greg, age twelve, thought, "The kids who were first made the rest of the group go faster." Heidi, age eleven, agreed. She said her other friends began to change because she and another girl started liking boys last year. "At first they teased us and said we were silly, but then they started liking them, too."

Gene, age thirty-nine, said, "I was always scared stiff of girls. I didn't know how to act with them. Most of my friends were interested in girls at least by junior high. But I didn't have my first date until I was twenty-three. My friends understood that I wasn't ready, and I understood that my friends were. It didn't bother my friendships."

I've heard mixed feelings about whether or not being interested in going out causes friendships to change. Gene's friends stayed the same even though he didn't date and they did. Other boys and girls have told me that they didn't spend as much time with their friends when their interests were no longer the same. I think much depends on how close you have been, whether you each understand that everyone has his or her own feelings, and how much each of you respects these feelings. Even best friends may not be interested at the same time.

Traci, age thirteen, said, "I'm interested in boys but my parents won't let me go out with anyone until I'm in the ninth grade. What a bummer!"

Jimmy, age fourteen, said, "My parents think it's okay for kids to date at my age. But I couldn't care less about girls right now. I wish they'd stop bugging me about it."

As you can see, some boys and girls are ready before their friends and parents, others not until way after. Some get interested (sometimes pressured) to begin going out because their friends have started; others feel more free to do what feels right to them. Of course, lots of friends can become interested all at once. It doesn't always have to be at different times.

Some kids are ready, but their parents aren't. Others are not ready, but their parents are. Have you ever discussed going out or dating with your parents? We'll talk more about this later.

The big question is how you feel about all of this. Even if you've been going out for years, it might be interesting to think some more about how you felt when you started. Who else of your friends was also interested? Who wasn't? Did anyone tease or give you a hard time?

If you haven't yet begun, it might help to keep telling yourself, "It's okay that I feel the way I feel." Try not to rush yourself. But also watch that you don't hold yourself back, even if you feel shy and a little scared. Think about Gene. He waited until he was twenty-three—not because he wanted to wait—but because he just was so nervous that he didn't try to take the first step.

It's very natural to be nervous. Keri, age fifteen, shared, "Before I went out, I didn't know how to act with just one boy. I always had lots of friends that were boys, but we all usually were together in a group. It's much different when you're alone. Most of my friends are scared of boys. You always think about what it's going to be like and what you're going to do. I think if you date even once, you won't be as scared the next time. I grew up so much even from one date."

Although Gene said he was "scared stiff of girls," he didn't have to wait until he wasn't scared anymore to get started with a special relationship. Lots of people like Gene think they have to be comfortable with everything. But we can't always expect to be comfortable with everything we do. If that were so, lots of people would be waiting their whole lives to get started.

So if your feelings for wanting to go out with someone have begun—the idea is to decide to push yourself to take the first step. Then, go for it!

Even if the first time asking someone to spend time with you is the scariest, you'll find—as Gene probably would have—that your confidence and your comfort will build. Just as with trying to make a new friend, if you ask someone out and that person doesn't seem interested, it doesn't mean there's anything wrong with you. It just means you haven't asked the right person yet and you need to look around for someone else to ask.

Keep in Mind . . .

A "going out" relationship, like any other relationship, starts best as a friendship that can build up over the time you spend together. Some kids think that the time they spend with this person always has to be "social," like partying or going on an "official date." But you can get to know each other just hanging out at home and bringing in a pizza. Or you might go to a sports event at your school or rent a movie. Think about what is fun to do. You can talk about this together. (And don't say *"nothing."* There's always *something* to do, no matter where you live. You may just need to be creative!)

You might consider taking a walk or hiking, playing tennis, mountain biking, Rollerblading, visiting a museum or other place of interest, fishing, golf, having a picnic, playing Frisbee. You can cook a meal together, bake cookies. You can volunteer together in your community. Perhaps you can work in a soup kitchen for those who are homeless or visit a nursing home. You can even go to the library and study together. Whatever you do, the time you spend will give you a chance to get to know each other better. The more time you spend, the more comfortable you'll probably feel.

You don't have to push your new relationship forward. If it seems to be something you both want, your relationship with this person will grow naturally as you spend more time together. If not, then you might as well know it sooner than later. Not every relationship works out.

The problem often is that too many kids really do rush into officially becoming boyfriends or girlfriends without getting to know who that person is and how it feels to spend more time together. And too many kids have friends who put a lot of pressure on them to move faster.

If you're not interested in going out, hold off and go at your own pace. Just because your friends are interested doesn't mean that you have to be. If you're not sure, take more time to think about it. Think twice if you feel forced. It may not be as much fun for you—or right for you just yet—if you let others tell you what to do and when.

If you've decided that you *are* interested, try to take it a day at a time, have fun, and see what happens.

How Can You Tell If Your Feelings Have Begun to Change?

- When you look at the girl who has been sitting in front of you for three months and realize you've never really seen her before, and she's kind of cute.
- When the boy who has been grabbing your scarf and throwing it around to his friends at recess decides to stop grabbing, and you wish he would do it again.
- When you notice that the girl who has been the only girl allowed on the boys' baseball team has started looking more like a girl and less like one of the boys.
- When you look at someone and think, "Oh, I'd just 'die' if he [or she] would come over and talk to me."
- When you start taking more showers and begin to pay attention to what you look like.
- When you start noticing other people's appearance, too.
- When there's more teasing, more phony phone calls to boys from girls or girls from boys.
- When you'd rather spend the afternoon with one girl or boy than be with your friends.
- When you think a lot about someone and write his or her name on your notebooks or on a secret piece of paper that only you or your close friends can see.
- When you dream about someone special. . . . When you get all fluttery when you see that person, maybe even blush.
- When you go out of your way to make sure that you "bump" into him or her while walking through the halls at school.
- When you spend even one minute hoping that he or

she would call you, or wishing that you'd have the
guts to call that person.

You and your friends might be able to add some more *whens* of your own to this list.

IMPORTANT NOTE: You needn't be concerned if you have never felt any of these feelings. Maybe your time for being interested in someone has not begun yet. Remember that each person's feelings are different. There aren't any rules about "when."

Try to be patient with yourself. Try to accept the way you feel, no matter how much interest your friends have. If they're really your friends, they'll respect your right to feel and be who you are and they won't try to push you if you're not ready. If they do push you, tell them to lay off. If they don't leave you alone about it, tell them again. They may not realize you're serious. If they keep at you, maybe you need to look for some new friends.

It's possible that you'll spend a little less time with your friends if they're with the boys or girls and you really don't want to be. But you might choose to hang around and just see how you feel with them. Maybe the feelings won't have started inside you, but if you try being around them, you might find it fun, anyway. Do whatever feels comfortable for you. Be patient with yourself. You've got your whole life ahead of you. You've got time to think about it.

How Can You Let Someone Know That You Like Her or Him?

When you decide to let someone know that you like her or him, you're deciding to take a chance that they'll like you or at least will think about wanting to spend extra time getting to know you better. It might help to remember that if you don't try, he or she may never know how you feel. If you'd like someone to know, then you have to make sure to let that person know—somehow.

Before you read these choices, it might be fun to try to make your own list of how you can let someone know.

Eleven-year-old Hillary suggested, "Just tell him!" While this is certainly the most direct way to make sure he or she knows, I've learned that this is one of the hardest for kids to do.

What's the concern? Once again, rejection. What if they say, "Thanks for telling me, but no thanks." What if they don't like you? What if they laugh? Actually they just might laugh if they're nervous—especially if they do like you.

If you don't think you can get up the courage to tell someone yourself in person, on the telephone, or in a note (watch what you say in notes; they have a sneaky way of getting around), then maybe you'll want to try something else.

Jody, age thirteen, says, "Tell your friend and have your friend tell him." Lots of boys and girls seem to feel this way is easier. Brian, age eleven, thinks that a good way is to tell someone's brother or sister that you like a person and have them find out if he or she likes you back.

Twenty-four-year-old Judy remembers, "The way everyone found out who liked who was when we passed notes around in class. You know, Judy likes Jimmy and so on. The only trouble was that you could get caught! Once a teacher took away a note I was passing to my friend and asked if I wanted everyone to know what it said. I was so embarrassed thinking she would read it out loud, but she never did! The boy I liked was in the same class and didn't know I liked him yet."

"Spread a rumor," said Danny, age ten. "Rumors usually spread all around the school very fast. You can tell your friend to start it." While it may be easier for you to let other kids tell your feelings instead of you, you're not as much in control of what's being said. By the time a rumor reaches *the* person, it may not even be what you wanted to say. So be careful about whom you trust to tell.

Jennifer, age twelve, thinks it's a good idea to ask *the* person if he or she wants to go into town (or to someone's house or anywhere) with you and your friends. "That way it will be a group and not as personal. Sometimes it's easier to start that way."

Danielle, age fourteen, said, "You can also flirt with someone you like. Tease, but be cute or funny about it."

Pay more attention to that person. Ask questions about what she or he is doing so you can show you're interested. Let someone know you notice her or him and do what you can to get that person to notice you too. Smile! Ask if she or he would like to study with you—or do any of those other activities I mentioned before.

Choose the way that feels best to you to let someone know you're interested. If one way doesn't work so well, try another and another. Or mix a few ways. Experiment! The more you try, probably, the easier it will become.

How You Might Know If Someone Likes You

Just take all the suggestions in the section you just read and turn them around. Instead of your doing something to try to let someone else know how you feel, they would be trying to let you know how they feel.

Here are a few tips to remember:

When it seems someone really is not interested in you because they're always teasing, that's the time to wonder if they really are interested but don't know how else to show it.

If it seems someone is hanging around you and may like you, you might try to help out. Understand that it may be very hard for the other person to talk to you about how he or she feels. Lots of people just don't know what to say and are afraid they'll act and sound like a jerk. The more sensitive and nice you are, the easier you will make it for others to share with you. In fact if you like them and they're not saying anything about liking you (but you think they do), instead of waiting, you can be the one to talk about it first.

Taking a Chance . . . Making the First Move

Some people don't take a chance on asking someone because they're so afraid that person will say no. They don't realize that by not asking, they're making sure the answer is no because they're not giving that person a chance to say yes. Did you follow me? The idea is that you've got nothing to lose and you just might win! If you don't try, the answer will surely be no. If you try, it could be yes. So, if you believe you're ready and have someone in mind whom you'd like to approach, why not take a chance? If you don't have anyone in mind, you can begin to look around and check out whom you might consider.

One more thing. Lots of kids think that in boy-girl relationships, it's the boy who is supposed to be the one to ask. While there are some people who still hold on to this idea, because that way of thinking is part of their culture or is the way they were taught, most people now feel that either the boy or girl—whichever one is interested—can ask. In fact, I've spoken with many boys who said they'd be relieved if a girl asked first.

Choosing Someone to Like

Just as you can look around for a new friend, you can also look around for a girlfriend or boyfriend. (You might find it helpful to review the steps for making a friend in Chapter 12, Friendship. This is not really different.) Remember to watch out for judging by things like clothes or looks that may not really tell you what kind of person he or she is.

I know that if, for example, a girl wears a lot of makeup, that might affect your opinion of her. You may not care what kind of person she is, if you don't like the way she presents herself. So it's tricky to decide what's important to consider and what really isn't. It's very personal.

Cindy, age seventeen, told me, "There was a boy in the sixth grade who dressed really shabbily. He was clean, but he didn't dress in the coolest clothes to come to school. My friends and I couldn't figure out if we really liked him because of the way he dressed. Yet he was nice. And I know that the way he dressed really stopped me from wanting to like him. Then we invited him to a party. He came dressed in the greatest-looking sweater and pants. No one was even sure if it was really him. He was gorgeous! When he told us that he didn't wear his good clothes to school because they were for special occasions, we were all really sorry about judging him." So you never know.

Some kids are so good-looking that many people feel they can't ever go up to them. They think he or she would *"never* go out with *ME*!" Tommy, age thirty-one, shared, "I was very lonely when I was growing up. I was too shy to ask anyone to go out with me, and I think because people thought I was so good-looking, they were afraid I would reject them."

The steps I suggested you try in order to make a friend are also the ones for going out. If someone says no, go on to the next and the next. Tommy's loneliness might help you realize that no matter what a person looks like, you should try. They may be so happy that you did. And if they're not, that's okay. You don't lose anything by trying.

Liking Someone Who Is the Same Sex as You Are: Homosexual Relationships

It's common during the growing-up years for you to feel that a person of the same sex is very special in your life. They can mean a lot to you. You'll probably want to do everything together.

It's possible that you will find it hard also to have a boyfriend or girlfriend when your feelings are so strong about this close friend. You might want to spend more time with that friend than with anyone else.

Most of the time, those kinds of feelings toward a close friend of the same sex change and kids start to become interested in "going out," dating and spending more and more time with kids of the other sex. But sometimes these feelings toward someone of the same sex continue to grow stronger and go beyond feelings of friendship to include sexual feelings as well.

A person who finds he or she has strong emotions, along with strong sexual feelings, for others of the same sex—and mainly or only seeks out this kind of relationship—is considered to be homosexual. A male who is homosexual is referred to as being *gay*. A female who is homosexual is referred to as being a *lesbian* (LEZ-bee-an). A male or female who has strong emotions along with strong sexual feelings for persons of either sex is referred to as *bisexual* (buy-SEX-u-al).

Some people don't understand, are uncomfortable with, or don't accept the idea of a homosexual relationship—or that someone is gay or lesbian. Fear of homosexuality is called *homophobia* (home-o-FOE-bee-uh). This is a big problem, because people who feel so strongly against homosexuality sometimes try to hurt those who are homosexual with words or physical actions. You may have heard the term "gay bashing," which refers to such disrespect and violence and has even resulted in murder.

Educational programs are continually being developed to help people of all ages understand that disrespect or violence in any form is unacceptable. No matter what our differences, all of us are in this world together. No matter who each person is or what kind of relationship they're in, everyone deserves to be valued and treated with respect. All people have the right to decide for themselves what is most meaningful and how they wish to live their lives, as long as they're not interfering with or harming anyone else.

So, if you don't relate to someone, don't have the same beliefs, don't accept the way that person relates to other people, or don't even like that person—you can still treat him or her with respect.

Sharing sexually with a person of the same sex just a few times doesn't make someone homosexual. Having sexual thoughts, dreams, or fantasies about someone of the same sex also doesn't mean a person is homosexual (even if those thoughts make you have sexual feelings that lead to orgasm).

It's common for many people of all ages to have different kinds of sexual thoughts that lead to sexual feelings. But that doesn't have to mean that they would want their sexual thoughts to come true. So just thinking about sexual sharing, no matter with whom, is quite different from actually wanting to share yourself in real life in a very close, personal, and sexual relationship with a person of the same sex.

It's also important to realize that if someone in your family—be it your parent, brother, sister, or any other relative—is gay or lesbian, it doesn't mean that you will be gay or lesbian.

An eighth-grade girl asked, "I've never gone out and probably won't for a while. Am I a lesbian?" If you're not interested in going out, while most of your friends are, it doesn't necessarily mean you're homosexual. There are lots of kids who couldn't care less about dating until at least their late teens, sometimes later. Remember, everyone is "ready" on his or her own time schedule.

Tom, age twenty-three, shared with me: "When I was a teenager and I first started feeling that I mainly wanted to be with guys . . . that scared me. I never thought of myself as homosexual and wondered if that's what I really was. It was a very confusing time. I faked liking girls with my friends because I was worried that they would stop being friends with me if they found out. I also was afraid the whole school would find out if I let anyone know. I ended up telling nobody until much later."

I spoke with Fran, now in her forties, who shared,"When I was seventeen, my first sexual experience was with a woman. That left me so confused and I had no one to talk to about it. I tried to kill myself because I didn't think I was normal. I didn't understand what I was feeling or why. Now I realize what I was feeling was very real and was very normal. It's so important to talk with somebody—anybody."

If you find that your feelings confuse you, I suggest you speak with your parents, school guidance counselor or psychologist, religious leader, family doctor, or other trusted adult. It may also be helpful to contact a gay and lesbian organization.

If you're not sure how to start a conversation in order to talk about your confusion, you might first say, "This is hard for me to tell you. I'm very confused and I need to talk. Can you help me?"

How to Let Someone Know You Don't Like Them Anymore

It's important to tell a person yourself (in private) that you don't like them anymore, rather than having a friend do it for you. Understand it will probably not be easy for someone to hear that you don't want to continue being her or his boyfriend or girlfriend anymore. It also may be hard for you to say what you want and need to say, even if you know that what you're doing is right for you. If they liked you a lot, you can figure they'll feel upset about breaking up, even if they don't show it.

Most kids tell me that they'd rather know it if someone doesn't want to go out with them anymore. So, be honest, but be sensitive. How you say what you need to say can make all the difference.

You might say, "I've been doing a lot of thinking. And I really feel I'm not ready to go out with only one person. I hope we still can be good friends." Or you can say, "I really like you and everything, but I don't think I want to be boyfriend and girlfriend anymore. I'd like to—or need to—just be friends. I hope you understand. I'm really sorry. I don't mean to hurt you." Or "It's just not the same for me anymore. And I didn't know how to tell you that. The last thing I'd ever want to do is to hurt you."

Even if you know what you need to say, it can be very hard to get the words out. But if you keep important feelings silent because you're afraid of hurting the other person too much, think about how much more it might hurt your relationship and that person if he or she never knows how you feel. Because the feelings can be so difficult to deal with, many people stay in relationships long after they're really over, just because it's too hard for them to break up.

How do you think it would feel to keep going out with a boyfriend or girlfriend you really didn't care for anymore—or feel it's not good or healthy for you to go out with anymore—just because you couldn't get the words out? How long would you keep going out, secretly not wanting to go out with that person? Is it really fair to anyone? How do you think you'd feel if someone kept on pretending with you?

Again, the key is *how* you say what you say. Be thoughtful and show that you care. Then go ahead and try to push yourself to say what you must. Sometimes you can't prevent hurting someone's feelings, even if you don't want to hurt them. That's an important lesson to learn. It not only affects your relationships with boyfriends or girlfriends, but it will help you be more honest with your parents, family, teachers, and friends.

You might be surprised at how much it can mean to really share deeply with someone on an honest level. You may find that you'll come to a new understanding that will help you feel much closer—or at least allow you to try to still be friends.

Breaking Up . . . Dealing with the Feelings

Even if you're the one who wants to break up with your girlfriend or boyfriend, and you know that person is just not right for you, or if you both really know it's time to stop going out, you may be surprised at how painful it will be to try to let go and move on. Especially if that person was your boyfriend or girlfriend for a long time, you might feel very lonely and sad, even sort of empty inside.

Some kids feel that they must not be important or worth anything if someone breaks up with them. They figure if the other person doesn't care about them in the same way anymore (and then doesn't want them back), they must not be very special. Breaking up does *not* mean you're less special. It just means that your relationship wasn't working. That's a very different thing.

It's understandable and natural for you to feel hurt or upset, even if you were the one to break up. Many kids (and adults) think, "I should be handling this better," or "I should be able to forget about him or her." Well, "shoulds" can make you feel worse. "Shoulds" can push you into believing that you're supposed to feel better much sooner than might be fair to expect. The truth is, it may take a while to get over that person. That's natural. Allow yourself the time. Try to let yourself feel your feelings.

It would be more surprising if you didn't feel sad ending a relationship that was important to you. The fact that it is so hard to deal with the feelings is a sign that all the time you spent with that person really did mean a lot. That's very special. It may help to remind yourself that you can always hold on to your memories, all the things you shared, all that you learned from being with each other, and trust that in time you'll be ready to go on.

You may be thinking right now, "That's easy for you to say!" But I really mean it. I don't pretend that it's easy to break up, no matter how much you understand. I can even think back to my own tears and how tough it was to go to school the next day and know that I would see him in most of my classes.

The hurt can last longer than you might expect. But if you find yourself believing that your whole world has fallen apart, try harder to hold on and think through the situation more clearly.

You'll find it really isn't the end of the world, no matter how much it may seem to be. It's just the end of a relationship that wasn't working, whatever the reason. And when you think about it, if your relationship is not right, if it doesn't feel good to both people, and *both* people don't want it, what are you really holding on to anyway? And if only one person wants a relationship, it's not a relationship.

If you find you're not able to concentrate in school and it's taking a very long time for you to be able to get past the hurt, then it may be important for you to talk with someone (besides your friends) in order to understand your feelings. There's no rule that you have to handle this alone. Talking about your feelings or writing them down can be very helpful.

Why not be good to yourself and reach out to your parents, older brother or sister, grandparents or other relatives, a school counselor or psychologist, teacher, friend's parent, or any other adult you trust will be there to listen and help you sort out your feelings. If you don't know what to say, you can start with, "I don't even know what to say to you . . . but I walk around thinking about ____ and I can't think about anything else. It hurts so much."

Also, it will probably take time to get used to not being boyfriend and girlfriend anymore. If you see each other in classes or after-school activities, you'll have a constant reminder. If you have the same friends, you'll probably still both hang out with those same people. And, if your "ex" boyfriend or girlfriend becomes interested in someone else pretty soon, it might be very strange and hard to see him or her with someone else.

Brian, age seventeen, recently told me he felt much worse seeing the girlfriend he broke up with walking with another boy just five days after they broke up. You never know, Brian. A new relationship may be the only way she can leave you behind. Deep down, she may still be crying. But she knows her relationship with you is over—at least for now—and there's no reason to hold herself back. It doesn't mean that she didn't care about you when you were together. It simply means there's no point—for either of you—in waiting around.

Staying friends after a breakup A lot of people think that "I hope we can stay friends" is just a "line" to try to make someone feel better about the breakup. For some, that's probably true. They may not have known what else to say.

Others really mean it. It's not that they want the person they broke up with completely out of their life. It's just that they don't want to go out anymore.

If you're in that situation, here are a few thoughts that might help. Even if you want to remain good friends, one or both of you may need time and "space" to deal with all the very real emotions that can go along with breaking up. So, if you have the same friends or always see each other in classes, it may help to say, for example: "I don't know about you, but it really feels awkward when we're with our friends. . . . I get the feeling that they don't really know how to deal with us not going out anymore, either. So, if I seem a little strange, that's really how I feel. I'm going to need time to get used to it. I know we said we should still call each other and see each other . . . but right now, I think it would be better if we didn't call. Let's check in with each other in a few weeks—maybe then it will be a little easier."

Saying something like that may not change how awkward you feel at first, but bringing those feelings out in the open can help take the edge off the awkwardness. Then no one has to pretend that things are okay and you're handling it better—when you're not.

Any change usually takes time to get used to . . . it's important to take the time!

If you're being abused by the person you're going out with (sometimes it's harder to break up) Abuse—in any form—is never okay. You don't deserve to be slapped around. You don't deserve to be abused verbally. You don't deserve to be abused sexually. You're worth more than that. Abuse is *not* a sign of love, caring, or respect. No one deserves to be abused.

Abuse is unacceptable. Some kids don't know any better because they grow up seeing their parents treat each other this way. So they think that's just the way things are. Some kids don't value themselves very much and feel if that they were "better" people, only then would they deserve to be treated better. Some kids are threatened—and even if they're not, they're scared to get out of the relationship.

Some people who hit with words or fists apologize, seem to feel terrible afterwards, promise they never meant to hurt you . . . until they do it again the next time.

Consider your own situation. Think about how you know you're being treated. Some people find it hard to admit they're being abused, because if they admitted it, then they'd have to do something about it— or feel foolish if they didn't.

If you're not being treated in a respectful way, you can choose not to take it. But I realize that choosing to walk away from an abusive relationship may be harder than just deciding to break up. Some people who are being abused are afraid of what will happen if they say anything. Even with court orders for protection, there can be violent reactions.

I recently heard about a high school student who broke up with her abusive boyfriend. Several male students she knew took turns walking her to and from school and taking her from one class to another throughout the day. It was like having a bodyguard. They kept switching off so that her old boyfriend wouldn't see her only with one person, think she was going out with someone new, and possibly beat him up.

The first step in getting out is to recognize that you're being abused and that this is not acceptable. The next step is to get advice from someone who is trained to help you take positive steps in the safest way possible. Even if you're scared, call a hotline related to preventing abuse or violence. Or speak with a counselor.

If you're worried about a friend who is staying in an abusive relationship, encourage your friend to get this kind of help. If your friend won't, you can call a hotline or speak with a counselor to deal with your own feelings and learn what might be most helpful to say or do.

It's okay to be scared, and certainly natural to feel that way. It's *not* okay to let fear keep you in an abusive situation.

"I'm never going to have another girlfriend/boyfriend because I don't want to be hurt again" It's natural for kids to feel that they never want to let themselves get close to someone again—because it's usually so hard and painful to break up. But the growing-up years just naturally involve breaking up and starting over again and again. This is the time to get an idea of the kind of person you really like to be close to, an important time to get to know and go out with many different people, learning from each relationship.

Just try to be smart about whom to give your heart to. Don't let anyone rush you into a relationship or make you get more seriously involved before you're ready. It takes time to get to know someone and come to trust that a person cares about you in a special way. It's important to know that relationships can (and must) be worked at, with both people giving of themselves, sharing, teaching, and learning about each other. You'll begin to have a sense of how much they care, how much of themselves they'll share with you, how well they treat you, how much they accept and appreciate you for who you are, how you feel when you're with them and when you're apart. And so you'll grow in your relationships and learn much more about yourself. And you'll get stronger (and wiser) with each experience.

So if it is time to break up and move on, remember—it's not you, it's not about blame—it's the relationship. The relationship is just not something to hold on to. It's also a matter of valuing yourself enough to listen to your own feelings and act upon what you know is right for you—even if that's hard.

Again, if only one person wants the relationship, it's not a relationship. So what would you be holding on to? You really can go forward, taking all you learned with you. It also might help to know that you're not alone. More than likely, you'll have lots of breaking-up-and-starting over company among your friends and classmates. That's just a part of growing up.

After the hurt eases, you may be very surprised at how relieved you are to be free. Besides, just think about how much fun it will be to look around in your classes, the halls, the lunchroom, or wherever, to see who else might be great to go out with. You can start to show an interest in anyone who seems nice. You never know who will be your next boyfriend or girlfriend. You never know who'll be standing around the next row of lockers just waiting to be met by you!

Be careful not to compare each person too closely. Don't expect your next girlfriend or boyfriend to be exactly like the last one. Every person is different. It takes time to get to know someone and let them know you. Just be yourself. You'll see, it probably won't be too long before you start again.

Boyfriends, Girlfriends, and Other Friends

"What if you like someone your friends don't like?" Tim, age eleven, said, "I like this girl, but my friends all think she's ugly and want me to go out with someone else."

That's an example of the judging that I've been talking about. Maybe if Tim's friends allowed themselves to get to know the girl he liked, without letting her looks get in the way, they'd think she's nice, too.

Tim can say to his friends, "Hey, I like her. So cut it out. It really bothers me when you say that. All you're doing is *looking* at her. You don't even know her."

Pressure from friends can be very strong. Would you stop going out with someone you liked just because your friends didn't like his or her looks? Even if they went beyond looks and still decided they didn't like her? Who do you think should decide whom you like, them or you?

If you're strong about your own feelings, I would hope your friends would respect you. If you respect your friends and if they're concerned about this person because they feel he or she is bad for you in some way—you might listen to what they say and consider it seriously. Sometimes it's hard to see how someone affects us the same way others can see by looking at a relationship from the outside.

After considering what your friends have said, the thing to ask yourself is, "What do I feel?" Be honest. Then make your own decision.

"What if you're dating someone of another race?" While some may be accepting, you may find that other people around you—even close friends—are uncomfortable with and won't understand your choice to go out with someone of another race.

Patty, age sixteen, told me, "My parents are giving me a real hard time because I'm going out with someone who is black. They won't even let him come to our house. They're so prejudiced. They don't even know him, but they want me to break up with him just because of his color. I don't know what I'm going to do."

Howie, age sixteen, shared, "My girlfriend's parents seem to like me so that's not a problem. But I think they're worried about what everyone else will think and how people will treat us because we're not the same race."

When it's parents who don't approve, that can make the situation more difficult. Some kids listen to their parents and eventually break up. Others feel that it's their relationship and it's not right for anyone—even parents—to make that decision for them. Still others are confused and feel torn between wanting to please their parents and wanting to satisfy themselves.

There are many different feelings about this—and the topic is very emotional. Some school populations and communities are more accepting of interracial relationships than others. Sometimes these relationships trigger fights and other kinds of violence.

If you're in an interracial relationship and your parents don't approve, you can try—if you haven't already—to bring up the subject in a peaceful way. You might say, "Mom/Dad, I love you and I know you want the best for me. And the last thing I want is for us to get in a fight. But I really like _____, and I know you don't approve. Can we at least talk about this?"

While I can't guarantee that your parents will be open to discussing this situation, at least you can try to start the conversation. You might find it easier to say what you wish in writing, give them your note, and plan to talk about it after they have had a chance to privately read what you have said.

A tenth grader who had been in an interracial relationship told me, "A lot of my friends didn't understand why I was going out with someone who was so different. But I told them that was my choice. If it wasn't right for them, that's their choice. This was my relationship, not theirs. So it was my decision to be in it. I wish everyone would just mind their own business. It would make things a lot easier. The gossip at my school is so bad."

It may be hard for people to understand that you're going out with a human person, not with a "color." While there seem to be more and more people who date those of another race, many remain uncomfortable with this.

It would be helpful if people would respect that each person deserves the freedom to make decisions for themselves, as long as that decision does not harm or interfere with anyone else.

"What if you don't have a boyfriend or girlfriend and most of your friends do?" Marni, age twelve, talked about how "out of it" she felt in the seventh grade. She wanted a boyfriend so badly but no one seemed interested in her. Most of her friends had boyfriends. Said Marni, "They would talk about their boyfriends at the lunch table all the time. They would hang out together in the afternoons after school. They'd go over to one person's house or walk into town together. But since I didn't have a boyfriend, I didn't go along. It felt awful. Finally, I found a boyfriend. I really didn't like him that much, but it was better than not having anyone at all."

How do you feel about wanting a boyfriend or girlfriend so badly that you take on whoever seems to be interested just to belong? It really can be painful to feel left out. But you can't always magically produce a boyfriend or girlfriend just because you're ready! You've got to look around, find someone interesting, and try to get to know that person first.

If you allow yourself to need a boyfriend in order to feel good about yourself with your friends, then you're forgetting that it's not having the boyfriend that makes you so special; it's being who you are. With or without a boyfriend, your importance doesn't ever have to change.

Imagine if having a boyfriend or having a girlfriend really did make you special. Would that mean if you didn't have a boyfriend or girl-friend, you couldn't be important? Or if you have a boyfriend one day, you're special, and then, if he breaks up with you the next day, you're not special anymore? Are you able now to understand how much power people give to others by letting them decide how special they are?

I can understand that it might feel awkward going to someone's house if everyone there is paired off. I guess it depends on what they're doing. If everyone is together with each other, you can think about being there, too. If they're just together with their boyfriends or girl-friends, you're probably better off finding something else to do.

Walking into town with a group of your friends and their boyfriends or girlfriends might not make you feel as left out as you think. More than likely you'll all know each other. You probably even grew up with many of the boys and girls. So why not join them? If you don't already know them, it would probably be nice to meet them. Have they said anything to you to make you think you should stay away?

Another way to deal with this is to find some other friends who don't have boyfriends or girlfriends either. I'm not suggesting you give up your friends. It's just that you might find you'll be spending less time with them—at least for a while.

There's also nothing wrong with taking a chance and just asking a boy or girl if he or she wants to come into town with you and your friends.

"If you like a boy and that boy is going out with another girl, should you tell him your feelings for him?" As always, you have several things to think about before choosing what to do. First—whether or not the other girl is a friend of yours—flirting with him and letting him know you like him would probably be thought of as a ratty thing to do.

Second, realize that anything you say to him might be told to her and many others. That might be embarrassing and could give you a reputation as a boyfriend stealer (not a good thing to be). Thirteen-year-old Andy states, "I don't think you should even hint at it. Because if anybody else finds out, then it will get around. That could be embarrassing to you and to that other person."

Jamie, age fourteen, feels, "If someone is going with someone else, you don't have to totally go in the background. You can get to know that person and be friends, but don't let anyone know you're making a play for them. You just have to wait!"

You never know. If you're nice and fun to be with, he just might look at you differently. You don't have to flirt to catch his interest. And there's no rule that says you can't be friendly. Just be you and hope he doesn't take too long with that other girl.

Most important is how *you* feel. No matter what cautions I or anyone else have offered, you may feel so strongly about him that you want to tell him, no matter what. As long as you understand and are willing to accept what might happen if you tell him your feelings, then go ahead and choose what you think is best for you. This is your own personal decision.

"If you and your friend like the same person, what should you do?" At your age, boyfriends and girlfriends usually come and go. But the friendships you make can last forever. It would be sad to let anything, including liking the same boy or girl, interfere with your friendships.

I suggest you talk with your friend about whom you like. With luck, both of you will have a good sense of humor! Maybe one of you likes that person more than the other. You could even flip a coin to choose who can keep liking him or her, but you still have to wait to see whom that person likes. Maybe you won't have to choose, after all. Maybe he or she already likes one of you more than the other. Maybe he or she doesn't like either of you!

"What if your boyfriend or girlfriend goes to a different school?" Darren, age fourteen, shared, "I have a girlfriend but she doesn't go to this school. And all my friends have girlfriends. I feel that when we have activities involving boys and girls, I won't have anyone to go with. I don't like anyone in this school as a girlfriend, so I feel I'll be left out." It often depends on what the activity is. Most of the time it doesn't matter if everyone's girlfriend or boyfriend is there, because you're all there together. And if you're really good friends, they'll be happy you're with them, girlfriend or not.

If you're concerned about being with someone, there's no reason not to ask a friend who's a girl or boy to go to those activities with you. Then you'll have company. As Jeff, age fourteen, said, "I asked a girl who's a friend of mine to go to a movie with me. We're not going out in school; we are just friends going out."

As you can see, spending time with someone doesn't always have to mean that you're boyfriend and girlfriend. You can still go places with other friends who are going out with each other and not feel left out.

What About Parties?

Boy-girl parties can begin as early as third grade with some groups. Have you ever gone to a boy-girl party? If you have, were most of the kids paired off or all together?

Katie, age twelve, said, "I was really embarrassed and bored at the party my friend had last weekend. There was one boy there without a girlfriend. We stayed in another room while the others turned the lights out and had kissing contests. I couldn't decide if I should have my parents pick me up or stay since it didn't seem to matter that I was there."

If most of the kids at a party are paired off in couples, it can be awkward to be one of the only people who is alone. I think in Katie's case, the fact that they turned off the lights made it more difficult to be there. If all her friends were just hanging around together, listening to music, dancing, and talking, she probably would have felt good about being there.

Sean, age twelve, told me how he felt pressured because he's friends with a group of kids who have had girlfriends for at least two years. They started having parties in the fourth grade. Sean just started going out with someone and felt very funny at the last party he went to. He said, "All my friends have had girlfriends for at least two years, but this was the first time I was with a girl. I felt funny being there when the lights were turned low. It was embarrassing. The other kids looked like they were kissing and holding each other close. I didn't want to do anything like that. Besides, I didn't really know how. So I asked the girl I was with if she wanted to go into the other room so we could just talk."

Wise move, Sean! As you can see, even if you're paired off, you can feel a bit funny, depending on what everyone else is doing. The best idea is to follow your gut sense as to what you'd like to do. Try to think of your choices, and then pick something that seems comfortable. In Sean's case, he chose to leave the room where the other couples were "kissing and holding." In Katie's situation, she and two others stayed in another room but weren't sure what they wanted to do. Sometimes it's harder to decide than other times.

Parents and Parties

Fourteen-year-old Alexis shared, "The only problem with having a party is that my parents come down so many times to check that no one is doing what they shouldn't. While I understand they have to check up every once in a while, they don't have to do it that often. They never allow us to have much privacy. It embarrasses me in front of my friends that they come down so many times. I'm always glad to go to parties at other kids' houses, so I won't have to worry about what my friends will think."

It would be a shame not to feel good about inviting your friends to your home. It can make a difference to you and your parents to let them know how you feel. It's hard for some parents to realize that their children must be given a little space and privacy. Perhaps the fear is that if they were to leave you alone, "with all that's going on among kids today," you or your friends would do something you'd all be sorry about. They've got to work at believing they can trust you, just like you've got to prove to them you deserve their trust. Perhaps an honest discussion with them will help to ease some of their concerns.

Sometimes it really has less to do with a parent's trust in their child and more to do with worrying that large numbers of kids (even close friends) can be hard to control. Also, depending on where you live, there may be laws that make your parents responsible for anything that happens to a kid who drinks alcohol in your home. That could be very serious because if anything happened to that person—if they got hurt or they caused someone else to get hurt—in your home or on the way home, your parents could be blamed—even if they were not home. Even if they have always told you drinking is not allowed. So there are many reasons it's a big decision for parents to allow their kids the freedom to have parties or even just to have a lot of kids who want to hang out at their home. Most parents don't want parties at their home if they're not there. They also don't want their kids to go to parties at a friend's home if parents aren't there.

It's important that you and your parents talk together in order to figure out what you can say or do to prevent problems with your friends and deal with any emergency if it happens. (Remember—for any emergency, you can dial 911 first. Also keep the phone numbers of your local police and fire department near the phone so you don't have to look them up. And keep handy a phone listing of neighbors, friends, and relatives.)

"My problem," said Peter, age twenty, "was when my friends showed up and my parents weren't home, and I had to tell them they couldn't come in. My parents made a rule that no more than three kids could come over to our house if they weren't home. And no girls! But it was really hard. What do you do when your closest friends are outside saying that your parents will never find out, and they can't believe you're actually going to listen? But I always worried about being caught, or that something would break, or they'd try to take my parents' booze. So I would shut the door and feel awful about it."

As hard as shutting the door might have been, I feel Peter was correct in respecting his parents' limits. It's his parents' house and it's their right to make the rules. He may not be happy about following them, but he can't always expect to be happy about everything. If his parents found out he didn't obey, they might have had a hard time trusting him about other things.

If Peter had explained his parents' rules before, it would probably have been easier not to let his friends in. That way his friends wouldn't have been surprised that he couldn't let them in. Peter could have just said, "Sorry, they're not home!" And his friends might have had an easier time accepting what they already knew to be a rule. If he believed the rules were too strict or hard to keep because of his friends, then it might have helped to talk with his parents.

Bobby, age fourteen, said, "I don't really want my friends to come in when there's so many. I've seen what they've done to other kids' houses and I don't even want to deal with that."

If it's too hard to tell your friends that they can't come in, you might find it easier to just blame it on your parents. For example, you can say, "I hate to say this, but I can't let you in. My parents would ground me if they ever found out!"

Parents and Going Out

Kenneth, age thirteen, said, "Every time I tell my father and brother who I like, they make fun of me and tease me about it. They don't realize that I'm serious."

Kenneth, I think it's very important for you to tell your father and brother how you feel. Let them know you are serious and feel bad every time they make fun. You might say, "I don't think you realize how serious I am. Every time you make fun of me, I get very upset. It really bothers me. If you don't stop, I'm not going to tell you anything serious anymore."

Samantha, age twelve, said, "My parents won't let me date. They think seventh grade is too early." Laurie, age eleven, told me, "My parents don't care!"

Kim, age eleven, said, "I'm afraid to talk to my mom or dad about liking someone. I'm afraid they're going to tell me that it's too early, that I have to wait."

Well, Kim, the fact is they may just tell you that. Different parents have different ideas about when going out or dating should begin. But you won't know what your own parents feel unless you take a chance and ask them. If you think they're being old-fashioned or unfair, tell them your feelings and see if you can reach some agreement.

Susie, age fifteen, told me that her parents would always say things like, "Do you know him? He's really cute . . . ," when they went with her to school events. Although she wasn't interested in having a boyfriend, she felt pressured when her parents said things like that. It seemed to her that her parents felt she should be liking someone already. Since it's possible that her parents have no idea how she feels, I talked with Susie about the importance of letting them know.

Carl, age thirteen, told me he spent two hours trying to convince the mother of a girl he liked to "let us go out with each other." He said, "But she wouldn't budge an inch. She still feels her daughter shouldn't date until the ninth grade. We're in eighth grade now. We can be friends and be together in school. But I can't really say that I'm dating her. What a bummer!"

Some parents are more strict than others. Have you ever talked with your parents about going out? It might be very interesting and helpful for you to ask them. When no one is rushing off, you'll have time to stay and talk with each other for a while—perhaps at the dinner table one night.

Even if you're not interested in going out with anyone yet, you can still talk with your parents about dating and when they feel it's okay for you to start. You might be surprised to find that your parents also had crushes and have great stories to share with you about first dates when they were your age. They might also share with you some helpful ideas and advice for when you do start going out.

CHAPTER 15

PEER PRESSURE, MAKING CHOICES

Before reading this chapter, please take a few minutes to think about whether you have ever done anything that you really didn't want to do but did anyway because your friends were doing it. That's what peer pressure is about.

It can affect your friendships and decisions about going out, smoking, drinking alcohol and using other drugs, having sex, how you dress, how you treat your family or other people. Since making choices can often be difficult and confusing, I hope this chapter will help you better understand what peer pressure is and how it can affect your choices. The more you understand, the more prepared you'll be to make healthy and safe decisions—and the truer you will be able to be to what you believe is right and safe for you, no matter what your friends are doing.

What's Peer Pressure?

If you take the two words separately, you'll find that *pressure* is the feeling of being forced, persuaded, or influenced by something. It can give you an uneasy feeling and sometimes cause you to do things that you really don't believe in and wouldn't usually do. A peer is someone who is about the same age as you are. *Peers* is another way of saying "other people your age." Peer pressure is felt when your friends try to influence you to say or do something, even if you don't want to and you feel you need to do it so you can stay friendly with them.

Maybe if you think carefully about each of the following questions, you'll get a better idea of how peer pressure works. You'll probably be surprised to realize how many different ways your friends have influenced you, even if you weren't aware of the pressure at the time.

Have you ever:

- Wanted to do something just because your friends were doing it, thinking if you didn't go along with them, they wouldn't accept you as much and you wouldn't stay their friend?
- Wanted to do something that no one else wanted to do but felt funny doing it because you didn't want anyone to call you dumb, silly, or say they wouldn't be your friend?
- Not wanted to do something that everyone was doing but did it anyway? (And didn't let them know you didn't want to do it, because you thought your friends would laugh, be angry, or not think you were the type to hang around with them anymore?)
- Not wanted to do something, told your friends you didn't want to, and found they said things like, "Oh, come on, why not?" "Oh, try it, just this once. . . . " "What, are you chicken?" "You're such a baby. . . . Why don't you just go home to your parents?"

If you said yes to any one of these considerations, you have felt peer pressure. Most kids, if not all, have felt it at one time or another. Adults have, too. You might already have found that some pressures are easier to deal with than others.

Dealing with Peer Pressure

Sometimes peer pressure can be very positive. It can cause you to work harder to reach goals that you might not ever have reached without the influence of that pressure.

Peer pressure can challenge and strengthen your confidence, help you learn more about who you are and what you believe, and teach you which friendships are real. But it also can be very confusing and sometimes painful.

At times, you'll probably find that friends may not be as nice or easy to be with as you'd like them to be, especially when you don't go along with them. So you'll end up having to make a choice between their feelings and yours. You may find it confusing to even figure out what your choices are. But trust that choices will be there if you think hard enough. And realize that you—not your friends—have the final word (of course, figuring in what rules your parents, teachers, or other adults have set for you).

Sometimes you may have the confidence to do what you feel is right, no matter what your friends think (even your best friend). Other times, you might feel that the pressure is too much and it's better to give in than fight it. Each choice will be up to you.

Dealing with peer pressure forces you to take a chance and see if your friends will respect your right to decide what's right for you. First you have to respect yourself.

Peer pressure can be felt in many ways. Even the same pressure in the same situation with the same friends will be felt differently by each person. It would be great if everyone learned that the only decisions a person has a right to make are his or her own. Friends can give advice and tell you what they think, but it's not fair for them to tell you what to do and how to do it and expect you'll listen. If you allow them to make your decisions, you're giving up your own power to choose.

This is a tough message, but if you don't learn to be strong about saying no (or yes) when you must, then you can end up being pressured into doing something very dangerous. The sooner you take charge of your own decisions, the easier it will be to act according to what you believe is right and what you know is safe.

Let's take a look at some of the different ways other kids have felt peer pressure. Maybe you've been in similar situations. In each case, I've suggested ways the boy or girl might have handled it differently. I hope the lists of other choices will help you better understand how each situation can be taken apart in order to figure out what you want to do. As always, it would be great if you can add other choices.

Tommy, age eleven, told me his parents are very strict and don't let him go to R-rated movies, though his friends can. His friends always tease him about not being as mature as they are, and they make sure to talk in front of him about the movies they've seen. That only makes him feel worse. Whenever he can, he tries to change the subject.

What else could Tommy do?

- Instead of changing the subject, he could tell them how he really feels.
- He could tell his friends that he feels they're talking about the movie in front of him on purpose.
- He could say to his friends that he can't help what rules his parents make. If he were allowed to go, he'd love to.
- He could let his friends know that their teasing and movie talk make him feel worse, and he'd like them to stop. (If they're really his good friends, they will. He may have to say this a few different times to let them know he's really serious.)
- If they don't stop teasing, he could start to look for some non-R-rated friends!
- He could talk with his parents about the fact that he feels he's old enough to go to that kind of a movie. Maybe they would agree to let him try one as long as they went with him, so they could be sure to answer any questions and see that he understands.

NOTE: If Tommy's parents won't even think about it, Tommy will have to try harder to accept that he'll have to wait for a while.

Jeannie, age thirteen, shared that she felt pressured when a girl she wanted to be friends with asked her for answers during a test at school. She'd never cheated before and didn't want to then, but she had a hard time deciding what to do. Since she wasn't very popular and wanted to make friends badly, she went ahead and let her copy.

Some thoughts about why Jeannie did what she did:
- She was worried that saying no would make the girl not want to be her friend.
- She thought that saying yes would be proof that she was a good friend to have.

What else could Jeannie have done if she didn't want to let her cheat?
- She could have said, "Quiet! We'll get in trouble. I'll be happy to help you with your homework after school if you still have any questions."
- Another possibility is: "I'm sorry, but I don't want to get into trouble."
- Or, "Please don't ask me anything, I really need to think."
- She could have ignored her and spoken to her after class.
- If there was no way to even whisper during the test (figure that most teachers who hear talking during a test will think that person is cheating), she could have shaken her head no. Then she could have talked with this girl right after class to explain that she didn't want to get into trouble and would be happy to help her after school or on the weekend.

What do you think you would have done?

Richard, age twenty, said, "One afternoon when I was in the eighth grade, I was at my friend's house with a group of other kids. They decided to try one of his parent's cigarettes that were lying around. They passed it from person to person, and when it came to me, I passed it on to the next person without trying it. (I knew it was wrong and didn't want to get in trouble.) They couldn't believe that I was such a wimp and kept telling me that for the rest of the afternoon. I don't know why I stayed."

Let's hear it for Richard; he had guts!
- It must have taken so much inner strength for Richard to have passed the cigarette without trying it (many kids would have been pressured into trying it).
- Richard had the confidence to take a stand for what he felt, even if it hurt to have his friends call him names all afternoon.
- I'm willing to bet there were other friends who wouldn't have tried smoking that afternoon, if they knew someone else wasn't going to try it either.
- If the name-calling got bad enough, Richard could have left.

What else could Richard have done?
- He could have left when they first began to talk about taking the cigarettes.
- He could have told his friends from the start that he didn't agree with what they were doing and would not go along with it.
- He could have told his friends their name-calling really bothered him and that he had a right to say no.
- He could have said he wouldn't stay if they continued to call him names.
- He could have tried to convince them not to smoke. (Kids may find it tough enough to make the decision not to smoke for themselves. The thought of telling friends not to smoke can be even harder. But it's certainly another choice to consider.)

Rachel, age fifteen, was at the movies with her boyfriend; they had been going out for eight months. During the movie, he put his arm over her shoulders and pulled her very close to him. He started moving his hands closer to her breasts. She had told him before that she wasn't ready for him to do that. She wanted him to stop and decided to get up, saying she had to go to the bathroom.

What else could Rachel have done?
- She could have put her hands on top of his and pushed them away.

- She could have told her boyfriend, *"No!"* or *"Stop!"* or "Don't go any further."
- She could have said to him, "I need you to go out in the hall with me." When they got there, she could have told him how upset she was that he tried to touch her again after she told him not to do that. She could also have told him that if he's not going to respect her feelings, then maybe they ought to break up.
- She could have said, "If you do that again, I'm not going to stay here with you."

Note: Sometimes it's really hard to know what to say at the very moment you're being pressured. Rachel did a really smart thing by getting up to go to the bathroom and giving herself a chance to think. She did what she had to do to get out of a situation that made her uncomfortable and upset.

Thirteen-year-old Mindy's story is another example of how friends can influence your decisions. She shared, "A couple of weeks ago, my mom bought me a great pair of purple overalls. Purple is my favorite color. I loved them and couldn't wait to wear them to school. As soon as I got to school the next day, kids started saying things like, 'That color is gross,' and 'I like your overalls but why purple?' I had a hard time stopping myself from crying. I was so embarrassed and so angry." Mindy decided she would wear them only at home and when her family went visiting.

Some purple truths:
- Even though she wanted to wear her overalls to school, how her friends felt about them was more important to her than how she felt.
- Her friends' remarks pressured her into keeping her new overalls private.

What could Mindy have said to her friends?
- "You may think they're gross, but I love them!"
- "Now that I know how you feel, you don't have to keep saying it."
- "I love them and I'm the one wearing them. I'll remember not to lend them to you."

Jeremy, age twelve, shared, "I don't like going down really steep places fast. Like, say I'm skiing. I like taking my time and going slowly. When I'm riding my bike with my friends, they will sometimes go down some very steep place. And even if I'm really scared and I don't want to do it at all, I'll go down it. Even if I hate it the whole way, I'll do it."

(Jeremy told me he mainly does it because he hates being teased and doesn't want the word to get around that he wouldn't do it.)

> *What could Jeremy have done besides go down the steep hill with his friends?*
> - He could have said, "No way! Go ahead if you want to but I won't!"
> - He could have told them, "I'll meet you at the bottom. I hate going down really steep places fast."
> - He could have asked his friends to go somewhere else or told them that he would lead the way as soon as he realized where he was headed.

How about trying to make your own list of choices for the next few situations. It might be interesting and fun to ask your friends to make their own lists, too. Then compare and talk about your answers. Pen or pencil ready? Here goes.

Scott, age fourteen, said that he felt pressured when all his friends wanted him to go out with a certain girl, and he didn't like her. What do you think Scott should have done? What could he have said to his friends?

Craig, age nine, felt pressured when the kids he was with wanted to sneak through his neighbor's yard and his parents had already told him not to do that. What might Craig have told his friends? What would you have done if you were Craig?

Liz, age fourteen, would have been very happy not getting a bra. She said she didn't even need or want one. But most of the girls in her gym class wore one and she felt she had to get one, too. What would you have done if you were Liz? What might you have felt?

Alan, age twelve, feels very embarrassed that he's not allowed to go to the candy store a few blocks from his house. Alan shared, "My parents think that too many rough kids hang out there, but most of my friends can go. It drives me crazy when we ride our bicycles home from school and my friends are making plans to go there." Is there something that Alan could say to his friends so that he doesn't have to be driven crazy hearing their plans? What might Alan say to his parents about his feelings? What would you do if you were Alan? Would you listen to your parents?

Rob, age thirteen, said, "I get very embarrassed sometimes when I go into town with my friends. They get bigger allowances than I do, and my parents don't believe in giving me any more money if I spend it all at once. A lot of my friends can't understand it when I can't have a second piece of pizza. Maybe it would be easier if I just say I'm not hungry." Do you think that would be a good thing to say? How else could Rob deal with this?

Danny, age fourteen, lives in an apartment building, down the hall from a boy who is a senior in high school. Danny had just left his friends and started walking home from town when this neighbor drove by and stopped to give him a ride home. Danny thought he smelled beer on his breath and saw there were some empty beer bottles thrown around the front floor of the car. Danny really wanted a ride because it was already past when he promised his dad he'd be home. What were Danny's choices? What might each choice mean? If you were Danny, what would you have said or done?

Charlene, age ten, loves to put peanut butter on her tuna fish sandwiches. The first time she brought one of these sandwiches to school, the kids at her lunch table said, "Gross me out! That's disgusting. How could you eat it like that?" Charlene answered, "Because I love it." Her friends said, "Well, you're crazy!" Charlene decided that she would eat peanut butter–tuna fish sandwiches only on the weekends, and she'd eat plain tuna fish during the week at school. Would you have still added peanut butter, no matter what your friends thought? Would you have put only a tiny bit of peanut butter on so they couldn't notice that much? What could Charlene have said to her friends to let them know how she felt and stop them from saying her sandwich was gross?

Now that you've had some practice in figuring out choices in many different kinds of peer pressure situations, the next step is to look more closely at what your choices might mean.

Just Knowing You Have a Choice Is Not Enough, You've Got to Look Ahead to What Your Choice Might Mean

To look ahead means to *anticipate* (an-TISS-i-pate) or try to guess ahead of time what the results of your choice might be. Think to yourself, "What will happen if . . ." For example:

This is what might have been rolling around in Richard's head as the cigarette was being passed around to him:

> *If I decide to smoke that cigarette:*
> a) I'm going to hate myself for giving in.
> b) My friends will think I'm cool.
> c) I could get into trouble.
> d) I might look dumb or foolish since I don't know what to do.
> e) Maybe I'll cough a lot or get nauseous [NAW-shuss: feeling like you need to vomit].
> f) If my friend's parents find out about this, they could tell my parents. And that could mean trouble.
> e) Maybe I'll really like it. Then what would I do?
>
> *If I don't try to smoke when the cigarette is passed to me:*
> a) I'll really be doing what I think is right.
> b) My friends will probably try to convince me that I should try it.

c) My friends will learn that I can be their friend but not feel I have to do what they do.

d) My friends might tease me and give me a hard time.

e) My friends might respect me and just keep passing it among themselves without trying to push me to do it.

f) My friends might feel I shouldn't be hanging around with them if I won't do what they do.

g) My parents would probably be very proud of me if I told them I didn't smoke when I could have tried.

h) I'll feel really good about myself for not giving in and sticking up for what I knew was right for me.

If I leave before they start smoking:

a) I won't be in an uncomfortable situation.

b) I'll feel relieved not to be part of something I know is not right.

c) Maybe my friends will talk about me when I leave— that I'm "chicken" or whatever.

d) I'd be taking a risk. Maybe they'll think I'm not cool enough to still be friends with them.

e) I won't get into trouble.

If I try to convince them not to try smoking:

a) They might think I'm a real goody-goody.

b) They might listen.

c) They might laugh at me for trying to stop them.

Let's pick apart one more situation so you can further practice figuring out choices and what they might mean. Go back to Danny's walk home and the possibility of getting into his neighbor's car when he knew that he had been drinking. If you haven't already thought about what choices would be important to consider in that situation, do that now before reading my list.

This is what Danny might have been thinking when he smelled his neighbor's breath from across the car—and then saw the empty beer bottles:

> *If I get in his car:*
> a) I'd be letting myself take a serious chance by doing something I know is not safe.
> b) I'd be really scared that we'd get into an accident because of all the beer he drank. I could die.
> c) Maybe it would be okay and we'd get home safely.
> d) He'd think I was cool and okay. And he'd give me more rides.
> e) I'd get home faster and my dad would be less angry with me.
> f) I wouldn't feel very good that I gave in and didn't stand up for what I knew was right and safe.

> *If I don't get in his car:*
> a) I'd get home later but I would definitely be safer. (I'll tell my dad that I made a safer choice, and I hope he'd feel relieved.)
> b) My neighbor might think I'm a wimp and not offer me other rides.
> c) I'd feel really good about myself for being strong about what I knew was right and safe.
> d) My dad would be proud of me and maybe even trust me more because I didn't take the risk.

What else do you think might be important to consider?

When It's Your Turn to Be "Tested"

If you're thinking, "I don't have to deal with this right now; my friends aren't doing anything that makes me feel pressured," you never know when it will be your turn to be "tested." Someday—maybe this year, maybe not until next year or the year after—you can count on being in a situation where either someone directly tries to pressure you or most other kids are doing something and you'll wonder if you need to do it, too. Maybe you'll be at school, maybe a friend's home, maybe at a party, a mall, a movie, or anywhere else. It's worth taking the time now to think about how you might handle different kinds of pressure situations.

If you're saying to yourself, "I'll just say no!" understand that it's easy sitting in a cozy place reading this book, *thinking* about what you would say or do. But when you actually find yourself faced with a real situation, it can be much tougher to be so strong. Especially if the people involved are your only friends.

It's even more important to be prepared to make choices because you probably won't have very long to make your decisions. Whether you're thinking about taking the drug that someone is trying to give you, smoking the cigarette that is being passed, letting someone's hand keep moving closer and closer to a very private, sexual place on your body, or getting in someone's car if you know they have been drinking, choices such as these often must be made in a few minutes' time, sometimes seconds. If you don't know what to say and don't even realize that you have a choice, then you may allow yourself to do something that could be very wrong for you, very dangerous, and possibly even deadly.

Keep listening for peer pressure stories from friends, classmates, perhaps an older (or younger) brother or sister. When they describe difficult situations and what they did to handle the pressure, that's a great time for you to also think about what you might have done. The more you practice thinking about what choices you have and figuring out what each choice might mean, the more ready you'll be to handle your own situations (even if they take you by surprise) in a way that is safe and good for you.

What You Can Say If You Don't Want to Give In to Peer Pressure

Here are some more ways to turn what you're feeling into words:
- "Stop pushing me."

- "No thanks."
- "I told you I don't want to do it."
- "You go ahead if you want to, but I'm not going with you. I'll catch you later."

Danny could have told his neighbor:
- "Thanks for asking but I really feel like walking."
  (Even if it was raining or snowing, he could have said that he loves walking in the snow!)
- "No thanks . . . hey, why don't you leave your car here and walk home with me. Someone can pick it up later. You don't seem like you're in such good shape to drive. It's not worth taking a chance."

If you feel that it's too hard to deal with what your friends are doing or about to do, you can always blame your parent. For example,
- "Oh, I can't believe what time it is! My parents told me I better get home early."
- "I wish I could stay, but I'm supposed to baby-sit for my little sister."

You could also say something like, "I gotta go . . . I haven't even started my book report yet." Whether you blame a parent or schoolwork, make up a doctor's appointment that you have to go to, or say that you have to visit a relative, the most important thing is that you *leave the situation.* Do what you have to do—say what you have to say to get out of there as quickly and easily as possible. Then, in the comfort of your own home, you can talk with your parent(s) about what else you could have said or done—and what you can do differently next time so that you don't find yourself in that situation in the first place.

What You Need to Know Before Making a Choice

- First, you need to have your facts straight. You need to understand information about what you're considering.
- Then think about choices and risks. What choices do you have?

- For each choice, ask yourself, "What will this choice mean?"
- Think through each choice, answering, "If I do or say this, then what could happen?"
- Think about how your decision might make you feel (proud, embarrassed, disappointed in yourself, ashamed, confident, left out, scared, relieved, great).
- How do you think people will respond to what you say or do (with surprise, anger, relief, happiness, disappointment, respect, maybe they won't want to be your friend anymore)?

What are your risks? How much could your choice affect you (or anyone else)? Just how serious is the decision?

Ask yourself, and answer honestly, "How much of a risk would I be taking?"
- A wrong decision (using certain drugs or drinking and driving) might lead you to the hospital or even the morgue. A wrong sexual decision might cause you to become infected with the HIV virus (which causes AIDS), which could have deadly results. Taking sexual risks could also result in other changes in your life that you're just not ready for and might always regret. But if it's just a decision to have a plain cheese because that's what most of your friends want instead of the pepperoni pizza that you really want, it won't harm you to give in.
- So you'll need to pick and choose which situations won't matter if you give in and which are much more serious. Consider each decision carefully. Be honest about what you know could be the result. Then be strong about what you know is right for you.
- And remember—bad things don't happen only to other people. Figure that *you* can be the "other person" to someone else. If you flirt with danger, you may win—

but you also might lose. There's no telling which times you might get away with what you're doing or which times you won't.

- The problem seems to be that a lot of kids believe that the dangers are real only for other people in other places. The attitude "It won't happen to me" or "It can't happen here, not to me," is very common.
- How serious do you feel you are about the possibility of unwanted results from taking risks? How serious do you think your friends are about what could happen if they take risks?

When you make your choice . . . Be clear in your communication. Make sure your words and nonverbal actions match what you feel and what you've decided. For your safety and even your survival, *no* has to mean NO. And you need to be sure when you say yes. If your brain and your voice say no and your actions say yes—then you'll be giving a mixed, confused, and unclear message. That can lead to trouble.

Remember how you can figure out what you need to say. First, think about what you're feeling, then turn your feelings into words. Here are some words to keep in mind that can help you say no to pressure:

- "NO."
- "I'm not comfortable."
- "No, you go ahead if you want to, but I don't."
- "Don't push me."
- "Please stop!"
- "I'm leaving."

If you're not sure, wait. Get more information before you decide. You can say, "I'm really not sure about this. I need to think about it. Please stop pressuring me." You can also decide to walk away.

Now you know that you can decide to be in complete control of what you allow yourself to do. The more you understand about what situations can lead to unwanted, possibly dangerous pressures, the more you'll be able to prevent yourself from being in those situations in the first place.

Believing the Risks Are Real

It makes me scared and deeply upset to know that most kids don't believe their decisions are so serious until something horribly tragic and unthinkable happens to them or someone close—a best friend gets killed in a drunk-driving accident or a relative is dying of AIDS. Only then do they believe. Too late.

Did you ever hear the term "Russian roulette"? That's when someone puts one bullet into a gun that holds six or more bullets, spins the chamber, points the gun at their head and pulls the trigger. So the idea is that the person who's playing this very deadly game hopes that when the trigger is pulled, that chamber will be one that's empty instead of the one that's loaded. If it's the loaded chamber, the person's brains get blown out. If not, the person lives.

It seems to me that kids are making their serious decisions as if they're playing Russian roulette. For example, every time someone gets into a car with a drunk driver (or drives when drunk), it's as if they're pulling the trigger of that gun. They could die (or at least get seriously hurt), kill someone else (or seriously hurt them), or be lucky enough to get home safely. It's a life-or-death gamble.

Consider this. Can I (or anyone) promise you that you definitely will get into an accident if you get into a car when the driver has been drinking? No, I can't. But I can promise you that you *might*. Will an accident happen the first time you get in that car? Maybe, maybe not. But it could. It may not happen until the third time. Or the thirty-fifth time.Or maybe not until the hundred and fortieth time. Or, if you're lucky, maybe never. But each time you take that kind of risk, the truth is you're taking a risk that could end your life—or someone else's.

Because so many people seem to drink and drive or take other risks and get away with them, a lot of kids ignore the truth about how serious those risks really are. Even if they do believe the risks are real, they don't think they will really happen to them.

What do you think it will take for you to believe that these risks are real? You'll have to be able to answer for yourself, "What are my risks? At what price do I do this?" What will it take for you to believe that the price is too high if you're playing with your life—or someone else's?

So, one more time—what will it take to prove to you that the risks are real? Will it take an overdose? A pregnancy? A terrible accident? Knowing someone who is dying of AIDS?

If your answer for yourself is that you never in your life would want a particular consequence or result to happen even once—then even one chance is too many.

What If You Make a Mistake?

Just because you understand your choices doesn't guarantee that your decision will always be the right one. You'll probably make some mistakes along the way. Everyone does. Adults, too. Even if you know what you need to say or do, it can be hard to get the words out, hard always to have the confidence to act upon what you know is right. And sometimes you might simply think you can get away with what you're doing "this one time."

Remember that you're human. If you make a mistake, try not to be too hard on yourself. Forgive yourself. All you can do is try your best and say you're sorry for being wrong. It doesn't mean you're a bad person because you made a bad decision. It just means you goofed, you messed up. Unfortunately some goofs are more serious than others. But, no matter what, if you're lucky enough to get another chance, you can learn from what you did, so you don't make the same mistake again.

Some people can't forgive themselves for their mistakes and feel guilty for a long time. They walk around saying to themselves, "I shouldn't have done that. If only I didn't . . ." And they can't seem to allow themselves to let go of their mistake, to put it behind them and start to go forward in their life.

If that's you, help yourself by talking with someone who is trained to help you understand your feelings and develop the tools to go forward in a more positive way (parents, school counselor, psychologist, religious leader, teacher). You don't deserve to be held back by a mistake. Besides, no one can go backwards. We can't change what we already did. But we can learn from it and go on.

Sometimes it's a kid's parents or friends who keep reminding them of what they did. As I talked about in Chapter 12, too many kids have to deal with years and years of having the burden of a bad reputation just because they did something a while ago that no one lets them forget. That's not fair. People can learn, they can even change. It can mean so much for others to give them a new chance.

Note: Remember, if you've had a reputation that doesn't feel good, just keep on being yourself. In time more and more people will get to know you as the person you are instead of the person they expect you to be because of the reputation.

If there's a particular person who is spreading rumors or talking about your personal life to "everyone," you can approach that person privately and let them know how much they're hurting you. You might tell them if they don't want to be your friend, that's fine. Just leave you alone. If you know or find out you've done something that has bothered them, you can apologize and add, "I hope we can try to leave what happened behind us and start again today."

As I've said many times, I can't promise you that if you tell someone how you feel, he or she will definitely stop hurting you. I can only promise that if you don't say anything, that person may not even know that you want them to stop.

You can also say to parents and friends: "I'm trying very hard to put what happened in the past. Please stop reminding me. It hurts too much and I need to go on."

If you make a mistake, you might find it a relief to be able to say:

- "I'm really sorry."
- "I guess I just didn't think it through. I never meant to hurt you."
- "I did a terrible thing and I'm so embarrassed. I hope you won't spread it around the school. It would mean a lot to me if you would just keep this between us."
- "Mom/Dad, I know you're going to be very angry because you told me never to do this. But I just didn't know how to get out of it. I wanted to listen to you and I feel horrible that I'm disappointing you. But please. Please don't get so angry that you won't be able to help me. I need you. And I'm so sorry."

- "Mom/Dad, I'm so afraid to tell you this. I'm afraid you'll judge me and think you'll never be able to trust me again."

If you're honest about your feelings, it will help you turn them into words to friends, girlfriends, boyfriends, parents, family, teachers, counselors, or anyone.

Remember that even if you can figure out what to say, that doesn't mean it will be easy to say it. It may be very hard. But that's okay. It's *not* okay to let being scared—or worrying about how your parent(s) will respond—stop you from saying what you need to say anyway. Push the words out if you have to. Write them down if you can't say them out loud. Say them any way you have to. Just don't keep them to yourself.

Being Able to Talk with Your Parent(s) and Get Help If You Make a Mistake

You may still be thinking, "I'll never be able to be so honest with my parents. They'll probably ground me until I'm thirty-five years old and never let me be with my friends again." Most kids tell me how hard it is to tell their parents about bad decisions, especially if they know their parents will be very angry, shocked, or upset. It's understandable that kids might be afraid to admit such serious concerns as being pregnant, using drugs, having an alcohol problem, stealing, or trying to commit suicide. But when you think about how painful, difficult, and dangerous it could be for a kid to deal with these things alone, it becomes clearer that parents (or some other adult) need to be given the chance to help.

Again, I'm not saying that telling your parents about your mistakes or other difficulties will be easy. It's fair to expect that they may be shocked or upset. But after the shock eases a bit, most parents want to be able to be there for their kids. The problem is too many kids never want to take a chance on how that shock will affect their parents. And too many parents want to help but don't always know how to let their kids know they really can come to them. And so, many kids stay silent, wishing they could talk with their parents, needing their help. And many parents wait silently, not really knowing how to bring up the subject with their kids—and not realizing that their kids are holding back.

If you haven't already talked with your parents about coming to them for help, don't wait for a serious mistake or any other difficult situation to happen. Talk with them now. Let them know how important they are to you and how badly you want to be able to come to them if you have a problem. Let them know if you're afraid of their reactions, afraid they'll judge you or your friends, afraid you won't be trusted. The more you and your parents talk about your feelings and theirs, the more you will be able to trust that you can tell them anything (even if it will upset them) and know that they'll be there for you.

Don't forget to thank parents or friends if they are understanding, for being there for you, for forgiving you, and for helping you to go forward.

If you find, after trying to talk with your parents, that you don't feel good about going to them for help, that they can't or won't be there for you and don't understand, realize that it doesn't mean you're not worth helping. Just that your parents might not be the ones to help.

Maybe your parents aren't comfortable with what you did, maybe their parents never helped them and so they don't know how (even if they want to help). Maybe they've got their own problems and don't have the energy to help you with yours. Maybe they're fed up because you always get into trouble. Maybe they can't make the time. Maybe they really don't care. But no matter what, you deserve to be helped. If not by them, by someone else.

It's great to be able to go to a friend for help. But when problems are more serious, besides speaking with close friends, it's also very important to speak with an adult. You have many other people just waiting to help you if you would let them try (other relatives, a school counselor, psychologist, social worker, teacher, someone at a health services clinic, a religious leader, family doctor, friend's parent).

If you can't relate to the first person, go on to the next and the next and the next until you find someone who can help. Don't give up looking for help. Don't allow yourself to deal with your situation alone. That can be very hard. You deserve to have a caring adult there for you to offer guidance, support, and help you deal with your feelings.

Taking Charge of Your Own Choices

Your parents (or anyone else) can tell you not to cross a busy street, not to go to a certain store, not to hang around with a certain group of kids, or not to smoke, not to drink or use other drugs, not to cheat, or not to have sex before you're an adult and are more ready to make that choice. You can know and understand what you've been taught. But when it comes to actually being faced with the situation, you're the one who will have to decide what you will or will not do. The choice will be yours to make.

It will be *you* going down that steep hill, *you* taking the chance that you might fall, *you* risking that you'll be left out, *you* taking the chance that you'll be caught, *you* facing the possibility that your friends will not talk to you for a few days, *you* taking the chance that what you're doing might be dangerous to you, *you* risking that your parents will be angry if they find out, *you* who will have to deal with all the feelings that can go along with doing something you know is not right for you. You will have to decide. And you will have to live with your decision, its *consequences* (con-si-KWEN-ses) or results—what happens because you let yourself do what you did—and then hope that you will learn from it so you can be wiser next time.

If you respect yourself strongly, then I hope you'll be very careful about going against your *values* (VAL-use), or what you feel is right or wrong, important or not important, unless you're sure that the time is right to do so. Not because someone else is pressuring you, but because you've had the freedom to think of all the reasons you should or shouldn't, and because you then made the choice yourself.

Walking Away from Your Only Friends

If you find that your friends are doing something too dangerous for you and you need to walk away, that may be very tough. You may feel scared and really alone. That's natural. But I hope you'll also feel proud of the strength you had to actually walk away.

It may take you a little while, but at least you know you have the power to start again with new friendships. You don't have to wait for someone to come up to you; you can walk up to someone and say hi. Remember to look in your classrooms, lunchrooms, halls, bus, and pick out that first person to approach. If he or she doesn't work out, look for the next, and the next. Remember, once someone starts showing an interest back, you'll be on your way.

You don't deserve to act in ways that you know are not you just to be accepted. You don't have to give in to pressure just because you're afraid to lose your friends. If they don't respect your right to choose, maybe they're not such good friends anyway.

Sometimes You May Be More Easily Pressured Than Other Times

Have you ever wondered why it is that sometimes you're more likely to give in to pressure than other times? It usually has to do with the way you feel about yourself at the moment. If you feel confident and good about yourself, you'll probably not give in so easily. If you are not confident and don't feel so good about yourself, you'll probably give in more easily. Most of the feelings you have about yourself may come from the way you feel about how you relate to your mother, father, brothers, sisters, relatives, friends, and teachers.

For example, even if your mother and/or father really love(s) you, if you feel unloved, then you might not feel as important. Maybe you would think that your parent's bad feelings were your fault. Maybe you'd think if you were just a little bit better as a kid, it would make your parents happy.

So, since you might have difficulty making your parents happy (with you), you might try to at least make everyone else, like your friends, happy. That's one of the reasons peer pressure can start, and you may give in to pressure that you might not agree to if you felt stronger and better about yourself.

If you don't feel confident that your friends like you for who you are, you might be more likely to go along with what they want you to do. You may think that going along with them, even if you don't want to, will help to make sure they'll still like you and help you feel more like you belong.

Now you know that friends who don't respect your right to make your own choices—and who like you only if you do what they tell you to—may not really be true friends. And they could be dangerous to hang around with.

Also, if you've had a bad experience because you made a decision that didn't turn out right, you might be more likely to let other people decide for you—so you don't have to be concerned about being wrong again. But letting others make your decisions means that you're giving up and missing out on a chance to test out your ability to think for yourself and become more confident, as you find you can trust your judgment. Each decision, whether it's right or wrong, will teach you something. If you let others decide for you, you give up your chance to learn, your chance to express yourself according to your own feelings.

Making Choices Will Become Easier as You Learn More About Your Values

It's hard to know exactly what you will do if your friends pressure you, as each situation will probably be a little different. Making choices will become easier as you learn more about your own sense of values. Sometimes what's right or wrong will be clear to you; other times you may not be so sure. Try not to rush into anything, especially if you feel you need more time to decide. If you can't make up your mind, it might be smarter to wait.

You may decide to wear a certain kind of shirt, beads on your sneakers, or the same jeans that everyone else seems to have (even if you don't like the style that much and you miss your purple overalls). But you may not choose to smoke or drink at your friend's house just because the other kids are doing it.

If you say no and find out that your friends (girlfriend, boyfriend, or anyone) don't respect your decision, even after you've told them you don't want to be pressured, then your sense of values and ability to think through your choices will help you know what you need to do. Your understanding of the risks involved will help you have the extra strength to make the right choice, even if you don't feel so confident at the moment.

It's hard to anticipate every single possible situation that will cause you to feel pressured or could possibly be dangerous. But the stronger you are about what you believe, the stronger you'll be about making the choice that seems right for you. The more you understand how to take each situation and figure out what choices you have to consider, the more likely you'll find a choice that is healthy for you.

CHAPTER 16

SEX

This chapter deals with sexual feelings, more pressures, and more choices. In Chapter 9, I spoke about sexual feelings that can be felt when a person is alone. In this chapter, I talk about when these feelings are felt in response to another person and shared.

How Can You Tell When You Have Sexual Feelings?

- When you have the desire to touch someone in a caring, personal way.
- When you want to share yourself with another person and allow them to touch you.
- When you feel tingly just looking at that other person.
- When you feel a warmth in your genital area just thinking about them.
- When you want to be held by that person.
- When you want to hold them.
- When you want to be close.

When Can You Expect to Have Sexual Feelings?

Once again, because each boy and girl is so different, it's impossible to say when. The most honest answer I can give you is that you'll feel them when you feel them, whenever that may be!

You may have been "going out" for some time and not have felt those feelings. You may not be "going out" with anyone and might already feel them toward a special person, whether or not that person even knows it.

As with all other changes of puberty (both physical and emotional), some boys and girls will have sexual interest in the beginning stages, and others won't have these feelings until much later. Your hormones have an influence here, too.

Since you can't predict when your sexual feelings will start, it wouldn't be fair or wise for you to sit around expecting them, wondering why they haven't begun and worrying if something is wrong with you because they haven't yet appeared.

Many boys and girls have shared how frustrating it has been for them to listen to their friends talk about what sexual things they did or would like to do with someone, and know that they've never had any of those feelings. Very often, in fact, they didn't even know what their friends were talking about!

John, age thirteen, said, "A lot of boys talk about wanting to do something with their girlfriend. I don't really think anyone has done anything. But I haven't ever wanted to do anything like that and I wonder when I'll get those feelings."

The truth is some kids really are doing what they talk about—and some are doing a lot but keeping it private. The high numbers of teenage pregnancies is proof enough that plenty of kids are "doing it." And, at the same time, many are not.

More important than figuring out who's being honest about their sexual stories—and who is just trying to be "cool," "with it," or trying to get a reaction—is learning about your own sexual feelings and your own sense of readiness. The more you understand about what you feel and the many ways you can express your feelings, and what may or may not be a wise sexual choice at your age, the better you'll be at making sexual decisions that are right for you. If you go at your own pace, you'll also find that you'll be more comfortable and have a lot more fun.

How do you think you compare sexually to your friends? Are you more or less interested or about the same? If there's a lot of sex talk, how does that make you feel? Do you feel pressured? Amused? Excited? Jealous? Comfortable? Embarrassed? Confused? Frustrated? Do you feel like you "should" be doing what they're talking about? Do you do most of the talking? If not, who does? Does what they're saying sound real to you?

Since everyone reading this book will be at a different stage, I'm going to start with beginning sexual feelings and the many different ways to express them. Then I'll move on. No matter where you're at, it may be interesting to follow along, starting with beginning ways to express your feelings—even if just to remember back to when you started. You'll probably have lots of memories, lots of your own stories that could fill these pages.

And if you haven't yet felt sexual feelings for another person, or think maybe you're just beginning to have such feelings, the next sections will help you understand how you might feel, how other kids feel, and how you can share what you feel (when you're ready).

How You Might Let Someone Know You Have Feelings for Them

HOLDING HANDS One of the ways kids (adults, too) show that they like each other in a special way is to hold hands or put an arm around each other.

Linda, age thirty, said, "It used to be such a big thing if a boy held your hand. Then you knew he 'liked' you and you always hoped people would see you walking together."

Jimmy, age fourteen, shared, "I haven't gone out with girls that much and it gets me nervous to try to hold hands. What if they don't want to hold mine?"

Jimmy, this is the same type of concern that I talked about in the friendship chapter. It has to do with rejection. What if she doesn't have the same feelings you do? It may help to realize that she might want to hold your hand in private but may be too embarrassed or uncomfortable about these new feelings to want to hold your hand in public. A good way to find out is to ask the person you like if he or she would like to hold hands with you. Chances are if she's showing any kind of interest in you, she'll be happy to hold your hand. If not, you might as well know it sooner than later.

Becky, age thirteen, said, "I love holding my boyfriend's hand. He's too shy to take my hand, so I just take his!"

Many boys are relieved when girls take the first step. Though old rules of *etiquette* (EH-ti-ket, social manners) state that girls should wait for the boy to act first, fewer and fewer people still believe that to be true. Many kids today are realizing that there doesn't have to be a rule as long as everyone respects one another. It's easier that way and it takes pressure off the boys. Also, girls don't have to sit around waiting; they can ask, too. Do you think you could be the one to ask? If not, why not?

Note: The same with telephone calls. I remember sitting around not wanting to leave the house just in case "he" called. Today, many girls just pick up the phone and call the boy themselves.

KISSING So many boys and girls have asked me when is the right age to start kissing the person you like. Since I've been told about Spin the Bottle games that were played as early as third grade, it would be hard to give you an age to go by.

Sometimes Spin the Bottle and other kissing games are practice to see if you think you'll like kissing someone for real. There's a difference between kissing games and really kissing someone you call your boyfriend or girlfriend. So often, in early kissing games, no one really kisses anyway.

Think back to the "going out" chapter, when I talked about when kids said they started having boyfriends or girlfriends. Sixth, seventh grade? Usually when you have reached the point where you're "going out" and have picked one person that you'd like to be with more than anyone else, you might be ready to kiss that person. But there isn't any rule, since many boys and girls are not ready until much later.

Besides, it doesn't matter much when other kids are ready. The important question is, "What about you?" You'll be ready when *you're* ready, no matter when anyone else is ready. As far as when it's okay for you to be ready, that's a good question to talk about with your parents.

If you're thinking to yourself, "There's no way I'm going to talk with my parents about kissing!" here's a great idea for dinner table conversation. "Hey, Dad. When was the first time you kissed a girl? Oh, would you pass the ketchup, please?" Or: "Mom, this is a little embarrassing, but did you ever play kissing games at parties? Can I have more salad, please?" If your parent falls off the chair, you'll know they were paying attention!

I was just kidding about the chair. But, really, do you see how you can slip in a question or two, if you're just sitting around together, having a meal, driving somewhere in the car, or helping in the kitchen? You'll find you really can learn a lot from your parents, if you try. But they may not be able to guess you're ready for certain answers unless you bring up the questions. It can also be a relief to know you can go to your parents for information about personal things (that your friends may already think you understand). If you find that your parents make a joke and fool around instead of giving you a serious, real answer, it may be that they're not comfortable with your question or with the fact that you were ready to ask. Let them know you want to be taken seriously.

Spin the Bottle is one of the very early kissing games (if you mention it to your parents, they'll probably smile and tell you some funny old stories). That's when a bunch of boys and girls sit around in a circle and one person spins a soda (pop) bottle in the middle. If a girl is spinning, the nearest boy that the bottle points to is "it." If a boy is spinning, the bottle has to point to a nearest girl. The person who spun the bottle and the person who's "it" then go to another room or behind a door or wherever, and are supposed to kiss. Or, as eleven-year-old Stephanie said, "You just run over and kiss. It only takes a couple of seconds!"

Mark, now twenty, remembers his first game of Spin the Bottle. Mark said, "I was so scared. I didn't know what to do. I thought of ducking or getting up to get a snack or something, but it was too late. The bottle pointed to me and my heart started beating so fast. The girl I was supposed to kiss went with me into the back room of my friend's basement and I told her I didn't know what to do. She said not to worry, just go like this (she puckered her lips to show me). Then she touched my lips with hers. That was my first kiss. I remember thinking, 'Hey, this is great! I like this! I hope I get picked again.' "

Judy, age thirty-two, shared, "One time, I was invited to a party at a girlfriend's house. And they did all those things like Spin the Bottle and Postman, where the person who got the 'letter' was supposed to go behind the door and kiss the 'postman.' " Judy said that when she was picked, the boy who went behind the door with her said, "Let's pretend we're kissing!"

Danny, age thirteen, said, "The big thing at our parties was kissing contests. We all sat around and timed how long the couples who were going together could kiss."

That kind of kissing, though lips were touching and the people were going out together, is more like a game. It's one of the ways that kids can find out if they want to think differently about kissing. It's also one of the ways kids lead into more tingly, sexual, one-to-one kissing. When will these feelings happen? For each boy and girl, the answer will be different.

Bobby, age fifteen, shared that his first "real" kissing was with a girl-friend at a party in the basement of his friend's house. All the lights were out and everyone was with someone. Bobby said, "We were holding each other, but no one really knew what to do. We were too scared to try anything else but kissing and it was nice to feel close. I remember peeking out from the corner of my eye to see what other people were doing."

TOUCHING Often kissing and being close can cause you to want to touch other parts of each other's bodies. Touching places like the breasts and the genitals can make boys or girls feel very aroused. Since these feelings are so personal, it's not surprising that different people will have different reactions. Such feelings can be exciting and confusing at the same time. Exciting, because they can stir up inner warmth in the genital area. Confusing, especially when a boy or girl has never felt them with another person before. Two people may feel very close and good but not be sure where the feelings will lead, or even if they should be having such feelings. Sometimes religious beliefs can add to the confusion if a person has been taught that these feelings are wrong. (It might help to talk with your parent or a religious leader so that you can understand your feelings and not feel guilty.)

When Sexual Feelings Build

When two people allow themselves to go that far sexually, the feelings can start to build and get stronger. Touching in this way can lead to orgasm (page 69). Sometimes the feelings can take people by surprise because they're so strong. The stronger the feelings, the harder they can be to control, and the harder it can be to stop. It's difficult to say "no" when the sharing feels so good.

Too many kids are positive they can handle these feelings and will be able to stop when they want to, but they really can't or won't. Too many are afraid that their girlfriend or boyfriend will be upset or won't "go out" with them anymore if they try to stop. Boys as well as girls might not want to be known as a "prude" (someone who won't share themselves sexually). Boys are often pressured into continuing even if they don't feel ready, don't want to, or aren't in the mood, because many people mistakenly expect that "boys always want sex." And so, to keep up the impression of being sexy and strong, they keep going, because to them it seems too much like being a loser to say, "Let's stop."

It would be sad for any boy or girl to end up in a situation where passion or pressures—instead of their brains—are telling them what to do. One tingly feeling can lead to another and another and another. It takes a very strong boy or girl to reach the point of having such feelings and be able to say in the middle of having them, "I think we'd better stop!" When you go past your comfort zone or past where you know you can handle what you're doing (or the possible results), that's when you can get into trouble.

Too often kids think that sexual intercourse (Chapter 2, page 18) is where all sexual feelings have to lead. Now you know this is just not true. You have many ways to express sexual feelings that can be more appropriate for your age and where you're at.

Feelings About Sexual Pressure

Pressure can rob you of your free choice, if you let it. Imagine being pressured into sexual sharing when you don't want to or aren't ready.

Here are some questions to think about:

- How good do you think it would feel to share sexually because of pressure?
- How much fun do you think you would have if you felt forced to share more than your comfort allows?
- How do you think you'd feel about your girlfriend or boyfriend if they kept trying to force you to share more?
- How much respect would they have for you?
- How much respect would you have for yourself if you gave in?
- If they don't go out with you again because you didn't share yourself more, how much do you think you meant to them? (Do you think they wanted to go out with you for who you are or for what they could get from you sexually?)
- How far would you let yourself go just because it's expected of you, not because you're ready and truly want to go further?
- What do you think would happen if you couldn't or didn't stop?

The decision to have sexual intercourse or share yourself sexually in any close way should not be about:

- being pressured into it
- thinking this will make you more important to the person you're going out with
- thinking that sexual intercourse is a ticket to self-esteem
- saying yes because you feel you "should"—due to pressure within yourself or from your partner
- just wanting to get it over with
- wanting to no longer feel left out when other people talk about sex
- allowing this to happen to you because you've been drinking or using other drugs and are no longer in control

Figure that at some point while growing up, you'll probably have to deal with sexual pressure—from the person you're going out with, talk among friends, as well as other influences such as movies. Many kids seem to think sex is just expected. That can create even more pressure and cause some kids to feel, "I'm the only one left who hasn't had sex!" or "What's wrong with me?" if they choose to wait.

Nothing is wrong. There are males as well as females who have not yet experienced sexual intercourse and choose to abstain from sex (not have sex) until they're married or at least until they're at an adult age. No one has a right to rush or pressure or force your decision about sexual sharing. No one has a right to make this decision for you. This is a very personal choice. You can choose to remain in control of what you allow yourself to do.

If you feel comfortable that you are sharing what you feel is right for you, according to your values—and you feel you can also handle what the consequences (emotional as well as physical) might be, then you'll have greater freedom to enjoy what you share.

If You're Going Out with Someone Younger or Older

Maggie is fifteen and her boyfriend is seventeen. When she started going out with him, she told me that she talked with him about not being comfortable going past a certain point sexually. She figured that he might expect her to do what older girls in his own class would do, but she wasn't ready. She felt a lot better letting him know her limits at the beginning of their relationship—before she started going out with him—so she wouldn't wonder all the time if he would be upset that she wasn't going farther. She told him, "If you can't handle that, then we shouldn't go out." He said he understood and it was okay.

Boys can also feel this pressure when they go out with girls who are older. Sometimes the pressure can be strong because boys seem to be expected to just "know" what they're doing sexually, even if they're younger. Of course that's not fair.

When Danny (now twenty-seven) was sixteen, he remembers feeling very clumsy and embarrassed when it came to sexual sharing with his girlfriend. He told me, "There I was. I had this great chance to finally 'do' something. And I didn't have any idea what to do. So I did nothing." Maybe you have felt the same way.

Jimmy, age fifteen, shared, "I don't know what to do with my girlfriend because we just started going out and she's much younger. I'm afraid to try anything." Kevin, age sixteen, told me, "It's really annoying. My girlfriend is younger than me and she's not ready for anything!"

Lots of boys who have gone out with someone younger have talked with me about their confusion as to what might be "right" to try. Many girls have also talked about such confusion when going out with someone older or younger.

It would help for boys and girls to understand that whether someone is younger or older, it would be wrong to have any expectations because of their age. The person you go out with could be an older person with less sexual experience or a younger person with more. The person with less experience could be more ready to share sexually than the person with more. Or the reverse could be true.

So, just knowing someone's age doesn't tell you anything except how old they are! Each person needs to be taken for who they are. If you're respectful of each other, talk about what you choose to share, ask and make sure that if it's okay to do what you'd like to do together, and honor what the other person says is their limit (how far they say it's okay to go and when they want to stop), then you'll be fine. If you know you've set limits that are right for you, you'll find that sexual sharing can be more fun and feel great. You'll be freer to share as much as you choose and be able to trust that your own limits will be respected.

What About Sexual Intercourse? What About Pregnancy?

I strongly believe that sexual intercourse is not for kids—and that the safest, most appropriate decision for kids to make is abstinence (choosing not to have sexual intercourse). But I know that no matter how strongly I feel or how strongly your own parents feel about this, the reality is that millions of kids don't agree. And so it's no wonder that unwanted results of sexual intercourse are happening as early as the upper elementary school, middle school, and junior high school levels. That scares me.

I can only hope you'll seriously read the following information so you can get your facts straight and your feelings sorted out. Even if you're thinking, "Here we go again. I've already heard this at least five hundred times!" you never know what you might learn a little differently. And it's important to double-check that the information you believe you know is as correct as it must be. You just might be reminded of something that can save you years of feeling sorry. I especially hope you'll be sure to pay close attention to all the risks of consequences you don't want in order to make safer, better, more appropriate sexual decisions for yourself.

No matter what I share with you, or how many times your parents, teachers, and other adults in your life talk with you about preventing unwanted sexual results, not using drugs, and not drinking (or using other drugs) and driving—the truth is, we're not going to be there with you when you end up having to make these serious decisions. I know I won't be at your parties, won't be in the car, at the movies, at the fraternity house (or wherever) with you and your girlfriend or boyfriend. Neither will your parents, teachers, or all the other adults in your life who are so concerned about what you're allowing yourself to do. You're going to be on your own when you make these serious decisions.

When your limits are tested, probably no one will be looking over your shoulder whispering, "Hey . . . wait. Are you sure you understand what you're about to let yourself do? Are you sure you really do understand the risks?" What you do will be your choice. And it's going to be up to you to make sure you keep yourself in control.

Even if you believe you're being responsible and serious about avoiding unwanted consequences, you may be basing your decisions on incorrect knowledge. If that's the case, you may still be taking serious risks. To be as safe as possible, take the time to read through the following information. That way, you can make sure that what you believe you already know is accurate and fully understood.

Risks Related to Sexual Intercourse

Pregnancy—A woman becomes pregnant when a male sperm enters an egg cell. An egg can be fertilized if it is present in the Fallopian tubes around the time of intercourse.

Sperm are able to stay alive inside a woman for several days after sexual intercourse. Even if the egg cell wasn't present in the Fallopian tube at the exact time of sexual intercourse, if it is released (this is called ovulation) days later, live sperm could still be there, able to penetrate the egg cell.

Some truths about becoming pregnant that are often misunderstood. A girl or woman *can* get pregnant:

a) If she has sexual intercourse just once (even the first time).

b) If she has sexual intercourse during her period. (Remember, it's possible the egg will be released several days later, when sperm cells are still alive.)

c) If she has intercourse sitting, lying, standing on her head, or in any other position.

d) If she doesn't actually have sexual intercourse but ejaculation happens near or just outside the opening of the vagina (sperm can "swim in").

e) Even if she's "just a kid." There's no big mystery about getting pregnant. It's very clear. If egg cells are being released and sperm cells are allowed "in," then any girl or woman is definitely taking a chance on becoming pregnant.

So, it's safest to figure that *any time* ejaculation happens inside the vagina or close enough (just outside the opening of the vagina) so that the sperm cells can "swim in," there is a chance that pregnancy will result.

Being pregnant and having a child can be incredibly wonderful when the experience comes at the right time in your life. But pregnancy and all the responsibilities of having and caring for a child can be a very difficult, even scary experience that's much too much to handle if it occurs before you're ready.

If you risk having sexual intercourse and become pregnant, you will not only have to deal with the pregnancy, but also with how having a baby changes your life.

Having a baby is a twenty-four-hour-a-day responsibility. Although they may be adorable, cuddly, fun, and very huggable, real babies are not like dolls. They can't be put away when you're finished playing with them. Besides being loved, babies need to be fed, clothed, and cared for completely. A baby's needs are more important than—and may keep you from—school, homework, parties, vacations, sports, movies . . . anything. And you've got to have enough money to be able to pay for a child's needs.

There are an increasing number of high schools that are offering baby and child care for young mothers so they can still go to school. That's a help. But it doesn't change all the other responsibilities and restrictions once the mother goes home. A kid who has a kid, even if she can continue in school, is still forced to grow up faster than she might ever have dreamed, ever have wanted. That doesn't mean she won't love her child. It just means the timing was too soon.

If a girl loves her child but doesn't love the fact that she has that child, then all her love may not be strong enough to prevent resentment and frustration from building up. It becomes easier to understand why many babies can become neglected and abused.

There are girls and boys who become parents when they're very young who do love their children and are able to find happiness as young parents. But for too many kids who really would love to have the freedom to grow up more slowly—and have the time to explore and decide what direction they wish to take in their lives—becoming pregnant and being a kid with a kid is a sad, often tragic mistake.

A better idea would be not to risk pregnancy in the first place.

Who Needs to Take Responsibility to Prevent Pregnancy from Happening?

Both partners—girls as well as boys. Some people say, "Oh, look what he did to her!" when they hear that a girl has gotten pregnant. But the truth is, except for forced sex (rape) situations, the girl allowed herself to risk becoming pregnant as much as the boy allowed the possibility of pregnancy to be risked.

Pregnancy is another risk that kids usually don't take seriously until it actually happens. Then it's too late. The only way to be sure to protect yourself from pregnancy is to first have your facts straight. Understand everything there is to know about conception and how to prevent pregnancy from happening. Then, you must be clear about what your limits need to be—and clearly let your partner know ahead of time what these limits are. That way there's no confusion, no mixed messages about sex. And then, stay in control (definitely don't get drunk or use other drugs) so that you can always know what you're allowing yourself to do.

How You Might Tell if You're Pregnant

- If you skip your period.
- If your breasts are sensitive and start feeling a bit fuller.
- If you're nauseous (sick to your stomach, possibly even feeling like vomiting). You might have heard the term "morning sickness." But this feeling can also be later in the day.
- If you're extra-tired much of the time.
- If it's harder to close your zippers and it seems that you're gaining weight.
- If you need to urinate more often than usual. (As a pregnancy progresses and the fetus continues to grow, the uterus enlarges and presses more and more on its next-door neighbor, the bladder. This doesn't interfere with the function of the bladder, but since the bladder stores urine, you end up having to urinate more and more frequently.)

If you have pain (often sharp) in the area of the lower abdomen (lower belly), and you know you risked becoming pregnant, this could mean you have a *tubal pregnancy* (TOO-bull). Instead of "planting" itself in the lining of the uterus, the fertilized egg cell plants itself in the Fallopian tube by mistake.

Because the Fallopian tube is not made to expand and expand as the uterus can, the developing egg cell if left untreated can cause the Fallopian tube to burst. If it does, poisons can get into the body and cause bad infections, even death.

A tubal pregnancy is an *emergency* and must be treated by a doctor right away. If you suspect you could be experiencing this condition, tell a parent and call your doctor immediately. You can go to the emergency room of a hospital for help.

(This is just another reason that it's so important to know as much as you can about your body and different signs of pregnancy and diseases, especially if you're sexually active.)

If you risk becoming pregnant, it's also important to be aware that smoking, drinking alcohol, using any drug, or taking in caffeine can seriously affect the development of a fetus. Even before you know you're pregnant, you could be harming your child.

It's also possible to be pregnant without a beginning sign. And it doesn't mean you're definitely pregnant if you have any of these signs. For example, when girls start getting their periods, it's common to skip a period and even skip again and again. In these cases, the skipping doesn't mean being pregnant.

The key question is whether or not you had sexual intercourse or if a boy ejaculated close to the opening of your vagina. If the answer is "yes," then it's certainly possible for you to be pregnant. If you then start noticing changes in your body, it's important for you to have a pregnancy test.

To test for pregnancy, you either must have a blood test (a sample of blood is taken by a needle placed in a vein in your arm) or a urine test (more people choose the urine test). The clinic or office where this will be done will give you special instructions, like making sure to take a sample of the first urination in the morning, how to keep it pure for testing, and so on.

There are also tests that you can buy in pharmacies and do yourself. But the instructions have to be followed perfectly, and the tests are not always completely accurate.

Besides the blood or urine test, you'll need to have a pelvic examination so that a doctor can actually check to see if there are any changes in the color of your cervix ("neck" of the uterus, page 16) and feel if your uterus seems a bit larger than its normal size. These changes will let the doctor make sure whether or not you're pregnant and can also give you a better idea as to how many weeks or months pregnant you are.

It's also important to have a pelvic exam once a year if you've started having sexual intercourse, to make sure that all is fine with your inside sexual organs. Many girls think, "I'm not going to let anyone examine me *there!*" But special instruments make this examination easier than you might imagine. The doctor examining you will probably be very sensitive to how nervous you might be and how much you might wish you weren't there—especially when it's your first visit. Have the doctor explain the whole exam to you, make sure you ask any questions (no question is too silly), and if you don't understand the answer, ask again.

You can look in the phone book under "Birth Control Information" to find listings for labs, clinics, and health centers that do pregnancy testing. You can call to find out what you need to know about taking the test, how much it will cost, how long you should wait to take the test after missing your period (usually ten days to two weeks, sometimes less), when you can be tested, and so on.

Feelings About Telling Your Parents, Feelings About Yourself

You may have strong feelings about telling your parents you're taking a pregnancy test, even stronger feelings if the test results are positive—not only about dealing with your parents' response but also how you feel about yourself.

A girl in the eighth grade asked me, "If you were pregnant and you were only thirteen and were three months along, would you tell your mother, even though your mother has warned you that if you ever got pregnant she would kill you, or do something threatening? And your best friend is the only one that knows. And she said she'd help you through it. What would you do? Please help me!"

Yes, I'd tell your mother (and father). No matter what she threatened, when it comes down to it, she needs to help you. And you need her help. She probably thought those threats would scare you enough to keep you away from having sexual intercourse.

My sense is that "threats" and "don'ts" from parents, teachers, or anyone else aren't powerful enough. Kids won't really make their own limits—and be strong about them—unless they truly believe that the limits are a must. By that I mean, unless they—*for themselves*—don't want to take a chance on results that could mess up their lives—or change their lives in a way they're just not ready for and don't want. Would threats from your parents be enough to scare you into making sexual limits and really being strict about those limits? What would it take?

It's great that the eighth grader's friend will be there to care, to talk with, to cry with. But that can't take the place of a parent's guidance and support. No, I don't pretend to know that girl's mother. And I can't promise that any parent would be happy about this situation. But the only way to find out if she'd really be there for her is to take a chance and let her know. She can say to her mom or dad (or both), "Mom, this is one of the hardest things I've ever had to tell you. I know I went against your wishes. You threatened me to make sure this didn't happen. But I hope you won't be so angry that you won't help me. I didn't mean to get pregnant. I guess I never believed it would happen to me. Please, I don't want to go to anyone else for help. Please help me."

And if her parent doesn't respond in a helpful way, she needs to seek out another adult: grandparent, aunt or uncle, older (adult-aged) brother or sister, religious leader, family doctor, school counselor, health or other teacher, school nurse. She can also find guidance at local health centers or clinics, or woman's health care and birth control information centers, and through organizations that offer referrals for residence homes for pregnant girls.

If you're wondering why I keep writing a similar list over and over again of whom you might approach for help, I'm hoping that the choices will become so familiar to you that you can always realize if one person isn't helpful, you can seek out the next and the next. You don't ever have to handle difficult situations alone. It may help to reread page 212 (in Chapter 15, "Peer Pressure"), in order to approach your parents (or anyone) honestly and directly when situations are very difficult.

It's also important to remember that a positive pregnancy test doesn't mean you're a bad person. You might have made a bad or unfortunate mistake, but not even a pregnancy years too early can take away from who you are, unless you let it. You can *decide* not to let it. Understand that somehow, you'll deal with this, because you have to. In one way or another. Reach out for support. Counseling can be very important, not only to make decisions related to the pregnancy but also to help you cope with your feelings and relationships, and move forward as best you can.

It's important to take seriously what people in these counseling sessions share with you. If they try to offer information about birth control or your own personal ability to set limits and you've "heard that before," try to let it "sink in" differently. Those counselors know that too many kids, no matter how sincere they are at the moment or how horrified they are about being pregnant at the moment, will actually allow themselves to become pregnant again, and sometimes again—even if they vowed they'd never do that again. Don't fall into the trap of being too casual. If it happened to you once, it can certainly happen again. If you let it. The idea is to be totally aware of and in control of what you allow yourself to do. You don't have to let yourself take even *one* chance.

If people around you push you away because you're pregnant (friends, close family members, or anyone), giving you the idea that they feel you're bad, no good, or an embarrassment to the family, just try to hold on. The more you understand that most people aren't prepared for things like this to happen to them, and that most people—even parents—may worry about "what the neighbors will think," the better chance you'll have to keep on feeling good about yourself (even if you feel bad about what has happened).

Many parents feel that what their children do is a reflection on how good they have been as parents. So they might find it hard to put aside any difficult feelings of anger or guilt in order to be able to concentrate on helping you. And, as always, there really are parents who will be there, no matter what. They'll offer support, go with you for tests, help arrange for counseling, and be there to talk with you to help you deal with this, no matter what the time of day or night.

Just remember that even "with it" parents might fall apart when faced with this kind of tough situation. It's hard to know how they'll handle it. The only thing for sure is that it has to be handled. And it's too much for you to handle by yourself.

One more thing. It's possible that a girl who becomes pregnant will be very angry with her boyfriend and blame him for "making" her pregnant. It's also possible for parents to say, "Look what he did to my daughter!"

Remember, it may be hard to face, but unless you're forced to have sex (that is, raped, page 274), you have a choice. And if you really let him make your sexual decisions for you, and you lacked the strength and ability to take charge of your own actions, you can learn to be stronger about your limits next time.

If Your Girlfriend Gets Pregnant
Jeff, now in his thirties, talked with me about the agony he experienced several years ago when a girl he went out with became pregnant. Said

Jeff, "She wasn't even my girlfriend. I just went out with her a few times. But she was sure that she was pregnant because of me and I knew that was possible. I was devastated, deeply upset. And I had a lot of trouble dealing with her decision to have an abortion. I'll never forget how I felt when she told me. I was sick inside. I kept thinking, 'I'm the father of that child. That's *my* child . . . who I'll never know.' I walked for hours that night and just cried."

Whether or not a boy has the opportunity to offer support and continue to be involved with his pregnant girlfriend, it can be very important for him to sort out and deal with his own feelings. Talking with parents or a counselor (or any of the people suggested in the previous section) can offer relief and understanding. These people can also supply information that will help prevent another unwanted pregnancy from happening.

If you need to approach parents or anyone for help, you can always hold on to this opening line: "This is very hard for me to say. But, I think that _____ is pregnant and I'm very upset. I need to talk with you. . . ."

If you're going to a counselor, you can say, "My girlfriend just found out she's pregnant and I'm having a hard time dealing with this."

Be sure that pregnancy is confirmed by a laboratory test, not a do-it-yourself home test.

Helping a Pregnant Friend or Girlfriend Get Help

If your girlfriend is getting help, good. If she's not planning to go for help, or is so confused that she doesn't know what to do or where to turn, it is extremely important to let a counselor, your parents, or whomever you can turn to, know. Then, besides dealing with your own feelings, you can get advice as to what you can say to your girlfriend so she can take the first step for help.

Just remember, as with any difficult problem that someone else must deal with for themselves, such as alcohol abuse, you can do only so much. You can't go for help *for* the other person. It's not your responsibility to act for your girlfriend, only to try to get her to act for herself. You can plead with her to try to go for counseling and at least try to talk with her parents. You can keep her company, hold her hand, listen to what she needs to share. But it's very tough to drag someone in for help against their will. Girls who are pregnant may shy away from going for help because they're so scared and don't know how to deal with how others will respond.

If you're frustrated and very upset that your girlfriend isn't getting the help she needs as quickly as you know she must, you might say (turning feelings into words):

"It's really hard for me to watch you go around making believe that there's no problem (or, not getting any help). I feel like shaking you and shouting, 'What are you doing to yourself . . . why aren't you dealing with this?' Maybe you think if you wait long enough, the pregnancy will just go away. It won't. It's real and it's just going to be a bigger and bigger problem unless you deal with this *now* and figure out what you need to do to take care of yourself. Too much time has already passed. If you're scared, I'll go with you to speak with someone. You don't have to deal with this by yourself."

The best you can do is remind her how important it is to get help *quickly*, offering as many suggestions as possible . . . and hope she'll act upon the suggestions.

Another choice, although difficult, is to talk with her parents and let them know how upset you are that she's not approaching them for help. This is very sensitive and, for most kids, probably very difficult. It's natural to feel that way. It also depends upon the kind of relationship you have with her and her parents. If you can't talk with them personally, you might ask a good friend of hers to approach them. It's not a good choice for her to go on without telling anyone.

If an Unplanned Pregnancy Happens

Once again, if you become pregnant, you should go for help. If your girlfriend becomes pregnant, you deserve similar support—either separately or together. It's of vital importance not to deal with this alone.

Here are some choices to consider:
- Give birth and raise your child as a single or married parent.
- Give birth and give your child up for adoption. This means you give up all rights to your child.

- Have an abortion.
  - An abortion is a procedure during which a doctor removes the embryo or fetus from the wall of the uterus so it won't develop any further. An abortion removes and ends a pregnancy.
  - Although abortion is legal in every state, the length of time during which a woman has the legal right to make this decision (starting from the beginning of pregnancy) varies from state to state. After this set time, the only reason an abortion can be allowed is if the mother's life is in danger.
  - Each state also differs on whether parental consent (permission) is required in order to have an abortion.

It's very important that each of these choices be explained, discussed, and thought through, if possible, with parents and family as well as a counselor—or at least with another adult who is trained to offer such guidance. While support from friends can mean a lot, it's necessary to seek out help from an adult when dealing with this kind of serious life decision.

With this kind of guidance a pregnant girl or the boy involved can better understand and be more prepared to deal with the issues and emotions and all the legal rules that apply to each choice.

These are some of the considerations that are important to think over when making a choice: feelings of all persons involved (the girl who is pregnant, the girl's parents, the boy who is involved, and all significant others), values, age, finances, family involvement, support, school, the health of the girl, and so forth. And, it is especially important to consider the welfare and physical and emotional health of the child (for example, who will have the ability to fully care for and meet the needs of that child).

What makes it so critical to examine each choice fully is that certain ones are for keeps. There's no taking the baby back months after he or she is given up for adoption (rules can vary in different states), no way to recapture the pregnancy that has been ended if a girl has an abortion.

Each choice has a very serious meaning. It will not only affect life at the moment but can make a difference in the the rest of that girl's (and boy's) life, as well as the life of their child. This decision can be very emotional. Understanding why a choice may be appropriate does not mean it will be easy to make or live with. Continued counseling or participation in a support group after a choice is made can be very helpful in working through all the feelings that might be involved.

Aside from health clinics, women's health-care centers, and family planning centers, referrals for counseling and other kinds of support can be gotten through religious organizations such as the Office of Family Ministries or the Jewish Family Services. You can also ask information for pregnancy hotlines.

More About Abortion
There are girls who think that if they get pregnant, it's no big deal, they'll just have an abortion. Those who feel this way often aren't aware of the difficult emotions that can be involved with such a decision. They often don't think about the fact that any procedure carries with it possible risks. And they seem to place little or no value on the meaning of conception.

There are many different feelings about abortion, as it is a very emotional topic. The following will give you an idea of what different people believe:

- There are people who are strongly against abortion and feel it should not be legal. They don't believe women should be able to have the freedom to choose to have an abortion. (This belief is often referred to as "pro-life.")
- There are people who are strongly in favor of abortion and feel it should be legal. They believe it is a woman's right to have the freedom to choose. (This belief is often referred to as "pro-choice.")
- There are people who feel that abortion is murder (and therefore morally wrong) because they feel a human life begins as soon as the egg cell has been fertilized (at conception).
- There are people who feel that abortion is not murder (and therefore not morally wrong) because they do not consider the developing egg a human being.

If you haven't already spoken about this with your parents, it would probably be worthwhile and interesting to do so. They may have similar or other feelings they would wish to talk about with you. Their feelings may strongly relate to their religious principles.

If a girl does choose to have an abortion—and the procedure is performed properly and the girl is in good health—it should not interfere with future ability to give birth. The earlier in the pregnancy an abortion is performed, the safer it is. The further along in a pregnancy an abortion takes place, the more complicated the procedure.

The best solution for the problem of unwanted pregnancy is not to get pregnant in the first place. You can decide not to allow yourself to take even one chance.

Preventing Pregnancy Through Birth Control

Birth control methods or *contraceptives* (con-tra-SEP-tives) are used as protection against becoming pregnant or causing someone to become pregnant. The very surest, 100 percent safest method of birth control is abstinence, simply *not* having sexual intercourse and *not* allowing ejaculation to happen very close to the opening of the vagina (remember, sperm can "swim in").

If partners choose to have sexual intercourse, there are several birth control methods that can offer preventive measures against risks and unwanted consequences. Although these methods can't guarantee absolute 100 percent protection as abstinence can, they can be very effective in preventing pregnancy as well as sexually transmitted infections, including HIV (the virus that causes AIDS) if used *properly* (when partners follow the exact instructions).

Here are some of the more popular methods:

THE CONDOM: Also called a "rubber," the condom offers good protection against pregnancy and is simple to use, harmless, and easily purchased at a pharmacy, discount store, "quick" stop, and elsewhere.

Most condoms are made of a thin but strong form of rubber called latex (LAY-tex). They're made to fit (roll onto) on the penis, and look like one finger of a rubber glove. With a condom, when a man ejaculates, his semen collects inside the tip of the condom instead of passing inside his partner.

Latex condoms are also very, very important to use as protection from HIV (the virus that causes AIDS [Acquired Immune Deficiency Syndrome]) and from other types of sexually transmitted diseases (diseases passed from one person to another during sex). Only latex condoms should be used, as these can significantly reduce the risk of pregnancy or infection.

The idea is that if sperm can't get to the egg, there will be no possibility of pregnancy. If you are protected from infected semen, discharges, or sores in the genital area that could be contagious (con-TAY-juss, "catching," able to spread infection), there is less chance of your getting sexually transmitted diseases.

This method of birth control is quite effective by itself but can be even more effective if a woman uses contraceptive foam, sponges, creams, or jellies at the same time a man uses a condom. Use of contraceptive creams or jellies on the condom itself can also add protection.

A female condom is available which is made of plastic and is designed to fit inside a woman's vagina. It is presently not considered as effective as the latex male condom.

CONTRACEPTIVE FOAMS, SPONGES, CREAMS, AND JELLIES These methods of birth control are simple for women to use, and can be bought without a prescription from a pharmacy. Using these in addition to the use of a condom by the male can further reduce risk.

Although each of them is slightly different, the main idea is that they are inserted into the vagina so the spermicides they contain can destroy the sperm and prevent them from going through the cervix. If sperm can't live and pass through to where they could meet the egg cell, there will be little or no possibility of pregnancy. Spermicide can also kill infectious agents. (But remember that using these *in addition* to a condom can further reduce risk of pregnancy or sexually transmitted diseases.)

BIRTH CONTROL PILLS When a woman takes hormone pills, her hormone level stays high throughout the month, fooling her body into behaving chemically as it would if it were pregnant. There is no chemical signal to remind the ovaries to ripen another egg cell. If no egg cell matures, there will be no ovulation (release of an egg). If no egg cell is released, there will be no egg that could be fertilized in the Fallopian tube. So even if sperm are present in the Fallopian tube, fertilization cannot take place.

So, the main idea of the pill is to prevent ovulation. If there is no egg cell, there will be no possibility of pregnancy. These pills, which can be very effective, must be prescribed by a doctor. They have some side effects and risks that are important for a doctor to explain before anyone decides to take them.

While birth control pills can be very effective in preventing pregnancy, they offer no protection from infection (HIV and other sexually transmitted diseases). That's why, as with the other methods discussed, it's very important to also use condom protection even if the woman is taking birth control pills.

THE DIAPHRAGM The diaphragm (DIE-uh-fram) is made of soft rubber shaped like a dome with a rim, and must be measured and fitted by a doctor.

It is inserted into a woman's vagina and moved into place so that it can block the cervix and prevent sperm from passing through. In order to be effective, it must be used with a spermicidal cream (the chemicals in the cream destroy sperm on contact).

Here, again, the idea is that if no sperm pass through toward the Fallopian tubes, they won't be able to fertilize an egg cell. Thus, no pregnancy.

The diaphragm combined with the condom offers very good protection from pregnancy, as long as it is used strictly according to the instructions.

THE RHYTHM METHOD Some people refer to this as the natural or calendar method.

The egg cell can live for about two days after it is released, and sperm cells can live inside a woman after ejaculation for about five or six days. So the idea of the rhythm method is to avoid having intercourse right before and during ovulation, and then wait long enough after so that the egg and sperm won't be there at the same time. *Caution:* I'm mentioning this method only because you may be one of those people who think, "Natural is best." It's risky to have the attitude, "All I have to do is not have intercourse when the egg is there and I'll be free to use nothing (no protection) the rest of the month!"

The special mathematical formula that helps figure which days of the month to avoid usually gives the amount of time to wait to have intercourse as about two weeks. And many young couples aren't so patient. However, even with this calendar method, there is no absolute guarantee that the egg won't be there anyway.

So if pregnancy would be a terrible mistake for you or your partner, this is definitely *not* a method to count on.

If, because of religious beliefs, this is the only method you can consider, speak with your doctor or birth control counselor in order to get more information about ways to be as exact as possible using the rhythm method.

WITHDRAWAL Another method that people think is a form of birth control, although it is *not—withdrawal*:
Many people think that if a boy or man just "pulls out," or removes his penis from the vagina before ejaculating, then pregnancy won't happen. But there is still a chance that it will.

Probably neither partner will notice the few drops of semen that leak out of the penis before ejaculation even happens (see Chapter 6, page 67). It's also possible for a little semen to drop on or near the opening of the vagina while the penis is being removed. Even if the penis is removed "in time" (before ejaculation), that little bit of semen can contain enough sperm to fertilize an egg cell (as well as transmit infection).

If no form of birth control is being used, withdrawing the penis before ejaculation is better than not trying at all to prevent pregnancy. But if you or your partner absolutely don't want to deal with a pregnancy, don't count on being safe by withdrawing.

Withdrawal also provides *no* protection against sexually transmitted diseases.

Using Birth Control Methods Properly Is a Must
Even if a method of birth control is considered to be very effective, it will not work well if the person using it doesn't fully understand what to do. For example, if a diaphragm is used without the contraceptive cream, it might as well be thrown out the window! It won't be of any

value. If the contraceptive foam isn't inserted as directed and within the exact time period specified (some must be inserted no more than fifteen minutes before intercourse), it won't offer the protection needed.

If you choose to have sexual intercourse, you need to know as much as you can. Even with the condom, which may seem so simple, it's not just a matter of buying one in a pharmacy and knowing that it rolls onto the penis. There's much more to be understood in order to get the best protection possible. Here's the kind of information that anyone who is buying or using a condom needs to know:

Selecting a condom/condom care
- Always use a latex condom (not a natural or lamb-skin condom).
- Use a U.S.-approved name-brand condom.
- Use a lubricated condom (do not use this for oral sex).
- Condom package should still be sealed (don't use condoms from a package that has been punctured).
- Do not use Vaseline or any other oil-based lubricant or lotion because it can destroy the latex (rubber) of the condom. (Oil-based lubricants are not okay to use; water-based lubricants are okay to use. It's easier to just use a lubricated condom and not have to figure out what is okay.)
- Heat and moisture can cause damage to a condom (so it's not a good idea to keep them in a wallet for a long time).
- It's important to check the expiration date on the condom package.
- If someone has an allergic response to a lubricated condom, a latex non-lubricated condom can be used with a spermicidal jelly. (Researchers are developing and studying condoms from various materials that can be used by people who are allergic to latex.)

Actual Condom Use
- Put on the condom before any sexual contact with a partner. (Before ejaculation, a small amount of fluid

passes out of the tip of the penis. Contact with this pre-ejaculatory fluid can put a partner at risk of infection and/or becoming pregnant. That's why there should be *no* contact without condom protection.)

- Pinch the tip of the condom before rolling it on, so it won't get an air bubble.
- Leave about one quarter to one half inch of space at the tip of the condom (some condoms already have a tip) so there is room for the semen that is ejaculated. So, a good rule is: Pinch about an inch at the tip (even if the condom already has a tip, it's important to do this). Then, roll the condom on all the way to the base of the penis, making certain enough room at the tip is left for the semen.
- Be careful that jewelry or sharp fingernails don't put a hole in the condom when putting it on.
- Hold the condom at the base of the penis when withdrawing after ejaculation, so that it doesn't slide off and remain inside, letting the semen leak out.
- The male should withdraw before he starts to lose his erection. After ejaculation, because of the loss of erection, the condom will not fit as snugly, which might cause leakage of semen.

To push the point, there may be more to know than you think. True, some methods are simpler than others. If you are sexually active, just make sure you get your facts straight. And don't rely on your partner to know them for you. Don't assume—even if your partner is much more sexually experienced or older—that he or she "must know." People of all ages can have incorrect information. People sometimes try to take advantage. The only way to protect yourself the best you can is to take responsibility for yourself.

To get further information about birth control (and sexually transmitted diseases), you can talk with a parent (and other adult relatives), doctor, your health teacher, or a counselor at a family planning or health clinic, as well as check the library or search the Internet with your parent.

A Word About Birth Control Choices

Besides knowing about the different birth control methods, it's also important to realize that one method might be wiser and more appropriate than another. Here are some more issues to think about:

Frequency of intercourse (how often?)
- For example, it might not be appropriate for a woman who has intercourse once or twice a month to take birth control pills every day and have to deal with all the possible side effects. In that case, a condom combined with foam can be a much wiser choice.

How many partners?
- The more partners, the greater the chance of risking sexually transmitted infection as well as other diseases. (So it's very important not to have multiple partners and to carefully consider any partner. It's also important to keep in mind that all it takes is just one partner to contract sexually transmitted diseases, including HIV, if that partner is infected.) No matter what form of birth control is used, it is essential to also use a condom.

How cooperative will your partner be in using your method of choice?
- Birth control devices are not very effective if left in drawers, glove compartments, or pocketbooks. If you feel pressured by your partner into not using what you're prepared to use, maybe it's time to think about your relationship and how much respect your partner really could have for you (and him- or herself) to want to take a chance. If you don't use your protection, how much respect could you have for yourself?

What about the cost?
- Family planning and health clinics often offer counseling, supplies, and doctor services at a lower cost. *Just remember:* It costs much much more to raise a

child than any amount of money you might have to spend on birth control.

Although these are just some of the concerns to think about, I hope you'll begin to understand that there is a great deal of planning involved when considering a method of birth control. Each type of protection and any related concerns can be sorted out one at a time. If you're not sure of what to use, that's an especially good time to seek out some professional advice. At the very least, try one of your parents.

Parents and Dealing with Birth Control

Choosing the appropriate method of birth control is a decision that many parents would probably want to be part of. Before you tune out this section, thinking, "Not my parents—you don't know them!" consider this. Even if their parents don't approve, don't agree, and are very upset that their child is having sexual intercourse so early, some kids might be very surprised to learn that parents would still want to go to the doctor (or wherever) with them to deal with the decision about birth control.

Many parents want to be there for support, want to make sure they're giving proper guidance, or simply want to keep their child company when they go to the doctor's office or clinic. But they worry that talking about it will make their child think, "My parents must think that it's okay for me to have sex." While I can't promise that your parents will want to help you with your birth control decision, I can promise that you'll never know how involved they might want to be unless you take a chance. Try talking with them. Dig a little at your inside feelings and turn them into words. You might say something like: "I know you don't approve of my having sex. But I really don't want to lie to you. Please, I need your advice. Would you go with me to the clinic? I'd feel a lot better not going by myself."

The difference here is that you're not asking for their approval. You're letting them know that *you* know they absolutely *don't approve.* If you both understand each other, you'll have a better chance to go forward together from there.

If your parent says no, at least you tried. Realize that this usually is a very difficult, sensitive issue. If he or she (or both) says yes, then you will have taken another step forward in your relationship with them, another step closer. That can mean a lot.

Just Knowing Facts About How to Reduce Risk Isn't Enough

For example, just knowing that it's dangerous to get into a car with a driver who has been drinking or using other drugs doesn't guarantee that someone won't get in that car anyway. Just knowing about condoms and additional forms of protection doesn't guarantee they will be used properly—or at all.

So, while it's critical to have accurate factual knowledge, actually being able to act upon that knowledge is a different issue. Beyond knowing the facts, staying in control of risk usually has to do with valuing and respecting oneself and the other person, having self-confidence, being able to communicate honestly and clearly, and believing that the risks are real. If you're sexually active or planning to be, it might be important to answer for yourself:

- Do you use protection *every* time you have sexual intercourse or have close enough sexual sharing that ejaculation is near the opening of the vagina?
- If you and your partner don't have protection with you, would you decide not to have sexual intercourse at that time?
- Have you ever been in a situation without protection where you said to yourself, "Just this once . . . I won't ever do it again"?
- Has your partner ever said to you, "Oh, come on, just this once . . ." and did you give in?
- Have you ever chosen not to use a method of protection that you actually did have with you because your girlfriend or boyfriend didn't like that method?
- Have you ever lied to your boyfriend about being protected, like saying, "Oh, don't worry, I'm on the pill," when you really weren't?
- Have you ever been too embarrassed to talk with your partner about the use of protection and how to reduce risks?

- Have you ever not asked your partner if she was protected, knowing that you weren't, because you figured if she wanted to have sex with you and didn't seem to care about being protected, that would be her problem?
- Have you ever been too uncomfortable to ask your partner if he or she has a sexually transmitted disease or has risked becoming infected?
- Have you ever suspected that your partner was not telling you the complete truth? What did you do about it?
- Have you ever allowed yourself to have sexual intercourse—or other close sexual contact—without having any idea whether your partner had any other sexual partners before you?
- Have you ever allowed yourself to have sexual intercourse or other sexual contact without knowing if your partner—or your partner's past sexual partners— ever injected drugs? (HIV, the virus that causes AIDS, can be passed from an HIV-infected person to someone else through shared use of needles. No matter which way a person becomes HIV infected, he or she can pass the infection on—in the same or a different way. So a person who becomes HIV infected through shared needles can pass the infection on through sexual contact. And a person who becomes HIV infected through sexual contact can pass the infection on by sharing needles.

If you answered yes to any of these questions, you've already put yourself at risk. Depending upon what you allowed yourself to do, it may be important to talk with your doctor or local health clinic about the need to be tested for infection, and, if appropriate, to have a pregnancy test.

As I explain in the sexually transmitted disease section (page 253), some STDs have no symptoms (signs). Therefore, it's possible for you or your partner to be infected and not show any signs of infection. That's why it's so important to answer for yourself whether you have taken even one chance to become infected. If so, it's wise to check yourself out. If left untreated, STDs can cause serious permanent damage.

Also, if your answer is yes to the question of whether you put yourself at risk, don't continue any sexual contact until you are properly tested and treated, if necessary.

If you risked, you can't undo what you already did. But you can learn from your mistake, be stronger about your limits and make new decisions that will be safer. You can choose not to continue doing what you now know can put you at risk. It's in your control. You can decide to make healthier choices. *You* are in charge of *you*. *You* are responsible for *you*.

As far as being able to be honest with your partner, I realize many people will read the above questions and think to themselves, "I could never talk about those things! I could never ask!" Remember that even if you're embarrassed or uncomfortable, you can start with, "This is really hard for me to ask you . . ." When you're dealing with the need to prevent pregnancy as well as infection that could be serious enough to kill you, you should not remain silent. You must talk about this.

If you're sexually active—or planning to be sexually active—you owe it to yourself (and your partner) to push yourself to ask and talk about protection, past sexual experience, how to reduce risks as much as is possible. If you can't talk about such closeness, you're not ready to be so close. (Even if you can talk about it, you may still decide to wait.)

One more thing. The truth is, even if you do ask, it's possible your partner could lie. And some partners may not really know the true answer. Some may think they're telling you the truth and not be aware that, for example, a past partner injected drugs. It's hard to know.

That reality can be uncomfortable, even scary. But the idea is, to the best of your ability, if you're planning to be sexually active you need to find out what you can, so you can at least try to be as safe as is possible. And if you always properly use a latex condom (using a condom with spermicide can help reduce risk even further), you'll be doing what you can to stay in control of your risk.

It may help to realize that females as well as males can buy condoms and be prepared. Males as well as females can buy the contraceptive foams, sponge, creams or jellies, as well as have the condom with them.

Males *and* females can take responsibility for being as well protected as possible by *not* counting on their partner to remember.

One of the more common reasons young people don't like to use birth control is that they feel most methods interrupt lovemaking and too many think that unwanted results "won't happen to me."

Again, partners need to seriously consider, "Can I handle any unwanted results of unprotected sexual intercourse?" If the answer is no—and partners choose to have sexual intercourse—then responsible use of protection from pregnancy, as well as sexually transmitted diseases, is a must.

"Real Sex"

Many people think that the only way to "have sex" or have "real sex" is to have sexual intercourse. It's important to realize that people can share in many different sexual ways other than sexual intercourse. Kissing, touching, holding the other person, and hugging can feel very sexual and are safer ways to share. Sometimes just being held can feel very, very close and good.

Even if a person has a disability and doesn't have any feeling in some parts of their body, it doesn't mean that person can't have sex or have sexual feelings by touching with other parts of the body. Each person can share sexually and feel sexual feelings in his or her own way. There's no one way. There's no "right" way except what each person feels is right for them.

So, sexual intercourse is *not* the only way to sexually share. It's a mistake to think that you're not doing "anything" if you're not having sexual intercourse. There's plenty else to do.

Oral Sex

Oral sex refers to one partner contacting the genitals of the other partner with their mouth. This kind of sharing is a very personal choice about which there are many different feelings. Some people find oral sex pleasurable, some never feel comfortable about it, and some believe such sharing is against their religious standards. It is usually an embarrassing topic for children and parents to discuss.

Many kids do not view oral sex as "sex" and think it's no big deal. Oral sex *is* sexual activity. Although there is no risk of pregnancy with oral sex, there is a risk of spreading or becoming infected with a sexually transmitted disease (including HIV) if one of the partners is infected. As with other close sexual sharing, having oral sex can also affect feelings and emotions. Respect for ones own sexual limits and the limits of others needs to be taken seriously. No one has a right to pressure someone else into having oral sex or any other form of sexual activity.

Partners having oral sex need to fully understand how it is possible to spread disease from one person to the other by mouth-to-genital contact and how they might be able to tell if their partner is infected. The problem is, some diseases have signs that are hard or sometimes impossible to notice. And some have no visible signs. It is wise for partners to wash their genitals before sharing in this way, but this cannot take the place of using proper protection—a non-lubricated latex condom (spermicide should not be used during oral sex).

Touching Doesn't Always Have to Be Sexual

Many people think that if they start touching someone, kiss, or even hold someone close, it means they have to get heavily involved with sexual sharing. It's nice to be close without feeling pressured to be more sexual, without concern that the other person expects sharing to go further.

Putting an arm around a shoulder or giving someone a hug can also feel good to a friend or relative. Touching doesn't always have to be sexual.

Moans and Groans

There are many movies that show couples having close sexual contact, even sexual intercourse. Very often, partners are shown moaning and groaning, rolling around together in very dramatic ways. Some moans are so loud that it seems like they could be heard for miles!

Be careful not to measure sexual feelings and responses by what you might see in the movies. Some people really do moan or sigh and are very active during sex. Still others feel good in a much more quiet way. It just depends upon the person. It also might depend upon such things as how tired they are, or how relaxed.

Lots of kids have asked me, "How will I know if I'm 'doing it' right?" There are no grades for sexual sharing. It's not a matter of questioning, "Is this right or wrong?" or "Am I good?" Rather, sexual sharing can be much more meaningful and less pressured if the concerns are: "How does this feel?" "How does my partner feel?" and "How can we work at sharing and learning together what feels even better to both of us?"

It would be unfair to expect that someone would "just know" how to make someone else feel good. Partners can teach each other which kind of touching is most pleasing to them. It takes time to get to know someone sexually, just as it takes time to get to know them in other ways.

There's always more to learn. Even adults who have been together for years and years can still learn more about each other, still try new ways of touching and sharing. Sexual learning need never stop, no matter how old you are.

My worry is that if kids decide they're ready for sex early, they won't be in the kind of mature relationship that allows them to have the freedom to learn about each other, slowly. Kids who have sex can end up being much more pressured to "be good" at sex instead of being able to appreciate what such closeness can mean. They often don't realize that what pleases one person might not please another in exactly the same way. They may end up forcing themselves to fake sexual reactions and fake feeling good just because they're afraid to hurt their partner's feelings and they want their partner to think they're a "good lover." So instead of feeling special about such closeness, they may secretly wish that it would be over very quickly. And they may think something is wrong with them because they're not responding the way they think they're "supposed" to.

It can help to talk with your parents (or a trusted adult) about the topic of sexual sharing, so they can let you know what they feel is important for you to understand—not only about sexual sharing itself, but also about trust, respect, and deep caring, according to the personal values and religious beliefs that they hope will be a part of you, too.

But just in case you (or they) are too embarrassed and they never get a chance to help you feel more prepared, it might help to understand that it's very natural to feel awkward, fumbling, and uncomfortable the "first time," even if it's your wedding night. Bells don't always ring; violins don't always play (you're not in a movie), even though sometimes for some people it's possible to imagine many different, wonderful things. It's fine to talk while sharing so deeply. You're also allowed to laugh and be silly, or even excuse yourself to go to the bathroom—this is a human experience. One touch can slowly lead to another and another, and so each partner will learn. Just be patient. Be careful about expecting, and concentrate more on appreciating. There aren't any rules except those that people make between themselves, privately.

It also might make partners feel more comfortable if they are able to say to each other, "I'm a little nervous," or "I never shared so closely with someone before," or "Tell me what feels good to you."

Sexually Transmitted Diseases (STDs)

Besides pregnancy, another possible unwanted result of sexual intercourse that has been mentioned is getting a sexually transmitted disease or STD (a disease that can be passed from one person to another during sex). You might have heard these diseases referred to as *venereal diseases* (vuh-NEAR-ee-al) or V.D., or sexually transmitted infections.

It's possible for STDs to be passed by kissing (mouth to mouth), oral sex (mouth to genitals), or through contact in any combination between the mouth, vagina, penis, and anus (rear opening). The fact that someone can actually get an STD from kissing means that every kid who has any kind of sexual contact needs to be responsible for knowing the STD warning signs that mean "Keep Away!" or to have an STD test. Only then will more people protect themselves from infection and at least get proper treatment as quickly as possible, before too much damage has happened.

Once again, the one sure way to be totally protected against becoming infected with a sexually transmitted disease is abstinence, avoiding sex or saying *no* to sex.

"Nice" people can get STDs Millions of people each year are infected with STDs. "Nice" people can pass them to others, "nice" people can become infected. If sexually active kids don't know to protect themselves against disease—or don't believe or aren't serious about the risk of infection—it's very possible that they will become infected. Adults can become infected, too.

No one is free from this possibility of infection if they're exposed. Not cheerleaders, starters on the football team, first singles on the tennis team, goody-goodies, bookworms, teacher's pets, baby-sitters, the lead in the school play, the class president, even a principal's son or daughter, even a principal, even a teacher, even a parent—if they take risks. *Anyone* can get a sexually transmitted disease—rich or poor, no matter what color, nationality, religion, or if they're on the honor roll or not. And there's no age limit. A person can have more than one STD at the same time.

It's very simple. STDs can be passed to a partner only by someone who is infected or someone who is a carrier. A carrier is a person who isn't actually suffering the effects of the disease but who is able to pass it to someone because it's in their body system. Once a person is exposed to an STD, he or she risks becoming infected.

Someone who gets an STD isn't bad or shameful. Whenever a person is exposed to disease, he or she might become infected. That's why protection is so important.

As with pregnancy, many people think, "It won't happen to me." They take sexual chances and lose. Very often they don't even realize they're taking a chance. They have no idea what signs of disease to look for, what to avoid, or how to protect themselves. If they actually notice a sore, for example, they might be too uncomfortable to ask their partner what it is for fear of hurting their partner's feelings. Or it's possible that one partner might keep their infection a secret from the other. There are so many ways a person might be exposed.

Finding an STD before it finds you There are several different types of STDs. Some have symptoms that are easy to notice. Some have symptoms that might look like those of other, nonsexual diseases—such as a rash, headache, fever, sore throat, or sores in the mouth. If a person doesn't realize they have any other changes, for instance in the genital area, they might think they simply have a sore throat. Some STDs have hidden signs that are usually impossible to notice (because the changes are inside the genital area where they can't really be seen or felt). Some have no signs.

Because infection from a sexually transmitted disease can cause serious permanent damage if left untreated, it's important to be aware of all the signs that could possibly mean a person is infected.

If you are sexually active, any of the following symptoms could mean STD infection:

for males:
- burning or pain when urinating
- any discharge from the penis (could be cloudy colored)

for females:
- discomfort or pain in the pelvic area
- burning urination
- an unusual discharge and/or strong odor from the vagina (Discharges are very common for young girls. If you know you have *not* had any sexual contact and you have a discharge, you don't have a sexually transmitted disease.)

for both males and females:
- any unusual skin change
- growths or bumps on the skin
- warts—can be shaped like cauliflower and may be flat or raised
- painful sores or bumps on the genitals (that might bleed, crack, or blister and then become open with pus)
- painless sores on the genitals, mouth, rectum, nipple, or elsewhere on the skin (sores will go away on their own and may be followed by other signs such as a skin rash, headaches, fever, and a sore throat)
- itching in pubic or other body hair
- itching, pain, or bleeding in the genital area

If you or your partner have any of these signs, stop any further sexual contact. Be sure to go to a doctor, health center, or clinic in order to be examined and tested. You need to start treatment as quickly as possible if you are infected. Don't diagnose (make the decision about whether or not you're infected) by yourself.

If you're not sure where to go for help, look in the Yellow Pages or call information for your local health department. You can also call the national STD hotline for advice (1-800-227-8922) or the National AIDS Hotline (1-800-342-2437; if either number changes, you can dial 1-800-555-1212 for new information).

For most STDs there are tests, lab cultures, or special examinations to figure out if a person is infected. But first they would have to realize that their symptoms mean they need a test. If there are no symptoms, the only way someone could find out quickly if infection is present is if a partner admits to being infected. Then they would know it's possible they are infected, too.

Most STDs are curable; some are not. Even if an STD is curable, if a person waits too long to get treatment, the damage that has already taken place can be permanent. For both men and women, an untreated STD can result in permanent damage to the reproductive organs, causing them to become sterile—not physically able to have a child.

Just as you can't diagnose an STD by yourself, you can't treat any STD yourself. Treatments include medications, injections, creams, and ointments. Many can work very quickly to cure the particular disease.

Sexually transmitted diseases caused by different types of bacteria can be cured. These include chlamydia (kluh-MID-ee-uh), gonorrhea (gon-uh-REE-uh) and syphilis (SIF-uh-luss). Antibiotics or other medications that need to be prescribed by a doctor must be taken in very specific doses, depending upon the kind of medication and the disease being treated. It's dangerous to use anyone else's prescription for treatment.

Sexually transmitted diseases caused by a virus include herpes (HER-peez), genital warts, and HIV infection (HIV is the virus that causes AIDS). These diseases need to be managed but as of now, cannot be cured. For example, for herpes there are some drugs and creams that can ease the discomfort from the sores and prevent further infections. Researchers continue to search for ways to improve treatment and find a cure.

Untreated STDs The possibility that a sexually transmitted disease might not be noticed or recognized is very disturbing because of the serious permanent damage certain STDs can cause. Besides the serious effects an untreated STD can have on the man or woman who is infected, it's also possible for an infected pregnant woman to pass her untreated STD on to her unborn fetus, causing serious damage.

Even when the beginning signs disappear—and even if symptoms may seem mild—an untreated infection can continue to do silent damage until it's bad enough to be noticed. And then it might be too late.

For instance, untreated chlamydia can cause damage to the reproductive (sexual) organs, causing the man or woman to become sterile. It can cause a woman to suffer from pelvic inflammatory disease (PID), and can also cause a tubal pregnancy. Untreated gonorrhea also can damage the reproductive organs of a male or female, causing sterility. Gonorrhea can also cause crippling arthritis. If genital warts are left untreated, they can multiply and grow bigger, and they can make childbirth and delivery more difficult. If syphilis goes untreated, it can, over many years' time, end up causing heart disease, blindness, insanity, and even death.

Because there is still no cure for herpes, those who have been infected need to be especially sure of their facts. Only then will they be able to exercise caution, knowing when to avoid sexual contact in order to reduce the chance of spreading the disease. A person who is infected with herpes must also learn how to avoid causing further infection in other parts of their own body. And it's important for a woman infected with herpes to be aware of how the virus can affect pregnancy as well as childbirth.

An untreated STD has a greater chance than a treated one of being passed from one person to another and another and another. Sexually transmitted diseases can cause a lot of damage. They're often uncomfortable, sometimes quite painful, and can have very serious results that can affect a person for a lifetime. That's why it's very important to have a complete understanding of each of these and other STDs.

Learning more about STDs As with seeking out complete information about birth control, you can talk to your parent, contact your doctor, family planning clinic, birth control center, local (sexual) health services, center for sexually transmitted diseases, health clinic (look in the Yellow Pages or ask telephone information), library, health teacher, or check the Internet with your parent in order to find good resources to explain the facts about STDs. You can also call the toll-free national STD Hotline; CDC, Atlanta, Georgia: 1-800-227-8922. (If this number changes, dial 1-800-555-1212 and ask for new information.).

Acting on what you know Take another look at the symptoms I mentioned that can signal an STD infection. Before reading ahead, think of which signs would make you stop and think about whether sexual sharing would be wise.

You now know to avoid any kind of sexual contact with someone who has sores (whether or not they're painful) on the genital area, mouth, breasts, or any other area of the body. You know that signs such as a rash or genital discharges and intense itching could possibly mean infection. Also, pain or discomfort in the lower abdominal area might signal a new infection, or one that has been there for a while but has only recently become noticeable because it wasn't treated earlier.

If you're sexually active, it's very important to have regular check-ups with your doctor at least once or twice a year. Remember that using a condom can offer the best available protection from disease.

Since an STD must be passed by an infected person or a carrier, the more sexual partners a person has, the greater the risk of infection. But keep in mind that all it takes is one infected partner to transmit his or her infection. The less well someone knows their partner, the more possible that the partner will keep their infection a secret.

Washing the genitals with soap and water after intercourse can add to the protection against sexually transmitted disease, but can't be counted on by itself.

Turning feelings into words If a person becomes infected with a sexually transmitted disease, it is *very important* to let any sex partners know (as well as the public health authorities). Then he or she can be sure to have the proper test and treatment in case of infection.

Too many people don't tell their partners about being infected. Some don't know they're infected, and some don't realize the seriousness of what could happen if the disease is left untreated. But they also don't tell because they're scared of what that person will think of them, or they worry that their partner will judge them as terrible or dirty and maybe will love them less—or won't go out with them any-more.

If you can't tell your partner directly, it might be easier to call an STD center, health board, or related birth control clinics. They can contact your partner(s) for you if you don't feel you can tell your partner yourself.

Turning feelings into words can work here, too. "This is hard for me to say, but . . ." or "I feel so horrible having to tell you this, but . . ."

What About AIDS?

AIDS, or acquired immune deficiency syndrome (a-kwi-urd im-MEWN dee-FISH-un-see SIN-drome) is caused by HIV, the human immunodeficiency virus (im-MEWN-oh-dee-FISH-un-see), which gets into the system when transmitted by an infected person. HIV is also called the AIDS virus. If a person is HIV infected, he or she is referred to as HIV positive.

When a person becomes infected, HIV can remain in the system for many years without causing any signs of illness. During that time, the infected person can look and feel fine. It often takes at least eight to ten years or even more before symptoms start to appear. During this period of no symptoms, the only way HIV infection can be detected is by tak-ing a special blood test (see page 266).

When a person becomes HIV infected, the virus gradually attacks and breaks down the person's immune system, which is the body's pro-tection against disease, and signs begin to show up. When the immune system reaches the point where it becomes seriously damaged and weak-ened, the HIV-infected person is diagnosed as having AIDS.

Both males and females can become infected with HIV. HIV infec-tion has nothing to do with your age, religion, skin color, race, what country you're from. It doesn't matter if you're a star athlete or an hon-est and caring person. People can get it whether they are gay or straight. The rule for becoming infected is very simple. If you risk HIV infection, no matter who you are, you may be a person who will develop AIDS.

Can AIDS be cured? Although there is a great deal of research being done, no cure for HIV infection or fully developed AIDS has been dis-covered yet. So for now, as with many other viruses, once HIV (the virus that causes AIDS) gets into a person's system, there is no way to get it out. And so far, there is no type of prevention method like a shot or vaccine (vack-SEEN) or medication that will protect people from becoming infected with HIV.

While the search for a cure goes on, there are now medications available to help people with HIV infection and those diagnosed with AIDS manage the disease as well as possible. So it is important for anyone who suspects he or she might have risked HIV infection to get tested (refer to blood test information, page 266). The sooner a doctor knows that someone is HIV positive, the sooner a treatment program can be set up for that person.

How AIDS can spread If a person is infected with HIV (the virus that causes AIDS), the virus can be found in transmittable amounts (enough to be able to cause someone to be infected) in their blood, semen, pre-seminal fluid (pre-ejaculatory fluid, pre-"come"), vaginal secretions, and breast milk.

The virus is spread when these bodily fluids from an infected person come into contact and get into the system of an uninfected person through mucous membrane (vagina, opening at the end of the penis, the anus or rectum, inside the mouth), through an open cut or sore, or by injecting drugs with a needle that has been been used by an infected person.

Behaviors/ways by which people put themselves at high risk for HIV infection
- Men or women having close sexual contact (penis with vagina, penis with anus or rectum, mouth with penis, vagina, anus or rectum), if one partner is infected—no matter what the sex of that partner or whether the partner is homosexual, heterosexual, or bisexual.
- Men or women injecting drugs with a needle that has been used by an HIV-infected person. Blood left in the needle from a person who is HIV infected can pass the virus directly into the blood of the next person who uses that needle.
- Men or women having sexual contact with a partner

who has used drugs by injection (such as someone who injects heroin or steroids) with a needle used by an HIV-infected person.

- HIV-infected-semen, vaginal fluids, or blood getting into an open cut or sore. (So "blood-brother" or "blood-sister" pacts are not a safe thing to do.)
- HIV passing from an infected pregnant woman to her unborn fetus.

Other ways of becoming infected:

- HIV passing from an infected woman to her child through breast feeding.
- In the past, people have become HIV-infected by HIV-infected blood transfusions. Today, hospitals and blood banks are required to screen and test blood. At this point, there is little risk of HIV transmission through blood transfusions. If you have any questions or concerns, check with your local doctor or blood bank.
Note: Donating blood will not put you at risk to become infected with HIV.

Also keep in mind:

- Don't share toothbrushes or razors with anyone. (Blood from bleeding gums or from shaving cuts can transmit HIV if the person is infected.)
- If you are getting your ears (or any part of your body) pierced or are being tattooed or having electrolysis, make sure the needles used are properly sterilized.
- If you're getting a manicure or pedicure, make sure that the instruments are sterilized. It's even safer to use your own instruments.
- If you are going to help someone who is bleeding, it's wise to avoid direct contact with the blood. (Latex gloves are an excellent choice for protection.) If you get blood on your skin, wash as soon as possible with soap and water.

- Be sure that needles used for injections are properly sterilized.

While drinking alcohol, smoking cocaine, inhaling crack, or using other drugs that are not injected are not directly associated with transmission of HIV infection, people who use them are likely to be less careful about having sex or using protection during sex and so are more likely to be at risk of infection.

What about kissing?: Although saliva can have small amounts of HIV in it if a person is infected, transmission through kissing (or spitting) is not likely. So far, there are no reported cases of HIV infection transmitted by just kissing.

However, you can put yourself at risk of becoming infected from kissing if you kiss an HIV-infected person who has a cut or sore in their mouth—and you have a cut or sore in your mouth. If HIV-infected blood from their mouth sores gets into the cut or sore in your mouth, infection could happen.

Most important is always to remember that there can be risk involved. If the person you're going to kiss has cuts or sores, it's not a good idea.

Extra caution about close sexual contact: Even without having sexual intercourse, if infected semen, pre-seminal fluid, or vaginal fluids contact the mucous membrane of a partner, HIV may be able to be absorbed into that person's system.

That means, for example, if a male ejaculates semen just outside the opening of the vagina—even if the penis never actually enters the vagina—there is still risk of HIV infection (since semen is a liquid, it could drip into the soft area in the opening of the vagina).

Even if ejaculation does not take place, it's important to protect yourself from the tiny drops of seminal fluid (pre-ejaculatory fluid or pre-"come," which is clear) that drip out before ejaculation happens. If a male is HIV-infected, even those few drops can transmit HIV infection to a partner.

So, *any* unprotected contact with the head of the penis (by mouth, vaginal opening, or anal opening) could put someone at risk for HIV infection.

What does this mean about protection? Here's a reminder If you're choosing to be sexually active, latex condoms are the best available protection against transmission of HIV and many other sexually transmitted diseases (such as gonorrhea, syphilis, and herpes, talked about on page 256).

Always use a latex condom during *any* kind of close sexual contact (with the mouth, penis, vagina, anus or rectum) to prevent semen or other bodily fluids to pass from an HIV-infected person to a partner. The condom needs to be used correctly and must be put on before *any* contact is made.

Dry latex condoms can be used for protection during oral sex so there is no contact with semen or pre-seminal fluid. Moisture barriers, such as dental dams or using a condom that has been opened up (like a flat piece of latex) can offer protection against vaginal and cervical secretions.

The more sexual partners a person has, the greater the chance that he or she will become infected with HIV. But all it takes is one partner who is infected to pass on this deadly virus.

If you're having sex, your risk of HIV infection is as great as if you were having sex with all your partner's past partners. Also, the more contacts a person has with the same infected person, the greater the chance of becoming infected with HIV.

What about kids who go to school with HIV infection or full-blown AIDS? Many people are scared that if a kid who is HIV positive or has developed AIDS goes to school, he or she will infect classmates, teachers, or anyone else around. You may have seen newspaper articles or heard news reports about how confused and upset people in different communities have been about this. AIDS in school is a very emotional concern. Many people think kids with HIV infection or those who actually have AIDS should not be allowed to attend school at all.

It's natural for people to be scared of such a dreaded infection—especially since it has already killed so many people. It's natural to think that you might be better off running in the other direction from any kid who is HIV positive or has progressed to have AIDS. It's also natural to be scared of AIDS because many people don't understand how it really spreads.

But the truth is, casual contact—like changing in the same locker room, sitting in the same classroom, sitting next to someone on a school bus trip, walking through the halls together, or even eating at the same lunch table with or hugging a kid who is HIV infected or has been diagnosed with AIDS—is not harmful or risky. Casual contact does not put someone at risk.

And kids with HIV generally will not be harmed by being in school with other kids. But they are more at risk for becoming sick, because their immune system is not as strong as that of other kids who are not HIV-infected. If they do get sick, it's harder for them to become well again. Their own doctors and appropriate school authorities can decide together what would be best for each individual.

A big problem A big problem is that because people who become infected with HIV might not see any signs of having this infection until many years later, they might continue to pass on their deadly virus, without knowing it, to more and more people—never realizing the damage that is being done.

The horrible truth is that there are thousands of people right now who are infected with HIV and don't know it. HIV infection and full-blown AIDS are very widespread already, and very serious. This means that thousands of people who think they're safe from AIDS (and may even tell their sexual partners they are safe), really aren't.

Think about why this is such important information. How can it help you to know this?

Protecting yourself from HIV Try to answer these questions before reading on:

- Do you know how you can protect yourself from becoming infected with HIV?
- How can you make sure you don't spread HIV infection to anyone else?

Probably you have figured out that the answer to the second question has to do with controlling your own risk of HIV infection. If you can protect yourself so you never become HIV infected, then you can also help stop the spread of AIDS to other people. HIV can be passed on only by someone infected with HIV.

Here are a few ways to control your own risk:

- You can decide if and when and with whom to have (or not to have) sex.

- You can make sure—because it would be risky to take even one chance on anyone being completely safe from HIV infection—to *always* use a latex condom if you have close sexual contact of any kind.
- You can decide not to mix alcohol or other drugs with having any kind of sex. (That way, you can always remain in control and careful.)
- You can make sure—if at any time your partner has been drinking or using other drugs—that you don't let him or her start any kind of sexual contact with you. (You may not be able to stay in command if your partner is out of control.)
- You can decide to not ever use an injectible drug unless prescribed and supervised by your doctor, and you can decide never to use a needle that someone else used to inject a drug.
- You can even decide not to have sexual contact simply because that's your right to decide—without needing to give a reason for saying "NO"

Review this list again. Also review the list of what researchers feel puts people at the most risk (page 260). What other points could you now add to this list?

While this list does not include every single possible situation to be aware of and watch out for, you now have a better idea of what I mean by staying in control of your risk.

Do you see that if you understand the ways HIV can be passed from an infected person, then you don't ever have to let yourself take even one chance that can cause you to become infected? You can choose to stay in control of what you allow yourself to do. You can choose not to risk.

How will you know if someone is "safe" from HIV infection or not? The truth is, you probably won't know. Remember, a person who is HIV infected can look and feel healthy for a very long time. So you can't tell if someone is infected just by looking them over. The person who is infected may truly not know they are infected, and may not know this for many years.

Others may know they're infected but choose not to tell anyone—not even a sexual partner. And they, too, might appear to be just fine. So, where does that leave you if you want always to be in control of your own risk?

Since you can't know if someone is infected just by looking and you can't control whether or not someone is being honest with you about being infected, your very safest and best protection from HIV is to conduct yourself as if everyone around you were HIV infected. If you're always protected, you won't let yourself take even one chance.

A dangerous attitude . . . In addition to understanding the facts about HIV infection and AIDS, and understanding what it means to stay in control so you don't put yourself at risk, a big part of what will keep you protected is your own attitude.

Many kids know that HIV is a deadly virus and realize that protection from HIV infection is truly a life-and-death decision. But they don't think HIV infection can happen to them.

So they end up not being careful about what they allow themselves to do and they don't take protection seriously—or use it at all. Pressure from peers who don't take the threat of AIDS seriously can also make it difficult to stay away from risk situations that can lead to HIV infection.

In the chapter on peer pressure, I asked you to ask yourself, "What will it take for me to believe the risks are real?" This is a good time for you to ask again.

Getting tested for AIDS If you're worried that your behavior might have already put you at high risk of becoming HIV infected, you can take a special blood test in order to check yourself out. Be careful not to allow yourself to repeat any behavior that might have put you (or anyone else) at risk of HIV infection.

While it can take up to six months after someone becomes HIV infected before the signs (changes in the blood) will actually show up on a test, you can still arrange for testing immediately. As the consideration of how much time has passed since your risky behavior is important, you'll need to share with the person at the testing site what you feel is the approximate date that you put yourself at risk.

You can call your state department of health to find out where the nearest testing site is located. While you can easily arrange for this blood test yourself, you can benefit greatly from discussing your concerns with someone who is trained to help you. You can speak with your health teacher, coach, a local health clinic, your doctor, the AIDS hotline, 1-800-342-AIDS. (If this number changes, you can dial 1-800-555-1212 for new information.) You can also call your local blood bank.

If a person takes the blood test before these changes have time to develop enough to be identified, the test result can be negative (indicating there is no infection) even if someone is actually infected. So, proper timing of the test is very important.

Sometimes it's possible that the test will pick up other changes that are not caused by HIV. So, if a person tests positive (indicating HIV infection), it's important for a follow-up test to be done to confirm that the positive result is correct.

If your test results are negative, and you're still worried that, because of the risk you took, you might actually be infected—wait another six months or so and arrange to get retested. Be cautious about not allowing yourself to participate in any further high-risk behavior that could lead to HIV infection. If your second test results come back negative, you can be reassured that you're not HIV infected. If you learn that you're not infected, be sure to stay strong about not putting yourself at risk again. Don't relax your guard against HIV infection.

The HIV test is a simple blood test that can be done anonymously (without identifying who you are), or at the very least, kept confidential (con-fih-DEN-shull), that is, it will be respected as information to be kept private between you and your doctor or clinic. There is usually a counselor—someone trained to talk with you about the blood test and what it means—who can be helpful to you before you take the test and after you learn the results, so you don't have to handle your concerns alone (and as I've suggested many times before, you can also seek out the support of the adults in your life who you trust).

If there is any reason to suspect the possibility of HIV infection for you or someone you're going out with, besides discussing the importance of a blood test, it would also be wise not to have any close sexual contact until you learn the test results.

If someone close to you is HIV positive or diagnosed with AIDS—or if you are

I spoke at length with Jennifer, whose brother has AIDS. She said:

> There are several important things to realize. The first is that being infected with HIV doesn't mean your life is over. HIV doesn't mean they're going to die tomorrow or next week or even next year.
>
> There are a lot of things that people can do to remain healthy and increase their odds. And as our knowledge progresses and we learn more about this disease, those people will be able to live even longer with this. Having a supportive network of friends and family is one of the most beneficial things a person living with HIV can do.
>
> The other thing for kids to understand is that people don't get AIDS by living in the same house with someone who has AIDS. Day-to-day life does not transmit the disease. So there's no reason in the world that people who have HIV or AIDS can't be good mothers or fathers, can't hug and kiss their children, can't take care of them or make them meals or do anything that good parents do. And likewise, if your brother or sister or friend has AIDS, you can still do all the things that brothers and sisters and friends do. You can play games and go out together and share a pizza and not have to worry about getting AIDS that way either.
>
> People with AIDS do become ill. And I think what we need to realize is that what they need when they become ill is what they've always needed in the past. They need someone to love them, and to be friends with, and to tell jokes to, and to cry with and share the sad times, too. Becoming ill doesn't change the person you are, and it doesn't change your basic needs as a person.

I also spoke with Henry, who has been HIV infected for many years and now has AIDS. He told me:

> I think one of the really important things other people need to know is that you're not going to die tomorrow. Because a lot of people think that if you have AIDS, you're going to die tomorrow—so they treat you as if you're going to die tomorrow.

It's almost like you're made of glass and they're afraid they're going to break you or something like that.

That was one of the things my friends were very good about. They realized I wasn't going to die right away. So we sort of got back to life as normal. They realized I was still the same person. So they knew there was no reason to treat me differently.

I think for people who find out they're HIV positive, realizing this is very important as well. Because attitude has a great deal to do with how long you live.

It's like a family disease for us. We all try to share in everything to deal with it and to help each other. It makes it easier. That's one of the reasons why support from your friends and family is so important.

I spoke with Dave, now thirty-four years old, whose friend died of AIDS last year. He said: "It was very important that we set up a strong communication system between us. That way, I would know all the issues related to how he was feeling or how he was responding to me as a friend.

"It was always important to not see my friend as a victim. That was one thing that he asked us never to do. He asked us never to feel sorry for him. Keeping his dignity was very important.

"There was one point where he was very, very sick. And he just kept on fighting to stay alive. He never really focused on what it was going to be like when he wasn't around. He always focused on life and living.

"I think people need to view those who have AIDS as living with AIDS rather than dying with AIDS."

Jennifer added: "People with AIDS who are ill may have their limitations placed on them by their doctors. They may be too tired to go out skiing or play Frisbee, but there are lots of things that you can still do. The most important thing is that you continue to spend time with the people you love. It would be the same if someone you love had cancer or any other life-threatening illness."

Even with love and support and open communication with family and friends, there still may be some tough feelings to handle. If you are having difficulty keeping a positive outlook, besides approaching family and friends, it can be important to speak with someone who is trained to help you (your doctor, health clinic, AIDS hotline, religious leader, health teacher, coach, school counselor, principal, or other administrator).

Your caring and concern for people with AIDS No matter how a person becomes HIV infected, it's very important for everyone to be sensitive, compassionate, and caring about people who are HIV positive and those who have developed full-blown AIDS. Such compassion also needs to be extended to their families and their other loved ones.

We are all in this world together and all of us can make a difference to one another. In addition to your genuine concern, you can consider volunteering at hospitals and AIDS clinics. Certainly any fund-raising efforts for AIDS research would be helpful and important. You can also get involved with AIDS education at your school and in your community.

The future AIDS is being widely researched. While it is understood that a virus causes AIDS, it is also possible that there are many additional factors that may have impact on how long people can live with the infection that doctors and researchers are just learning about. Be on the lookout for new information and new discoveries about HIV and AIDS.

Hepatitis B

Hepatitis B is a virus that is passed from an infected person through blood and *all* bodily fluids (including tears and saliva). HBV stands for the Hepatitis B Virus. While HIV (the virus that causes AIDS) attacks an infected person's immune system, HBV affects a person's liver.

As with HIV, HBV is not spread through casual contact. The same precautions for preventing HIV infection also apply here and you need to be extra aware and extra careful since HBV causes all bodily fluids to be infected. So, for example, don't share chewing gum.

The majority of people with HBV become infected through sexual contact. In many cases, how a person becomes infected is not known. HBV is even more contagious than HIV.

The only way someone can know for sure if they are infected with HBV is by taking a blood test. Most people who are infected with HBV don't have clearly noticeable symptoms and don't know they have been infected.

When people do have symptoms of HBV infection, these might include loss of appetite, pain in the abdomen (stomach), nausea, vomiting, and jaundice (yellowness of the skin). Symptoms can sometimes be so severe that people infected with HBV can be very sick for weeks, months, or even longer.

Some people infected with HBV are carriers. That means that, although the infection is in their blood and bodily fluids, they don't ever have symptoms or get sick but can pass the infection on to other people.

Hepatitis B is the only sexually transmitted disease which is preventable through vaccination (getting a shot so you can be protected). If you're choosing to be sexually active, it's an excellent decision to be vaccinated. You can ask your doctor or health clinic about arranging to be vaccinated.

For more detailed information about Hepatitis B, you can call the National STD Hotline at 1-800-227-8922 and the American Liver Foundation at 1-800-223-0179. (If either of these numbers change, you can call 1-800-555-1212 for new information.)

Unwanted Emotional Consequences of Sexual Intercourse

Think about what it might mean to share so closely and completely with another person. Have you ever stopped to consider what would make you feel "right" about going further and further sexually? What would make you feel comfortable? What might cause you to feel sorry, ashamed, disappointed, guilty, used, angry, unhappy, upset, anxious, scared, cause you to lose respect for yourself, or cause any other difficult or uncomfortable feelings?

Here are some emotional results that other kids told me would make them wish they had *never* shared so closely:

- If, after you let yourself share, the person doesn't ever go out with you again, and probably was just with you for what they could get sexually.
- If the person you shared with talks to other people about what you did together and it gets around school or even just to close friends.

- If the person you've been going out with wants to break up because you won't share more sexually. (Valerie, age 15, said, "It kind of makes you think that the only thing important about going out with you is your body . . . not *you*.")
- If you went further than you know was comfortable or right for you.
- If you did something that you don't respect yourself for.
- If you did something that might give you a bad reputation.
- If you know you're just letting your partner do what they want to do sexually because you're afraid if you don't, they won't go out with you.

Far too many kids don't think about their own feelings and choices, and the consequences of their sexual sharing, until after they can't change what they've done. These emotional concerns can also result from oral sex and other close sexual contact.

Making Sexual Decisions

Here are a few questions that might help you dig a little deeper into what you need to understand about yourself so that when the time comes for you to make a sexual decision, you'll be sure of staying within *your* own limits.

Note: If you wait until you're sitting in the backseat of a car, hanging out at her house, in the darkened end of a basement where there's a party and "everybody" is making out, or walking to the beach with a sleeping bag in one hand and your boyfriend in the other, it may be too late to start figuring this out.

Try to decide how you feel about your own sexual limits—to the extent that you can. Consider for yourself:

- How far is it "right" to go?
- How much touching? Where?

- How do you feel sexual sharing changes a relationship?
- How strong do you think you are about your limits?
- What relationship or situation could influence you to go further?

Your sense of when you will be ready to allow yourself to touch and be close will probably depend on so many things, such as: your age and the age of the person you're going out with; maturity; readiness—what you think you can handle; your personal values, standards, and self-respect; and what your parents, religious leaders, and teachers have taught you. Being close is a personal decision that also has to do with how comfortable you are with that other person and how much trust and respect there is between you.

The truth is, no matter how much you understand about yourself, setting sexual limits and making sexual decisions can be very confusing. Movies, magazines, radio, books, and TV often give young kids the message "sex is okay" and that can add to the confusion. Parents, teachers, and religious leaders are likely to be telling you that sex should be saved until you're married or at least until you're an adult and can deal with the emotions of such closeness in a responsible way. And there you are, in the middle, wondering what's right.

More pressure and confusion can come from all the talk about sex. As I've said before, even when kids aren't doing anything, they often feel the need to sound as if they do a lot. Sexual talk often influences kids to go further sexually because they don't want to feel left out. Sometimes this pressure influences kids to let their girlfriend or boyfriend make sexual decisions for them. (The less personal control you have of your decisions, the greater the chance that you'll have to deal with unwanted physical and emotional results.)

Some boys and girls have talked with me about being upset (or wondering if they should be upset) because they aren't interested in or ready to share closely with anyone. They just don't seem to have the same feelings as many of their friends. This is okay! Again, for *both* boys and girls, each person's time of readiness for wanting to be close is different. You may be interested earlier than your friends, about the same time, or not until many years later.

I know I've said this again and again, but I also know that it's hard to be at a "different place" than most of the kids you hang out with. So I'm hoping if I keep reminding you that each person will be ready at their own time, then maybe you'll accept where you're at and not push yourself, or anyone else, further.

When you do feel ready, to help you decide how much sexual sharing is appropriate, you can answer for yourself:

- Am I about to do (or doing) what I truly believe is right for me? Can I handle any unwanted risks?
- Am I respecting myself and the other person?
- Have I talked about this with the person I'm going to share myself with?
- Am I being pressured into doing something that I'm just not ready for or don't want to do?
- Have we decided how we're going to reduce the risks?

Sometimes People Are Forced into a Sexual Act Against Their Will

Rape is a criminal act. It occurs when a person is forced to have sexual intercourse against their will, without their permission. It's an invasion of someone else's body that can be physically dangerous and emotionally devastating and disturbing. Rape is considered to be a crime of violence and power.

While many people are raped by strangers, very often a person is raped by someone they know *(acquaintance rape)* or someone they're going out with *(date rape)*. Date and acquaintance rape are more common than most people realize. While the majority of rape victims are females, both males and females can be victims of rape, and both males and females can be rapists. Even someone who is married can be raped by a marriage partner if sex is forced.

Many people don't understand that it is considered rape if someone has sexual intercourse with a person who is so drunk that he or she is not capable of making a clear-headed decision to have sexual intercourse (or is high or sleeping or in any other such condition). The key issues that determine whether someone is raped or not have to do with *will* and *consent*—whether someone has clearly given permission to have sexual intercourse.

That means, if someone wants to have sexual intercourse with someone else, the *only* way it's okay to go ahead is if the person gives clear permission (says it's okay). If sexual intercourse takes place without clearly stated permission—that's considered rape.

So, once again, if someone is totally drunk, high, or even sleeping—and is in no condition to give consent—having sexual intercourse with a person in that condition is rape. Just because someone doesn't or isn't able to say "no," that doesn't mean "yes" to sex.

And, kissing, molesting, pinching, fondling, and sexual touching of any nature without the person's will and consent can be considered sexual assault or harassment. That includes unwanted sexual attention to someone else's body by touching or words. (That means no putting hands on someone's butt, no snapping bra straps or jock straps, no staring at or making negative or unwanted sexual comments about someone or their body.)

If someone is paying this kind of unwanted attention to you, clearly tell them you want them to stop. If they continue, tell them again—and make sure to say you're serious. If they don't stop, let someone who can help you deal with this situation know (an adult, such as your parent or teacher). This kind of behavior is unacceptable and, depending upon what the person is doing to you, can be against the law. (See page 279 for ways of asking for help even if you're scared.)

Sometimes kids try to get back at other kids or teachers by falsely accusing them of doing something that really didn't happen. Since sexual harassment, assault, or rape (or other abuse of any kind) is very serious—and can have very serious consequences—any accusation is a serious responsibility and needs to be truthful.

As you get older, you need to be aware of what messages you're giving to other people through what you say, how you act, and how you dress. Sometimes teasing and flirting can give the idea that you're very interested in having sex, when you don't mean that at all. And although you might feel that what you wear is your own business, some people make judgments that low-cut means you want sex, or tight pants means "I'm hot." Whether you believe they're right or wrong for viewing you this way, it's important to realize that's what others might think.

The more you understand and anticipate how others might see you, the more aware you will be about how they might react. That will help you be more prepared to avoid, or at least get away from, situations that could be dangerous for you.

Carin, now in her thirties, shared: "Most of the boys I hung out with as friends were just interested in sex. And I was just interested in playing sports with them. So sometimes I would find myself in situations where we'd be hanging out for a long time and they would misunderstand my feelings for them. I trusted them because they were my friends and I figured, 'Oh, we're just fooling around. Nothing's really going to happen.' And things happened to me. So, no matter how hard it is, you've got to talk with each other and tell each other how you're feeling. If it feels like it's going to be an unsafe situation, leave. Because young boys and their hormones are hard to control. They often don't listen to girls when they say no. They figure you must mean, 'Oh, not now.' Or, 'Just a little bit.' Or, 'You could try and see what happens. . . .' The thing I think would have helped me not get in so many of those date rape situations is if I went with my instincts. If it feels unsafe, then it is."

It's also important to keep your eyes and ears open for verbal and nonverbal messages from other people. For example, if you're being guided into an area where no one else seems to be around, try to avoid going there. If you move someone's hand away and they don't stop, that is an "alert" signal. Be careful whom you trust.

It's critical to understand that date rape and acquaintance rape are very real. There is a serious need for awareness and caution. Date or acquaintance rape can also result in HIV or other STD infections—for the violator as well as the victim. Be sure to attend programs in your school and community in order to learn more about how to best protect yourself, what situations put you more at risk, and how to attempt to handle them if you find yourself in trouble.

I hope that the following guidelines will help make a difference in your ability to prevent date or acquaintance rape from happening. Add anything else to this list that you can. Share these ideas with your friends.

Preventing date or acquaintance rape:
- It is very important to set clear sexual limits.

- Be aware of mixed messages that you might be giving, verbally as well as nonverbally. *No* has to mean no.
- If your partner says no, respect that limit. Don't push any further. Accept that your partner means no.
- If you're not comfortable with someone—or if you're not comfortable with some action or response—listen to those warning signals. You're better off not putting yourself in a situation alone with that person—stay around other people. Or you may be best off leaving the situation that you're in.
- Don't leave a party or go off to a secluded area with no one else around with someone you don't know well. And even if you do know someone well, remain aware and alert.

Keep In Mind

- No matter what a woman is wearing, her clothing doesn't mean she's asking to be violated sexually.
- No matter how much a person flirts, that still doesn't make it okay to violate them sexually.
- Alcohol and other drugs can lower your control, loosen or do away with sexual limits, increase risk, cause someone to be out of control.
- If you choose to drink, it's safer to open your own can or bottle. Don't take a drink that has already been opened.
- If you had sexual intercourse with someone in the past, that doesn't give you the right to expect to have it again unless the person clearly consents.
- If you say no to sex, make it clear that you're not saying no to your partner, personally. (Explain that it's just that you don't want to have sex. It has nothing to do with wanting to be with him or her.)

Rape by strangers is also very common. The more you keep a "safety mind-set" (meaning—never let up your guard, always be cautious), the safer you will be. More examples—don't walk around (or jog) by yourself at night, get your keys out ahead of time when you approach home or your car, always lock car doors. The idea is to "think safety" at all times.

The best protection starts with believing that the risks are real. Then do everything you can to remain aware and in control of what you allow yourself to do. It's also a great idea to take a class in some type of self-protection.

If someone is a victim of rape So many rapes go unreported. If someone is a victim of rape, it's important for them not to handle the experience alone. There are rape crisis centers, rape hotlines, local hospital emergency rooms, and health clinics. It's very important for a victim to call as soon as possible after being raped to learn what to do about evidence (such as not showering or bathing or cleaning themselves or their clothes). They'll also explain why it is important to report the rape, whether or not the victim decides to bring charges against the attacker.

It's very important for anyone who is raped to get help from someone who is trained to deal with the very difficult feelings that can be involved. Beyond approaching a rape crisis center, it's also important to contact your parent or other trusted adult in order to get the kind of personal support you need.

If you have a friend who tells you he or she has been raped, encourage your friend to report the rape when it occurs. Many people are very uncomfortable about reporting rape, especially when it involves someone they know.

I've spoken with so many students who told me I was the first person they let know that they had been raped—and how painfully difficult this was to handle. Again, rape is a violent, criminal act, a terrible violation. Don't even think of dealing with this by yourself.

Rape by Family Members

It might shock you to know that many girls and boys are raped by family members, such as older brothers, fathers, mothers, uncles, aunts, even grandparents. Some kids agree to have sex with them (or their friends or other adults) because they're threatened or are told this is the right thing to do. It's *not*.

Someone close might also say, "If you love me, you'll let me do this." (See page 282 for ways to say stop.)

Some kids are actually threatened with, "If you tell, I'll hurt you," or even "I'll kill you." Or they may simply be told, "You'd better not tell anyone!" Lots of kids don't know what else to do but give in. And it's common to be scared of telling even if they're not threatened. They're scared of what the abuser will do to them, scared that the person they go to for help will be angry or won't believe them or won't help them. Very often boys and girls who are sexually abused just don't know what to do to get help.

You probably can't imagine sexual activity with a relative happening, but it does. Or, perhaps you know only too well that this can happen. Just in case anyone tries to convince you it's natural and okay, it's definitely *not!* The name for this type of sexual activity between family members is *incest* (IN-sest).

If you are being forced to have sex against your will or are being abused sexually in any way by a stranger, someone you know, or a family member, it's very important that you tell someone, even if you were warned not to do so. Tell your other parent, a grandparent, or other relative, a trusted teacher, coach, your religious leader, guidance counselor, a friend's parent, or any other adult you trust. If that person doesn't believe you the first time, tell them again. If they don't listen, tell someone else.

Even if you know what must be said, actually getting the words out can be very hard. But it's important for anyone who is abused not to be silenced by the threats, not to let feeling scared hold them back from getting help. Even if the person abusing you is someone you love, any form of abuse is not right. Abuse is not acceptable. It's also against the law.

You may be thinking, "But it's my teacher. . . . How could I tell anyone?" Or, "It's my religious leader. I'd better keep silent." Or, "But, my family loves my uncle. They'll all be mad at me for telling them something that will keep him away." Or, "My mother will never believe me that my father would do that. It will hurt too much if she didn't believe me." Remember—in *any* case of this kind—if a family member or other adult has touched you in a sexual way or you are raped, you first need to realize it wasn't your fault. You're not to blame, and don't let anyone blame this on you!

Then remember—you need to speak to someone who can help you, so the abuse can be stopped. If you don't know who to turn to or what to say and you're very scared—it's okay to be scared. It's just not okay to let feeling scared prevent you from getting the help you need. You don't have to wait until you don't feel scared anymore. It's natural to feel scared. And, that's just what you can start with. "I'm really scared to tell you this." Or, "I'm afraid that you won't believe me." Or, "Please help me."

If you can't find someone close to you who will listen, you can call the operator to get information for any hotlines that offer help for kids who are abused in your area. You can also dial your own area code in the state where you live and add 555-1212 for information about where you can get help in your state.

Or you can call 1-800-555-1212 and ask for information on national hotlines that relate to child abuse or domestic or family violence. The operator will probably first ask you what your area code is so you can be given the correct number for your state. An 800 telephone number will not cost any money to dial. The person who answers is trained to help you and give you advice about what you can do next. One useful number is the Child Help I.O.F. National Child Abuse Hotline (1-800-4ACHILD [422-4453]; if this number changes, you can dial 1-800-555-1212 for new information).

You Can Change Your Mind

If you allow yourself to go further sexually and you realize afterward that this kind of sharing is not something you want for yourself at the time, you have a right to change your mind.

Even if you went further sexually with one person, it doesn't have to mean that you wish to share in the same way with someone else. *You* can make your own rules about sharing how much, with whom, and when.

It might interest you to know that there are many groups of young people in different parts of our country who are joining abstinence groups in order to support each other in their choice of abstinence (not having sex).

If you realize that you allowed yourself to share more than you really are ready for, you can tell your partner, "I've been thinking. What we did together really felt good. But it's too much for me to handle right now. I hope you understand."

Don't be surprised if your partner "tests" you to see if you really mean what you say. You may have to set your limits more than once to make sure they know that you really mean it. Once you repeat yourself, you'll know how much your partner respects you by how hard they try to push you to change your mind. If they stop going out with you, that will give you important information. Maybe sex was more important to them than you as a person.

I Want to Keep Going Out with You, But . . .

If you're just doing something sexual to make someone like you or to prove that you like them or try to be popular, then take a step back and ask yourself, "Is it really worth it?"

Although such sexual sharing might feel good while it lasts, unless you really thought about respecting your feelings before saying yes, you may have some doubts about how you feel about yourself afterwards.

If someone likes you for being you, then they should accept that it's your right to decide what you're ready to do and they won't try to push you (no matter what their friends or your friends are or are not doing).

What Can You Do When You Feel Pressured Sexually?

Jill, age fourteen, asked, "What do you do when boys want to have sex but you think it's wrong?" Leslie, age thirteen, asked, "How do you deal with boys who want to have sex and you don't?" Many girls have asked me how to deal with the sexual pressure they feel when boys want to touch or see parts of their bodies that they're not ready to share.

Boys have talked about pressure, too. Much of this pressure has to do with thinking they were expected to "make a sexual move" or "try something sexual," whether or not they wanted to, were ready for it, or even knew what to do. Some boys talked about finding it hard to say no when girls put sexual pressure on them.

Brian, age thirty-two, told me: "I went out with one girl who really was tired of me going so slow [sexually]. And she wanted me to be more aggressive [active, faster] with her. But I didn't trust her. She didn't treat me and react to me the same way each time I was with her. I wanted to find out if I could be comfortable with her before I shared more. She said to me, 'I may get bored.' But I'm not going to speed myself up because she's threatening me. If she feels our relationship is important, she'll be patient."

Many boys and girls talked about not knowing what to say or do in order to stop once the feelings were started.

Here are some possible ways to say NO:
- "NO!"
- "NO!"
- "NO!"
- "NO!"

Get the idea?

Here are some possible ways to say STOP:
- "STOP!"
- "STOP!"
- "STOP!"
- "STOP!"

This can also be used with "Please" or "Let's."

You might also say:
- "I hope you understand but I'm just not ready."
- "I really don't want to right now."
- "Please don't push me; I don't want to go any further."
- "Cut it out!"
- "This is much more than I can handle."
- "Enough!"
- "I'm really not interested in getting involved right now."
- "If you really respect me, you'll stop."
- "Keep your hands off me!"
- "I'm going home. . . ."

Another way to let someone know how you feel is telling them with motions instead of words. This is called communicating or speaking nonverbally (non-VER-buh-lee). Instead of saying "stop" with your voice, you can put up your hand, push a hand away, or even shake your head no. If your motions are clear, they'll get the message.

If you have already experienced feelings of sexual pressure, you'll probably find it easy to understand what I've been saying. If you can't relate to and have never felt sexual pressure, you can file this information away in your mind to be used at a later time.

Note: If you do feel good about what you are sharing with another person, it's nice to let them know. You can say something like, "That feels good," or "I like the way you did that," or "I really like it when you hold my hand."

Caring About Others

As important as it is to respect yourself and your own values, it's also important to respect and care about others. Just as other people do not have the right to pressure you into choices that aren't comfortable for you, you need to be concerned about how you treat other people.

Try to be sensitive to other people's feelings. Accept their right to their own values and beliefs, just as you hope they accept yours.

It will help to remember that it's often hard for people to share their true feelings. Especially with sexual sharing, it's common for people to keep their feelings inside rather than admit them aloud. Listen carefully to what they're saying verbally and nonverbally. If you sense their discomfort or concern, you might help them out by saying: "You seem uncomfortable, is everything okay?" "Is something bothering you?" "Do you want to stop?"

If you are not sure about what they're feeling, care enough to ask.

Parents and Sexual Feelings

Many kids think if there are four children in the family, their parents "did it" (had sexual intercourse) four times, three children, three times, and so on. But it might interest you to know that parents can continue to share themselves sexually for the rest of their lives together.

You might be saying to yourself, "Not my parents! I never see them even hold hands in front of me." I'm not making this point to interfere with your parents' privacy. But if you realize that your parents are sexual people, too, perhaps you'll feel more comfortable talking with them about things you never knew you could.

Here are some examples of how you might start a conversation with your parents:

- "This is hard for me to say."
- "I'm embarrassed to ask you this."
- "I know we've never talked about these things before, but I'd like to."
- "Please, I need to talk with you. I'm so scared and I don't know what to do. I made a really bad mistake. Please help me. . . ."
- "I know you might not think I'm old enough to talk about these things, but everyone talks about them and I'm not sure of what they mean."

Whatever you're feeling, remember to try to turn your feelings into words.

Give your parents a chance, if you haven't already. They would probably be happy to be able to help you, offer advice, or at least be a caring ear for your concerns. And they'd probably be very happy that you trusted them.

If your parents have been silent and have never talked with you about sexual facts and feelings, it's possible they're uncomfortable, too (they may never have spoken about this with *their* parents). Even if they're very interested and want so much to talk with you, it may seem strange and awkward for them to be talking with their own children about such grown-up things. They may not know how to approach you, just as you may be unsure of what to say to them.

Also, some parents worry about children knowing too much too soon. If your parents hold back information, it may help you to understand that they may be concerned about this. If you feel you need more information and sense they're not giving you the full explanation, ask more questions and let them know *you* know there's more.

Those parents who worry about how much their children learn might think that as soon as their child knows about sexual feelings and sexual intercourse, they'll probably run right out and try it. They may not realize that the only way for their child to make responsible decisions is if he or she understands the facts, feelings, choices, and possible wanted or unwanted results, as well as what all of these might mean.

If you have tried to talk to your parents and they refuse to discuss sexual topics with you, you might tell them once again how much it means to you to be able to go to them with your concerns rather than to anyone else. Sharing this section, the whole chapter, or any other part of this book might also help open up conversation between you and your parents. If you still have difficulty talking with them, at least you will have tried very hard to make them understand. Perhaps you can try to talk to them again in a few days or weeks.

If this is your situation, you might consider talking about your feelings, questions, and concerns with another trusted adult.

Be careful when taking facts from your friends. Sometimes they'll be correct and sometimes not. If you still need more information about any topic, you can also ask your school or public librarian to help you.

A Final Plea

Take a step back and seriously review your own thoughts and feelings regarding going out, sexual sharing, and what your own values are. Identify what you feel are your sexual limits. Challenge yourself. Try to imagine what kind of relationship or situation would ever allow you to be tempted to go beyond where you know it's important to stop.

Please, care enough about yourself to at least take the time to think seriously about what chances you're taking and how you might feel if unwanted results happened to you or your partner. Think about what changes might be important for you to make so that you avoid taking serious chances.

And remember: You have a right to your own sense of self-respect. You have a right to your own feelings of readiness. You have a right to be strong about your values. No relationship can be so important that it should push you over the edge of your own readiness or what you deep down feel is right for you at your age.

Unwanted results can happen to anyone. Even you. If you let them. It's up to you to say no to unwanted results. Isn't it a relief to know that you can?

CHAPTER 17

COMPARING CLOTHES, GRADES, AND LOOKS, COMPETING IN SPORTS AND TRYOUTS

Have you ever felt terrific because finally your grade was as good as or higher than the class brain's? Have you ever looked at someone and said to yourself (or to others), "It's disgusting that her hair looks so perfect all the time," and wondered, "Why doesn't mine?"

Have you ever stopped yourself from trying out for cheerleading, a part in your school play, or an athletic team because you felt other people would probably get picked instead of you? Have you ever felt terrible because you didn't have the sneakers that "everyone" was wearing?

It's natural for you to compare yourself with others. It's another way to learn about who you are and where you stand among your peers. If you think you measure up, that may make a big difference in how great you feel about yourself. If you think you don't measure up, you might make the sad mistake of wishing you were someone else instead of accepting, appreciating, and valuing who you really are.

Competition is a part of everyone's life. It can make you try harder and be able to do things better than you might ever have done them. It can also make you feel you shouldn't try at all.

Clothes

Clothes can make you look dressed up, grown-up, sloppy, sexy, comfortable, stiff, silly, handsome, beautiful, rich, poor, "with it," or "out of it." Some kids don't care at all about clothes; others are thinking it might be fun to test out a new look. Still others think clothes are very important. What do clothes mean to you?

Many times kids will judge others mainly by their clothes, never bothering to learn about the person inside. But clothes can tell only so much about a person. While clothes can give hints about how neat a boy or girl is and whether his or her tastes are similar, they can't tell what kind of friend that person would be. People don't always wear clothes that reflect their inside beauty.

Still, there's a lot of peer pressure about clothes, a lot of comparing. For example, some kids think if they wear jeans with designer labels on them, that makes them better than someone else who doesn't. And those kids who want very much to be accepted think if they run out and buy the same jeans with the same labels, then the "better" people will like them.

It's too bad more kids don't realize that better labels don't make better people. Some people are not as beautiful as their clothes! Besides, it's not the clothes you become friendly with, it's the person inside the clothes. When was the last time you threw a ball to a uniform, told a secret to a T-shirt, or asked a sweater to go for pizza?

Some kids have the courage to wear whatever they wish, even if it's different. Many others try to dress like everyone else—labels or not—hoping that will give them a better chance to be accepted.

As you read about the many different feelings kids have shared with me about clothes, try to take a few guesses as to why they feel the way they do. It might give you some extra understanding about your own feelings.

Maggie, age eleven, said, "Most of the time I wear jeans and sweatshirts to school. But my mom bought me a mini-skirt outfit that I've been wanting for a long time. When I wore it to school, one of the girls in my class said that my shoes didn't match my mini-skirt.

"I was so embarrassed and wondered how many other kids also thought my shoes didn't match. Some of the kids in my school seem to have a different pair of shoes for each thing they wear! Well, I have my sneakers and one pair of shoes. I just couldn't wear my mini to school again. I didn't want to think that kids would be checking to see if I matched.

"My parents say they spent too much money on it for me to leave it in my closet. I told them I'd save it for when we go visiting, but I just can't wear it to school. It makes me sad—angry, too. But I can't."

Peter, age thirteen, told me, "I've been paying more attention to how I look. I can't believe that I, the shopping hater, asked to go shopping a few weeks ago. I think my parents must have freaked after all those years of arguing with them when they forced me to go for clothes. Maybe it's because of the girls. I don't know. But all of a sudden I care about how other people see me. It also makes me feel good to look good."

Barry, age twelve, said, "I always loved getting hand-me-downs from my cousins. Even though they weren't new, it made me feel good to have some different things to wear." Jessica, age ten, said, "I hate getting hand-me-downs. I never get to pick what I like. I never get to wear something new. I understand there are a lot of kids in my family and clothes cost a lot of money, but sometimes I wish just once I could get a whole bunch of clothes that are mine and no one else's first!"

Lawrence, age thirteen, said, "I've heard some kids say, 'Oh, John? He's so popular, he could wear anything he wants.' If he wanted to wear a skirt to school, I don't think kids would tease him!"

Mrs. H., age forty-five, said, "My daughter drives me crazy with her clothes sometimes. It's so hard to say no to her because I know she'll probably storm out of the room and make it unpleasant for everyone else in the family to be around her. But there's a limit to what she can get. She tries to make me feel guilty by saying things like, 'Oh, please, everyone is wearing it, and I want it so badly. It's not fair. It's going to be your fault if everyone doesn't think I look good.' "

Christine, age twelve, said, "All the girls who have nice clothes think they're such hotshots."

Bobby, age twelve, said, "I don't pay clothes much attention. When I wake up, I just grab whatever is at the top of my drawer and put it on."

Susan, age ten, told me that she thinks clothes are important and carefully plans what she's going to wear the next day in school. Each night she lines up her clothes very neatly near her bed. Sometimes she has fun making the clothes look like they're on a make-believe person.

Nancy, age fifteen, remembers a time in the sixth grade when she was really growing out of her old jeans and badly needed a new pair. Her mom finally got the chance to take her shopping, and it took a long time to find a pair that fit well.

It happened to have a designer label, but she bought it because it was the best-fitting pair, not because of the label. She felt great when she arrived at school the next day. She knew her jeans looked good, and the feeling made her smile to herself.

As soon as she put her coat in her locker, kids started commenting on her jeans. They teased her about the label, called her snobby, and it didn't take long for her inside smile to turn to inside tears!

Said Nancy, "After I felt so hurt, I started to get angry. I know why I got them. They fit better than any other pair in the store. And they were more comfortable. Why does everyone always have something to say about everyone else? Anyway, I decided that I wasn't going to let them make a big deal out of this, so I told them to shut up about it. After a couple of days, they left me alone."

Isn't it interesting how one scrunched-up nose or a few words can make someone not want to wear something? The kids who can take the judging are usually those who feel pretty confident about themselves. Others, who feel less sure, probably wish they could run right back home, open their closet door, jump in, and stay there! But, even if someone is confident enough not to be shaken by the judging, negative judgments don't feel good to anybody.

If you're one of those kids who thinks hanging out means hiding in your closet, think again. So maybe your family doesn't have the kind of money to buy you T-shirts in every color or fifteen new pairs of shoes to match each skirt. Maybe while you're waiting for hand-me-downs, your jacket from two years ago looks like it's been used as third base in too many games. Maybe that's embarrassing to you and doesn't make you feel very good about yourself.

Remember when I talked about things you can control and things you can't? You can't help it if your parents don't have the money to buy you great clothes. Even if they did, you'd find that after a while, the clothes wouldn't mean as much as who you are. That, you can control.

It would help if, when parents choose to buy their children tons of clothes, they would remember to also teach them respect for others—no matter how much they have. Just as many kids feel that the designer labels make them "better," they often think that having a lot of clothes makes them better than someone else who has less. Kids need to understand that clothes don't "make" the person. Clothes are just clothes! (We'll talk more about this in "Getting Past Differences," Chapter 25.)

So, how much importance do you place on clothes? Here are some questions that will help you think about your answer:

- How much checking do you do to see how your clothes look compared to everyone else's?
- If kids you wanted to be friendly with were all wearing the same thing and you didn't have it, would you feel it was important to ask your parents to buy it for you?
- If you liked wearing clothes that are a little different than those around you, would you be confident enough to wear them anyway? (How concerned would you be about people making comments, teasing, or looking at you as if you had six eyebrows?)
- How important are clothes when you're trying to decide whether or not you want to be friendly with a person? Would a person's clothes prevent you from wanting to get to know someone?

Much of what you might feel can result from the influence your parents have on you. Sometimes it's not the boy or girl who thinks of comparing; it's the parents who ask, point out, and make it important to talk about how much money clothes cost. It may be hard to separate what you feel from what your parents feel and are teaching you.

Sometimes your parents and friends may have a strong say in the kinds of clothes you wear. Even when you don't realize you're letting them choose for you, there may be a little tiny voice in your head that's saying, "Oh, come on, pick this style. You know the other one's just not 'you.' "

But that may not be your voice. It may really be theirs, but you think it's yours. Or you know it's theirs, but you believe that they know what's best for you. So, you listen.

The truth is, along with changes in your emotions and your body, it's likely that your tastes will change, too. If you're a sweatshirt person but have a secret feeling you'd like to see what a frilly blouse looks like, or if you always wear football jerseys or T-shirts and you wonder how you'd look in a crew-neck sweater with a shirt underneath, take a chance. Experiment. At least allow yourself to try it on, so you can see how it looks and feels.

Your friends may tease you and ask if you're going to church or something. But if you know you feel good, that's what counts. In time they'll get used to your new look and may even decide to try it.

Grades

Eleven-year-old Leslie said, "There's one girl in my class who always gets hundreds on everything in social studies. When I ask her what she got, she tells me one hundred, and I give her a look. I say, 'of course.' And then she gives me a look."

Mindy, age nine, told me, "We have a lot of smarty pants in our school . . . people who get hundred averages in everything. Some of them are nice but a lot of them brag about their grades."

Tommy, age ten, said, "I hate it when my teacher reads the grades out loud. I get pretty low grades, and she always ends up reading mine last or almost last. I know the kids in my class think I'm stupid compared to them. I think so, too."

Cindy, age thirteen, told me, "Sometimes I feel like lying because it makes me feel funny to always get one of the highest grades in the class. Then people look at me and make faces and say to each other, 'I knew it!' I'll bet they think I'm the teacher's pet or something."

Scott, age twelve, said, "My friends and I always compare grades after a test. If I got a lower grade and everyone else did, too, I don't feel so bad. Then when I have to tell my parents, I can tell them that the class really didn't do that well or that I'm not the only one to have gotten a grade like that."

David, age thirteen, told me, "I'm in competition all the time for grades with this kid in my class. My father always asks me about my grades. I tell my dad and he always asks what did that other kid get. If he does better than me, my father always asks why. It just drives me up a wall. Sometimes I'd just rather not deal with it."

I asked David if all the pressure is from his father or if some of it is from himself. David answered, "Sometimes I pressure myself just as much as my parents pressure me. I always try to get better than him. Every time I get a better grade than him I'm always very happy because he's a genius. He stays home every day and studies. And I don't even do close to that because half the time I'm out in the afternoon."

"I always feel awful when I have to take tests," said Bonnie, who's eleven. "My sister had the same teacher three years ago and got very good grades. I always feel that the teacher compares me to her and expects my grades to be as good as my sister's."

So often kids feel the higher the grade, the better the person—sort of like designer labels on jeans: better label, better person. Not so! They're always asking each other, "What did you get?" or, "Let me see your paper."

If your grade was higher, you probably wouldn't mind showing it. In fact, you might tell your classmates before they had a chance to ask. A higher grade can make you feel proud, relieved, really good, and prevent hassles with your parents. You, your classmates, teachers, and parents might think that higher grades make you a better person.

A higher grade might also make you feel like tiptoeing out of the classroom, hoping no one asks you what you earned. Many would rather keep their higher grade private because they don't want to be known as the "class brain."

If you get a lower grade, you may not want anyone to know. Those are the test papers that kids sometimes try to stuff in someone else's garbage can on the way home, praying that the teacher won't call their parents to tell them what the grade is. (That's probably why many teachers ask their students to bring the paper back signed by a parent.)

Lower grades can make you feel frustrated, embarrassed, confused, upset—and stupid. Kids who get mostly lower grades often do not have a high opinion of themselves. They may not think they're as good as everyone else. They may even say they hate school (really, they hate how it feels to get those lower grades) and stop trying.

It's hard to feel good about trying when you don't think you're "worth it." A lot of kids end up thinking, "Why should I bother? I guess I'm just not a good student."

Did you ever think that maybe your 75 percent is a very good grade for you? That's not to say you shouldn't try to get a 77 or an 80 or even higher. But maybe you'll never get in the 90s—it might be unfair and unrealistic to expect that you should. It doesn't mean you're a bad student and everyone else who gets higher grades is better than you. It simply means that's the level you're working at right now, and you can try to advance yourself from there as best you can—at your own rate. No matter what your grade, you can work hard and be a good student. You have a right to be proud of yourself and feel successful at your own level. The problem comes when people compare and think they should be working at everyone else's level.

The next time you find yourself about to make a negative comment on someone's lower grade, stop! If your friends bug you about your grade, tell them to bug off. The next time you start getting down on yourself, remember that you're not your friends; you're not your brother or sister, you're you. If you can honestly say you tried your best, that's all you can hope to do. And that's a lot.

So instead of chipping away at your good feelings and letting yourself believe you're not as good as others, realize you're as good as *anyone* anywhere. No matter who, no matter what. Your specialness—how worthwhile, valuable or important you are—doesn't depend on grades or anything else.

And if you don't do as well as you feel is within you, you know you have the power to learn from your mistakes. Ask your parents or teachers to explain them to you, if you're not sure why you made them. With some extra effort and extra help, you can hope to do better next time.

The only person it's fair for you to compete with is *you*. Challenge yourself! And if you want to compare, check back and see if you improved your own grade. Even if you raise your grade one point, I hope you can allow yourself to be proud. Next time you can try for another point and then another and another. There's no telling how far you can go . . . point by point by point.

If you've sincerely tried your hardest and your parents still tell you how disappointed they are in you, asking why you can't do as well as your brother or sister, it's important to tell them your feelings about being pressured and compared. They may have no idea how you feel. Instead of spending so much time talking about what you're not able to do, suggest to them that they teach you better ways to approach your studying and organize your time. That can help you feel more confident and prepared to do your work.

A higher or lower grade doesn't say anything about how much fun a person is to be with, if they're kind, or if they would make a good friend. Maybe if friends, parents, sisters, brothers, and teachers would try even harder to accept that each person is different, there would be less teasing, fewer bad feelings, and less pressure.

Sports

Most boys and girls love sports. Only some kids are really good at them. Others are okay. And still others are what lots of people call uncoordinated. These differences have created many kinds of feelings and pressures.

Robert, age twenty-nine, shared, "I never had someone to play ball with when I was growing up. My father was always too busy and my older brother wasn't an athlete. He was always playing his guitar or going on dates or hanging out with his friends. I missed it."

Joan, age eighteen, told me, "The first time I tried to play volleyball in gym class, I was in the seventh grade. I couldn't get the ball more than halfway up toward the net. I was smaller than most of the other kids and everybody laughed. They didn't even hide their laughter. Every time it was my turn to serve, I couldn't do any better. Every time I stepped up to try, they started whispering and laughing again. Even though the teacher told them to be nice, I became the class joke."

Abby, age twelve, said, "When we pick teams, I'm one of the last to be picked. It's not that I'm bad at sports. It's just that I'm not one of the popular kids. Most of the time, they're the captains or they'll whisper to the person who is the captain."

Mrs. T. age sixty-three, said that when her son was in eighth grade, he played Little League baseball. He wasn't a good athlete, but he liked the game. "The coach's son, David, came to the door one day, just before it was time to sign up again in the ninth grade. He said, 'Hi, Mrs. T., do you know if Charlie [her son] is going to play ball again this year?' I told him I was pretty sure he wasn't. David said, 'Good. He was the worst on the team!' " Neither of them knew that Charlie was standing right behind his mother and heard every word.

Richie, age thirteen, said, "I'm really nervous about making the basketball team this year. I was on it last year, but I just blew tryouts. I have another chance later in the week. I'll be so embarrassed in front of everyone if I don't make it again and kids from a lower grade make it instead of me."

George, age thirty-four, said, "I remember standing by the backstop at my elementary school playground, watching kids yell at each other or pick on some boy for not being a good player. I never understood why kids were so cruel. The bad player was really nice but just couldn't play baseball."

Danny, age fourteen, said, "Since I made the team, people seem to be acting differently toward me. Some of the popular girls actually talked to me at lunch yesterday."

Barry, age fifteen, said, "In the sixth grade, it was the 'in' group that played semi-hardball before school. That was *the* group! If you didn't play, you were not part of the crowd. There was always a lot of pressure about that."

Lenny, age twenty-nine, said, "I think if I had been more into sports, I wouldn't have got into so much trouble. I just never felt I was good enough to play. So I hung around with the gangs instead."

Alan, age thirteen, said, "I was playing first singles for my school tennis team last fall. The kid I was supposed to play walked onto the court, and my friends and I looked at each other and had a hard time holding in our laughs. He was kind of fat and we were sure he wouldn't even be able to run for a ball. I figured the match would be a piece of cake! Well, he beat me. I guess you can never tell by looking at someone how good they'll be."

Robin, age eleven, said, "People were always making fun of me when I played after-school sports, so I stopped playing. My parents said I could take dance lessons. I'm doing really well. Now, even if kids tease me about not being good in gym class, it doesn't make me feel bad because I know that I'm good at my dancing."

Mary, age ten, told me, "I was playing goalie at our play-off soccer game last week. We beat that team already but couldn't make a goal this time. That was okay because neither could they. So the score was tied at zero to zero. Just before the game ended, they tried to score again and I don't know what happened. I just couldn't stop it. So they scored and won the game. Everybody was saying things like, 'Didn't you see it coming?' and 'I can't believe you missed it!' I felt awful."

If you're a good athlete, you probably already know how important sports ability can be. To many kids, even if your grades are lower, somehow being good at sports is more important. You're still respected, often envied (that means people are jealous of you), often very popular, just about always included, and never picked last.

If you're not good at sports, you may well understand the pain of being left out, the embarrassment of being teased, the feeling of being laughed at, or overhearing teammates say that they would have won the game if it wasn't for you.

While good athletes seem to play whatever they want, poor athletes may choose never to play at all, even if they want very much to play. It takes a lot of guts to get out on a court or a field and know that you can't completely trust yourself to catch the ball. But you don't have to catch it every time. Even professional athletes drop balls every once in a while! Not everybody is good at everything. But everybody can try. And every person deserves to be on a team, if he or she is interested.

If you can't make a school team, there are plenty of chances in gym class, in after-school sign-up sports (often called intramurals), and with your friends at a playground or in the street. You can also get together with kids who are not the top athletes and have a game at your own playing level, where there might be less pressure. Just because you're not a super-jock doesn't mean you shouldn't play at all.

If you don't want to play a team sport, you can play what's known as an individual sport—one that you can do by yourself. You can jog and no one need judge how far or how fast you run. You can swim without judges. You can roller-skate, Rollerblade, ice-skate, or skateboard. You can take long walks and just take in the fresh air, think a little bit, and feel refreshed. You can go fishing or biking. You can swim or ride a horse. You can try golf and all kinds of dance. You can work out and do many different types of exercise for your body. You can also hit a ball against a wall by yourself and improve your tennis arm. You can ski.

Some recreation centers offer free or low-cost lessons in many different activities. Even if your parents or older brother or sister aren't athletes or don't have time, you might be able to ask one of your friends, another relative, a neighbor, a friend's parent, or a teacher to help you learn a skill. Sometimes you need to let your parents, sister, or brother know that you're interested. Don't expect them to magically guess what you wish they would do.

Perhaps one of the most helpful things to remember is that even though everyone is different, everyone has a right to enjoy playing. Once again, "good athlete" doesn't have to mean "better person." It's who you are, not how you play, that makes you special.

If you're a strong athlete, you can help by saying "Nice try" to someone who messes up a play, setting a great example for others on the team. You might be very surprised when you see that the more encouragement you give, the freer your teammates will probably be to try. The more pressured, the more they might tighten up and make mistakes because they're so nervous and upset. Each person's positive attitude can be a big help, not only for the person who's trying so hard, but also for team spirit.

Looks

Everyone is beautiful. But not everyone believes it. People look at others to check and make sure about their own looks. They compare. Depending upon how other people look, they may still think they're beautiful, decide that they're less beautiful, or maybe think they're not beautiful at all. In fact, many people really believe they're ugly!

That's very sad. If you think you're ugly, you probably don't feel so good about yourself. You may shy away from people. You may keep to yourself. You may not think other kids would want to be your friend or go out with you. You may not ever give yourself and others a chance to appreciate how special you are.

There are some people who look physically beautiful and yet, because the way they dress may not be so cool, because they're not particularly good at sports, because they tend to be quiet and shy, or because they're not around enough people so that friends can say to them, "Hey, you know something, you're really cute!" they don't think they're good-looking. When kids don't get this kind of *feedback* (when someone gives you information about yourself), they often don't feel that their body and face is a good as anyone else's. So, they think they're ugly because no one ever tells them they're good looking.

Lois, age thirty-three, remembers that when she was in junior high school, one of the most popular girls had short, stubby legs and blond hair. She said to her friend one day, "So-and-so has got the nicest legs! They're short and fat. I only wish I could have short and fat legs. Then maybe I could be popular."

Sometimes kids who are not in the popular group think if they had a particular feature that the popular kids had, then maybe they'd be popular, too. Lois didn't realize that people don't become friends with legs, anyway. Whether they were short, long, fat, skinny, just didn't matter. Yet it seemed so important at the time.

When Lois got to high school, she looked at that girl's legs and thought, "How could she have been popular with those legs?" But in junior high, she had thought, "Maybe if I had that kind of legs, I'd be popular too."

Sometimes when people don't feel so good about themselves, it's hard for them to see the truth. While your body is in the process of growing, it may just be that your arms or legs are a little bit lankier and longer. During the time your body is getting used to the changes that have taken place, you might even find yourself tripping over your own feet. If you're thinking that you're ugly, it may just be that you're not as graceful as you once were and will be again when you get used to your new size and shape.

Every person can have an inside beauty no matter what his or her outside looks like. If people are beautiful on the outside, that might make them nice to look at, but it won't mean for sure that they're nice to know. They *may* be nice, but that's not because of their looks. Feeling good about knowing them has much less to do with their face, their hair, their body, their clothes, and much more to do with what kind of person they are on the inside. What makes a person beautiful is something that can't be seen—until you begin to get to know them for who they are.

You may be saying, "But I'm really ugly." If you're talking about the feeling that your outside looks are ugly, well, maybe it's time to deal with that feeling a little differently.

First of all, is it your ears that you don't like? Your eyebrows? Your chin? Your cheekbones? Your neck? Your hair? Your legs? Your rear end? Your thighs? Your hands? Are you overweight? Skinny? Are your knees kind of funny looking? Too many pimples? Too many freckles? Do you feel you're too short? Are you too developed or not developed enough? Is your nose too wide, too long, too bumpy, too pointy?

Though it may be hard to be honest about this, can you figure out exactly what it is that gives you the "uglies"? It might help to write down your own private ugly list, so you can understand your feelings a little better. Think carefully about what you come up with and then try to decide which things you might be able to change and which you can't.

Since it wouldn't be fair or helpful to pressure yourself to change everything at once, pick one thing to start with. For example do you think you would feel better about yourself if you lost a few pounds? If so, you can decide to change your eating habits and ask your parents to help by buying and guiding you to eat the right things and stay healthy while you lose weight. Maybe a new hairstyle or a change in the type of clothes you wear would freshen up your look. Getting involved with some kind of physical activity might also help.

If your ugly list is mostly made up of things you can't change, then you've got some work to do. A can't-change example would be that you can't switch your legs for new ones, stretch your neck, or speed up or slow down your development. But you might be happily surprised anyway. Just realizing what you cannot change can be the relief that will allow you to stop dwelling on it and go on to other things.

You've got to start, even if it's little by little, trying to accept each thing that you cannot change as the part of you that's always going to stay the same, no matter what you do about it. If you don't, you may never feel good about yourself.

So which will it be: feeling ugly forever, or finding the beauty in yourself that nothing on the outside can touch? You can start right this minute if you want to.

Though I just talked mostly about people who don't have good feelings about their looks, there are lots of people who do. Those are the people who feel beautiful inside as well as outside. Yet there are some people who look beautiful but don't feel very beautiful. They don't see themselves as beautiful.

Vicki, age thirteen, said that her mother always told her that she was pretty. But she never believed her mother because Vicki was 5 foot 8 inches tall, had long and swinging arms that were very gawky, and was a twig. She used to walk with her shoulders slouched so that no one would see she was not developed. She wore glasses and some people called her "four eyes." Very few of her friends said she was pretty and she didn't feel pretty. Her ugly inside feelings made her outside looks and personality kind of dull.

It took Vicki until high school to realize that she could grow out of gawky feelings, get new frames for her glasses, get a sensational haircut, and learn how to apply makeup. It was her inside confidence that made her outside looks and personality sparkle and come to life. She started to feel beautiful inside and outside.

Other people may be very happy with the way they look compared to everyone else. But they're not happy with themselves. Even with their good looks, they may be lonely.

You see, people need more than looks to fill emptiness, more than looks to make friends. As you read the different feelings shared by boys and girls as well as adults, you'll get an even better idea of how outside looks can affect the way people feel about themselves and others.

Patty, age thirteen, said, "I'm pretty conscious of the way I look. I've broken my nose a few times. There are really weird people in my school. They stick notes in my locker and call me birdie and stuff like that. If there's a kid that I like, I feel like covering my nose."

(We may see ourselves differently from the way anyone else sees us. A nose that seems too long on our own face may be passed right by without a blink by others.)

Patty doesn't realize that her nose is not who she is. Besides, if people can't see past the end of her nose, it's probably not worth bothering to spend time with them anyway.

Gerard, age eighteen, said, "Sometimes I wish I wasn't so good-looking. I get the feeling that people are afraid to come up to me because their looks are not as good as mine. Maybe they think I won't talk to them. Even when I go up to them, they seem to get a little nervous, like they have to watch how they act or what they say."

Maureen, age ten, said, "My friends always tease me about being fat. What really hurts is that they do it behind my back. Sometimes I hear them talking about me. They say I eat three candy bars at lunch, when I really don't. They eat more candy bars than I do and none of them are fat. It makes me feel horrible, and it's also not fair that I eat less and am fat and they eat more and they're skinny."

Billy, age twelve, said, "I hate it when the kids tease this girl in my lunchroom. She has white hair and is kind of weird looking but she's nice. I had to do a project with her."

Samantha, age eleven, told me, "I wish I could have hair like my friends. Mine is kinky and like Brillo. My white girlfriends have soft, silky hair, and mine is never going to be like theirs. Sometimes it makes me feel so ugly, but at other times when I cornrow it, it's really funky and I love it."

Andrea, age forty-eight, remembers feeling very embarrassed about her legs. Said Andrea, "They reminded me of tree trunks. That's why I hated gym. We had to wear a silly-looking short gymsuit that made my legs look even worse. I made excuses not to play whenever I could."

Craig, age fifteen, said, "When the girls come over to our lunch table, I know they're coming to see my friends and not me. The guys I'm friendly with are really good-looking and I'm kind of puny next to them."

Chris, age fourteen, said, "I am extremely short and need to grow. Everyone calls me Pee-wee. It's sort of become like a nickname by now and I really don't like it. But everybody thinks I do."

Diane, age fourteen, said, "I get so angry when I wake up with pimples on my face. They make me feel so ugly. Until they're gone, I just feel like burying my head or wearing a mask whenever someone talks to me close up. I wish we got them on our knees instead of our faces!"

"My best friend is so beautiful," said Marni, age thirteen. "All the boys follow her around. I know I'll never be beautiful. I don't know whether to love her or hate her sometimes."

As you can see, too many people don't understand that outside beauty is not as important as a person's feelings and who they are. They tease, often cause embarrassment, and help to create ugly feelings.

If you think that outside beauty is all it takes to be beautiful, what happens to the person who is born with a birthmark covering much of his or her face? What about the person who is injured and has a permanent facial scar? The person who loses a leg, is paralyzed and must remain in a wheelchair, or has a deformed arm or any other disability? Does that mean the person can never be beautiful? No! Everyone can develop their inner beauty, if they believe they can.

It's hard for kids (and many adults) to realize that beauty is such a personal thing. No two people see things quite the same way. What one person may believe is beautiful, another may not. Isn't it a shame that so many people see themselves only through other people's eyes? They allow other people to judge if they're beautiful or not. And they judge themselves by other people's looks.

If only more people could realize they have the power to decide to see themselves—and appreciate themselves—through their own eyes. They only need to look inside themselves to see how beautiful they really are—no matter what their shape or size, or how they look on the outside. No matter what anyone else says.

A special note about permanently changing your looks In this day and age, doctors can perform special surgery to change just about every possible part of the body in order to make it appear more the way a person wishes it would be.

Cosmetic surgery should not be considered lightly, as if you were just going out and changing a pair of jeans. Like all surgery, it has risks and it has benefits. Also, surgery can be expensive.

I would strongly suggest that you sit with your uncomfortable feelings about your nose or any other body part for a long, long time in order to make sure that having such surgery is really what you want to do. (Of course, this must be discussed with and arranged by your parents or other adult you may live with.) Wouldn't it be sad to find out after surgery that it wasn't ever your nose that was bothering you, but instead that you were unhappy with yourself inside?

If it turns out, after much thought and discussion with your parents and doctors, that changing a physical part of you through surgery is what you want for yourself, you now know that it's likely that such a choice can be possible.

Competition During Tryouts

Tryouts—whether for a part in your school play, getting on a sports team, becoming a cheerleader, becoming a school officer, being elected representative to student government, or getting a solo in a chorus concert—can be a real test of how good you feel about yourself.

Tryouts test your confidence; they test your cool. Some kids who are really good at what they're trying out for are a disaster at tryouts! That's probably because they "choke." As thirteen-year-old John said, "I always fold in tryouts."

"Tryouts make me nervous," said Donna, age twelve. "Tryouts can really be embarrassing because everyone will be watching you and maybe everybody else will make it and you won't," said Allison, age twelve. Robby, age eleven, said, "I always worry that everyone will be better."

After all the talk we've done about trying not to judge—that's just what tryouts set out to do. When you sign up or appear for a tryout, you are asking to be judged. You're taking a risk. You're saying, "This is me; this is what I can do; these are my talents; this is how good I am, now judge me!" You're allowing yourself to compete and be compared with everyone else who wants to get the same position. Tryouts can be very exciting and very scary. Tryouts take guts!

Yes, everyone may be better than you at the tryouts. Yes, most of the kids might be picked instead of you. Yes, it can be scary and even embarrassing to put yourself through such a test. But just because tryouts are not the most comfortable thing to do, that doesn't mean that they're not good for you.

To be able to get up in front of judges and your peers and at least try, says a lot for the kind of strength and confidence that you have. As I've said so many times, each person is different. Each person has his or her own abilities, and some people are better than others at certain things. But everyone can try.

Some people who want very much to try out don't. They're the ones who especially don't feel very confident. They may not want to deal with worrying that other kids will laugh at them or spread around the school how poorly they did. So they stay away. My guess is, if people respect them and like them as people, then no matter how poor they are at tryouts, they'll be loved anyway. Others will probably even feel, "Good for them that they had the guts to be here."

You might hear someone say, "I'm not going to try out because I'm not going to make it anyway. So it's stupid to try out." Well, if they don't try out, they definitely will not make it. If they try out, at least they have a chance. And since they don't feel they'll make it, they won't be disappointed or surprised when they don't. So why not try? They have nothing to lose and might just gain!

Tryouts can teach you a lot as well as be fun; some kids love to watch how everyone else does. Proving to yourself that you can actually get up in front of a group of people and take the chance can help strengthen your confidence. I spoke with a girl who ran for vice president of her school several months ago. She wanted to win but really didn't expect to. When she found out she lost, she wasn't so upset because she felt so good about having the guts to run. She proved to herself that she could try. She had never done anything like that before.

Trying out lets you see what skill level the other kids seem to have (even though some kids "fold" and aren't really showing the judges how good they can be). Some people are surprised to find that they're not as bad as they thought they were. In fact, they're pretty good, compared to the other kids who tried out. All this time, they never thought they could come close. So the experience of trying out gives you a chance to compare your skill level and get a sense of where you stand.

If you try out, you can also learn more about what the judges are looking for. By watching the other kids perform and learning who is picked, you can put the two together and figure out what was important to the judges and what wasn't. Then you can practice and be much better prepared next time.

It might help to realize that sometimes judging isn't as fair as you'd like to think it would be. Since we're dealing with judges who are human beings, there are personal human feelings that sometimes can get in the way of fair judging. As thirteen-year-old Marcy said, "Some teachers will give kids parts because they like them and have them in class, not because they're better than the other kids who tried out."

Even though I'd like to believe that most judges try to be fair, sometimes kids are picked who shouldn't have been picked, and kids are left out who should have been included. But that's life—who ever said everything was going to be fair?

Fourteen-year-old Mitchell said, "At the younger grades, usually the most popular kid is voted for representative or school office. Even if they're not good. When kids get a little older, it doesn't matter as much if the person is popular; people are more likely to pick the better person for the job."

Donna, age fourteen, said, "I can't believe it. I practiced all last year and the beginning of this year to try to make cheerleading and I screwed up at the tryouts. I was so nervous!"

Jessie, age thirteen, said, "It's really bad when you make a team and everyone knows—and so do you—that the only reason why you made it was because you're the teacher's pet or your sister was good."

Patricia, age eleven, said, "Sometimes it's hard to decide if you want to try out, even if you know you're really good and you will probably make it. If none of your friends make it, then you won't know anyone else on the team."

Charles, age twelve, said, "It's embarrassing when you tell everyone that you know you're going to make it and someone else won't. And then you don't make it and they do."

Bobby, age fourteen, said, "I can't stand the pressure at tryouts. Especially when everyone expects you to make the team. I wish no one else would have to watch."

Susie, age twelve, told me, "My friends got really jealous when I was picked for cheerleading and they didn't make it."

Nine-year-old Seth said, "If you start bragging about getting on the team and you spread around school that you expect to get it, then you might be embarrassed if you don't get picked."

Thirteen-year-old Andy said, "One of the problems with tryouts is the waiting, knowing that the list is going to be posted after fourth period."

Hank, age thirteen, said, "I was really angry that this kid got picked instead of me. I know I'm better than he is. I just can't understand it."

Gail, age eleven, told me, "Everyone thought the girl who was running for president would get it because all the boys would vote for her. She has tits! But she lost, anyway."

Judging Yourself—Needing to Be "Perfect"

Now that you have a better understanding of the different ways people compare themselves with one another and how they make judgments from their comparisons, there's one more thing to consider.

That is, sometimes you can judge yourself more harshly than anyone else judges you. Some kids can never be "perfect" enough for themselves, and that adds a great deal of pressure and frustration to anything that they're doing. They never quite measure up to their own standards for themselves, so it's hard to feel good.

They may get very, very upset if they receive 95 rather than 100, may expect themselves never to make mistakes, always to look their best, never to miss a ball, always to handle whatever is required of them. Even if everyone around them, including parents and teachers, begs them, "Please take it easy on yourself!" "So, you made a mistake. . . . It's okay. It's no big deal." Or, "I'm so proud of you. I just wish you could be proud of yourself."

There really will be times when you won't do as well as you would like. You may not have the particular talent, or you may simply fall short of what you know you're able to do. All of us, adults included, experience times such as those.

But you can only do the best you can at any given moment. Even kids who understand that's true might find it hard to "give themselves a break," appreciate that they did their best, and realize they can learn something positive from every experience. (In fact, sometimes the biggest disappointments can teach us the most powerful life lessons.)

If you're saying to yourself right now, "That's me! I know I always need to be perfect," take a few moments to think about what makes you feel that way. Is it that you feel perfection is the measure for who you are? For whether or not kids will like you and include you? For how your parents or other family members feel about you?

By now I hope you understand more fully that your worth is something that is not measured by performance of any kind. You're valuable and important and special, no matter what—it has nothing to do with grades, looks, tryouts, sports ability, or anything else.

If you know you're being hard on yourself, the first step toward easing up is to admit it. The next step is to decide you want to do something about it. Then, take each situation as it comes and try to respond in a more accepting, positive way.

It may help to understand that just because you've made the decision to go easier on yourself may not change how you first feel when your performance falls short of your expectations. Your instant response may still be to get down on yourself because you're so used to doing that. While you may not be able to prevent those first "down" feelings, what you do about those feelings is what can begin to change.

At those moments when you find you're being hard on yourself again, it can help to talk to yourself and say, "Hold it. You need to *chill!* Take it easy. You know you tried your best. Come on, stop making yourself feel miserable. *Enough!* You deserve to feel good about how hard you tried."

I'm not suggesting that making this type of change is easy. And it may take a while before those "getting down on yourself" feelings completely stop, especially if you've been judging yourself so harshly for a long time. It can help a great deal to talk about your feelings with parents, teachers, counselors at school, and other adults who are trained to help you see things differently—and develop the ability to act upon your feelings in a more positive way.

The more you understand that it's simply not fair or realistic to expect that you will always shine, always handle it, always be perfect, always be Number One, the more relieved you'll begin to feel—the more you'll be able to appreciate all that you are.

Chapter 18

GROWING UP DRUGGED UP, DRINKING, AND SMOKING

Drugs are chemical substances that people take into their bodies. Some drugs fight sickness (as with antibiotics). Some drugs relax muscles or ease pain. Some drugs change a person's moods and feelings.

When you consider that even aspirin, caffeine, alcohol, and tobacco are drugs, you can realize that drugs are everywhere in our society. We're a drug-using society!

All drugs can have serious risks—whether they are created in a laboratory or come from plants, whether they are legal or illegal. Illegal drugs are not only harmful but they are also wrong to use because they are against the law.

Date-rape, accidents, fights, pregnancy, sexually transmitted infections (including HIV, the virus that causes AIDS), stealing, breaking the law—these can all result from involvement with alcohol and other drugs. And drugs can kill. Drugs can also be a factor that contributes towards someone killing themselves (committing suicide). Most kids know that drug use can be dangerous. Yet the truth is, many kids abuse drugs anyway.

This chapter will explain different kinds of drugs and their effects, why kids take them, and how they can affect people's lives.

Risk-Taking and Drug Abuse

I'm not saying that all drugs are bad. Drugs that are prescribed by doctors can be very important for fighting disease and getting people back to health. However even if a drug is taken properly (as directed by a doctor) it's possible that a person can be allergic to that drug, without knowing it. People's bodies can change over time and their response to medications can change. So it's very important to be careful about *any* drug use—even aspirin.

Over-the-counter drugs (the ones that can be bought without permission from a doctor), such as aspirin, can also be abused. For example, if someone has a bad headache and takes four aspirin instead of one or two as directed, that's abuse.

Instead of using prescribed drugs for the reason they were given (for getting healthy), some people abuse them to change moods and feelings. Any time these drugs are taken for a reason other than what they were meant for, drug use becomes drug abuse. People end up using prescription drugs as they do illegal drugs, for the purpose of getting high (to purposely alter their state of mind, "get a buzz," change their moods and feelings).

Many kids aren't aware of or don't take seriously the fact that drug abuse can lead to addiction (when someone needs to keep taking drugs, is dependent on them—psychologically, physically, or both), and that with abuse of illegal drugs, there is the additional risk of going to jail. People who abuse drugs can also overdose and die. (This can happen from abusing drugs only one time.)

Even when the consequences of drug abuse are not as serious as causing someone's death, they can still be harmful and interrupt a person's life. Drugs can destroy family relationships, friendships, or any chance of being able to concentrate on work in school, and cause people to be fired from jobs.

The risks involved with drug abuse are troubling for people of any age, but especially for kids who are trying to grow up feeling good.

When Kids Begin to Abuse Drugs

Whether it's sniffing glue, drinking wine coolers or beer, or smoking a joint (marijuana cigarette: mar-uh-WAN-uh, discussed on page 318) at a party, many kids are attracted to drugs by the excitement of doing something they're not supposed to be doing. Some kids are just curious. Some are bored and feel like there's nothing else to do. Others try drugs because they want to fit in and seem cool.

Fourteen-year-old Mara talked with me about the first time she smoked a joint: "I always said I'm never going to do it. I'm never going to try it. But this year, I knew some people who were smoking pot. One close friend did it a lot. I would always tell him not to smoke, but he'd always say it's so great. I guess I just wanted to see what it felt like."

Sometimes the reasons why kids experiment and start to abuse drugs are more complicated. Kids who turn to drugs might not even be aware that their drug use really has to do with trying to cope with difficult and painful situations in their lives. Death, divorce, parents drinking, fighting at home, loneliness, problems with friends or with boyfriends or girlfriends, and problems with school can be very confusing and frustrating.

In these situations, kids may look to drugs as an escape from reality. Or they may take drugs as a cry for help, in an attempt to get parents and others to pay attention to them. Or, when kids are angry, they may take drugs to rebel or lash out at "society" and everyone in it.

These reasons might also combine with the ones already mentioned, such as wanting to seem cool.

Some kids experiment with alcohol or other drugs once or twice and decide it's not for them. But many others find that they do like the feeling drugs give them. For them, the first couple of times is only the beginning.

When Drugs Become a Habit

Experimenting with drugs can lead to more and more drug usage and very often, kids end up getting hooked. This is exactly what happened to Mara.

She shared:

The first time I smoked, nothing happened to me. The same with the second and the third time. So I just kept doing it until something happened. I think the fourth time I did it—I felt it. I think I was scared because I'd smoked a lot and felt very weird. I thought I was out of control. But then I just tried to relax, listened to some music, and was okay. After that I made an agreement with myself.

I wasn't going to go look for it, but if someone had it, then I'd do it. What happened was there was a lot of pot available to me. Kids could buy it pretty easily if they knew the right people.

So I just started doing it more and more. I got very caught up in it. I thought about it all the time. It was constantly on my mind. I was constantly waiting for the next time I was going to do it, thinking about when, where, with whom?

But then I said, I've got to stop. The stopping started with me when I realized how much it had taken me over. But what forced the stopping was my parents. I got punished because they found pot in my drawer. That was the worst thing that ever happened to me. Now they don't trust me anymore. My parents said if they ever saw it again, they'd punish me for an even longer time. The most important thing to me is my freedom to go out with my friends, and my parents grounded me. I couldn't go out to parties and I had to come home right after school.

I wanted to stop or at least cut down. I knew it was better for me. I got no pressure from my friends when I stopped. If anything, they were telling me I'd better not smoke anymore. They gave me a lot of support.

Now we almost never do it. Once in a while, but hardly ever. I would never have believed I could have gotten so caught up with smoking pot. I didn't realize what I was getting into until I was there. It just happened. I didn't even see it happen and then didn't really know what to do about it. I always said it would never happen to me! Now I'm fine. My grades are even higher. I can't say I'm not going to do it anymore. I might. But I'm never going to let it control me again. It will be my choice, not because I think I have to use it. I'll be controlling it."

Mara really meant what she said. But even with the best intentions, the truth is, once someone starts using drugs regularly, stopping or cutting back isn't easy to do. When people like or need the experience of doing drugs, it's very common for them to need them more and more.

It's like when someone takes a pain-killing drug to make the pain go away. When drug wears off, the pain can seem even worse. At that point, they want to take more of the drug.

This is similar to what happens when kids get hooked on alcohol or other drugs. Even if there's no pain, they might simply like the feeling of being high or "buzzed," so that being straight (not high) becomes not good enough, not fun enough. And they need more and more of the drug so they always can be high.

Robert, age seventeen, said: "When I was in tenth grade, my good friend's older brother got him into pot. I was curious so I started to smoke, too. I liked the feeling of being stoned. I thought the whole scene was really cool. But as time went by, my friend and a few other friends were getting stoned like twelve times a day. They totally became pot-heads and couch-potatoes. All they did was smoke pot and watch TV.

"My friend quit the baseball team and his personality really changed. I didn't feel comfortable in that scene any more. And I had to get away from them. Now I think pot is a pretty scary thing."

Robert's story is very common. People who start to drink or take other drugs often get so hooked (dependent upon drugs, mentally or mentally and physically) that they're drunk or high all the time. It's actually possible for people to reach a point where they can't get through their day without using alcohol or other drugs.

The More Needy, the More Desperate . . . the More Violence

The more you need the drug(s) you're taking, the more money you'll have to spend on buying drugs. Kids who become dependent on drugs might find they're so needy and so desperate that they'll do anything to get money to be able to get more of the drug—even if that means they have to steal money from their parents, family, friends, or neighbors, or even trade sexual acts for money.

One can only imagine how parents would feel about learning their child has stolen from them. Even "nice" kids can become liars and robbers when they need drugs to survive.

Mrs. N.'s son is still in jail because he was heavily into drugs and stole from a neighbor's house and got caught. She said, "I wish my son were here to talk to you. He writes me these letters that sound so good because he can't get the stuff. He says he's going to change. I don't know what he's going to do when he gets out of jail. He says one thing and then does another. It's so hard. I search for answers all the time. I can't help but feeling that there's some way that we're at fault. It's not true. But it's hard not feeling that way."

Some kids become pushers (drug dealers). They sell drugs, even to kids who are much younger, just to make enough money to buy more and support their own drug habit. It's also possible they'll make a big profit.

Selling drugs is a very serious offence. It's against the law. The penalties for getting caught dealing in drugs are getting stiffer and stiffer. So are the penalties for using illegal drugs.

Add to these concerns the serious reality of all the drug-related violence. I spoke at length with Kelvin, who works at a hospital. He told me, "What I see at the hospital are kids who are leading a life that's going to lead them to drugs, jail, or an early death. I remember one young man who I saw for the first time when he was ten. He had gotten stabbed in the side because he was selling drugs on someone else's territory, someone else's drug spot."

It is sad that so many kids don't realize, don't understand, or just can't admit that their drug use is leading them down a troubled road to no control. It's hard to feel good about chipping away at who you really are. It's hard to admit that drugs control everything you do. You really end up giving up yourself. That's what's so tragic.

What will it take for you to believe that anyone can become a drug abuser? Even you, no matter how much you might start out by saying, "I'll never do that," "I'll just say no," or "That will never happen to me. I can stop." Drugs can suck you in. They're very persuasive. They fool you into believing that you have to count on them to feel good. They tease you into believing that you need them to feel "cool" or to belong.

Drug dealers can be persuasive, too. People who are trying hard to get you involved just love to have company. They also love your money. They might even give you a free first "sample," promising that you don't have to buy anything from them if you don't like it. The problem is that the initial effects may make you mellow, may help you "chill out," and may be very attractive. And you just might want more.

It's very common to start out saying, "Well, I'm not going to look for it, but if it's there, well then okay." And, just like with Mara, drugs just happen to be around more and more. She never planned it that way, but she also didn't say no.

Staying Safe from Drugs—Controlling Your Risks

I don't pretend that refusing drugs will be easy. In fact, depending upon what your friends or someone you're going out with are doing, staying away from drugs might be uncomfortable and very tough. If your friends are drug users, they might pressure you or at least encourage you to join them.

It may be hard to be the only one at a party who doesn't want to drink, smoke pot, or use whatever else is there. (You can refer to Chapter 15, on peer pressure, to review ways to deal with pressure from peers.) But if your friends are really good friends, they'll respect your choices and won't push you. The main thing is that you need to (and certainly deserve to) respect and value yourself.

If you're drunk or high and not in control of what you're doing, the consequences can be dangerous to yourself and those around you. As I said in the beginning of this chapter, date-rape, accidents, fights and other types of violence, pregnancy, sexually transmitted infections (including HIV), stealing, breaking the law—can all result from involvement with drugs. Because of drugs, you could lose your driver's license, get kicked out of school, be put in jail. Drugs can break up friendships, break up dating relationships, break up families. Drugs can also kill.

Even when people aren't involved with drugs, drugs can be the cause of their death anyway. You may have heard news reports or know someone personally who has gotten killed because they were innocent bystanders—just in the way—of drug-related shootings or other types of violence. While it's difficult to be able to predict those types of sudden violent attacks, you can still do the best you can to stay safe by staying in control of yourself.

You can decide to never put yourself at risk. You can decide to refuse drugs. You can decide to not allow yourself to be around others who are abusing drugs. You can decide not to get into a car with someone who has been drinking or using other drugs. You can decide not to put yourself in a situation where alcohol or use of other drugs could cause someone to take sexual advantage of you—or where you would be out of control to the point that you would take sexual advantage of someone else. You can always keep in mind that what you allow yourself to do is completely up to you and no one has a right to choose for you.

Clearly the absolute safest decision is not to use drugs at all. But if you are considering drug use—for your own survival you need to make sure you understand all of the risks involved. Don't just take your friend's, girlfriend's or boyfriend's word that you'll be okay on whatever drug it is you're thinking of trying.

If you're choosing to use drugs, make sure you fully understand the facts about the particular drugs you're thinking of taking and how those drugs could affect you. You also need to consider who you're going to be using drugs with and whether you're going to be in a safe environment. But even if you know the facts, are aware of the risks, and have carefully considered your circumstances, the truth is that with any illegal drugs you can't be positive as to the exact strength and purity of what you're taking. You could still get much more than you bargained for—much more than you're prepared to handle—and much more than you would have ever wanted.

Don't wait until after an unwanted result happens to take charge of what you let yourself do. You can stay safe and healthy if you believe the risks related to drugs are very serious—and could actually happen to you if you take even one chance. You can be safe if you make safe choices and behave in a responsible way.

Different Drugs and Their Effects

In order to make responsible choices and not put yourself at risk, it's important to know the facts about different kinds of drugs.

Alcohol and Other Downers

One of the most interesting things about alcohol is that it's a depressant drug that slows down the central nervous system (brain and spinal cord). In smaller amounts (like one or two beers), it makes people feel mellow, relaxed, giggly, and talkative. That's why it may seem like a stimulant. Yet it's really putting to sleep the policeman in your brain (the part that makes you listen to reason).

Even what may seem like small amounts of alcohol can have a strong effect on people. Lisa, age fifteen, told me, "If I drink one beer, the room starts spinning!"

The more a person drinks, the more you can see that the drug is really a depressant. It's likely that a person's speech will become slurred, they'll have difficulty in walking, they'll think they're very funny and they'll talk louder than they have to.

Sometimes the alcohol can cause difficulty beyond your control. You may have acted and appeared normal while drinking, yet you may have no memory of what you did while you drank. This is called a blackout and can happen if you drink heavily. (You can see why reaching this point can lead to date-rape and other serious consequences.)

Drinking may even cause loss of consciousness. This is your body's way of preventing you from doing it more harm. It's screaming, "No More!" If you're unconscious, you can't drink anymore. Another way that your body may protect you from doing it in is to cause you to vomit (nature's way of saying "slow down," to prevent the alcohol from getting through your stomach). Sometimes your body has more wisdom than your brain does.

You may be wondering how, if you do get drunk, you (or your friend) can make yourself sober again. People have some interesting ideas about ways to make a person sober up more quickly. But there is no quick way to rid your body of the intoxicating effects of alcohol.

People mistakenly think that if you take a cold shower or drink lots of coffee, you'll get rid of the alcohol that's in your body more quickly. This is not correct. Coffee will make you wide awake and drunk, and the shower will make you wet and drunk.

The body can get rid of only one drink (a can of beer, a glass of wine, or about one ounce of the hard stuff—like vodka or rum—mixed with water or soda) every hour. There is nothing you can do to speed this up. Even taking yourself on an evening jog will not help.

If you wake up with a hangover (feeling awful the next morning because of drinking too much the night before), it will take its own time before you feel better.

A lot of kids are *binge drinking* (drinking a lot of alcohol in a short amount of time). If you start pouring too much alcohol into yourself, the body can't get rid of it fast enough. Binge drinking changes the rules and can have very serious results. If you drink a beer or two, get a headache, and don't feel well, that's one thing. But if you drink heavily, the chance of acute alcohol poisoning is higher. This happens when a person drinks way too much alcohol, past what the body can detoxify or get rid of, so that he or she either goes unconscious or has respiratory failure (is unable to breath) and dies.

Another danger is vomiting. Because alcohol is a depressant, it shuts down some of the body's natural voluntary and involuntary mechanisms. If you vomit, your body may not recognize what it's doing and at the same time, may try to take a breath. That could lead to choking and death if there's not someone there to help you.

Last year, a star high-school athlete at a Midwest high school died as a result of this situation. It happened after binge drinking. His friends, caring about him, put him to bed, thinking he would just sleep it off. He vomited, sucked in his own vomit, choked, and died.

Other depressant drugs can result in the same feelings. They can have the same effect on the body, and are often more powerful than alcohol.

Depressants, sometimes called "downers," slow down and depress the central nervous system. (We will talk more about downers later). One major problem that you ought to be aware of is this: If you mix other downers with alcohol, you may be in for some serious trouble, even death.

Here's the problem. In mathematics, we're taught that one and one equals two. But one and one does not equal two when you are dealing with drugs. The effect of one downer and one beer may be like doubling or tripling the effect on the brain. Under the influence of depressants, body functions (like breathing and heartbeat) slow down and can even stop, causing death.

When people mix alcohol with other drugs, this is called *potentiation* (po-ten-she-AY-shun) or *synergism* (SIN-ner-jiz-um).

Alcohol and other downers, unlike marijuana, have one extra property. The more you use of these drugs, the more you're going to need of them to get the same effect, even at low levels. So, if you've been used to drinking two beers every day for one week, you may need to drink two and one-half beers the following week in order to get the same feelings you got from two beers the week before. This is called *developing a tolerance for the drug*.

As your tolerance increases, your body may start to physically crave the drug. This happens when you are using alcohol or downers very often and you're using heavy amounts.

If you stop taking these drugs, you might find yourself shaking, feeling hyper, sweating, feeling irritable, having a rapid pulse, and perhaps having convulsions (like a marionette puppet that's gone crazy). These are the withdrawal symptoms I mentioned before. Withdrawal can be very dangerous and can result in death.

Therefore, if you've been abusing alcohol and downers and want to stop, speak with your parents and your doctor to get yourself the help you need to stop drinking (or using other drugs) with minimal risks to your health.

Hallucinogens

A *hallucinogen* (huh-LOOSE-in-uh-jen) or psychedelic (sie-ki-DELL-ik) is a type of drug that can cause a person to feel, hear, see, and smell things that aren't really there. It just seems they are because the drug alters (changes) the senses. It also can affect a person's sense of judgment and coordination. Usually the person using the drug knows that they're seeing hallucinations, but sometimes the visions can seem very real. These effects can make it especially dangerous if a person drives a car, works with machinery, or does anything else that requires clear, accurate judgment. Other than hallucinogens used in research or controlled medical treatment, these drugs can only be gotten illegally and are easily abused.

MARIJUANA Marijuana, also called pot, grass, or reefer, is a drug in the *hallucinogen* grouping. It comes from a plant that is illegal to grow in the United States, and people usually smoke it to get high or stoned.

If you hear someone talking about smoking a "blunt," that's a marijuana joint that's rolled in a cigar wrapper. People may also refer to a "bong," which is a device like a pipe through which the pot smoker inhales.

The problem with smoking marijuana is that since it is illegal and can be gotten from many different sources, very few people know what's actually in it or how strong it is. They don't know whether it is mixed with something else that can be dangerous (that's called "laced"), if it is sprayed with some pesticides (used to kill insects, bacteria, or harmful animals) that can be very hazardous to your health, or if it is stronger than they even suspect it might be.

If you smoke marijuana, you may get a rushing feeling (like feeling you're nauseous and floating in the air and are not able to stop the feelings from happening). It may become difficult to concentrate on what it was you wanted to say. It becomes hard to put thoughts together, hard to know what you just said.

Often, if you get a bad feeling in your head while smoking pot, it's hard to get rid of the feeling—it seems to stay with you for a very long time. You can also get paranoid and think people are out to get you. This, of course, is not true, it's just the effect of the drug.

Marijuana can also affect short-term memory, make you feel stupid, laugh at things that wouldn't be funny if you weren't stoned. It can make you feel giddy and disoriented. Being stoned might affect your sense of time and space. Being so disoriented and having your mental state so altered can be exciting for some people and very scary for others.

Smoking pot can also give you a case of the munchies. If you're concerned about gaining weight, you might consider the fact that marijuana can put extra pounds on you because it makes it difficult not to raid the refrigerator and everything around it.

Another problem with smoking pot is that it can make you feel like doing nothing. It may be that you've got nothing to do, so what's the harm? However, all of us have responsibilities, whether they be cleaning our room, mowing the lawn, taking care of our brothers or sisters, babysitting, delivering newspapers, working on relationships with friends and parents, or going to school and doing homework.

All these things do take motivation (you've got to want to do them). Smoking pot can really prevent you from doing these things. That's why smoking pot over a long period of time can be so damaging to your life.

It first was believed that there were very few physical consequences of smoking pot. However, new facts seem to suggest that smoking pot may cause lung damage equal to the damage cigarettes cause. It may also have an effect on hormone levels, sperm count, and sexual functioning.

Marijuana is a psychologically addictive drug. That means that people can become very attached to or dependent on it. They begin to feel that they need the drug to get through the day.

This is different from other drugs, such as heroin, which can be not only psychologically but physically addicting. With physical addiction, the body itself actually craves the drug and begins to need it in order to keep on functioning. Without it, the person sometimes suffers horrible withdrawal symptoms, such as shaking, sweating, and vomiting.

Addiction to marijuana, while it's not physical, can still be very powerful.

LSD AND MUSHROOMS One powerful hallucinogen is a chemical drug that is often called LSD or "acid." It has no color, taste, or odor, and is usually sold in liquid form. A "tab of acid" refers to a tiny piece of paper with a drop of liquid LSD on it that is then placed in a person's mouth. Taking acid is also referred to as "dropping acid," "dosing," or "taking a trip."

Acid trips can be extremely powerful, and can cause someone to lose touch with reality for as long as twenty-four hours. LSD can cause the person who takes it to experience many different sensations, thoughts, and hallucinations (fake visions—seeing, hearing, or sensing things that seem real but aren't really there).

While the people who choose to take LSD are usually seeking to experience these visions, it's also possible they'll get more than they wanted, expected, or could handle. Sometimes acid trips can become extremely frightening or disturbing. These are referred to as "bad trips." With larger quantities of LSD, a person can have convulsions (severe shaking) and delirium (sort of like a storm in the brain).

It's possible that the feelings and hallucinations from an acid trip can come back suddenly and without warning to a person, a few days, weeks, months, even more than a year after the trip was taken. These "flashbacks" can be a serious problem.

Certain types of mushrooms (which are grown in manure) can cause similar effects to LSD when eaten. These are commonly referred to as "shrooms" or "boomers."

ECSTASY Ecstasy, also known as X or XTC, is a drug that has become very popular with young people. It is often used at clubs or all night parties called "raves" that have loud music and flashing lights. This is because ecstasy makes the senses seem more intense and keeps the user awake for many hours.

People on ecstasy often feel less insecure and less shy. However, ecstasy can also be very destructive. It increases heart rate and blood pressure and destroys brain cells. People who take ecstasy can get "rushes" that involve panic or anxiety attacks. Also, after using this drug, a person can experience severe depression.

A lot of what is sold as ecstasy is not pure ecstasy, but a combination of all sorts of other stimulant drugs and other ingredients that can lead to an overdose. This is a very dangerous drug.

Downers

There are several different types of "downers" or depressant drugs in addition to alcohol.

BARBITURATES These depressant drugs are very widely abused. You might have heard of pills called such slang names as "reds," "blues," "goofballs," or "yellows." When prescribed by doctors, barbiturates (bar-BICH-ur-its) ease anxiety, reduce tension, and help a person sleep (sleeping pills). There are many hundreds of barbiturates that have important medical uses. But when these drugs are abused, the results can be serious.

Tolerance to these drugs can build and build and eventually reach a point where the dose can kill. The combination of barbiturates with alcohol, even in small amounts, can be very dangerous, possibly fatal (cause death). Overdoses of barbiturates are a common method of committing suicide. People might also kill themselves by accident (if they were too doped up and didn't realize how many pills they were taking).

Withdrawal for barbiturate addicts can be very, very severe.

NARCOTICS You might have heard the term *narcotics*, which refers to a large group of depressant-type drugs. When used in medical treatment, narcotics are especially important as painkillers. If you ever experienced extreme pain, such as you might from certain major operations, your doctor might have tried to dull the pain with an injection of *morphine* (MORE-feen), a strong narcotic found in the opium poppy.

Narcotics are also useful to help relieve coughs. Strong cough syrups often contain the narcotic *codeine* (CO-deen). Almost all narcotics used in medicine (except for mild cough syrups containing small amounts of codeine) can be bought only with a doctor's prescription. When abused, narcotics—like other depressant drugs—can be very dangerous, very deadly. An overdose of narcotics can kill. (You might have heard the term "to OD on drugs.")

Narcotic drugs can be even deadlier when they are injected with a needle. Remember, unclean or contaminated needles can pass HIV, the virus that causes AIDS (see page 259) from a person who is infected to someone else. Shooting drugs with a needle through the vein is called "mainlining."

HEROIN One illegal narcotic drug that is usually shot directly into the bloodstream with a needle is heroin (HAIR-o-win). Shooting heroin usually makes someone feel that "all is fine with the world," without their being completely connected to it. Heroin is made from morphine and is usually sold as a whitish powder. Most of the time, a person buying heroin "on the street" will not be buying pure heroin. It is almost always "cut"—mixed, reduced, diluted—with other chemicals, which are often unsafe. Just as with all drugs that are bought off the street, a person can't be exactly sure of the strength or purity of the product. In the case of heroin, a drastic change in content from what the addict is used to can result in death.

Regular heroin users can quickly become addicted and build a high tolerance for the drug. Heroin addicts will experience serious withdrawal symptoms if and when they stop taking the drug.

Uppers

Uppers are drugs that can stimulate the central nervous system and make you feel as if you were walking on air. They pep people up, make them awake, talkative, less bored, and make them feel that they have the power to do anything they want.

The problem with doing uppers for a long period of time is that it becomes impossible to sleep. That's why so many people who use uppers drink alcohol to go to sleep, take uppers in the morning to wake up, use alcohol to go to sleep, and so on. This dangerous stress on the body can lead to the morgue (a place where they put the dead).

Often if a person is using only uppers, like cocaine, *amphetamines* (am-FET-uh-means), or diet pills, and wants to stop using them, their body may crash. Crashing means that your body can no longer keep up at the pace it's been operating on, and you need to sleep for many days.

Taking uppers can cause major problems with your heart and lungs. It can also cause mental problems: make you edgy, anxious, nervous, and unable to tell the difference between what's real and what's not.

Just as with alcohol, anyone who feels the need to keep using uppers may find themselves becoming dependent on them and needing more and more of the drug in order to get the same effects. Having to leave the arms of the drugs can sometimes be very hard.

COCAINE Cocaine or "coke" is a strong stimulant that is highly abused, very expensive, and sold illegally in the form of a white powder. It is snorted (sniffed) or injected. When injected, it is often combined with other dangerous drugs, such as heroin. Cocaine causes a person to feel mentally and physically "up." This "high" feeling wears off fairly quickly (about thirty minutes to an hour), at which point the user will feel let down or even depressed. Then it's common for a person to sniff some more to get those good "up" feelings back.

Cocaine abusers often find that they get much more than good feelings from repeated doses. Sniffing for a long period of time can cause the breakdown and burning of the membranes of the nose.

With cocaine use, the body's functions, such as pulse and heartbeat, are speeded up. Sometimes a person's body or heart can't handle this and gets going too fast. This can result in a heart attack—an overdose of cocaine can result in death.

WHAT ABOUT CRACK? Crack is cocaine that is processed using baking soda. That changes it from a not-so-pure powder (cocaine—illegally sold—is usually mixed with other substances) to a more pure form of cocaine that can be smoked. This is called "free-basing." "Rocks" of crack (it looks like tiny rocks) are sold in vials (small tubes). Since they're small, they can be hidden in cigarettes.

When someone smokes crack, a much stronger (more pure) dose of cocaine is sent to the brain faster than if snorted. That's what makes crack so dangerous and deadly. The effect is quick and can be very addictive. An intense "high" feeling is felt after only a few seconds and might last about ten minutes, long enough to make someone violent, long enough to cause very serious damage. Crack is a killer.

Sniffing Aerosol Sprays, Paint, Gasoline, Freon

If abused, each of these or any other inhalants (in-HAY-lunts: a substance that is breathed in) will affect you a bit differently. The most important thing that you need to know is they are some of the most common, yet some of the most dangerous drugs young people encounter. If you sniff the vapors, chemicals, gases, and other harmful ingredients that were meant for cars or other things besides people, you could seriously damage your ability to breathe. You could also experience reactions such as blurred vision and lessened muscular coordination. Sniffing inhalants for a long period of time can cause serious damage to the lungs and other organs. You could die even if you're sniffing for the first time, as high doses can result in heart failure.

Don't let anyone fool you. Believe that drugs can be deadly. For additional information about alcohol and other drugs, you can call the National Clearinghouse for Alcohol and Drug Information: 1-800-729-6686. (If this number changes, call 1-800-555-1212 for the new number.) You can also check the Internet with your parent. Only if you're informed about what drugs are, how they can affect you, what they look like, and how they can be sold, will you be able to know for sure what to stay away from—even if someone you know and trust is trying to convince you that what they offer is okay and will be safe. You'll know better.

What's So Bad About Drugs—Learning About Growing Up While Being High

The problem with using alcohol and other drugs is that you learn many of your growing up tasks while you are high. This is called *state-dependent learning*. That means, your learning is dependent upon the state you're in, which can be straight (not under the influence of drugs) or high (under the influence of drugs).

Alcohol and other drugs can change and stretch out your emotions. They can make you sleepy, happy, giggly, filled with fear, *paranoid* (thinking everyone is watching you and talking about you or even out to get you), give you false courage or take courage away, make your anger turn into violence, make your sadness worse, and make your loneliness deeper. They can change all your feelings. And yet, at the same time, you may still feel very much a part of the group that's using drugs.

It's a problem when you've done your growing up high. If you were high when you practiced asking girls out, took a test, made friends, took dares, played a sport, and made a decision about what to do, where to go, how to act, how to feel—it's the drug-affected you who has acted—not the real you.

If you've grown up high, over time, it will become difficult to do things straight. You know what it feels like to do things high, but the more you do your daily activities high, the less practice you get doing them straight. This can become very scary. Let me give you an example. If you've ever broken your leg and been in a cast, you know it's very difficult to learn how to walk around in that cast. But like most things, you learned to adjust. You managed to walk around with the cast, impaired as you were, hard as it was. Imagine that this is similar to becoming accustomed to being high.

Once the cast comes off (once you stop using drugs), it's difficult to walk again. You'll have to exercise the leg and strengthen it because it's weak and has been out of practice. Well, after using drugs for a while and then stopping, your personality is weak and it's difficult to trust the decisions that you're going to have to make.

You'll have to learn how to make choices, pick and choose wisely, and deal with more confused emotions than you ever had to before using the drugs, because you are continuing to grow up. It will be hard to trust your judgment because you're not used to facing yourself, making difficult decisions, and being accountable for what you do.

If you started using alcohol and other drugs at twelve and stopped using them at fifteen, there are three years of your life in which you did everything as a drug-dependent person. So, as far as your emotions are concerned, when you stop using drugs, you almost have to continue developing back where you left off at age twelve.

It can be hard to play catch-up. And it's going to take effort and learning from mistakes. But sometimes the things that are most worthwhile are hard.

If You Think You Have a Drug Problem

Even if people close to you might be telling you they're worried about you and urging you to go for help, it can be very hard to admit that you have a drug problem. But for your own survival, you need to take the first step to stop your drug habit. You need to ask for help.

If drugs are controlling you, there are many people who can offer support and understanding, and help you deal with your problem. In addition to the usual list of helpful people, such as parents and other relatives, school counselors and psychologists, there are people who are specially trained to offer help with drug abuse. If your school doesn't have a separate counselor who works with drug-related problems, the school office (also check guidance and health) can more than likely give you this information.

There are also national, state, and local drug hotlines. You can look in your telephone book or ask an operator to get these numbers. For local information, dial 0. For your state hotlines, dial your local area code plus 555-1212. Also dial 1-800-555-1212 for other drug-related help numbers. A very helpful resource is the Crisis Hotline (1-800-444-9999).

In addition, many clinics and drug treatment centers offer assistance and advice. Some are associated with hospitals, some aren't. These will be listed in the telephone book or can be found through telephone information. You can also consider calling the Girls and Boys Town National Hotline, which is for boys, girls, and families (1-800-448-3000). If this number or the one for the Crisis Hotline changes, dial 1-800-555-1212 for new information.

Once again, it's okay to say, "It's hard for me to say this. I'm having trouble with drugs . . . I need to talk. Can you help me?" It's not okay to stay on drugs. It's not okay to destroy yourself. It's not okay to walk around not asking for help! Even if everything and everyone around you makes you feel like you're not important enough to be helped, you are. Even if you've been "crying out" by using drugs and no one has listened.

Think about what you might feel that would make it hard for you to go to someone for help if you have a drug problem. Here are some answers other kids have shared:

- afraid that the person you approach won't take you seriously
- afraid that the person won't understand
- afraid that the person won't really care

- afraid that the person won't keep your problem private
- afraid that the person would judge you and label you in a negative way
- afraid that you'd pour your guts out and then find out you weren't talking to the right person and then you'd have to tell your whole long story over again to someone else

All of these feelings and concerns are very natural. But even if you're uncomfortable and afraid, the most important thing is to get help. If you know that you have a drug problem, you need to reach out and risk telling someone who can help.

Make a list of the places you can go for help in your school, town, and the nearby communities. Then go down the list and pick out someone to reach out to. It's a good idea to give special consideration to those who regularly help kids with drug problems. That will give you a better chance of getting the kind of help you need.

If the first person you approach doesn't work out, don't give up—reach out to someone else—remember, it's most important that you get help. You're worth it.

You can start with, "This is very hard for me to say . . ." And then you can go on to explain, "I have a problem with drugs and I need your help." You'll probably find it will be a great relief to know that you no longer have to deal with your drug problem alone.

One more thing. An eighth-grade boy said to me, "If you talk with the school counselor, somebody will probably see you go there. Then they'll know you have a problem. And they'll tell other people they saw you."

The truth is, if you go for help, someone might see you. It's hard to be invisible in school halls. Instead of judging and whispering and telling other kids they saw you, it would be great if they would be sensitive enough to just say to themselves, "Good for them. It's great that they're getting help!" and then respect your privacy.

Students go to counselors all the time for lots of reasons—family, school, personal—and it's nobody else's business. Even if people do talk, don't let what they say stop you from getting the help you need. You can't control how others respect you or your privacy—but you always can be in control of how you respect and care about yourself. So no matter what, be sure to get help.

How Can You Help a Friend?

If it's your friend who has a drug problem, you may or may not be able to convince that person to talk with someone who can help. You can tell them you're very worried, let them know you'll walk them to a counselor's door, or beg them to stop using drugs, but it's going to be up to them to actually make a move for help. You can't do it for them. That's the frustrating part. And until they admit they have a problem, they may not even want to talk with you about it.

Be careful about believing that it's your responsibility to solve your friend's drug problem. It can be scary and frustrating to stand by, knowing your friend seems to be destroying himself or herself with drugs. However, if your friend doesn't seem to want to go for help, the worst choice is for you to be silent.

Most kids are afraid to say anything because they're worried that will ruin the friendship. But most kids would rather have an angry friend than an out-of-control or dead friend. So, if you can't get your friend to go for help, the best you can do is seek out your own parents or talk with a counselor to deal with what *you're* feeling about your friend . . . as well as explore other ways to help (such as possibly approaching your friend's parents).

If you end up bringing the problem out in the open with your friend's parents, don't be surprised if your friend gets very angry. Secretly he or she may be relieved, but it may be too hard to admit at the moment. Maybe someday, your friend will thank you. Even if you end up losing the friendship, at least you'll always be able to know that you cared enough to take a chance to help him or her.

People have to want to help themselves. If you're upset about the fact that your parents smoke, you can urge them to stop, but you can't stop *for* them. They have to want to stop badly enough to be ready to do something about it. And surely you can't diet for somebody. The same holds true if your friend is abusing drugs. You can't stop your friend if your friend doesn't want to stop or isn't ready.

Besides, you can't hold your friend's hand every single minute, just as your parent can't hold yours. Growing up means learning to accept responsibility for our own actions. Friends who use drugs need to accept the consequences of that use—even if that means losing you as a friend.

Don't be afraid to do the best thing a person can do for a friend: Help them end a drug use habit. Tell an adult who can help. (Keep in mind that adults who are trained to help kids with drug problems also know that it's important to respect privacy.)

Stopping Can Be Harder Than You Might Think

John's mother talked with me about the two years he spent at a drug rehabilitation center when he was around sixteen. She told me that he came back drug-free and planned to stay that way. Then the other kids in the town didn't want to trust him and accept him because of all the bad stuff that he had pulled since he was eleven years old. The kids who were on drugs were happy to accept him back because they had someone else to lean on. So, although he wanted to get a fresh start, he ended up going back to drugs.

John's mother shared: "You have to be so strong. It's difficult to turn your back on drugs, even if your body is rid of the drugs and has been for a while. When John came back home, he was labeled. All the other kids knew him as trouble. That's a difficult thing to turn your back on. He couldn't help allowing himself to have that label put back on him."

As in John's situation, there can be many obstacles to staying drug-free. After abusing drugs and going through a drug rehabilitation program, dealing with day-to-day life at school (and home) can be hard. Relapsing (going back to drug abuse) is common. It's very important that there be helpful, caring people around to give support.

If you know someone in your school or community who has just returned from a drug rehabilitation program, you can help make a difference in their life. You can appreciate that it takes a great deal of courage to face a drug problem and go through rehabilitation. You can give that person a new chance and not judge him or her by old reputations or labels.

Even if you don't wish to become friends, you can be friendly. A simple, "Hi, how are you doing?" in the halls at school can be very welcoming and may mean more than you realize.

If You Find That Your Parent Is Using Drugs

If you find that your parent is using drugs—smoking pot, snorting cocaine, or using other drugs—this may come as a great shock, especially if they have been telling you to stay away from drugs.

You may wonder whether to let them know you found out, be disappointed that their "image" has been broken, and be very upset that they might be doing something dangerous to themselves. You may also be confused, thinking, "Hey, if they can do it, why can't I?"

Although it's hard to know how your parents would respond, it would probably be a relief to be able to share your feelings with them instead of keeping it a secret that you know. If at all possible, you would probably be most relieved to get your feelings out and tell them that you're really upset that they're using the substance.

Remember, you can't say *no* to drugs for your parents. They have to say it for themselves. But you do have the freedom to say *no* for yourself, no matter what your parent does.

If your parents' drug use becomes a serious family problem, look at the section "What You Can Do If Your Family Is Drugged Up" for suggestions about how you can handle this situation.

Al-Anon Family Support can help you with family problems caused by alcohol. Their toll free number is 1-800-344-2666 twenty-four hours a day. (If this number changes, dial 1-800-555-1212 and ask for new information.)

Growing Up Drinking

All people drink. We drink water, soda (pop), fruit juice, and a variety of other beverages. They quench or satisfy our thirst. And yet alcohol is not for quenching thirst. People usually drink alcohol because it makes them feel mellow, or high, or "buzzed," rather than just to satisfy their thirst.

By itself, alcohol is a clear liquid that doesn't taste good at all. That's why companies add flavors and colors to make drinks look and taste appealing. Some companies even add fruit juice and other "healthy-sounding" ingredients. Keep in mind that no matter what form it's in, it is still alcohol.

Alcohol is probably the most popular legal drug available to adults. Each state makes its own laws about the age when a person is allowed to buy alcoholic beverages. (As of now, in all states the age is twenty-one.) You may know kids who can get alcohol from older brothers, sisters, or friends by asking people to go into liquor stores for them, or by using proof of age that is fake or not their own.

Because alcohol is legal, parents often think that if their kids are going to take any drug, they're better off drinking alcohol than smoking pot or taking other illegal drugs. But, like other drugs, alcohol can be addictive. Alcohol can also kill.

Mary told me that when she was fifteen years old, her older brother, who was in the bar business, told her if she wanted to get high, she should go into his bar to drink. He felt that at least he could keep an eye on her, and she wouldn't be taking those other dangerous drugs.

Mary is now recovering from alcoholism. Alcoholism is a disease that causes emotional and physical dependency on alcohol. Alcohol causes all sorts of problems because the alcoholic is under its influence much of the time.

Millions of people each year are affected by the drug alcohol. There are a lot of related accidents in the home and on the highways. Divorced, broken, or angry and hostile homes, lost jobs, failure at school, illnesses, and death can also result from abusing alcohol.

In some families, one or both parents suffer from the disease of alcoholism, which can cause very painful feelings for all the kids and anyone else in the family. While the decision to drink alcohol, how much to drink and the consequences of your own drinking are in your control, the decision about whether a parent drinks is not in your control. They are the ones who are doing the drinking.

What is in your control is how you feel about their drinking and whether or not you will go to someone for help to deal with your feelings about living with a parent who drinks too much.

Growing Up in a Family with Drug Problems

Because a parent with a drug or drinking problem is not really in a position to think straight, it may be hard to get along with that parent in a way that feels good. The drugs may make that parent unfair, unable to show love, and neglectful; they may yell a lot and embarrass you in front of your friends. Chances are that family rules and decisions made by a drugged parent will not be fair. After all, his or her feelings and emotions are stretched out from using alcohol or drugs for quite some time.

They may make a rule when they are not under the influence of alcohol or other drugs. Yet their thinking even then will still be affected by the many times they have used the alcohol or other drugs.

Every kid in a drugged family has his or her own way of coping with the situation at home. Some kids will try to make things better by being the best in school, the most popular (although he or she may not want to bring friends home), the best in sports, and generally, an all-around super person. They hope that maybe because of their efforts, their mom or dad (or both) will stop drinking.

What they might tell themselves is, "A kid who does this well in school and with friends can't really come from such a bad family."

Growing up trying to make your mom or dad not drink is a real burden. It can hurt a lot. The family gives so few good feelings back while you keep feeding them with the wonderful things you do. The hurt feelings get buried, and the world only sees how good and responsible you are.

Lisa, age twelve, the oldest child in an alcoholic family, felt that by being a cheerleader, cleaning her room all the time, and being Daddy's favorite, she could in some way get him to stop drinking. She so badly wanted the family not to fight and to be okay. She wished she could bring her friends home. The more she tried to make her family better by trying to stop fights and pleasing her father by getting good grades in school, the more she felt helpless and unable to do anything right. Even though Lisa feels she is smart, she has this nagging feeling that she hasn't done enough.

Some kids in an alcoholic family can start getting into trouble at school, begin to use alcohol and other drugs, run away from home, get pregnant, get into trouble with the law, and if they're "really bright," be the leader of a troubled group of kids.

When this happens, the mom or dad who is drugged can easily say the family mess is because of their troubled kid. Don't you believe it! It's the other way around. This troubled kid is angry about having to get their attention by leaving the family and using drugs and trouble as a way of getting attention.

The truth is they would love for the family to get better. They would love to have their mom or dad be like other moms and dads. They wish their mom or dad did not drink.

Patrick, age nineteen, always remembers hating his older brother, who could do no wrong. Patrick thinks that his parents thought that the moon, sun, and stars rose and set over his brother's head! Patrick feels guilty about not loving his older brother but feels it was "a bummer" being number two. When Patrick used to make his father, who was an alcoholic, get him out of bed in the morning, come down to school after he was thrown out, or go to court to help him after he broke store windows, at least he felt he was getting some attention.

But his father's drinking never changed. Patrick started to use drugs and alcohol very heavily and all the family problems were blamed on him. Patrick is still very angry at his father for being so two-faced. He says, "My father can only see my problem; he can't see his own. I hate him for that."

Meg, age seventeen, spoke about always running away from home, even if it was just for half an hour. She hated her house. If she could have lived underneath her bed to escape the family pain (the yelling, screaming, and fighting), she would have. She could do nothing as well as her older sister. So she decided, without being aware of it, that she would make her own way in the world.

She decided that having a life with her boyfriend was where she was going to get her attention. She started using drugs heavily, got pregnant, ran away from home for good, all the while knowing that she hated herself for her behavior. But she could see no way out of it.

Although Meg is back at home and understands that her behavior comes from living in an alcoholic family, she's still too angry at her mother to do anything about her own behavior.

Sometimes the younger kids in an alcoholic family may find themselves playing alone, spending most of their time in their rooms, and not being sure of what's really going on in the family. Very often no one seems to worry about them, because they're so quiet. However, just because they're quiet and seem to behave, it doesn't mean they're not feeling anything. They're often fearful deep inside, and may have little success in making friends because they spend so much time alone with their imaginary friends. (It's less embarrassing to bring an imaginary friend into a drugged home.)

Nicole, age eleven, stays away from the fighting in her house and sits in her room watching television with her dog (who is her best friend). She does this all the time. Even when it's sunny out and all the kids are playing outside, Nicole feels that her room, television, and dog are her best friends.

No one seems to pay very much attention to her. They figure because she's so quiet and doesn't give anyone trouble, she has no problems. When you ask Nicole how she feels about her father's drinking, she shrugs her shoulders and says (with her face down), "It doesn't bother me."

Nicole wishes she could really have a best friend besides her dog.

Sometimes children in an alcoholic family can seem like they have no problems in the world. They are often the class clown, are usually joking, and are sometimes unable to sit still. A child in an alcoholic family may not be aware of the drinking problem in the family if he or she is very young. And family members may take great pains to protect such a young child from the major family secret.

These children can feel that the family members are trying to protect them by telling them that there is nothing wrong in their family. But deep down inside, they may feel very anxious and scared that maybe there really is something wrong that no one is telling them.

Mark, age seven, the youngest child in an alcoholic family, can't sit still for one moment. He's either spilling milk, making silly faces, or driving every adult in the house crazy. He's cute and loving and everyone likes him. But no one takes him too seriously.

Because they may be so nervous that something might be wrong, kids of alcoholic parents can appear to be busy cracking jokes and running around like chickens without heads. Every once in a while, family members might like to laugh at these jokes. The problem occurs when no one takes these children seriously, and they really can't tell anyone about their nervousness.

These are some common responses of children in alcoholic families. Remember that each child in this kind of situation will respond in his or her own way. There are no rules.

What You Can Do If Your Family Has a Drug Problem

The number-one rule in families that are drugged up seems to be that you're not supposed to talk about what's going on in the family: not with other people in the family and not with outsiders.

Sometimes you hear this rule from your mother and your father, and sometimes you know deep down inside that's the way it's supposed to be (it's unspoken). What this rule does is to prevent you from getting help with your painful feelings. It also prevents the family from having a chance to get better.

You might be saying to yourself, "My family is the only family where this is going on." You should know that growing up in a drugged up family is probably one of the major family problems in the United States. Many kids have the exact same feelings as you. The problem is that so many of these kids have the same rules of silence. So it becomes very difficult to break the rules and find out that other kids are suffering, too.

Kids who are fed up, kids who are asked by their teacher or the courts, "What's going on in your family?" are the kids who usually break the family silence by finally telling someone what's going on. Other kids may not say one word, even to their best friends, and may really think the family's problems are all their fault.

If you're thinking, "But I don't have such strength, I'm really scared," it may help to understand that deep down, you really do. Even if it may not seem that way. Besides, it's natural to be scared. In this situation, most kids are. So, you have to push yourself to tell someone. It's your right to get help. You don't have to keep quiet. You deserve to have the chance to try to understand your feelings, how to respond in a way that will work better for you. You deserve to try to find some peace for yourself.

The best thing you can do for yourself and your drugged-up family is to break the rule of silence. It is important for you to tell your mother or father (if one of them is not drinking or abusing other drugs) that you are unhappy, confused, sad, fearful, and nervous about the family situation, and you think the *family* needs to get help—not just the drugged person.

If this is too much of a risk, you must at least get help for yourself and those family members who want to come along. You can speak to a school counselor or social worker, a religious leader, or your family doctor.

One of the best things you can do is to pick up the telephone and call one of the drug helplines on pages 543–44, Alateen, or Al-Anon Family Support. Alateen is an organization which offers support for kids who are growing up up in a family where there is a drinking problem. There are meetings of Alateen in many communities. Parents and other adults who have to deal with the person who has the drinking problem can go to Al-Anon meetings so that they, too, can talk about their feelings and get help. Al-Anon Family Support can also help you with family problems caused by alcohol. Their toll-free number is 1-800-344-2666, 24 hours a day. (If this number changes, call 1-800-555-1212 for new information.)

If the drugged-up person makes the decision that they can no longer live with stretched-out emotions, doesn't like what's happened to their personality, and doesn't want to create any more problems for themselves or their family, they can get help by going to Alcoholics Anonymous (AA).

These meetings can be found in many neighborhoods. Just look for the telephone number in your local phone book or dial 0 for Operator and ask how to get information. There are all sorts of meetings and plenty of wonderful, good, loving people who will reach out to help you when you walk through the door.

Sometimes things that are best for us to do aren't the most comfortable. But that doesn't mean you shouldn't go ahead and do them. You deserve to take steps for yourself to help you grow up and feel good. You're worth it. Go for help.

Drinking and Driving

While you might not understand or relate to what it's like to live in a drugged-up family, you may have been touched by the effects of alcohol in a different way.

Although you might not be old enough to drive, and it's certainly not legal for you to drink, you may suffer from the consequences of someone who is old enough to drink and old enough to drive, putting the two together. How is this possible?

Robert, now twenty-eight, said, "When I was in the ninth grade, my good friend and his father were spending a Sunday afternoon together. They were sitting in their car at a red light, standing absolutely still, when a drunk driver speeding from behind crashed into them. They were doing nothing wrong and they were both killed. The drunk driver wasn't hurt at all."

Camille, age eighteen, started to cry when she talked about her sister, a new driver, whose car was hit in the rear by a nineteen-year-old guy, a drunk driver, and how her sister's car was smashed into a tree like an accordion with her sister's body crushed inside. To make Camille's anger worse, the nineteen-year-old drunk driver was given a mild punishment and had to pay a small fine. Camille felt that something more should have been done to the driver.

This is a harsh reminder that, even if you don't drink, you can be seriously affected by someone who does. The effects of someone drinking can fall not only on that person but on everyone around them.

The problem comes a little closer to you when you need to take a ride from someone you know who may have been drinking. Steven, age fourteen, shared, "I didn't know what to do. Last weekend my older brother said he'd pick me up at my friend's party. When I heard the horn, I looked out to find that my brother's friend was driving instead of my brother. When I got closer to the car, I saw there were beer cans all over the front seat and I knew they had been drinking. His friend who was driving seemed okay but it bothered me. I got in the car anyway, hoping we'd get home without hitting something."

Betsy, age seventeen, said that there were times when her boyfriend had too much too drink and she felt scared riding with him. She thought he'd feel bad or get mad and not want to go out with her anymore if she told him she'd rather walk or call her parents to take them home. So she got into his car and hoped they'd get home safely.

You may get home safely the first time, and the second, and the third. Or you might not. Every time you ride with someone who has been drinking or using other drugs, you're taking a chance that you might not make it back home. The problem is that even though most kids know this, they don't seem to believe the risks are real until something happens to them or someone they know. Then it's too late.

When you get a driver's license, if you've been drinking you may think that the best way to not hurt someone and not get arrested for drinking and driving is to let someone else who has been drinking drive home. You may not get arrested. You may not hurt someone. But if the driver gets into an accident, he or she may take you along.

Mark, age twenty, said, "My friend was driving my pickup truck and we both had some beers. The ride home was pretty straight and easy. It was just our luck that we ran into the only parked car off the road. My pickup truck was wrecked! I spent the night in the hospital, and my friend spent the night in jail. My friend and I were very lucky. The fact that two girls from my high school died in a drinking-driving accident earlier in the year didn't have as much effect on me as when something actually happened to me. I'm really starting to look at things differently."

Many people who have been drinking and feel that they are mellow and not intoxicated think that they can make it home because their home is such a short distance away. Some people feel it's too embarrassing to admit that they can't drive home because they've been drinking. They may be concerned that their friends are going to laugh at them about not being able to handle drinking and driving at the same time. Others are embarrassed in front of a boyfriend or girlfriend, especially since they don't want this person to think less of them. Still others may think, "If I brought my car here, I have a responsibility to get it home, no matter what shape I'm in."

Others may even think there's absolutely nothing wrong with drinking and driving and will continue to until they get caught. Did you know that people who say they will drink and drive until they get caught usually continue to drink and drive even after they are caught? In spite of injury to themselves and others, embarrassment, shame, a possible jail sentence, guilt, or money trouble, some people never learn.

What you can do about the drinking-driving situation Many kids are finally starting to look at the drinking and driving problem very seriously. Usually these kids have been personally affected by this problem.

Doug, age eighteen, talked with me about his two closest friends who were killed last year. "Their car smashed into a tree off a winding road on the way home after a night of partying and drinking a lot of beer. Both were great guys, liked by everyone. Both were seniors in high school, really cared about their grades, and we were all looking forward to graduation. We went to school together each morning, partied together, spent a lot of time together. They were my closest friends. I really think as many people as possible should learn from what happened so they won't have to go through the horrible grief I experienced."

Doug and his friends started a driver-doesn't-drink rule and haven't broken it since. This rule means that the driver for the night (or day or whenever) doesn't drink even a sip of an alcoholic beverage and is responsible for getting everyone home safely.

Said Doug, "My friends are now really aware of drinking and driving. So is our whole high school class, for that matter. The problem is that's where it stopped. The younger classes, I'm afraid, just did not learn. I hope many people read your book so they'll know."

The simplest and most obvious way to prevent drunk driving is not to drink in the first place—or never to get in a car with someone who is drinking (or using other drugs) and driving. However, if someone chooses to drink, another way that you can prevent drunk driving is to call a parent. There are many community groups where parents have gotten together with the police and have arranged a special force of people who will be on call for any kids in their town who need to be picked up because they feel they should not drive home alone or with someone else who has been drinking.

You can also spend the night with your friends instead of taking a chance on anyone driving you home. Be sure to call your parents to let them know you're okay. You can explain that you're staying over and your friend's parents will look after you for the evening (that's important for them to do).

Some kids worry about how their parents will respond if they get that kind of a call in the middle of the night. They find it especially hard to admit that they, their friends, or both have been drinking. While most parents will probably not be happy about the drinking—and would probably wish it wasn't so late—they will be relieved that you called.

They'd rather have their kid safe and deal with the issue of drinking at another time, after you've gotten home safely.

It takes a lot of guts to do the next prevention measure. And you usually need two friends to help! If a friend of yours wants to leave a party and you think that the friend is in no condition to drive, have two friends walk arm in arm with the drunk person while you remove the car keys from his or her hand or pocket.

Convince them to spend the night even though they tell you everything is fine or might even be yelling at you. Call their parents to tell them that their kid is okay, and don't pay much attention to how much your friend might say he or she hates you. He'll probably thank you in the morning. And even if not, trust that you did the right thing to prevent this person from putting themselves and other people at risk.

You might be thinking that only bad people do these things. Being "bad" has nothing to do with drinking and driving. Even if you work hard in school, love your parents, always baby-sit for your little brother or sister, are a good friend, say your prayers regularly, and have wonderful goals and dreams—each time you risk driving drunk or high, you're taking a chance you (or someone else) might not get home. Trees aren't choosy. Neither are parked cars. Hospital visits are not as good as dates and parties. And funerals are not fun. (This might be a good time to reread what I said about Russian Roulette on page 209.)

Drinking and driving affects all of us. We are all responsible and we all must do something about it. Isn't it sad that most of the people who make sure to do something about the drinking-driving problem are those who have been personally touched by it, like Doug? Why does it have to take tragedies for most kids to believe that accidents can really happen?

Tobacco

Whether people smoke cigarettes or chew or "dip" smokeless tobacco, they are putting themselves at serious risk. There is no safe form of tobacco use. Yet, because the consequences of using tobacco usually take a while (sometimes many years into later adulthood) to begin to show up, kids often don't view tobacco as a problem drug.

Despite the fact that there is a movement in our country against smoking and most public places are becoming "no smoking" areas, many kids still pick up the habit.

Cigarettes and smokeless tobacco are easily available to kids and a great many kids still think using tobacco makes them cool.

People who are using tobacco are not usually casual about their use. Many smokers smoke a lot, sometimes several packs a day. They may rely on tobacco to settle their nerves, keep them more calm in stressful situations, and even prevent them from gaining weight.

Take a few minutes to think about how you feel about smoking cigarettes or using smokeless tobacco. How do you feel about the smoke going in and out of your nose and lungs? How do you feel about being in a smoke-filled room when you don't smoke or when you do smoke? If your parents smoke, how does that make you feel? How do you feel about your friends smoking? How do you feel about being near someone who is spitting tobacco juice? What kind of consequences do you think smoking or using smokeless tobacco would have for you?

Risk-taking and Smoking

Unlike the risks of drinking and using other drugs, the risks of smoking cigarettes might seem like something that has nothing to do with your life right now. Because you may not actually "see" any unhealthy results, you might find it hard to take seriously the consequences that are associated with inhaling the chemicals in tobacco into your body.

You need to know and take seriously that the chemicals in tobacco are highly addictive and can:

- Lower a person's energy.
- Make a person's blood vessels (roadways through which the blood travels around the body) constrict or grow narrower so that the heart has to work harder to pump the blood through.
- Cause lung damage (cigarette smoking is believed to be the main cause of lung cancer in people).
- Cause heart problems.
- Cause breathing problems. (Many people who play sports have noticed that smoking has made them get out of breath sooner. Smoking can also lead to

breathing problems that cause people not even to be able to walk up a flight of stairs.)
- Lower the weight of a newborn baby born to a woman who smoked during pregnancy.
- Cause smoker's cough (This is often *chronic* [KRON-ick] or lasts a long time, doesn't heal, and stays with the smoker.)
- Take years off a smoker's life.

Smoking cigarettes can not only have serious health effects on people who smoke but also affect others, through "second-hand smoke" (smoke inhaled from other people's cigarettes).

You may have heard your parents and other adults say they wish they had stopped smoking years ago. You might also have heard people say, "If only I could stop . . ."

And yet, in spite of all the health risks, in spite of listening to older people talk about how much they hate their smoking habit, in spite of educational programs teaching you about the dangers of smoking, you might still smoke. For more information on ways smoking affects your health, you can call the American Heart Association (1-800-242-8721). If the number changes, call 1-800-555-1212 for information.

Smokeless Tobacco

As I've already said, there is no safe form of tobacco use. That includes using smokeless tobacco (snuff and chewing tobacco). This is often referred to as chewing or spitting tobacco. Many kids think that as long as they're not smoking cigarettes, they're not taking serious risks. That's not true.

As with smoking cigarettes, using smokeless tobacco can lead to very serious results. These include cancer and other health problems in the mouth (affecting the cheeks, lips, tongue and gums) as well as other areas of the body. Smokeless tobacco can also stain and decay teeth and affect a person's breath.

Feelings and Pressures Related to Smoking

There are so many different feelings and different types of pressures related to smoking. The more you explore these pressures the more ready you will be to deal with them if they ever happen to you.

Steve, age thirteen, said, "I always saw my parents smoke and have wanted to try smoking since I was little. It seemed like the big person's thing to do!"

Beth, age fourteen, told me, "Some of the kids I hang around with started smoking. I'm not sure what to do because I don't want to feel left out, but I really don't want to smoke."

Vicki, age nine, said, "I don't ever want to smoke. My mother and my father smoke and I hate it when the smoke goes in my nose. I don't know how they can sit there with the smoke in their faces all the time."

Sammy, age eleven, shared that he's upset because his father smokes so much. His father coughs all the time and still smokes. Sammy's very worried that the smoking will make his father's cough worse.

Sharon, age fifteen, said, "I smoke because I like to, not because it looks cool or anything like that. My parents won't let me smoke in front of them, so I have to sneak."

Roger, age forty, said, "When I was younger, my parents told me I could smoke in front of them if I wanted to. I think they took all the fun out of it by giving me permission. I never smoked until years later."

Earl, now age twenty-five, shared: "When I grew up, I believed very strongly that smoking was wrong. I didn't even take a single puff of a cigarette until I was nineteen years old. Then one night at a bar, I decided that I had been silly. And that not only was it time to try smoking, but that I was going to see what it was like to be a smoker.

"I smoked ten cigarettes in one night. It kind of made me feel sick and gave me a head rush. But I was determined. Over the next several days, I kept forgetting that I was supposed to be smoking cigarettes. A day would go by, and I'd say to myself, 'Oh, shoot, I was supposed to smoke!' I eventually had to admit to myself that I don't like smoking. I don't like how it tastes or feels in my throat. And I guess I must be a nonsmoker."

Betsy, age twelve, told me, "I'm really afraid of what's going to happen in the girls' bathroom at the junior high school next year. I've heard people say that you can get pressured to smoke if you walk in there."

Carol, age thirty-eight, remembers, "I was one of the first and only people to have a car in high school. Every morning a lot of the kids sat in my car and smoked before school started. I didn't smoke and didn't feel pressured to smoke even though they did. I admit that for a while, it was important to let them use my car because they were my friends and I didn't want to say no to them. But finally I told them I hated the smoke and didn't want them to smoke in my car anymore. I said they'd have to find somewhere else to smoke.

"It was really interesting. I found out who my friends were. Some of the girls used me and didn't have much to do with me after I told them to stay away from my car. Other girls continued to be my friends."

Alexis, age fourteen, who always hated smoking and whose parents never smoked but whose aunt did, started smoking. Even though Alexis was coughing a lot and hated it, she did it because a boy she really liked smoked.

She felt that in order to get him to like her better, she should do the same things that he did. So she continued to smoke in front of him. She would never smoke alone.

Then her girlfriends, who were feeling the same way she was feeling, started to smoke in front of each other but still not alone. Now a new pressure was added. Not only did Alexis smoke in front of her boyfriend, but she felt she had to smoke in front of her girlfriends. She didn't have any idea that they were all feeling the same pressure.

After a while, Alexis started doing a lot of her activities with a cigarette in her hand. She started to feel grown-up like her aunt. In time, she decided that smoking was not for her. But she never really felt it very strongly.

So when a new boyfriend came along who always had a cigarette hanging out of his mouth, once again, Alexis felt the need to smoke. The smoking started to become a real habit. She smoked—needing to—not wanting to.

I hope by now that if your friends are smoking and you really don't want to, you'll have a better idea about how to say no. (For a reminder of what you might say or do if you feel pressure to smoke, turn back to "Peer Pressure, Making Choices," Chapter 15.)

Living in a Cloud of Smoke

If you are like many other people, you may think that what you can't see or feel probably won't hurt you. If you smoke, you might be saying, "I'll give up smoking when and if I can see that it has caused some harmful consequences to my body."

You may figure that when you start to notice these changes, it will be time enough to promise to be good to your body by not smoking anymore. But the truth is, by then it may be too late to undo the damage that smoking has already brought about, too late to ever again be able to do physical activities the way you would wish—if you can still do them at all.

And the following social and physical results, while they may not be as serious as consequences such as heart or lung disease, are still very real and may affect you even if you're not a smoker yourself.

First of all, let's talk about the lingering odor in your hair. You may spend hours each day trying to get your hair to look and smell nice. Yet the smoke in cigarettes, cigars, and pipes manages to get on your hair and stays there until you wash it again. Smokers' hair often smells like old sweat socks that have just been used to clean out ashtrays. If that sounds gross, that's what it's like to be around smokers' hair—gross!

Next, let's deal with breath. Phew! Lots of kids don't like to kiss smokers because their breath smells like a cesspool that has backed up. Get the picture?

A smoker's clothing often has that lingering smell of stale cigarettes. And even if you wear cologne or perfume, your body may smell like perfume on the old sweat socks that have been used to clean the ashtrays.

The unfortunate part is that many smokers have no idea they smell so bad. That's because one of the consequences of smoking is that it can lessen your sense of smell and taste. Smoking also can cause fingers to smell and fingers and teeth to be stained a yellowish color. Yuck.

Lauren, age sixteen, finds it very difficult to tell her girlfriends that they stink. She wants to be their friend and doesn't want to push them away, but her other nonsmoking friends have just about had it with the way her smoking friends smell. She likes her friends but hates their odors.

Allison, age fourteen, decided that she doesn't want to kiss her boyfriend anymore. He used to smell so nice but now he started smoking and uses breath spray to cover up the odor of tobacco. Allison gets nauseous from the breath spray and tobacco. Her feelings are beginning to change toward him.

Jason, age thirteen, can't stand when his father, a cigar smoker, tries to kiss him. He loves the fact that his father wants to kiss him and really would like to kiss him back. But he makes the excuse that he's too old for kissing and would rather shake hands. His father's cigar smell turns him off.

Sean, age ten, heard his brother, a nonsmoker, fighting with his girlfriend about her smoking. His brother said that his girlfriend was starting to become a turn-off. Even though she thought she looked cool and glamorous, getting close to her was disgusting. She always stank of tobacco chemicals and it was hard to be physical with her.

I should warn you that the people who advertise cigarettes are doing the best they can to make you think that smoking will make you very sexy, popular, desirable, and successful. They're very clever in their commercials. They would like to keep you drugged in a cloud of smoke so that they can continue making money. Now you know that the truth is death and disease are very real consequences of tobacco use.

If you have never smoked, you can decide never to start. If you smoke, you can decide to stop. It's up to you—no matter what anyone else is doing.

Chapter 19

YOUR PARENTS

Many kids say that they feel great about their parents. One nine-year-old girl said, "We get along. We're very close. I can say anything I want to them and they'll listen. They spend a lot of time with me. They don't pressure me. They're great!" Kids who feel this way are usually more secure, calm, happier, and more confident. They feel loved.

Too many other kids have told me that they wish they could feel closer to their parents. Charlie, age eleven, said, "I can't talk with my mom and my dad. They don't understand me. They're always bugging me about something. They're hardly ever home. I don't think I'll ever be able to talk with them." Kids who feel that way are often sadder, more unhappy, more insecure, lonely, angry, scared, and frustrated. As much as they might love their parents, and as much as their parents might really love them, these kids may not feel loved.

How do you feel about your parents? Are you happy with the relationship you have with them? What do you wish you could change? What have you wanted to say but just not been able to get out the words? What about your parents makes you feel good? What makes you feel bad?

This chapter will give you a chance to think about all the feelings you have that relate to your own parents or other adults in your life who may be caring for you as a parent. Trying to understand these feelings and learning how to deal with them better is very important.

If you haven't been writing down your feelings in a notebook as you read, this might be a good time to start. That way, when it's time to talk with your parents about anything, you'll have all your feelings in front of you and you can make sure not to leave anything out.

It may interest you to know that so many parents over the years have shared with me how difficult it is for them to say "I love you" to their children. Many of them said that their own parents hardly ever said it to them and didn't openly express affection. Lots of parents also said that they don't feel comfortable giving their kids a hug or kiss.

So it doesn't have to mean a parent doesn't love you if they don't tell you how much you mean to them. They may love you a lot but just not be able to show it. That's another reason talking can help. Let them know that you notice they haven't said "I love you" for a long time— and how much you want to hear it. That may be just the opening line that will help them talk with you about their uncomfortable feelings.

Talking with Your Parents

If you can talk openly with your parents and trust they'll care enough to listen, that's very special. The sad thing is that most of the boys and girls I've spoken to can't talk openly with their parents or don't think they can.

Statements such as "I'm nervous when I have to talk with my parents"; "My parents don't understand how I feel. I try to talk things over with them but they treat me like a baby"; "I'm afraid to talk with my parents"; "I have trouble talking to my mom. I don't know what to say to her"; "I have a question to ask my mother, but I think that she'll say I'm too young to know"; and "I can't talk to my dad" can give you a clue as to why so many feelings stay hidden. Maybe you've had some of these feelings.

Even when kids want very much to talk and parents want very much to listen, there still can be silence. Why? Well, kids are often scared, embarrassed, afraid their parents won't understand, will be angry, will punish them, or won't take them seriously. Very often children and parents just don't know what words to use or what questions to ask.

You'll find it easier to be open and honest if you keep reminding yourself that the words are right inside you. So you never have to be stuck for what to say—not with your parents, your friends, your teachers, your boyfriend or girlfriend, not with the President of the United States, or anyone! Just think about how you feel and then turn your feelings into words.

If you feel embarrassed, you can say, "Mom, Dad, I'm really embarrassed to say this . . ." If you feel scared, you can say, "Mom, Dad, I'm scared to tell you this . . ." If you're concerned they won't take you seriously, you can tell them, "I'm worried you won't realize how serious I am about this . . ." If you think they'll be mad, you can say, "I hope you won't get mad when I say this. I don't mean to upset you . . ." If you're ashamed, you can tell them you're ashamed. And so on.

It's very important for you to let your parents know about your feelings. They may not be able to guess, even if you're close to each other and understand each other well. And it doesn't have to mean your parent loves you less or isn't paying attention to you if he or she can't guess how you feel. The only way to be sure your parents know how you feel is to tell them. Aloud or in writing. It may not be easy to get the words out, even if you know what to say. But the more you push yourself to get those hidden feelings out, the better the chance you and your parents will have to understand each other and try to get closer.

Here are some more suggestions:

- If your parents upset you, you can say, "When you said [or did] that, I was really upset. You may not have meant it that way, but that's how I felt . . ."
- If your parents hurt you, you can say, "When you did that, I felt very hurt . . ."
- If you think they were unfair, you can say, "I don't think you were fair . . ."
- If they blamed you for something you didn't do, you can say, "I don't understand why you blamed me for that. I didn't do it . . ."
- If you feel they don't understand, you can say, "Mom,

Dad, I get the feeling that you just don't understand how I feel . . ."

- If you think they're going to think you're too young to know, you can say, "You're probably going to think I'm too young to know, but I'm really not. If you won't talk to me about this, I'll be forced to go to someone else . . . and it's very important to me that I hear it from you."

Anything you feel can be turned into words. Even if you can't figure out how you feel, you can say, "I don't know what to say," or "I don't know how to tell you this," or "Is it okay that we don't talk? I need time to think about how I feel. I'm not sure."

Figure that it's very hard for parents to always be wise and able to know how their kids feel, especially when so many kids hide their feelings and look just fine on the outside—even when they're crying on the inside.

Being comfortable Now that you know how you might approach your parents (or anyone) and what you can say, it might help for you to think more about what topics are harder to discuss than others.

Kids have told me they have difficulty talking with their parents about their bodies, their development, sex, dating, report cards and test grades, "crushes" on teachers, drinking and other drugs, smoking, mistakes, if friends have gotten in trouble, divorce, death, and so many other things. This is very natural.

Parents are people just like everybody else. They, too, may get embarrassed and uncomfortable about a lot of topics that you'll want to talk about. They might even be more embarrassed than their kids!

But that doesn't mean that you shouldn't try to talk with them about these things. It's okay to be uncomfortable. It's not okay to let uncomfortable feelings prevent you from talking about something that is very important to share.

Needing all the answers I think it would help for you to understand that some parents don't feel good talking with their children about certain things because they think they need to know all the answers. They aren't comfortable when they don't.

Your parents would probably be relieved if you told them, "I know you probably can't answer all my questions. But that's okay. I'm really happy I can ask."

Besides talking with each other, you and your parent(s) can go to the library together and find books on the subjects about which you need to know more. You may also have some good resource books at home. You can read together, learn together. In addition to getting helpful information, you might even find that you'll feel closer.

Your mother, father, or both? Which parent can you talk with more easily? Maybe you're one of those kids who can talk with either parent. Maybe you can talk comfortably with your mother, maybe only with your father.

The more I talk with kids, the more I find that girls continue to think that it's kind of strange to talk with their dads about periods, bras, and things like that. Boys often feel the same way about talking with their moms about wet dreams and erections, and so on. Not all boys and not all girls feel this way. But many do.

With so many kids living in single-parent households, there are going to be girls who live only with their fathers and boys who live only with their mothers. (And girls will continue to have man teachers; boys will be in classes with woman teachers.) The earlier you realize that there is no rule that girls must speak only with women and boys only with men, the earlier you might feel that you can take a chance on sharing feelings and asking questions.

Girls and boys can speak with moms and dads, man and woman teachers, and so on. Besides, while dads and other men don't get periods, they know about them! And moms and other women know about boys' development. It usually means a lot to parents when their child shares those and other kind of personal things with them.

Perhaps the next time you find yourself holding back, you'll push yourself to try to say what you think you can't. Remember, just because you're not comfortable doesn't mean you shouldn't try. Say it quickly if you have to, but say it! You might be wonderfully surprised at how much closer you'll feel to that parent.

Talking can be without words You're giving messages all the time, both verbally and nonverbally (without words). Sometimes the nonverbal messages can be much louder than the verbal ones.

For instance, did you ever see someone act really upset? They might have a deep frown, tightened-up mouth, and seem as if they're holding back their tears. And when you ask them, "What's wrong?" they say, "Nothing!" Well, you know very well something's wrong; they're just not telling you.

Or if someone gives you a huge smile and a great big hug, the message is love. They don't really have to say anything after doing that. They've already given you their message loud and clear. That's a good thing to remember in case you feel funny saying "I love you" out loud. Now you know you can give an "I love you" message even without words.

You'd be surprised how much you can learn about your parents and how much you are telling them, perhaps without even realizing it. If they're paying attention, parents can probably sense when you're happy or sense when something is wrong with you, even if you don't say anything. If you pay attention, you can probably learn a lot about what your parents feel. You can sense their feelings from how they act, the expressions on their faces, and whether or not they seem tense or relaxed. If you're not sure about what you're sensing, or if you're upset or confused, ask them if everything is okay. Tell them your feelings! Maybe there's something to be concerned about, but maybe not. The only way to be sure is to check it out, to ask.

(Remember: Although nonverbal messages can tell people a lot, it's still possible that your parent—or anyone else—won't guess how you feel. It doesn't mean they don't care or aren't paying attention if they don't guess how you feel. They simply may not guess.)

Sometimes parents want to protect their children from sad feelings and difficult situations. So they tell their kids, "Everything is fine, nothing is wrong," when inside, they're really very upset. They often don't realize how important it is to let their child know what's going on, even if it hurts. Most kids are very sensitive to their parent's stress. And, if left uninformed as to why their parent seems so upset, they often worry that something even worse has happened.

If your mom or dad says everything is okay and you still feel you're not able to trust that it is, you might say, "I know you're saying things are fine. But I have a feeling that may not be true. I'm worried that you're afraid I'll be too upset or too scared if you tell me what's really going on. I'd rather know than not know, even if I'll be very upset. Please tell me the truth."

You may want to add: "It's hard for me to do my work at school because I worry so much. I really need to know—what's going on?" You can also remind your parents that if you're old enough to sense their strain, you're probably old enough to get an honest answer. It doesn't mean they have to give you every detail. Just that you need to understand.

Parents may also worry that crying in front of their children will get them more upset. Many are afraid to explain problems because they don't know if they can trust themselves to stay calm and not break down in tears in the middle of what they need to say. Others think they have to be strong all the time, always "handling it," setting a strong example for their kids. If only more parents would be able to let themselves cry with their kids when their feelings hurt. It can be a relief for parents (and their kids) if they let out the real feelings which are inside—and don't feel they have to pretend things are fine when they're really not.

Besides, what kind of message do you think a parent being able to handle "everything" would give to you? Would you think *you* always had to be able to handle everything, too? That's a pretty big burden.

Let your parents know that even if there aren't any words said aloud, their feelings are coming through loud and clear on their face, in their eyes, in their tone of voice, and in how they seem to respond. Tell them you really need to talk about this with them.

Maybe the truth isn't as bad as what you think it is. If it is, why should they have to deal with it alone, without your support? And if you don't tell them that you're worried, you'll continue to walk around, worrying silently, without *their* support.

Parents and kids can gain strength from supporting each other. Sometimes, it's the kids who have to make the first move.

When You Can't Talk with Your Parents: When They Don't Pay Attention

While most parents would do anything to be able to talk with their children in a meaningful way, the disturbing truth is that some parents really don't care. I can't pretend that they all do. That can be very sad and deeply painful for the child who wants a parent so badly, who wants to reach out and know the parent will be there.

But all you can do is express your pain and let them know how much you feel hurt by their words, actions, or neglect. You can let them know how much you want more of a relationship with them. But they're the ones who'll have to make the decision to change, to pay more attention, to set more time aside so you can be together. You can stomp around, slam doors, kick, scream, and cry yourself to sleep every night, but nothing will change unless they decide to change themselves. You can't do it for them.

The more you try to get your parents to love you and the more you don't succeed, the more you may feel that you're not lovable or important. It would be helpful to remember that, even though your parents may not be able to talk with you or spend time with you, that doesn't mean you're not lovable. It just may mean that the people (your parents) who by all rights deserve to love and care for you—either don't want to or aren't able. And it just may mean that there is nothing you personally can do to change the situation or make the feelings different between you.

So many kids don't understand this and depend on their parents' love to prove to them that they're still important. Now you know that someone else loving or caring for you—even your parent—is not a measure of your importance. You're important with or without their love.

Sometimes parents spend more time with their friends and much less time with their own kids. They can spend hours and hours on the telephone or with friends who have come to visit, and when you want to talk with them, somehow they're always too busy.

When Sharon was thirteen, she said that her mother would spend hours in the kitchen drinking coffee with her neighbor. Every time Sharon wanted to talk with her mother about anything, her mother would "shh" her and say, "Can't you see I'm talking? Don't interrupt me!" Sharon would wait for hours to get to talk with her mother because it seemed like any time she approached her would be an interruption. It got to the point where Sharon realized that her mother thought her friends were more important than Sharon and her problems were.

To tell your parent that you'd like to talk with him or her more, sometimes writing your feelings in notes can be easier. Then you can take the time to say all the things you need to say, without feeling like you're interrupting. You can give your notes to your parent and hope to talk together after they've been read.

If Sharon turned her feelings into words, she could have said: "Mom, every time I try to talk with you, it seems like I'm interrupting. You're always busy with your friends and you have so little time for me. That makes me feel like you don't care about me and I'm very sad. I wish we could spend more time together. I need you."

All Sharon could have done is let her mother know how she felt and how she wished she could feel better about their relationship. The rest was up to her mother. If her mother still spent more time with her friends than with Sharon, I hope Sharon could still hold on to how special she is and appreciate that she at least did what she could to let her mom know how she feels.

A girl in the eighth grade told me that more than anything, she wanted her mother to pay attention to her. She said, "My mother promised me that her boyfriend wouldn't get in the way of our relationship. And he did. I hardly ever see her. She doesn't spend any time with me. Only him. I tried drugs. I tried running away. I tried committing suicide. And nothing got her attention."

While I helped her understand how she could express her feelings to her mother, the truth is there's no way to control whether her mother will change. So instead of destroying her life because her mother doesn't have the sensitivity or ability to give her what she wants so badly—love, affection, and time together—she needs to hold on.

She needs to realize she's not more or less important because her mother pays more or less attention. She's important, no matter what. And if she's dealing with difficult, painful feelings about how her mother doesn't pay her any attention, it's important that she speak with an adult (like a grandparent or school counselor) who can help her understand and go on with her own life as best she can.

Each child has to try harder to hold onto his or her inner strength and somehow get through childhood. And when neglected kids become adults, they can be stronger and wiser from all the hurt feelings they had to handle while growing up. They'll be that much more able to understand how much it means to give of themselves to the people in their life, especially to their own children.

Once again, being rejected doesn't make you less lovable, only less loved or more neglected by that parent. There's a big difference. Also, the parent may love you very much. It may just be your parent's own situation that is preventing him or her from paying you the attention that you deserve. And so just try as best you can to go on with your life, seeking out other people who do care—and are able to show it.

While you're waiting and hoping to talk, you can reach out to the other parent, an older brother or sister, a loving grandparent or other relative, religious leader, a trusted teacher, school counselor, or even your friend's parent. They won't take the place of your parent. No one can, exactly. But at least you'll be able to get guidance in how to deal with your day-to-day feelings and situations in a way that will be helpful to you. And you'll be able to feel more secure in knowing there are other people who care.

When Parents Don't Listen

There are several different ways that parents don't listen. Johnny, age eleven, told me, "I can't stand it when I'm trying to tell my father something important and he keeps on reading his newspaper. When I ask him if he's listening, he says, 'Of course. I can do both things at once!' But I never get the feeling he's really hearing me."

Joanne, age thirteen, said, "I wish my mother would listen more. She hardly ever looks up from her book when I talk to her (she's always reading). She says things like, 'Ummm,' 'hmmmm,' and 'oh,' and then ends up saying, 'I'm sorry to hear that.' But then she says nothing else."

Pete, age twelve, said, "I know my parents try to listen to me. But my younger sisters and brothers always need attention and it's always so noisy. I hardly ever get a chance to talk with them by myself."

Nancy, age ten, said, "Sometimes I have to say things five times before my father will look up from his TV program and give a grunt."

In every one of these situations, Nancy, Pete, Joanne, and Johnny can let their parents know how they feel. Here's how:

> **JOHNNY:** "Dad, a lot of times when I try to talk to you and you keep reading the paper, it seems like you're not listening to me. I know you tell me that you can do both things at once, but it really bothers me."

JOANNE: "Mom, I really wish you would listen more. After I tell you something, you say, 'Oh' and 'Ummm', and even, 'Oh, that's too bad,' but you don't say anything else, and I need more. Please don't read when I talk with you."

Another way Johnny and Joanne and Pete can ask to talk is to "allow for" what their parent is doing, for example:

JOHNNY: "Could you please call me when you finish reading the paper? I need to talk with you."

JOANNE: "I really need to talk with you. When might be a good time?"

PETE: "It's so hard to talk with you when ____ always need your attention. When you put them to bed, could we sit down together alone?"

Nancy can turn her feelings directly into words:

NANCY: "Dad, sometimes I have to say things five times before you look up from your TV show."

Or here are two other possibilities for Nancy:

- Give her dad a big hug and whisper into his ear, "Do you mind taking a TV break to talk with me now?"
- If she can wait, "Dad, please let me know when your program is over. I need to talk with you. I'll be in my room . . ."

Sometimes, even if a parent would really like to take the time to listen, they just can't.

Your mother or father may work long hours out of your home and may not be able to see you very often. They may hardly ever come home for dinner, or maybe they travel a lot. Even if you feel close and comfortable with each other, it's hard to share if they're not around.

At those times, you can write down your feelings in a note to them so they can read it when they come home. Maybe you can set aside a certain time over the weekend, like Sunday morning breakfast or Sunday evening after dinner, as a catch-up time. Though you'd like to talk with each other more often, knowing that you're doing your best to use the time you do have will help you feel better.

Sometimes when your parents are around and do listen, they just may not "hear" you. They might say, "Oh, it's ridiculous for you to feel that way," or "You shouldn't let that bother you." When anyone, even your parent, says that you shouldn't feel a certain way and you know you do, that's when the sirens need to go off! You can tell them, "I know you think I shouldn't feel this way, but I *do*. Could you please help me?"

Sometimes parents listen but they don't take what their kids say seriously. They make light of what really is important to their child. If this happens to you, it's important to let your parents know. For example: "It's very hard to talk with you when you keep making jokes and don't take me seriously. It hurts when you do that. I wanted a serious answer. It makes me think that I shouldn't bother trying to tell you what I feel."

Spending Time with Your Parents

Many kids have told me that they wish their parents would spend more time with them. Sometimes this is impossible, but many times it just takes being smarter about the time you do have.

Too often when people have only ten or fifteen minutes, they think it's not enough time to do anything. But it's plenty of time to walk around the block, sit in your yard, kitchen, or living room to talk, catch up, and let each other each other know about the day you've had so far. It's time enough to give a hug and tell someone you miss them and wish you could spend more time together.

You might find yourself jealous of other kids whose parents are out in the street playing ball with them for hours at a time.

You may be sad when your parents aren't able to come to back-to-school night, sports events, school concerts, dance recitals, or any other event. But be careful not to measure your parents' love or how important they feel you are by whether or not they attend. Chances are they really wish they could be there. They're probably sad about it, too.

Time with Friends or Time with Parents?

With all the talk about communicating with your parents, sharing your feelings, sharing your time, it's important to point out (if you haven't noticed already) that it's natural for kids to want to spend more and more time with their friends. Even if that takes away from some of the time they could spend with their parents (and family). That doesn't mean they love their parents any less. It's simply a part of growing up.

Also, parents may find their children aren't telling them as much as they did when they were younger. Here, too, it probably doesn't mean that their children trust or love their parents any less. And it doesn't mean that they have failed as parents. As children get older, it's natural for them to want to share certain things with friends, often instead of sharing with their parents.

As long as you feel you can and will share with your parents when you want or need to do so—especially if there are any serious concerns—then that's fine. It's not fine when you want to share and don't feel you can.

If you're wondering how your parents feel about the time you spend with your friends, ask them. If you're feeling guilty about wanting to accept your friend's dinner invitation instead of having dinner with your family, talk with your parents about your feelings.

If you're upset about something and would rather talk with your friends about it at that time, just be honest about your feelings. You can tell your parents that you're really upset, but need to talk to your friend so you can straighten it out. Tell them if you need them you'll let them know, and you feel good knowing that you can come to them. You can even thank them for understanding and give them a hug.

When Parents Fight

Robin, age eleven, shared, "I'm very upset about my parents. Lately they've been fighting more and more and this worries me. It makes me scared. Does a lot of fighting mean they might get a divorce? When I hear them starting, I go to my room and turn up my radio real loud so I don't hear them. This helps, but the trouble is that I still know they're fighting. My brother says not to worry about it, but I can't help it."

Though there are plenty of parents who have gotten divorced after too much fighting, fighting doesn't have to mean divorce. It's natural for people to fight sometimes. Most kids fight with their sister, brother, or friends every once in a while. That doesn't mean they don't love each other and don't want to be friends anymore.

If your parents are fighting more than ever, it may mean that either one or both of your parents could be tense about something that has little or nothing to do with their marriage, but they're just taking it out on each other. Or, they could really be upset with each other. Whatever it is may take a little while to work out. Breaking up their marriage may not even be in their thoughts, although their fighting may sound awful.

I don't agree with Robin's brother. I think if you're worried about your parents' fighting and what it means, that worry will probably stay with you all or most of the time. It's hard to just turn the worry off.

The truth is, it's also possible that your parents really are having a rough time with each other, and that they really are thinking about divorce. Unless you talk with your parents, you're just guessing.

It may be very hard for you to ask your parents about their fighting, and you may be scared to learn their answer. But consider this. If things are fine between them and they're just grouchy and strained for other reasons, wouldn't you be relieved to find out? If their marriage is in trouble, then why should you handle all the tough feelings alone?

It's important that you let them know how upset you are about their fighting and that you think it's getting worse. Tell them that you're worried all the time and need to know the truth about what's going on between them. (Divorced parents are discussed in Chapter 20.)

Sometimes when parents fight, the fighting is very hurtful. When one parent abuses the other—or if parents abuse each other—with words or fists, that can be very frightening and confusing. It can be even harder if this abuse takes place in front of the kids.

Jamie, age fifteen, told me, "My father hits my mother sometimes. Especially if he's been drinking. I don't understand why my mother stays with him. Once he pushed her so hard that she fell and broke her arm. He said he was really sorry, but I know he's going to hurt her again. He's been sorry before. And he's always hurt her again. I'm so scared for my mom."

As with problems related to alcohol or sexual abuse, many kids think they must be silent about what is going on. If this is happening with your parents, you need to know that it's not your fault. And it's very important not to stay silent. Let someone know what is going on so you can get the help you need to deal with this situation in the safest possible way, and not have to handle it alone.

Here again, consider the adults you can trust. You can approach grandparents, aunts or uncles, older brothers or sisters, your school counselor or social worker, teacher, coach, religious leader, family doctor, friend's parent. You can also dial 0 and ask the operator how you can get information to call a domestic violence (family violence) hotline or other related help lines. If you haven't already taken the first step to get help, do it now.

When Your Parents Punish You

Some parents punish; others don't believe in it. Some are more fair than others. Perhaps the most helpful suggestion about this would be to deal honestly with any feelings you have about punishments that are given to you.

If you don't think your parents are being fair, say so. Maybe you can come up with a suggestion that you think is more appropriate. Taking away the use of electronic games, being grounded, lowering curfew (what time you have to return home after being out), not having friends over, not watching TV, allowing less computer time, or making kids go to bed earlier seem to be among the most common punishments from parents.

It's interesting how some boys and girls are relieved to be punished. Somehow it gets really tough to be able to say to a friend, "I can't meet you tonight" or "I can't go out." It's easier to blame the controls on parents.

As much as Mara (from Chapter 18) hated being grounded from seeing her friends after her mom discovered marijuana in her drawer, she admitted to me that she was happy she didn't have to make up excuses to not do drugs. Being grounded was the control that she couldn't place on herself, at least in the beginning.

If you're ever punished and don't understand why, ask your parents to explain why they did what they did. If you know what their rules are ahead of time, you might find it easier to avoid being punished. If you know the rules and choose to break them anyway, then you only have yourself to blame for any punishment. You'll have to live with the consequences of your choices.

When Parents Don't Make Rules

Patricia, age twenty, told me that she never really knew what was expected of her because her mother never told her when to come home, how to act, and what was good or bad behavior. Patricia was left to decide all her own rules. She realized that she made up rules for herself that were more difficult than any rules her parents could have made her follow. She always felt guilty when she broke one of her own rules and always felt that she had to be perfect. She wished that her mother had given her guidelines to follow. She said, "I'm probably harder on myself than my mother would ever be."

Most kids who have spoken with me about this said they'd rather have rules than not, "as long as they're fair" and "not too old-fashioned." The limits often make it easier to make decisions.

Sometimes it's the child whose parents do not enforce any rules who cries out for attention (like James's friend who smoked so much pot, in "Growing Up Drugged Up"). Kids seem to get the message that parents care more if they bother to set limits.

If your parents have not given you any guides for your behavior, and you feel you want and need them, let them know. If your parents have set limits that you feel are fair, they would probably feel great hearing that from you. If you think they're unfair, you owe it to your parents and yourself to tell them. They may not realize how you feel and may reconsider their rules. If they still don't change, at least you know you expressed to them what you feel.

When Your Parents Blame You for Something You Didn't Do

What do you do if you feel you're blamed unfairly? How about, "Mom, Dad, I really don't think you're being fair. You're blaming me for something I didn't do!" "I don't understand why you blame me when it's really not my fault. You haven't even given me a chance to explain. You only listened to them."

Sometimes you can know that you've been blamed unfairly and there's very little you can do about it. If your brother or sister gets to your parents first or yells the loudest, your parents may side with them instead of you. It's really helpful when parents don't side with anybody. But, as you might have already found out, that may not be the case.

Sara, who is the oldest, used to get blamed for starting all the fights between her and her middle sister. Her sister would go running to Sara's mother and say that Sara picked on her, hit her, was being mean, didn't want to play with her, left her out, was being nasty, pinched her, took her doll, and locked her out of the room. Sara's mother would always take her kid sister's side. She'd yell at Sara, slap her, tell her she was rotten, ask how she could do that to her younger sister, and say she should know better.

Sara's younger sister used to watch her mother scream and beat Sara up. She sometimes felt delight that Sara was getting beaten up, but most of the time she felt guilty because, after all, Sara was her older sister and wasn't always that bad to her, anyway.

There was very little Sara could do to prevent herself from getting blamed in this situation. Her younger sister was the only one who could call off the war. Sara was angry for a very long time at her mother and her sister for being a team against her.

Sometimes the oldest child in a family gets blamed because parents expect them to know better. They expect more of them. If you feel your younger brothers and sisters get you in trouble all the time, it's important to let your parents know. Though at times they may not listen (like Sara's mother), maybe they'll be able to help you figure out a plan so the blaming will stop, or at least be less.

I'll talk more about brothers and sisters, and being the oldest, middle, youngest, or an only child, in Chapter 21, Family Feelings.

When Parents Don't Agree

"If one parent says no about going out and one parent says yes, which one do I listen to?" That question, asked of me by a girl in the sixth grade, is a great example of how confusing it can be when parents don't agree.

Whom do you listen to? Well, I guess many kids would say, "Listen to the parent who says what you want to hear!" But it's usually not as easy as that. Sometimes kids have guilt feelings, such as, "If I listen to my mom, then maybe my dad will think I love her more." It can become a game. Sometimes parents test to see who their child listens to. But in that kind of game there are no winners. There are only more confused feelings.

This situation doesn't have to turn into a game of who loves whom more. It's very natural for parents not to agree on everything. In fact, I'd be surprised if they did. Think of your own friendships. Do you really agree with your close friends on everything?

It's important that you let your parents know how confused you get when they don't agree. Tell them you're not sure whom you should listen to when they disagree, and ask them what they suggest you should do.

If they're allowing you to make more and more decisions on your own, perhaps you need to listen to both of them and then think more about what you feel. Then make up your mind.

When Parents Embarrass You

When you were little, do you remember learning nursery rhymes or starting to count? Did your parents say, "Oh, Debby learned how to say another rhyme this week. Say the rhyme, Debby!" And you (make believe you're Debby) said, "Okay, Mommy or Daddy, rhyme, rhyme, rhyme . . ."

When you got a little older, maybe they left nursery rhymes and went on to asking you to play the piano for company or telling you to explain how well you did on your report card. Some kids love to explain how well they did on their report card. Some kids love to perform like that. Maybe you did. Maybe you still do.

But others hate it! As soon as their parents come toward them and they know they have company over, they run the other way because they know that their parents will ask them to do something.

You can privately tell your parents that you hate being asked to perform. Let them know it embarrasses you and ask if they would please stop. Explain that you'll be happy to come out and say hi, but ask them please not to ask you to do anything else.

There are other ways parents can embarrass you. They can fight when your friends are over. In front of a friend, they can yell at you and say personal things that you don't want anyone to hear. They can tell a new friend how much you've been wanting them to come over. They can talk too loud if you're in a restaurant or in a department store, be more dressed up than anyone else, be drunk in front of your friends, get in a fight with a person at a store, make you come home earlier than anyone else, make you wear your boots when everyone else doesn't have to. If you feel your parents embarrass you in any way, what would you include on your own list?

Many kids have a hard time being honest about being embarrassed because they don't want to hurt their parents' feelings or possibly even make them angry. The key is *how* you let them know. You can be sensitive, private, put your arm around your parent and say in a loving way, for example, "Dad, I just didn't know how to tell you this because I'd never want to hurt your feelings. But I feel like crawling under the table when you say things like that in front of my friends. Please wait until we're alone."

If you don't let your parents know how you feel, they may never be able to guess.

If Parents Abuse You

Just in case you're not sure, it's not normal or right for a parent to beat you, pinch you, push you around, make you go long hours without food, make sexual advances toward you, say nasty, mean things to you, or do anything else that abuses you in any way.

Some kids think this kind of behavior is okay because they've never known anything different. Some think it's okay because they are told—and feel—that it's their fault and they deserve it. That's not true. Abuse from parents is not a kid's fault. Abuse in any form is not right or okay. Abuse is also against the law.

Part of the problem in dealing with such abuse is that kids fear their parent will find out if they tell someone. (Remember the code of silence in Chapter 18?) The other part is knowing who to tell in order to get help and then taking the first step to let this helping person know what's going on—and that help is needed.

If you're being abused in any way, you need to talk with someone who can help you. Aside from your other parent, grandparent, aunt or uncle, school counselor, guidance counselor, school nurse, trusted teacher, coach, religious leader, friend's parents, and family doctor, each state in the United States has its own helping agencies. In many towns, you'll find child abuse or neglect hotlines as well as those for domestic violence (violence happening at home, in the family). If you can't find one, you might look in your yellow or blue pages for any type of child protective services. Under state agencies, you might try youth or children's services, social services, family services, health or mental services. They can probably direct you to the right person to call. If you can't find a listing, dial 0 for operator and ask. You can also check for local help services with the secretary in your school office or with the library. Or call the Child Help I.O.F. National Child Abuse Hotline (1-800-4ACHILD [422-4453]. If this number changes, dial 1-800-555-1212 for new information.).

Once again, many kids don't break the silence. It's up to you to decide if your parents treat you in a way that feels good, bad, or dangerous. If you realize you're being abused, you deserve not to be treated that way. If you feel abused—and wonder if it's true that you actually are being abused—it's important that you talk with someone who is trained to help you.

I know I've said this many times before, but it's important to keep reminding yourself that you're not less important or less lovable because your parent abuses you. It's that your parent isn't able to or doesn't wish to give you the love that you deserve to be given. It's not you, it's your parent who is the problem. And it's not fair or right for your parent to continue to take out his or her problem on you. If you're being abused in any way, call someone who will help you!

Here again, if you're scared, that's just what you can say: "I'm really scared and I need help. Can you help me?"

When Parents Are Overprotective

A different kind of problem occurs when kids feel their parents try to protect them too much.

Sean, age thirteen, asked, "How can I get my parents to stop treating me like I'm younger than I am? They tell me to act my age and then they treat me like a six-year-old."

Fifteen-year-old Aimee said, "Everyone hates the way their parents always ask, Where are you going, What are you doing, Who will you be with, How long are you going to stay there, When will you come home? My parents aren't on my back too much as long as I call and tell them where I am."

Gary, age sixteen, shared, "My parents are worried about me driving with my friends because of all the accidents that have been happening. I'm at the point lately where I don't drive with certain people anyway. But how do I tell them to lay off with this pressure?"

If your parents are overprotective, it may be that they won't let you cross a street by yourself, won't let you go fishing alone with your friend, won't let you go to the candy store hangout, won't let you travel by bus or train to the nearest big city by yourself, won't let you go to the mall, or won't let you stay out as late as most of your friends.

But they can also be overprotective in different ways that are not always as easy to see or understand. Karen's story will give you an example of what I mean. When Karen was thirteen years old, she went shopping with her mother (as usual) for a special dress for her aunt's wedding. Before her mother could decide on which dress to buy for Karen, she asked eight women in the dressing room which dress they thought looked best. Karen has become very used to allowing strangers in dressing rooms to decide what clothing she should wear.

Her mother does this because she's so concerned to have everything Karen wears and does be just right. She leaves little or no room for Karen to even try to make her own decisions—this is overprotection. When it comes time for Karen to make choices, she usually checks with each of her friends just to make sure she's doing the right thing.

By being overprotective, Karen's mother has not given her the chance to learn how to be responsible for her own actions, even if they turn out wrong. As a result, Karen has become fearful of making a mistake and lacks confidence and practice in being able to think through each choice in order to figure out which one may be better.

Overprotection can also take the form of shielding a daughter from getting hurt by her boyfriend. When Ann's boyfriend broke up with her, her mother spent days sitting with her telling her that the boyfriend was really a creep, was really no good, wasn't good enough for her, and was a downright bum! Ann didn't really feel that way about her boyfriend. She knew he was wrong to break up with her the way he did, but she felt her mother was trying to take her side too strongly—over-protection. Maybe Ann would have gotten stronger sooner if she weren't so protected.

Some parents don't know how or when to let go in order to allow their child the room to grow more independent. Some parents find letting go hard because they can't imagine their little boy or little girl is growing up.

Too many parents don't realize that you must feel all kinds of emotions, even the ones that hurt, in order to gain confidence and learn how to cope with all life's experiences. Life isn't all fun, games, and laughter. There will definitely be times of hurt and sadness in all of our lives. If Ann doesn't learn how to handle hurt now, she may continue to have a hard time as an adult, when there won't always be someone there to sit and hold her hand.

If you feel your parents aren't giving you any room to breathe, talk with them about your feelings. Maybe they'll back off a little bit, maybe not. But at least you will have tried. It may take a while for your parents to become used to the idea that you're going to disappear around the corner, go about your day or evening on your own, and return home later—whether on your bicycle or in your girlfriend's or boyfriend's car. Even if they trust you, they may still need to see for themselves that you've returned safely. (Don't be surprised if you find them wide awake, waiting for you to walk through the door!) This is not surprising when you think about how many kids get hurt or killed in drinking-driving or other drug-related accidents.

It may take a while for you to prove to them that they can trust you. It may take some figuring to reach a good balance between your parents' comfort and your freedom. As Aimee said, "Most parents at least want to know where you are and when they can expect you home." If you know you'll be late, it's just plain courteous to call and let them know so they don't worry. It's not only respectful, it's smart! They'll know you're respecting their feelings.

Parents can be especially overprotective if you have a disability, and they feel they have to protect you because your disability won't allow you to care for yourself. I'll talk more about this in Chapter 23, "Having a Disability."

Still other parents are overprotective because a sister or brother has died and they want to hold on to you so that nothing happens to you, too. (They may be *extra* strict about where you can go and who with.)

What If Parents Nag You?

- "Are you going out with your hair that way?"
- "When is your book report due?"
- "Did you take out the garbage?"
- "Don't forget to walk the dog!"

Nag, nag, nag. . . . If you're nagged by your parents, how does that make you feel? If you're like most kids I've spoken with, you probably can't stand being nagged. Did you ever stop to realize that parents can't stand nagging their kids?

Do you think it's pleasant for a parent to keep saying, "Clean up your room!" "Did you do your homework?" over and over again? Do you think a parent feels great knowing that every time he or she has to remind you about the same thing, you're going to be mad or respond in some other unpleasant way?

Maybe a truce is in order. Maybe you can sit down with each other and say something like, "I know you probably don't like nagging me, and I hate being nagged. So what can we do? How can we deal with things a little better?"

It can be helpful for parents, as well as kids, to write a "nagging" list (actually write things down on paper) of what parents seem to feel they need to say over and over again. Kids and parents can then compare lists and talk together about how to make positive changes.

When Parents Go Out of Town and Leave You in the Care of Others—or When You Take Care of Other Kids

Before your parents leave, be sure to get the rules straight with your baby-sitter, grandparents, or anyone. Be sure you get permission ahead of time for anything you might need or want to do.

Think ahead. That way you won't find yourself in the middle of conversations like:

> **YOU:** "But my mom and dad always let me do that."

> **BABY-SITTER:** "Well, they didn't tell me you could, so you'll have to wait until they come home."

Your parent might appreciate being reminded of the need to consider leaving a medical authorization letter with the person caring for you (or with a close relative or friend) who will be home while they're away. This is especially important if your parent might be difficult to contact, such as if your mom or dad is out of the country, and there is a medical emergency decision that needs to be made.

It's a serious responsibility to take care of someone else's kids. You probably already know that if you do some baby-sitting or if you have been a camp counselor. It's important to get a written list of instructions from the parent(s) or other adult in charge, to know and understand the needs of each child—and where you can get help (for example, phone 911) if something goes wrong.

When Parents Work Outside the Home

Lots of changes have taken place over the past few years. More mothers are working outside the home than ever before. Food, clothing, and everything else have gotten more and more expensive. With unemployment such a difficult problem and with the rise in single-parent families, there is an even greater need for parents to bring in as much income as is possible.

While some parents are able to conduct business in or at least from their home, most parents work outside the home. Even when earning additional money is not a concern, mothers may choose to work out of the home because it's another way to explore and make use of their talents. Sometimes it's the dad who remains home with the children and the mom who works out of the home. Each family situation is different.

That might mean you will have to make your own breakfast, lunch, and at times, even dinner. When you come home from school, you may be coming home to an empty house or apartment. Many kids like being independent and are able to appreciate what their parents are doing. However, there can also be a lot of loneliness, frustration, anger, and resentment. Some kids feel much better if they can at least speak to their parent on the telephone when they arrive home from school. If this would make a difference for you, let your parent know.

Even though many kids are proud of what their parent is doing, they'd like a parent home, especially right after school. It's tough not to be able to spend time with your parent the way you want and need to. But, unfortunately, you can't always have what you want, even though you and your parent would wish things could be different.

It can also be tough for parents to balance their time. Very often they feel frustrated, too, and wish they could spend more time with their kids. They especially wish they could be home right after school. Perhaps it would help for you to understand how some parents feel about their working situations and how they feel it affects their children:

- "All day long I work with children who have special needs and find I have the patience of Job (pronounced "Jobe"—a leader in the Bible who handled tough times with strength]. When I get home, my two children [one of whom has a disability] arrive home from school and all my patience goes out the window!"
- "I am the single parent of three children [ages four to ten], and I work full time. When I get home, it seems my children all want to talk at once. So no matter how I try to give each one a chance, the others keep talking. How do I get each one to listen to the other?"
- "What can I do to lessen the guilt feelings I have because I work until five o'clock? I wish we didn't need the money so much because I hate not being home for my kids after school."
- "My four kids [ages four to eight] are so excited to see me when I get home [five o'clock]. By that time, I'm tired from fighting traffic, rude people, and other

things. I need to unwind before I hear the excitement and screaming and fights for attention. Sometimes I feel like sneaking home! They get very upset and un-understanding if I don't devote my entire attention as I walk in."

- "I think my working away from home has made my kids independent. They call me to see what they can make for dinner. We all manage. We all help each other out. The time that is available to be together is used in a more creative way. With two incomes in the family, we're able to do more things with our children and we all appreciate that."

Just as it's important for kids to share their feelings with parents, it's also important for parents to let their kids know how they feel. Parents, too, can turn their feelings into words. If they're frustrated, parents can say so. If they find it hard to balance their time and wish they could be there more for their kids, they can talk about this with their children. If they've had a hectic day, they can tell their kids how they'd love to relax a little before being ready to listen. It would also be great if parents remembered to thank their kids for working together in such a helpful way. If your parents don't share their feelings, it might be a good idea to ask them to read this section.

If your mom, dad, or both parents work away from your home and their schedules keep them away for long hours, let them know how you wish you could spend more time with them, if you feel that way. Maybe you could all figure out when to set aside time over the weekend to be together.

Some families find it very helpful to have a "family meeting," per-haps on Sunday evening, in order to talk about family matters and everyone's schedule for the coming week. That way, parents can be reminded of car pools or if supplies need to be bought for school. Set-ting that kind of time aside also gives parents and kids a chance to check their schedule for the coming week and figure out when they can look forward to spending time together.

It would probably help you a great deal if you tried harder to under-stand what your parents might be feeling about work schedules and the amount of time that it's possible for them to spend with you. It would definitely help your parents if you could be more sensitive to how hard it can be for them to balance their time and how pressured they might feel.

If parents rush in from their job, rush to make dinner, and seem like they're tense (remember to check out those nonverbal messages), you can go over to them and give them a huge hug and say, "It's okay. You don't have to rush so much. We can all wait a little while for dinner. Can I help you?" While you're helping, you can tell each other about your day, share what you didn't have time to say before, and catch-up with each other.

One more thing: I spoke with Andrea, age fifteen, who told me, "All of my friends' moms have a job and mine doesn't. She has always stayed home with us and been a housewife. When my friends talk about their mom's jobs, I feel kind of funny. I think they think because my mom doesn't work, she's not as important as their moms. Or maybe even not as smart. But my mom really is smart. And she's always been there for me and my brothers and sisters."

There are still people who think that being a "housewife" or "home-maker" doesn't count as much as having a job that earns money. And, that being a housewife or homemaker makes that mom less important than a mom who actually "works" and earns money. That's just not true.

You may have heard someone say, "My mother doesn't work." That's also not true. Raising and nurturing a family, taking care of a home and being there for kids is a very full-time job! In fact, when parents decide they need or want someone else to care for their children and care for their home, that usually costs a lot of money.

So, with or without an actual salary, mothers (and fathers) who work hard caring for their families deserve to be respected—for who they are and for all they do.

If Your Parent Goes to College

Parents who return to college or go for the first time often find it difficult to juggle commuting (traveling to and from school), classes, studying, and jobs, as well as be there for the family.

Many parents who are attending college worry about spending less time with their kids. You might suggest that your parent do his or her homework while you're doing yours. Sort of like having a study hall together! You might even offer advice about how to write papers or study for tests, since many parents haven't been to school for a long time . . . and may not remember.

You can help! The more that you and the other members of your family plan and work together to make sure needs are being met, the more freedom your parent will have to make the most out of college—and the more time there can be to spend with each other.

When Parents Are Unemployed

If your mom or dad has lost her or his job for whatever reason, that may make them pretty tense. They may be edgy, upset, worried, and just not their normal selves.

They may or may not try to hide their concern, depending upon how old you are and how much they usually share. They probably will be careful not to make you overly upset about the money situation.

Even if they don't say a word, if you sense that something has changed, it would probably be very helpful to you and to them if you mentioned what you sense. Some clues are: sleeping much later than ever before, being around more when you get home from school, or drinking more alcohol.

It's often a relief to parents to be honest about a family situation. That way they don't have to pretend. They can tell you straight out that there is really no extra money for the movies this weekend, or maybe you'd better wait until next week or the week after to buy a new pair of shoes.

It can also be a great relief for each person in the family to pitch in and work together to bring in extra cash. Kids who are old enough can try to find a job after school or on weekends to help out. Even if you're younger, you might find that neighbors will pay you to walk their dog, water their plants, mow their lawn, feed their fish, shovel their walk when it snows, shop for groceries, or do other errands.

Parents who are unemployed often find it hard still to believe in their self-worth, hard to believe that they're still valuable as a person. Job loss often has nothing to do with their skills and is not a measure of intelligence. Sometimes things just don't work out. It can just be a matter of luck, as when a factory your parent works for has to close because the company is not doing as much business as it used to, or if a budget doesn't pass and that causes your parent's job to be cut. It may take a while for your parent to find a new business situation, perhaps even a new career direction.

It would be very helpful to give a lot of messages that mean, "I love you, I care. Even if you lost your job, you're still important to me." You can say that verbally, with words, or nonverbally, with hugs and looks or maybe a comforting hand on the shoulder. It may also help to encourage your parent to keep on trying, keep on looking, and not give up on themselves.

Some kids are embarrassed to tell other kids that their parent is unemployed. Maybe they're worried that others will think less of them and judge their parent as a failure.

Similar feelings have been expressed by kids who have been teased about their parent's occupation. John, age fifteen, told me, "I have a hard time when my friends make fun of my father's job. I laugh with them but I really don't think what they're saying is funny. Besides, my father is working two jobs, just to handle everything since my mom got sick. I don't even want to tell my friends he's doing that! My dad is doing the best he can. I have a lot of respect for him. I wish everyone would just understand and keep their mouths shut."

No matter how much John knows his friend's judgments aren't true, it can still be hard to take when people make remarks that hurt. If John could tell his friends what he's feeling, it would help them understand better.

If John doesn't let his friends know his true feelings—and he just keeps laughing—John's friends won't know he feels what they're saying is hurtful, and they won't know he really wants them to stop.

If Your Parents Are Much Older

"I really love your grandfather!" said Barry's friend. The problem was that it wasn't Barry's grandfather but his father. For the moment, Barry couldn't decide if he should let his friend know.

Some kids have parents who are older than most other kids' parents. Although some kids find this embarrassing, others seem to be able to understand that this is just the way life is. The age of a parent doesn't have anything to do with how well they understand you, how close you are able to be with each other, or how active and young at heart your parent is. All those people who keep saying that age is a "state of mind" are very wise!

The truth is that there are parents and other people who are younger in age but act like they're much much older. And there are older people who would shock anyone if they told their age because they look and behave so much younger.

Once again, there are certain things in life we cannot control. Certainly, we have no say over the age of our parents. What we can control is how we relate to them and all that we share.

When Parents Are Single

This may be a result of separation, divorce, or death of the other parent. It's also possible that your parent never got married in the first place.

I'll talk more about having a single parent and dealing with divorce and stepfamily situations in the next chapter. For now, if you have a single parent, take the time to think about your relationship. How close do you feel to that parent? How has the fact that your parent is single affected your own life—and your life together? If your other parent is single or has remarried and there are now other siblings, how has that affected you?

If you had the power to change one thing about your relationship with your single parent, what would it be? (Please don't answer, "I'd like my parents to be back together." You may feel that way, as so many kids do. But that's not within any kid's control.) I'm asking you about what you feel you'd wish to change—personally and privately, between you and your single parent. For example, do you wish you could be closer? If your parent is dating, do you feel good about the person he or she is going out with? Are you concerned about your parent being okay if you're thinking that in a few years, you'll be going to college or moving out to live and work somewhere else? Is your parent in college, trying to juggle kids, classes, studying, a job and still find time to breathe? Are you able to be as honest as you want and need to be? Think about it.

If you're not saying all you want and need to say to your single parent, it's important that you push yourself to do so—for yourself, as well as for your parent. Now might be an excellent time to see how you can turn your feelings into words—by writing your mom or dad a note, or saying what you feel, aloud. Why not ask your parent when you can next spend some private time. (Remember, if it's hard to say what you feel, that's just how you can begin: "This is hard for me to say . . .")

When Parents Are Different from Each Other, or When Families Are Blended

Parents can be different in many ways. For example, one might be much older than the other. One might be of a different racial background or have different religious beliefs than the other. One might come from a different country and speak very little English; the other might have been born in the United States. There are so many possible differences.

Children in any family might also have differences in language, religion, race, nationality, and other features. For example, if a mother and father are of different racial backgrounds, some children in the family might have lighter shades of skin and others might be darker. If parents have different religious beliefs, kids may find that they'll be taught to observe a combination of religious traditions and beliefs (for example, they may celebrate both Christmas and Hanukkah in their home).

There might be stepbrothers or stepsisters from a different marriage who are the same age and in the same grade at school as other kids in the family. When parents remarry, they often start a new family, even if they have children who are much older. With the opportunity to adopt or have foster children from different parts of the world, any family might have a mix of children from different cultures and places.

Parents hope and may even expect that everyone in the family will get along with each other, no matter how different each person's background is—or at what age kids become part of the family. Sometimes feelings are loving and everyone feels like a family from the start. Other times, the adjustment to living with each other and being a part of the same family is not as smooth. There may be anger, resentment, concern that parents or other relatives favor one kid over another. Kids may or may not get along.

Even if kids from different backgrounds in the same family get along, other kids in the community might not be as accepting of all these differences. That situation can also make it hard to feel good.

If you're in a family where there are such differences, consider your own feelings about being part of your family. If you have feelings that are difficult to handle about your family—and perhaps find it hard to feel good about yourself—it's important for you to talk with someone who can help you understand and deal with your feelings.

Besides speaking with adult relatives, you can talk with a school counselor, school social worker, trusted teacher, or religious leader. You might also call an operator (dial 0) and ask for information about who you can call who deals with family or social services.

Whether your family is like the families of most kids you know or very different from theirs, it is my hope that you can understand and value what being part of a family means. There's a lot of teasing that kids have to take because of all kinds of differences, including differences having to do with family. Those kids who are teased would feel so much better if the teasing stopped and, instead, people would just accept and respect each other's differences.

When Parents Are the Same Sex—If Your Parents Are Gay or Lesbian

Here again, we're dealing with family differences. In this case, it has to do with a parent's relationship with someone of the same sex. If your parent is homosexual, it's possible that you're living with your parent and your parent's partner of the same sex—being raised by two mothers or two fathers. I spoke with Susan, age twelve, who shared:

> When I found out, I think I was about seven or eight. And I had gone to my mom. And her partner was there, and I asked what the word *gay* meant. I said, "Is it Greek or something like that?" I didn't really know what it was.

And they proceeded to tell me what it was. They said it's when two people of the same sex love each other, whether it's two males or two females. And they proceeded to tell me the people I knew around me who were gay, which was one of my uncles, one of my aunts, my chiropractor. And then my mom started to cry, which was one of the only times I saw her cry. And she told me how she and the person we had been living with for eight years were together.

And I don't really know what I felt. I know that I was confused and I was scared, but I knew that I'd have to deal with it. And after that, for about a year, it was a real bad year for me. I wouldn't open up. I'd be real scared about it and stuff.

I never really knew what it was. And all the kids would say, "eeeeeuuuuuu" about it and they made jokes about it. And I would go along with the jokes. And I realized, how am I going to deal with it? Meaning, now that everyone is telling jokes about it, and everyone thinks it's so funny. And now I realize that someone so close to me—my mom—is what they're laughing about.

The first time I told three of my friends, I told them about my uncle, because they were telling jokes about being gay. And I told them this is really hard for me and if you want to make jokes about it, don't do it around me because my uncle is gay. Because I didn't want to tell them about my mom yet. I thought they wouldn't come to my house anymore if they knew my mom was gay.

The summer I went to sleep-away camp for the first time, I had already been in therapy for two years. I went for two months and most of the people I was in a bunk with only stayed for one month. But I just became such good friends with them that I knew I could tell them.

At first I told one of my best friends up there and I was crying. And everyone in the bunk saw I was crying and asked, "What's wrong, what's wrong?"

So I just told them, "Nothing." And my friend said, "Just leave her alone." And the day after that, three of my other best friends were on my bed. And we were talking, and the friend I told was there, too. And I told them about my mom and started to cry again.

After that, I became more comfortable and I told my whole bunk, which was about twelve people. And they asked why I was crying about it. I asked them if they were still my friends, or if they thought I was weird or something. Or if they'd still come to my house. And all of them said, not at all (to being weird), we're still your best friends. It doesn't matter, it's not your fault. This will be my fourth year at that camp and I'm still extremely close with all of them.

If someone has a gay parent living with them, my advice would be to try to deal with it the best that you can. And if you feel you can't talk with anybody, at least talk with your parent about it.

Susan and I talked for quite a while about how important it was to her that her friends were very accepting of her mother. Because of all the jokes she kept hearing, she figured that kids feel that being a lesbian is bad. So that would mean they'd think her mother is bad. But she found that wasn't the case. It's just that people talk, and people don't understand.

Susan continued to tell me about an experience that happened to her in school. She shared:

My teacher gave us the assignment to do a family tree in the seventh grade. She said we should add our mom, dad, sisters, brothers, aunts, uncles and grandparents. And that's all.

I had come home to tell my mom about the project that I had to do that weekend. And she was like, "All right, I'll help you." But the person who we were living with (her partner) was very upset because she was never able to have kids for medical reasons. And she thought of me as her own. Because she had raised me for ten years already (she moved in when I was two).

And she said that she thought that I should be ready to put her—as my second mother—on a poster for the whole school to see. And I told her I wasn't ready. It would be in front of the whole school of five hundred people and questions would start flying around. And my mom agreed with me. So then it was like a battle between me and my mom against her.

And she was so upset for about two weeks. I handed in the project without her on it. But I had told her that a piece of paper doesn't really mean anything. That she should know in her heart how important she really is to me. And her argument to that was that my mom got all the credit and satisfaction for raising me and she got no recognition at all. I just explained to her while I could understand that she would want recognition, I simply wasn't ready. And I don't think I ever will be ready to tell my whole school.

In second grade, my friend's mom died. And the following week we had to do a Mother's Day poem. And my teacher said to my friend, "You're excused." In front of the whole class. And that night, she called me crying. And I thought it was just terrible.

And my advice to teachers is don't give a family tree project because it can hurt someone who has a death in their family and it can hurt someone like me.

I also spoke with Alex, who shared with me the difficulty and confusion he experienced in dealing with having a mother who is a lesbian. He learned about his mother's homosexuality when he was eight or nine years old but it wasn't until the eighth grade that he was able to tell a friend. He dealt with his situation by not telling anybody. Soon after telling that first friend, he was able to tell another. Now he's in high school and talked to me about the experience he had when he told his girlfriend:

Last year, I probably took the next big step in terms of opening up to people about my mother. That was in the midst of a relationship with a girl that seemed to be becoming fairly serious. I decided it was very hard to keep it a secret from her. The idea of telling about my mother to a girlfriend made me extremely nervous. And one day, we were just lying around and talking, and all of a sudden I announced that I was going to tell her a secret. I told her it was a secret. I couldn't even have her look at me, I made her look away.

I don't think she really could have understood why I was crying. You know when you hold something in for about five years, and you finally let it out—and you don't know how it's going to be when you let it out—and you find out that it's not such a deep dark secret anymore. . . . The burden was lifted then more than it ever had been lifted before. I felt much closer with her and much better about myself. There I was with a girl. And although she knew about my mother, it still remained that it was fine between us. And it was clear that although my mother was what she was, I was who I was. And it wouldn't be this thing that would reflect on me.

Telling her not only added to our relationship. It made us more comfortable around each other. After telling her that, I knew I could always trust her. We remained together for a while. But even after we broke up, we stayed extremely close. Even now, although she's an ex-girlfriend, I know I can always go to her. I know that never, ever would have happened if I didn't tell her.

Alex has a certain friend who is like a brother to him, but he still hasn't told him about his mother. Alex said, "I've told very few people, but it's surprising that *he* doesn't know because he's the person I talk to more than anyone. But he's narrow-minded when it comes to dealing with the subject of homosexuality." Although Alex said he might tell him someday, he doesn't see that there is anything to gain by it now.

Insults can be especially difficult to take when they deal with something personal about a kid's family. Whether it's your friend's parent's homosexuality or anyone else's, you can make a positive difference. You can be respectful.

Alex said, "If there's one thing I would share with other kids who might be in the same situation, it's to communicate with your parents and how important that is. Also, it was very important for me to talk with a therapist. For a long time that was only person I could really talk to about this."

He continued:

It's a big deal coming from a point where I couldn't tell anyone to being able to tell my girlfriend. I'm in a position now with my mother where I can immediately express what I'm feeling. Now it's come to the point where if I'm really upset, I can talk with her. And it really makes me happy that she's at the point where if she's upset, she'll come to me.

This was a hard decision for my mom. It wasn't like, "Oh, I'm so glad I'm a lesbian." It was really hard. It was more like, "I'm not going to deny myself something just because society might not tolerate me." The real difference is that she gets something out of her decision. She's found someone that she loves. All I've gotten out of it is that she got divorced.

It must have been difficult for my father to have been married for so many years, have a kid with a person, and then find out she's a lesbian. My father remarried and now I have a brother and sister. They made it worth it to me.

If you're in this situation and find you can't communicate with your parent as you would wish, it's important to talk with a counselor, relative, religious leader, or other trusted adult. Some kids feel it's hard to approach relatives for help if they don't know about—or know about but don't accept—their parent's homosexuality.

If the first person you approach doesn't work out, remember to keep trying another and another. The main concern is that you don't handle difficult feelings and situations alone.

If Your Parent Goes to Prison

I spoke with Michael, now in his fifties, who spent time in prison a few years ago. He said, "When I found out I was definitely going to prison, I got scared. I worried that it was going to affect my relationship with my kids. Although I didn't have a problem being honest with them, my concern was how they really felt about it and how it really was going to affect them while I was in prison. Because on the surface, they said, 'Don't worry about it. I still love you. Everything is going to be okay.' But I wondered if that's how they really felt. I worried that they'd think less of me. And I hoped when I got out they'd at least respect that I paid dearly for my mistake—and they'd give me a chance to start over."

I also spoke with several kids whose fathers spent time in prison. As with any other situation that is so personal, you'll see that each handled this experience in a different way.

Beth is now nineteen. Her father was in prison a few years ago. She told me, "I felt that he was in a strange environment. He was there and he was among them, but he wasn't one of them. I definitely felt sad for him, seeing him in those disgusting clothes, knowing that he was very intelligent. It was pathetic. It's difficult after you see your father in prison to ever respect him in the same way or see him in the same way. I mean, that's the lowest a person could go. It didn't take away how I felt about him. It just placed him at a different level."

I asked her how she handled this in relation to her friends. She said,

"Their lives all of a sudden seemed perfect and a lot of things they were dealing with seemed petty and superficial. I also became resentful of how easy their lives were as opposed to mine. Sort of like, give me a break. They have no idea. Like the fact that my friends could go out and buy any CD they wanted and it didn't matter. And I was waitressing and counting every penny. I'm not glad it happened. But in the long run, I'm much more appreciative and hardworking. I'm more careful and realistic."

Jenny, sixteen, whose father was in prison last year, said, "I hardly told anyone and I never talked about it. I didn't feel that I wanted to sit down and cry with my friends. I just guess I wanted to keep it to myself. If I went through it again, I would definitely talk more about it. Because I held it in, it was like I was fake. It was the first secret I ever had."

Jenny's brother, Steve, is now in his twenties. He handled their father's time in prison very differently than his sister. Steve told me:

> I felt like my family life was pretty secure and strong growing up. Then when dad went away to prison, it was like everything was just uprooted, like clumps of dirt were flying everywhere. It just made me feel like the very ground that I used to stand on was ripped up. It made me feel very old. Sort of like I wasn't a kid anymore. Of course I loved my dad and I felt so badly for him. But also, there was bitterness and anger and frustration. It was a mess. But I also want to say that we did get through it. And it forced the family to really rally together and I think we came out of the whole ordeal probably stronger for it.
>
> It's interesting. My sister didn't tell anyone. And I think she was surprised to find how freely I discussed it with people. She felt it was a much more private thing but I felt it made it easier for me to be honest. Actually, it was really very interesting to see how many other people had either friends or family, uncles, who had also gone to jail. I think she had a harder time because she didn't talk about it. By being able to talk about it, it wasn't as scary for me.

While it's not a kid's fault if their parent does something against the law and has to spend time in jail or prison, it certainly can affect them—and family life—very deeply. The feelings can be very mixed, very emotional, and often difficult to handle. No matter what your age, it's important for you not to handle it alone. It can be a relief to let friends know so you don't have to pretend. And it certainly can be helpful to talk with someone, such as a school counselor, who is trained to help you understand and deal better with your situation.

When Parents Are Ill

When a parent is ill—not just with headaches (which can sometimes be pretty bad) or a passing cold, but the kind of illness that makes you worry about them all the time—additional stress can be put on the family. Illness may require your parent to go into the hospital, make your parent weaker than usual, keep him or her in bed or at least in your home for many months, or in extreme cases, result in death.

First of all, I just want you to know that I know this is not an easy topic. It can be very painful and scary. No one likes to see their parent ill, no matter how old you are, no matter how old your parent is. Sometimes parents are confused as to whether they should even tell their children about their illness. They don't want to upset them.

Though I imagine there are kids somewhere who would rather not know, I have found that most kids would rather know than not know. As upsetting as it can be to hear the truth, it's worse to have to guess because that can sometimes make the illness seem worse than it really is. And sometimes the illness *is* more serious than you can guess.

An eleven-year-old girl shared, "My mom has a ruptured disc and she might get an operation that's new to the doctor that's going to do it. She might be allergic to the stuff that they are going to inject into her. If she is, she might not survive. I'm scared! Without my mom, I don't know what I would do!"

This is the kind of fear that words may not be able to take away. Don't let anyone tell you this is not scary. It *is* scary to know how risky the operation might be. It is scary to think about what life would be like if the operation doesn't go well. It is scary and painful to imagine not having your mother with you. That's the kind of thing that can be learned only when the time comes.

But since her mother's health and survival is in the doctor's hands, there's not much more this girl can do, except trust and (depending on her beliefs) pray that the doctor will take care of her mother in the best way possible. She can also talk with her mom, tell her how much she loves her and even tell her how scared she is. Her mom would probably be so relieved to be able to talk about this with her daughter.

Seanne, age twelve, told me that her mother has been very ill for the past three years. She's been in and out of hospitals. Every time the doctors think they've found out what's making her so sick, they realize it's probably something else, and they have had to do many tests. And many operations. Things have been very tense. Seanne said, "In all this time, I've only seen my mother cry once! I just can't understand why she hasn't cried more. I always go into my room to cry, so I don't upset her. But I felt so much better—it was a relief when I saw her cry."

I suggested to Seanne that she talk with her mom about how she always needs to hold back her feelings. Yes, it may make her mom cry if Seanne cries in front of her. But you know, that might also make them even closer and more free to talk about what they're really thinking and feeling instead of always trying to hide their emotions.

Seanne could also say to her mother, "Mom, I get the feeling that you're very upset and maybe you don't want to make me upset if you cry or let me know. But I want to be there for you—you've always been there for me. Please let me . . . it's okay to cry."

Neither parents nor kids have to handle their feelings alone unless they truly want to. Many people find strength in prayers and being part of a community of worship.

One more thing: All you have to do is turn on your radio, read a newspaper, listen to the news on TV, and you're bound to hear about another accident, another illness that resulted in death. We wish we could keep the people we love forever. As hard as it may be to accept, life isn't forever—not for your parents, not for you, not for anyone.

But knowing that we all have only a certain amount of time together doesn't have to be so sad. In fact, that's perhaps the greatest, most wonderful challenge of all. The challenge is to make each day as special as it can be. Though we can't control the amount of time we may have with those we love, we can control how we spend that time.

You can let people know you love them. Actually say, "I love you" every once in a while. Try harder to share your feelings. Try to appreciate even the little things. Learn as much as you can about each other. Share all that you can share.

Then if someone close is taken from you earlier than you ever expected, at least you can appreciate knowing that you lived each day with them as fully as you could. You won't have to look back and say, "I wish I had said _____ to them" or "I wish I had spent more time."

Remember, though, it wouldn't be fair to you to be filled with guilt and walk around feeling horrible for years because you weren't speaking to each other or weren't getting along well at the exact moment he or she died. It would also not be fair to you to blame yourself because you didn't say, "I love you" one more time. We can only do the best we can. Time passes quickly, even when we try to appreciate each moment, each person. It's easy to get caught up in fast-moving schedules, lots of activities at school, homework, plans with friends.

But, at least you can be reminded of a most important lesson: You can't change yesterday, only learn from it. Try not to blame yourself for what you didn't or couldn't do. It's today! So just learn from what you think you missed and go forward, wiser. Think of all the people you still have around whom you're going to try harder to appreciate.

You may not think you can live without one parent or the other. But the fact is, if the situation happens, you will. You'll have no choice. You'll have to. You can get strength from the special memories you shared and wink at your parent's picture every day. You can get strength from your family and friends who will be there with you so you can talk about your feelings and know you're not alone. You can gain strength from all your parent taught you, all you and your parent shared. So, although you can't hold on to them physically, you'll always carry a part of them deep inside of you. That part can stay with you forever.

What did I leave out? Only you can answer that. Think about your own parents. Think about what you love about them, think about what you wish you could change between you, how you wish they would change. What changes can be worked at? What do you have to work harder to try to accept? Writing down these feelings can be very helpful.

The next step will be to trust that you have the inner strength to talk privately with your parents about what concerns you. Remember, it's okay to be uncomfortable. It's not okay to let being uncomfortable stop you from saying what would be important for you to say—and important for your parent to hear.

If you're one of those lucky people who already knows the warmth and close feelings that can come from being open and trusting with a parent, also know that no matter how close you are, you can always become closer.

No matter what it is you need or want to say, if you say it respectfully, if you say it in a caring way, then your parents are more likely to listen and understand.

If you hold back and think you shouldn't say something because you may hurt them, just know that hurt is a part of life, and most people, including parents, would rather know what you're feeling. You can't always prevent it when you wish you could. But even pain can teach you a lot and help you get closer. You'll probably be surprised at how many things you can talk about with your parents that you never thought you could say.

CHAPTER 20

DEALING WITH SEPARATION, DIVORCE, SINGLE PARENTS, AND STEPFAMILIES

This chapter will help you better understand the hurts and the changes that are so much a part of separation and divorce.

If your parents are apart or are talking about separating or getting a divorce, I hope my words, along with the chance to learn how other kids feel, will help you strengthen your ability to accept what you cannot change and realize how you can let go of any bad family feelings, and try to find family happiness in new ways.

Separation and Divorce Hurt

Pain, loneliness, sadness, frustration, fear, anger, guilt, confusion—if you're one of the thousands of kids whose parents have separated or gotten divorced, you've probably felt most of those feelings. If you haven't felt them yourself, chances are you know someone who has.

Mindy, age twelve, asked, "How can I express my feelings to my parents about how I love them so much and I don't want them to get a divorce?"

Stephen, age eleven, shared, "My mother and father are divorced and my mother is married again. I haven't seen my father in two years and he never calls. I'm not sure if I should love him or not. Right now I think I hate him."

Joe, age thirty-nine, told me, "I came home from work one day and found my kids were next door and my wife was gone. There were things leading up to this, but she never told me she was leaving. It was a very emotional time for me as well as the kids. A few days after my wife left, my son woke up and said to me, 'Mommy's never coming back.' I'll never forget hearing that. I didn't want to believe it. Neither did he. And all we could do was just sit there together and cry."

Separation and divorce hurt. They hurt the parents who no longer can live together in a way that feels good. And they especially hurt the children.

It's Not Your Fault—It's Not Within Your Power

Wouldn't it be great if kids of unhappy parents had the power to make their parents happy again? Lots of kids try, but end up blaming themselves for not being able to make their parents stay together. They often feel guilty because they think that all the fighting must be their fault. After all, why would their parents have gotten married in the first place if they didn't love each other? They think, "It must be me." Or, "It must be because of my sister and brother. I hate them." Or, "Maybe if I loved them more . . ." Or, "Maybe if I were a better person . . ." Perhaps you have felt the same way.

But no matter how much you love your parents, how high your grades are in school, how much you help clean your home, or how much you baby-sit for your younger brother or sister, you don't have power over your parents' relationship with each other.

Consider that your parents can't make a person be your friend, and they can't make someone like you as a boyfriend or girlfriend. You need to work out your own relationships for yourself. They can encourage you, say they'd love for you to get along with someone better, even suggest ways for you to try to patch things up between you. But they can't do it for you. The same is true for your parents' relationship with each other. You can't do it for them.

Eric, age eleven, said, "My parents are separated and sometimes I feel left out or not cared for. I always want to be with both parents but I can't. How can I change it?"

Eric, I wish I could tell you what you want to know. But I can't. What happens between your parents is not up to you. It's only up to them. The truth is something that you probably don't want to hear. The truth is that you may never have your parents back together again. If they do get back together, it won't be because of anything that you can do. Change has got to come from them. Your wanting it so badly is not enough.

It's very sad to imagine that any boy or girl would make the mistake of blaming themselves or their sister or brother for difficulty that is so much beyond their control. It's also a shame so much energy is wasted trying to change something that's not theirs to change.

Parents can become unhappy with each other all by themselves. If anything is going to change in a relationship between parents, it's the parents who will have to work out their differences.

But Kids Have a Different Kind of Power

Though kids don't have the power to get their parents back together, that doesn't mean they're completely powerless. They do have power within themselves. More power than they might think they have, especially when everything seems like it's crumbling all around them.

A boy's or girl's inner power can get even stronger if it takes in more "fuel." The fuel is information that will help kids understand what's really going on between their parents and how this might affect them, now as well as in the future. Although it won't take away the hurt, it may add strength for kids to know that many kids of all ages are hurting for the same reasons. They're not as alone as they might think. And lots of kids who survived the hurt would probably be willing to share what they felt and what helped them handle their parents' divorce.

Separation Can Be an Ending or a Beginning

Parents may decide to separate for many different reasons. Maybe they have been fighting for years and finally decided that they've had it.

Maybe there's never been fighting and they really still love each other as people, but they just can't live with each other as husband and wife. Maybe one of them has changed so much from who they were when both got married that they can't live with the person the other has become.

Maybe one parent did something to violate the other's trust. Maybe they've become strangers to each other. Maybe there are money problems that come between them. Maybe there's jealousy. Maybe there's no longer any kindness. Maybe there's hardly any communication. Maybe they don't know how to talk with each other. Maybe they don't want to try. Maybe they just don't have the same values anymore. Maybe one parent is sneaking off to see another man or another woman behind the other parent's back. (Maybe your father or mother knows). Maybe one of your parents has come to terms with their homosexuality. Maybe one parent is taking a lot of drugs or drinking heavily and is ruining any chance of a good relationship. Maybe it's too painful for the other parent to stay around and watch while they destroy themselves. Maybe one parent is abusing the other with words or fists or other actions.

Sometimes parents talk openly with their children about the possibility of separation. Sometimes it comes as a great shock the day or night before one of them is going to leave. Sometimes a kid doesn't have any clue until he or she walks into the home and finds bags packed or the other parent sitting there with reddened eyes.

Very often a kid can sense the strain between his or her parents. Remember, nonverbal messages can be very loud. But just because you sense a strain, it doesn't mean your parents are about to split up. It may mean there's pressure at the office, money pressure, or someone who is ill, or they might be tired, and so on.

The best thing is to be honest about what you feel. Sometimes parents try to protect their children by not including them in personal problems. When the kid brings up the concern, it's often a relief to everyone and much less of a worry than they may have thought.

If there's really trouble between them, parents often don't know how to tell their kids. So they might not say anything until they have to, which may mean the day one of them walks out.

Separation can rock anyone's sense of security. It can mean a broken home, broken dreams, confusion, anger, hurt, and maybe some guilt.

Separation can also be a relief to kids who always hear their parents fighting. Many boys and girls have told me, "If they're staying together because of me, I wish they wouldn't. It's too hard to be around them this way." Let's take a closer look at what else separation can mean.

Separation can give each parent the space or distance they need to sort out their feelings and decide that they really do want to try again. Separation may give them the private time they need to figure out what went wrong and realize they need to make changes if the marriage is ever going to stay together. They may return after a few days or not until weeks or months later. In this case, separation may have shaken up each parent enough emotionally to make them want to work even harder to make their marriage work.

But while you can hope that a parent will return or that the parent who stays will want the other parent to come back, you can't count on it. Separation has no guarantees. Even though it's possible for separation to force a new beginning, it also can signal the end. That's the part that's toughest to accept.

The parent who left, or even the parent who stayed, can decide that he or she would rather stay separated. Even though the parent is sad about the breakup, even though he or she wishes the marriage would have worked, even though he or she is pained that it has to have a troubling effect on any children in the family, the parent might prefer to be alone than be together fighting. Or he or she might want to be alone rather than be with someone he or she can no longer respect, trust, and love. Or the parent might want to be alone rather than be with someone who doesn't share in working together to make the relationship a happier one. Or?

As you probably have learned from your own friendships, a relationship must work two ways. If only one person cares, then it's hard to keep up the friendship. If only one person tries hard to get to know the other person better, or if only one person decides to share more personal things, then it's hard to be close. If only one person is honest, then it's hard to trust. If only one person wants the relationship, it's not a relationship. Two people have to want it for it to have a chance to work.

Sometimes marriages are like that. Only the mother or only the father may be the giving partner. The other may not give at all or at least not very much. So only when both parents decide they want to try to become more sensitive to each other, only when both parents decide they're going to work at communicating better, will there be hope of working out differences.

Are you beginning to understand better why kids don't have the power to make their parents get along?

Sometimes It Will Help to Walk on Tiptoe

Justin, age ten, said, "My mom and dad are separated and my mom is a total grouch! What should I do?"

It's very hard to talk with anyone while they're upset or angry. Maybe it's not fair to expect that your parents are going to be their old, normal, nongrouch selves during this very hard time in their lives.

If they're fighting, it's not a good idea to bother them. You'd be wise to tiptoe around, helping out with chores, helping out with the other kids in your family, just doing whatever you can to keep everything else calm, even though your parents are not.

You can also turn up the TV or radio very loud, go take a shower, take a walk or jog around the corner, go out and shoot baskets, jump rope, or do any kind of physical activity to take your mind off things and help you get your frustrations out.

You may even find yourself feeling grouchy and upset, especially if your parents fight a lot or you're very scared about what's happening— and especially if you're very angry. If you accidentally blame your sister or brother for your parents' problem, you may find yourself hitting them extra hard or yelling extra loud at them. Neither you nor your sister or brother may realize that the hits, screams, and yells were probably meant for your parents. (It's just easier to hit a sister or brother than a parent.)

Depending on how lonely you feel and how much you wish someone would just hold you and tell you everything is going to be okay, depending on how angry you are and how much you need to lash out, depending on how much attention you need—you may just find yourself sitting in the principal's office for throwing spitballs at some kid. The sad thing is, no one (not even you) may have understood that the spitballs were really aimed at your parents.

Probably you'd be wise to put up your antennae and keep them up. Be sensitive to those moments that are more calm. That's when it will be okay to try to talk with either parent or at least to the parent whom you're living with.

Don't be surprised if you find your parent crying. Try not to worry about holding back your tears if you feel like crying, too. That's very natural and is a great way to get out your emotions. If you're worried that you'll upset your parent if you start crying, just remember that the more you can honestly share, the better you will be able to understand each other's feelings and the closer you may become. Your parent might feel better that he or she no longer has to pretend about how upset he or she is. Some things in life are very sad.

Very Important Message

- Just because your parents are not getting along, that doesn't have to change their love for you.
- Just because your parents don't love each other anymore, that doesn't have to change their love for you.
- Just because you're angry at them, and might even say you hate them, doesn't mean you don't really love them. It's possible to love and be angry at someone at the very same time.

Talking About This Can Be Hard

If you find there are no calm moments, or you just can't talk with your mother or father, it's important to try to speak with an older brother, sister, aunt, uncle, grandparent, trusted teacher, coach, guidance counselor, school counselor, psychologist, social worker, principal, religious leader, friend's parent, or another adult you respect and trust.

Though the talking may not change your parents' situation, it can help you better understand, accept, and deal with what's happening to you and your family. Getting your feelings out can also be a great relief.

Many children wonder if they should tell their friends about their home situation. That's a very personal decision. There aren't any rules. It would probably be helpful to have a friend your own age whom you can turn to when you feel like talking or just be with, even if you're silent—knowing they understand and care about you.

It can be a special comfort to know that you can speak openly with a close friend whom you can trust. A trusted friend will understand that it doesn't mean your parents are bad people just because they're having trouble getting along.

A close friend whose parents are already separated or divorced can be a great help as they can share their own feelings with you and let you know what you might expect. They'll also remind you that you're not the only person in the world to experience those feelings.

It's always good to write your feelings down on paper. You can even write a story or a poem, if you like.

If you're very confused and find you're getting more and more upset, or if you're having trouble getting your feelings out, it might be important to talk with someone who is trained to help kids with such feelings. They may be able to offer guidance that will lessen your confusion and help you get along better each day. Your school psychologist or counselor might be helpful. If you can, try to let your parents know how bad you feel, and maybe they can arrange for you to speak with the right person.

Some parents don't realize that older kids, as well as younger ones, can be deeply upset and have a difficult time adjusting to their parents' divorce or separation. They often think older kids can handle it better. If you don't tell them you're hurting, they may interpret your silence as proof that you're fine.

Remember, admitting that you're having trouble with your feelings is not a sign of weakness. It takes a very strong person to admit that he or she needs help.

When Parents Are Divorced

While a separation may mean there's hope, a divorce must be considered final (there are some parents who get back together after getting divorced, but you can't expect this to happen). All the feelings I've mentioned so far belong here, too.

Divorce makes it official and legal that parents are not married anymore. Here, too, some parents tell their children from the very beginning of difficulty, and some parents don't tell them until the divorce is in process.

Marlene, age eleven, shared a very sad experience she had when she was away at summer camp three years ago. Said Marlene, "One of the girls in my bunk got a letter from her mother telling her that her parents had gotten a divorce. She told her in a letter! The girl didn't even know that her parents had any problems. The whole bunk was so upset for her. She started crying, and we all started crying with her. I didn't know how to help her. On visiting day, her mother brought her up so many presents and so much food that they couldn't even fit it on her bed. I think she was trying to make up for the divorce."

My guess is that it was easier for the mother to wait for her daughter to go to camp than to tell her in person. Marlene said the letter came about two weeks after camp started.

It would have been helpful if someone had taught her parents that running away from painful situations is not the answer. There's very little that's going to soften the blow of being told your family is about to split apart. That girl might have felt better crying in her parents' arms, rather than in her bunk away from them at camp.

It would help for parents to tell kids as early as they know. That way the whole family can deal openly with the situation. Each family member can talk about his or her feelings and the children can get involved with plans that must be made.

I know there are kids who don't want to hear that their parents are having problems. They may shut them out, not listen, maybe even try to run away. But no matter how far they run, or if they take drugs or drink alcohol to run away, the problem will still be there when they get back—or even if they don't come back! Though it may be very painful, probably the best thing to do is to stay and face it.

You know those presents piled up on the girl's bed at camp? Well, her mother is one of many, many mothers and fathers who try to make up for the hurt, try to win their child's love, and try to feel less guilty by giving presents. Some parents even try to outdo the other parent to make them seem better. Be careful not to allow the presents to become a measure of love.

It would help if parents could understand that candy, clothes, movies, vacations, toys, money, and food—things—can't take the place of the family being together. I realize that most kids feel presents are nice to have. But keep your eyes open to how much is being given to you and how often you get gifts. That can teach you a lot about what your parent might be feeling. Maybe you can even talk about it.

Who Will You Live With?

Sometimes parents agree about who should care for the children after they get divorced; sometimes they end up having an angry custody battle in court (that means they're fighting about who should have legal control of the children). Still other times parents give their kids a choice of which parent they want to live with. Such a decision can be very painful and confusing, especially when you want to live with both.

Jimmy, age twelve, said, "My mother and father got a divorce a few years ago. Now my father is getting married again and he wants me to live with him. Who should I go with, my mom or my dad?"

Go with the parent who can take better care of you. Go with the one it feels better to be with. What's your gut feeling, Jimmy?

Cathy, age twenty, was visiting her father when I met her. She and her mother, stepfather, and six-year-old stepbrother live in a different state. Cathy said, "My parents decided to split when I was twelve. They gave us a choice of who we wanted to live with. My younger brother and I went to live with my mother. My older sister (she was seventeen at the time) went off on her own. My other sister went to live with my father because she could never get along with my mother. I visit my father and stay with him for a few weeks every chance I can."

Scott, age eleven, shared, "My father and mother got divorced when I wasn't born yet. I didn't see my father until I was seven. Last year my mother couldn't handle me and my sisters, so she turned us over to my father. They had to go to court but my mother didn't show up and they had to arrest her for a little while. Now my father won't let me or my sisters call her or see her. It's like she is dead. My baby brother lives with my mother. I wish I could see them. I love both of them a lot. I would like them to come back together and get married again. But I love my father and my mother a lot. My sister hates my mother now. But I love her a lot."

Do you think it's any wonder that Scott has trouble concentrating on his schoolwork? I can't even begin to imagine the pain he feels, the sadness of wanting to see his mother but not being able to. Maybe if he told his father honestly that he loves him very much, but that he also loves his mother and it would mean so much to speak with her on the telephone, then maybe his father might let him call her. (It doesn't have to mean that Scott loves his father less because he wants to contact his mother. Maybe it would help if his father was reminded of this.)

A girl in the fifth grade said, "My mother and father are divorced. I live with my granny. I have problems talking to my mother and father."

Sometimes grandparents, aunts, uncles, or even a parent's close friend may take over custody if neither parent is able to.

In some cases, like Joe's, there's no choice to be made. His wife left seven years ago, leaving him to take care of their two sons. Joe feels that he has grown closer to his sons in a very special way. So even though the divorce was hard to deal with, a lot of good came out of it.

As you can see, there are many different kinds of arrangements. Each one is a little different; each brings with it different feelings. Though all new arrangements will take some time to get used to, some aren't as tough to deal with as others. Being able to talk about your feelings, even when they hurt and might make you cry (remember, crying can be a great release for getting feelings out), can be very helpful.

One More Thing: Lots of kids who have to choose whether they want to live with their mother or father really do know their answer. But they're afraid to tell their parents because they don't want them to think they love one more than the other. They don't want to hurt their parents' feelings and they certainly don't want to make them mad. So maybe they'll just say, "I don't know," when deep inside, they really know.

If you're given such a choice, remember to put your feelings into words. It may hurt to say certain things out loud. But think about how much more it will hurt if you let your parents make a decision for you and you end up with the parent you didn't want to live with.

If you have feelings, let them be known. If you don't share how you feel, you may be sorry for a long time.

Where Will You Live and How Often Will You Visit Your Other Parent?

You might stay in the home you've always lived in or move out. Sometimes the move is to another, often smaller, home or apartment (possibly to cut down on expenses) right in the same town. Sometimes the move is much farther away.

Where you live and how far the other parent moves will affect how often you see that parent. Seeing him or her will also depend upon what visiting rules might be in your parents' written divorce decree (order of the court). For example, if your mother has custody, the decree might say that your father is allowed to visit with you every weekend, every other weekend, every Tuesday and Thursday, on certain holidays, during the summer, and so on.

Donna, age ten, asks, "How can I talk to my father? My parents are divorced and my father is in California." Since she lives in New York, it's very difficult and expensive to visit him. She told me she's been very upset that he hasn't called her very often. He says that it's expensive to call. I suggested she write him, which she did. But he didn't answer her letters. Donna had a hard time dealing with how much it hurt her not to hear from him and how badly she wanted him to show he cares. How could Donna turn these feelings into words?

As much as I hate to say this, some parents really don't care. They just want to do their own thing, start all over, try to forget, and run away from their responsibilities.

Dayna, age fourteen, told me:

My mother left us because of her career and because she wanted to be her own person. She wanted to have more freedom to come and go, go to classes, and go to work. Ever since she started her job, we felt we lost her. It was too late. She knew that she wanted to leave and she didn't want to have a family anymore. She'd come home and make dinner. Then she'd leave. She saw her friends and other men. She was hardly ever home. We saw my mother maybe one night a week. She never gave us a lot of attention. She never hugged us or kissed us. Never even a pat on the head.

She left the day before finals. That really screwed us up! But we're okay now. My father is seeing a woman. She's the nicest person in the world, and she's trying to make up for all the hurt.

When some parents leave, they stay away forever, even if that means they won't see their children again. While they probably still love their children, maybe they just can't deal with any part of their life the way it was and they have to get away. I'm at a loss to offer words that can ease the sense of loss children (and the other parent) must feel when this happens. It's natural for this to make kids feel very sad, very deserted, very angry and, at least at the time the parent leaves, very alone.

If your parent leaves, it will be most helpful to be able to talk about your feelings openly with an adult you trust (you can start with the parent who is still with you). Since you can't bring your parent back, at least you can try to understand and gain strength to live your life as well as possible without them.

But many parents do try to stay close to their children. Even if they aren't close by, they really try to keep in touch and arrange to see them whenever possible. If you're able to e-mail, it can be even easier to keep up active contact.

A friend of mine who has joint custody of her sons (even though she and her husband are divorced, they still share in raising their sons) said that her sons are free to travel back and forth between her home, where the children live, and her husband's home, about one and one-half hours away. They know how to travel by bus and train, and see their father quite often. They have no strict rules about when. They just go and come when they wish. It's very easy that way and everyone still gets along. In fact, they all spent last Christmas together. While some divorces are nasty, others can be more agreeable, supportive and, generally, positive.

Gary, age twelve, told me he sees his father every weekend. But he hates it when his father's new girlfriend is there. He wishes he could be with him alone, even though she seems nice.

Michelle, age fourteen, says, "Now that my parents are divorced, at least my father has to make time to see me. I spend more time with him than I ever did when my parents were married. We've gotten closer."

If your parents are divorced and you want to communicate with your other parent more, it may help to realize that even if you don't see them, you can talk with them on the telephone, through letters or e-mails. You can also write poems, send audiocassettes or videotapes, draw pictures, or possibly even have a video visit.

Don't expect parents to guess what you're feeling unless you tell them. Don't expect them to know—without being told—how badly you want to see more of them. Even if the visiting rules won't allow more visits, you can tell that parent how much you miss them. It's okay to say you're sad. It's okay to say you're unhappy about everything. It's okay to cry. It's also okay to feel relieved. The important thing is how you deal with your feelings, and that you know you don't have to deal with them alone.

Reminder: Even if you talk (or write) honestly to your parent, no one can promise that your parent will make the changes you wish, such as pay you more attention. But unless you tell your parent how you feel, he or she might not ever know.

Visiting Can Be Confusing

Mrs. P. has custody of her son. Her son lives with her and her new husband (his stepfather) during the week and visits his father every weekend. She told me that every time her son returns from a weekend with his father, he's upset and often seems angry with her.

Sometimes a child's anger can be from not being able to accept the parents' divorce. A child may blame one parent or another for breaking up the marriage, especially if one parent tries to influence the child to believe the other is at fault. One parent might try to turn the child against the other parent. That can make kids feel very confused (and even angrier).

I already mentioned that presents are sometimes given to make a parent feel less guilty, to bribe, or try to make it seem that they are more loving than the other parent who hasn't given as much.

Sometimes values are different in the mother's house and the father's house. One parent may let the child stay up all night; the other parent may say, "Lights out at ten o'clock!" One parent may say it's okay to watch a sexy movie; the other might think the child is too young.

While parents can feel differently even when they're not divorced, usually they try to work out their feelings and decide together what they'll teach their children. In a divorce situation, one parent will not necessarily check with the other about what's being taught. The parent might just do what they believe is right and may even think that allowing extra privileges or being less strict will make the child love him or her and want to visit more. There can be a lot of competition and comparing between parents, too.

Learning completely different ideas about what's right and what's wrong and living by a different set of rules with each parent can be very confusing. It may be hard for kids to keep track of which rules go with which house.

What do you think kids might say to both parents if they were confused or upset about the differences?

Being Patient with Your Single Parent

Whether because of divorce or death of their husband or wife, a man or woman who becomes a single parent may take a while to get used to the idea, especially if he or she has been married for years.

When people are married and their relationship is special, the husband and wife not only share their love, they are best friends. They trust each other with the most private secrets, they love to spend time with each other, laugh, and have fun. They can talk with each other about anything and sit together in silence without having to speak. They can count on each other, can share their sadness, their joy, their dreams.

When the relationship is no longer special, and they grow apart to the point of separating or getting a divorce, it may take a while before they're ready to even think of sharing so closely with another person.

Each parent will take his or her own time getting used to living on his or her own. Many kids worry about if their parents will still be able to care for themselves, and if they'll be okay. These feelings may be especially strong for boys and girls who attend boarding school and are required to live away from home. College students have expressed similar concerns about leaving a single parent home alone.

It may help to understand that, just as no parent can live their children's life for them, parents must stand on their own in order to go forward in a different way. Even if a parent is sad and upset, it doesn't mean he or she won't be able to find strength to be okay and move on with their own life. It's natural to be sad and upset about upsetting things. It would probably be more surprising if your parent weren't upset! Even if you don't live with that parent, you can still be supportive through phone calls, letters or e-mails. That can mean so much.

It would be impossible to guess how much time it will take for a parent to be ready to begin looking for another partner, someone to be close with again. Dealing with past hurts and the tremendous sense of loss is something that is very personal. Some parents will need more time to adjust than others. It may take them an even longer time to reach the point of being ready to share their lives in that way again.

It's also possible that parents will surprise themselves, their kids, and everyone around them by finding someone new more quickly than anyone might have expected. In these cases, it just might be that the other person "found" them!

Even when parents start reaching out for new relationships, it doesn't mean they have forgotten or have "gotten over" the other parent who is no longer with them . . . just that they were ready to try to move forward in their life.

It can help for kids to be patient with their single parents. At a recent lecture, a single woman told me her kids can't understand why she isn't dating. Her ex-husband (the man she divorced) has been dating for a while and even introduces his dates to his kids. She just isn't ready to date yet and doesn't want to be pushed. Yet her kids won't stop asking her why. Some kids are more ready for their parents to date than others.

It can also help for kids to try a little harder to understand that their mother and father probably spent a lot of time together. Just as kids need their friends, it's important for a mother or father to have a relationship that feels good.

Diane, now in her forties, shared, "My grandfather started 'seeing'a woman a few months after my grandmother died. I was in the seventh grade at the time and remember that my whole family was upset about how soon this was after my grandmother's death and how he should have waited longer. Looking back, I think it was probably wrong of all of us to judge his new relationship the way we did. He seemed to have a wonderful life with my grandmother. They were very close. I suppose it wasn't his fault that this woman appeared when she did. Maybe we all would have been more understanding if we realized that it was my grandfather's right to choose a companion—and realized his need to have one. It didn't mean he loved my grandmother less and surely didn't change his love for us. It's good that he found someone else to spend his life with so he wasn't alone."

So, if you find it difficult to accept your parent's need to find other adult people to be with, try to remind yourself that adults can be lonely, too. Just as adults can't completely fill in your loneliness if you feel you have no friends, you can't fill theirs. You need people your age, and your parent needs someone who's also an adult. It doesn't mean they love you less because they want and need a friend. If anything, when they feel good about themselves and their new lives, they'll likely be able to give of themselves to you more.

When Parents Start Going Out: Your Parent's Girlfriend or Boyfriend

No part of divorce is easy. Perhaps parents' dating is one of the harder parts since it makes it even more real that parents aren't together anymore. Many boys and girls whose parents have started dating have said it's very strange to see their mother or father with a different man or woman.

If your mother or father has started to go out with other people, you have probably had many different feelings about it. You might be very relieved and happy to see your parent date. Or you may resent their date, even if the person is nice, just because you don't want to see your parent with anyone else but your "real" mother or father. You may be jealous that this man or woman is taking away some of your private time with your parents. You may be scared that your parent will end up marrying this person. You might find that you're having a hard time being nice.

Maybe you need to know that parents are often scared, too. They wonder and worry about how their children are going to feel. They, too, know that dating someone else makes their divorce seem more final.

Resentment, jealousy, anger, and being scared or frustrated can naturally interfere with being nice. It can also be confusing to know how to introduce your mother's or father's date to a friend. You may find it embarrassing or awkward for other people to learn that your parents aren't together anymore. When your parent starts to date, the divorce becomes more public, more known.

Perhaps it will help to think about how your parents might be feeling. No doubt, they will feel strange about dating, especially if they were married for many years. Dating is something they probably haven't done since they were much younger.

Maybe this is the first time in months—or years—that they were actually able to have a pleasant time with an adult who respects them and is truly interested in being with them.

When a parent has dated someone for a while and likes them very much, they may decide it's time to invite them home to spend the night. Many parents are not sure how their children will react to their decision to share themselves in that way. Many parents are confused about what they need to explain to their kids so that they'll understand why this is important to them.

Bobby, age fifteen, lives with his father. He told me that he and his father have gotten very close since his parents' divorce. Bobby told me, "It's great. My dad and I talk about our dates like two buddies after we come in. Even though I know he's my father, we're having fun and have really become more like friends. He even asks my advice!"

Stacey, age twelve, is an only child. Her parents got divorced several years ago and her father moved away. Since he left, Stacey and her mother have gotten very close. With her father gone, Stacey felt free to come into her mother's bed and sleep there for the rest of the night if she had a nightmare. In fact, she kind of looked forward to going into her mother's bed. It made her feel safe and close to her mother.

When Stacey's mother's boyfriend moved in with them, everything changed. Stacey no longer felt she could go into her mother's bedroom. Her mother's boyfriend had taken her place. She was jealous and very upset. She especially resented him telling her what to do around the house. "After all," said Stacey, "he's not my real father. He has no business telling me what to do."

Stacey tried speaking to her mother about this and things got a little better. She still felt she wasn't as important as she used to be when it was just the two of them, Stacey and her mother.

Stacey admitted that it wasn't really the boyfriend who bothered her. It was the whole idea of having to share her mother. She didn't want to. She had given up too much already.

Holding in any of these feelings will not be as helpful to you or your parent as will talking about them honestly and openly at a time when both of you can be alone with each other. If you can't talk with your parent, go on to your list of other trusted adults.

When a Parent Gets Married Again

If your parents are separated or divorced, have you thought about what you might feel if either parent marries again? (Think about this now if you haven't already.)

If your mother or father has remarried, what were your feelings when you first learned they were getting married? What are your feelings now?

It's normal to be confused, scared, and even resentful. It's also normal to be excited and feel wonderful that you're going to have an extra parent who will live with you, care for you, be there for you, and get along in a loving way with your mom or dad.

Notice I said "extra parent." That's because a new marriage doesn't mean that your birth mom or dad will now have to take a backseat. It simply means you'll have one more parent, called a stepparent (the name given to the person your mother or father remarries). He or she doesn't replace your original parent. No one can. Rather, a stepparent is taking his or her own place in the hopes that all of you will have a better life together than you would have if you had remained apart.

Stepparents and Stepfamilies

Some kids feel close to their new stepparent very quickly. Others find it hard to give their new stepparent a chance. Some kids are confused about how to act toward them. They wonder if it's okay to try to like them.

If the parent whom you're not living with gets married, you may be concerned that if you like your new stepparent too much, your parents will decide you should live with the married parent instead of staying where you are.

If you like the stepparent too much, you might feel guilty or concerned that your birth parent might be jealous or worried that you like the stepparent more than your birth parent.

Boys and girls are often not sure what to call the stepparent. Mom? Dad? Their first name? That's something that it helps to talk about.

There are stepparents who will be kind, caring, and will love you as if you're their own child. Others are not so loving.

A girl in the sixth grade shared, "I have a stepmother. She doesn't like me and she treats me awful. She has children of her own and none of them likes me. She always lets her kids do everything. But not me."

What would you do if you were this girl? One of the important choices to consider would be to speak with your father (privately). You could also speak with your stepmother and ask her if you've done something to make her upset with you. You might tell her if that's so, you didn't ever mean to get her upset and you'd like to try to get along better.

Talking about getting along won't always make the bad feelings go away. The truth is sometimes kids don't get along with their stepparent, just as some kids don't get along with their birth parents. And sometimes they get along even better than they did with their birth parents. As you know, relationships must work two ways in order for them to feel as good as possible. If you're trying hard and your stepparent doesn't seem to care, the sad thing is that you may never feel good about your relationship with your stepparent. And they may continue to treat you unfairly. Your birth mother or father probably will do his or her best to help communicate how you would like to be treated better.

Once again, violence (abuse—beating you up with words or fists or belts—or any type of forced sex) is not and should not be considered acceptable, natural, or right. Abuse is also against the law.

Besides telling me about her parents' divorce, twenty-year-old Cathy also talked about how scared she is of her stepfather. He's an alcoholic and he beats her mother. Sometimes he tries to beat Cathy. But when he starts in, she just hides. She said she's afraid to move out but would really like to. She's afraid of what her stepfather will do to her mother if she's not there.

I suggested to Cathy that as much as she may not like it and as much as it may seem wrong, her mother has made a choice, at least for now. Just as her mother has to take responsibility for her own life and her own choices, so does Cathy have the right to choose for herself. As painful as it will probably be to leave, knowing how her mother is treated, how long do you think it fair for Cathy to live at home so she can protect her mother? Cathy said she's saving up money so she can move out someday, and then she'll see. Cathy might find it helpful to call Al-Anon or Alateen.

Cathy, as well as her mother, can also get help by dialing 0 and asking information about the nearest Domestic [family, in the home] Violence Hotline. Cathy's mother may not be able to control her husband. But she doesn't have to allow herself to keep taking the abuse. This hotline can help her begin to take steps toward being able to handle her situation in a better, safer way—so that she can stop being abused.

I'd like to believe that, in most cases, a stepparent wants a good relationship, too. It's not so easy to fill in the gap of all the years they didn't know you. It will take you and your stepparent time to learn about each other and become sensitive to each other's feelings and needs. It will take time to learn what each of you expects, as each family has been living by its own set of rules. It will take patience and the ability to forgive each other for not knowing what will hurt and not knowing how to handle situations that are new. Everyone will need time to learn to get along.

As far as your stepbrother(s) or stepsister(s) is concerned, there are families who come together who can get along beautifully right away. Especially when a child has always wanted a brother or sister and will now finally have one. Or, for the first time, they'll have someone to live with who's closer to their age. But it's also very natural for them to feel jealous, resentful, and angry. It's not always so easy for two families to come together and expect to get along immediately.

It's also possible that new stepbrothers and sisters have actually grown up in the same town and have known each other for many years before becoming part of the same family. If they have been friends, it may be fun and easy to get along. If not, the adjustment may be that much harder (especially if kids at school say things like, "I can't believe ____ is now your brother!").

Comparisons and competition can easily get in the way of friendship. If a stepsister or stepbrother is considered to be better-looking, smarter, more popular, a better athlete, or a better piano player, or anything else, there might be jealousy and resentment.

If stepsisters or stepbrothers feel you are taking away some of their mother's or father's love, they may even say they hate you (you may say you feel the same way about them). While I suppose it's possible that you really hate each other, I'm willing to bet that it's not so much the stepsister or stepbrother who's hated but more the whole idea of change, being forced to live with someone and call them family, and no longer having your parent all to yourself.

Some stepfamilies get along easily. It may take a while for others to learn to live together in a way that feels good. If your stepfamily is having difficulty getting along, you can talk about this with your mom and dad, stepmother or stepfather. You might find it helpful to have a step-family meeting so that everyone can talk together about what they like, what bothers them, what they wish could change, and other issues.

If your family still can't get along, it might be very important for your parents to check out what kind of counseling for stepfamilies can be offered to you in your town. In some communities, there are step-family organizations that can offer extra guidance.

While Divorce May Seem Like the Worst Thing That Could Happen, It's Sometimes a Blessing, Even for Kids

If parents are fighting much of the time, if there's a lot of pressure, if your parents really don't want to be together, if they're miserable being married to each other, if they just want to get away from it all, or if they still care very much about each other but just can't live together as man and wife, then maybe separation or divorce will be a blessing. Even if separating hurts.

Joe, age thirty-eight, shared, "During the first two years after my wife left me, I thought being divorced was the worst thing that could have happened to me in my life. By the time the third year began, I knew it was the best thing that could have happened to me."

As much as you want something to work, you can't force it. It goes back to what I said in the beginning of this chapter about relationships needing to be two-way. If they're not, then how long do you think it would be worth staying married to someone if they stopped loving you, stopped wanting to work at being able to communicate better, stopped wanting to please you, stopped wanting to be sensitive to your needs, stopped wanting to accept you for who you are?

Sometimes marriages don't work because one or both partners expect so much of the other person that they're sure to be disappointed. Their expectations aren't fair or real (just as sometimes your parents or teachers or friends expect too much of you and then are disappointed that you didn't live up to what they expected). So the husband or wife is never satisfied.

Or maybe the husband or wife thought that the other person would change (would be different) once they were married. (It's not a good idea to count on someone else to change. That person might change, but that's not in your control. You can control only your own changes. The same is true for any parent who decided to get married expecting that their husband or wife would change—and finding that they never did.)

Since each person is different, each relationship is different, as is each parent's reason for staying together or splitting up.

One more thing: Mara, age twenty, told me, "I don't think I ever want to get married because I'm afraid I'll end up getting divorced, like my parents." If your parents, older sister or brother get separated or divorced, that doesn't mean that if you get married someday, you'll get divorced, too. Divorce is not "catching."

What happens with your parents (or anyone else you know) has to do with their relationship with each other. You have the ability to work at and establish your own adult relationship. You can learn from your parents' mistakes and try not to repeat them for yourself. You can also hold on to what seems positive. But your relationship will be your own.

So Much Has to Do with Your Attitude

Your attitude can influence whether you feel good or bad about anything that happens to you. It can have a strong effect on how you and your family are able to adjust to change. You may have heard people say, "It's all in the way you look at it!"

For whatever goes on in your life, it's important to figure out and understand the difference between what you can control and what you can't. For example, you can't control whether your parents will stay married or not. That's up to your parents. But, while you can't control what happens between your parents, you can control how you respond to what's happening between your parents.

You *can*, to the best of your ability, continue to share your own life with each parent, even if he or she lives far away from you. You *can* choose to be honest with each of your parents about your feelings. You *can* choose to make the best of your new situation, and try to get along as well as possible with your new family (if you have one). And, you *can* approach someone who can help you if you're having a difficult time adjusting to your situation. That still leaves you in control.

CHAPTER 21

FAMILY FEELINGS

Your family feelings aren't just from today. They come from years of sharing many different experiences with all the people in your family: some that make you smile and feel good, others that are sad, and still others that make you wish you had huge fangs so you could run around and growl at everyone.

Think back as far as you can remember and try to pick out special family moments that have made a difference to you, moments which have affected your family feelings. Things like climbing into your parents' bed so they could protect you from the thunder, visiting your grandma and smelling her super-terrific-grandma-type chocolate cake, the first time you saw your baby sister or brother, the first time you were allowed to drive the tractor by yourself, going fishing with your dad or grandpa, finally learning how to ride a two-wheel bicycle, a special birthday party, holiday dinner, being sent to your room for being bad, being told your pet was very sick, family outings, and more.

Some of these may be on your list of memories. But the best thing to do would be to make your own list. Take a few moments now to think. Along with each experience that comes to your mind, try to remember the feelings that went along with it. You might have felt happy, excited, surprised, sad, disappointed, angry, scared, proud, grown-up, and so on.

As I've been writing this, suggesting that you write your own list, things keep popping into my head—my own grandmother's chocolate cake and her second-day chicken soup, being homesick for my parents the first summer I went away to camp, the day we were supposed to go to the amusement park and my father had to work at the last minute and we couldn't go, the time in the third grade when I pushed someone off the top of the monkey bars on the playground because she was teasing my sister, the day my grandmother died when I was in the ninth grade, my mom's chocolate chip cookies, being scolded for squeezing my sister's arm and cursing at her, my dog's bad breath, playing tennis with my uncle, the comfort of being able to knock on my parents' door at any time in the middle of the night if I was upset and felt like talking, being so scared when my father got very badly burned, singing with my sister when we did the dishes, when my grandparents took me (by myself) on an airplane to visit my cousins who lived far away, throwing dolls across the room at my sister in the dark, secretly hanging upside down at the top of the stairs with my brothers and sister so we could hear my parents' friends tell dirty jokes, dressing my little brother up in funny clothes.

It's amazing how every one of us has our own list. No two lists can be exactly the same, even if you're a twin. That's because each person has his or her own feelings, responses, and memories. Even the same experiences will be felt and remembered differently by each person. Some of the memories might be wonderfully happy ones, others may still cause you to ache inside. But all the experiences have helped to make you and me who we are today. What we feel for our family is like no other emotion in the whole world. Our family can make us feel secure, special, loved, happy, and make us have a deep sense that, no matter what, we belong and will be cared for.

But not all children (or adults) have such family feelings. Some lists will be filled mostly with sadness, dreams that never came true, love that wasn't shared, loneliness, distance, and fighting.

I've found that when kids feel good about their family, they can feel freer to enjoy their friends, concentrate on their work at school, and more fully participate in other activities. If they're pressured, worried, scared, insecure, or unloved at home, everything else will probably seem much less important.

It seems underneath everything is the need for family. Even if kids run away from their families, my guess is that they wish they didn't have to feel that way. They wish they could be closer and feel good, so they could stay. Even if parents are not close with their children, or if sisters and brothers stop talking to each other, I've never spoken with anyone who hasn't at least wished it could be different.

Family Means Different Things to Different People

Some people have family feelings for others who are not related but who feel and act as if they are. It seems that whoever can give you the caring, time, love, and security that is so important to your feeling good can become like family.

Even orphans find that the other orphans, as well as the adults who care for them, can feel like family.

There are stepfamilies who enjoy closer family feelings with one another than they ever did with the family members who were born together. Families with adopted children, many from all over the world, have the ability to develop family feelings that are special. So many foster parents take other people's children, raise them, and love them as if they were their own.

One woman in her sixties whose sister and brother are no longer talking to her feels that certain friends have become like sisters to her. She said about her friends, "There is nothing that we wouldn't have given up if we needed each other. That's dedication, a feeling of true loyalty, a feeling that if your hand is out, you know you can count on each other. But my own sister and brother never gave me that feeling. Because you're a sister doesn't mean that you're going to have family feelings. I once was at an airport when a man was waiting to see his brother who he hadn't seen for twenty-five years. The brother was not allowed to leave his country during these years and had just gotten permission to get out. When his brother came off the plane, they embraced; they cried; they yelled, they hugged, it was the most emotional experience I have ever seen. There's nothing to replace flesh and blood if the feelings are there. But if the feelings are not there, it doesn't matter if you're flesh and blood or not."

She and her friends are closer, spend more time together, are more trusting, and are more there for each other than she and her own sister and brother ever were. Her friends have become her family.

Just because someone is related to you doesn't guarantee that you'll be able to have warm, close family feelings with them. That would be nice. But that's not the way things are for everyone. All you have to do is think about the divorce rate, the kids who run away, or the kids who feel they need alcohol or other drugs to drown their loneliness so they don't have to deal with it, and you'll know that being able to feel close and secure is a gift to be treasured and not ever to be taken for granted.

When Family Feelings Are Not Good

Though it's sad to admit, there are some families that will probably never feel good, no matter how hard anyone tries.

Concerns that can make it hard to feel good:
- constant fighting
- money pressures
- failure
- neglect (nobody pays attention)
- no communication
- little kindness or understanding
- drug or alcohol problems
- illness
- unemployment
- abuse
- loneliness
- jealousy

Some parents never really wanted to have a family in the first place. Others who really love their children may just not be capable of taking care of them in a way that feels good to anyone.

Boys and girls growing up in a home where family feelings are not good will probably find it hard to be happy. They may not be able to concentrate in school, may bully other kids, show off, or misbehave in class. So often they do this to try to get the attention they aren't getting at home. Some will not even show up at school. They'll hang out in the streets and just try to survive.

Some kids from homes that don't feel good will just get unhappier, angrier, and lonelier over the years, especially if their family situation doesn't change. They may run away from home at an early age or get married earlier than they normally would (even if they aren't really in love), just to get away from their parents and their unhappy family life. They may turn to alcohol or other drugs, and may even commit crimes—because they're so angry, hungry, neglected.

Some kids from unhappy homes are able to find happiness with other families. Gary, age nineteen, told me, "When I was growing up, I loved going to my friend's house for dinner on Friday nights. I never felt good with my family. My older brother was always out with his friends, and my parents . . . well, my father drank a lot, and my mother was so afraid of my father that it was miserable even being around them. I felt sad. I didn't want to be there. But it was different in my friend's house. He had two little sisters who became very attached to me. They always wanted to sit on my lap, and I loved reading to them. He had a younger brother who always teased him. But I loved hearing it because it was fun to be with what seemed like a normal family. I became very close with his mother and father and was always welcome there. I don't know what I would have done if I didn't have them to go to. They were like my adopted family. But they felt more like my family than my own family did."

One woman shared that her friend (we'll call her Joan) had a baby-sitter who started baby-sitting for Joan's three sons from the time she was ten or eleven. The baby-sitter's mother had died of cancer, and her father physically abused her. Finally, because of all the abuse and unhappiness, the baby-sitter just couldn't live with her father anymore. Joan, her husband, and her children had grown to love this girl and decided to legally adopt her as part of their family.

That was many years ago and this girl is now expecting a baby of her own. She most likely learned from the family who adopted her that there really is goodness in the world—and she'll be able to give her own child all that she missed getting from her birth parents.

Another woman talked about a girl who was loved by her mother but was very neglected. Her father had died and her mother, who was a child herself, was just not capable of taking care of her three children. Though the girl had been a very good student, she started dropping out of school. She slept in basements, garages, or wherever she could instead of going home. A teacher at school realized there was a problem and tried to reach her and encourage her to come to school. At least if she was in school, he could give her support, talk with her, and try to keep an eye on her, which he did. This girl's situation touched him. And as time went on, his feelings about wanting to help her grew even stronger. One day, she came home with him, supposedly to baby-sit for his children, and she's been a part of his family ever since. Though her mother loved her, she was more than happy to have someone take the burden of caring for her off her hands.

According to this woman, "There are all different types of love. To say 'I love you' doesn't mean 'I want to—or am able to—care for you, be with you, or spend time with you.' "

How lucky these two girls were to have such special people reach out and bless them with the warmth, care, and love that is so much a part of family life that feels good. Their new families became closer to them, gave them the time, and answered their needs in a way that their birth families never could.

Unfortunately, not all children who are unhappy at home are lucky enough to have loving families to visit whenever they wish or to be taken in and raised by families who love them as their own. But all children who feel frustrated, sad, angry, unloved, neglected, lonely, or troubled about any part of their family life can at least try to better understand their feelings and learn new ways to cope with their family situation.

If you have such feelings, it is important to talk with someone who cares and is trained to listen and offer guidance. I know I keep repeating the list of people to go to for help, but maybe if I write it often enough, you'll begin to really believe that there are choices.

No one needs to deal with these difficult situations alone. You can speak with an aunt, uncle, older brother or sister, grandparent, teacher or coach, principal, religious leader, guidance counselor, school psychologist, school social worker, friend's parent, or other trusted adult. You can also check your local telephone book to find children's, family, or social services that can help.

If you're from an unhappy home, it may help to remind yourself that it's not your fault. If a parent is ill, or there's very little money, or your parents don't get along, or your parents neglect you, or they have an alcohol problem, or they get into trouble with the police, it's not your fault. It doesn't mean you're not special; it just means that sometimes life can be pretty hard.

Some Families Who Think They Can't Feel Better Really Can

Though certain families may never feel better, others who think they can't really can! In order to feel better, family members first have to admit that they don't feel good and they'd like things to be different. Then they have to agree to work together so that change can take place and feelings can improve.

Trying to change will take a lot of teaching and honest talking. It will probably mean taking risks and taking chances to say what you need to say. Even if being honest might hurt, through sharing these feelings, family members can learn to be more sensitive to each other.

Change will also require patience. If you figure it's taken years to develop the bad feelings you have, figure also that making positive changes will take time. Even if everyone agrees they wish to make these changes, they'll still take time. At first, it may seem like you're only taking tiny baby steps forward. Just remember, moving forward in any way, no matter how slowly, is better than standing still with bad feelings—or worse, moving backwards. Any change takes time.

Some families find family counseling—when the whole family gets advice from someone who is trained to listen and offer guidance—can be very helpful.

You Can't Choose Your Family

Have you ever said to yourself or heard someone say, "Oh, if only my mother was like that." Or, "I wish my brother would switch places with my friend's brother. Why do I have to be so unlucky?"

Well, family is different from friends. While you can choose your friends, you're stuck with family! You can't switch brothers, change mothers, or go shopping for a different sister.

Like it or not, you got what you got. So you might as well try to feel as good as you can about the way they are instead of spending so much time wishing they were different or someone else. The day you begin to accept them for who they are, you might begin to feel better about them.

Brothers and Sisters

If you have a brother or sister, think about what he or she means to you. Do your thoughts make you feel good, sad, frustrated, angry, cheated, or do they give you a bad case of the creeps? How do you think your brother or sister feels about you? If you're an only child, what are your feelings about not having a brother or sister?

Brother-sister feelings are affected by many things, such as who was born first, who's in the middle, who's the youngest, how many years are between you, how your parents treat you, and how your parents treat your siblings (your brothers and sisters).

If you were several years older when your sister or brother was born, you might have been very excited about having a new brother or sister. You most likely couldn't wait to help feed, dress, diaper, bathe, and play with him or her. You probably thought your new little brother or sister was so cute (much better than even your best doll or stuffed animal) and felt great about being such a number-one helper to your mom and dad. If you didn't feel that way, how did you feel?

If you were closer in age to your new brother or sister, you may have been excited and happy, but you also could have been very jealous. Now your mom and dad were going to take much of the attention that was supposed to be for you and give it to your new brother or sister. You might even have felt you hated him or her!

"When Carol was born, I was three years old," said Elaine, now age thirty-four. "Everyone was paying attention to her. I didn't realize why I felt so jealous at the time, but I thought it would be fun to stick her finger in the closet door! I took her out of the crib, and when no one was watching, put her on the floor, stuck her hand in the closet and closed it. I guess I thought that the baby's hand should have a new shape. Then I told my mother and said that I did it. She said, 'You didn't.' I said, 'I did it.' And then she said, 'It was an accident.' She didn't want to believe I could have done such a dangerous, horrible thing on purpose. And I kept saying, 'No, I did this. I did this.' I really hated my sister. If I could have beaten her up, I think I would have."

Not all kids go as far as to put baby's fingers in the closet door. But, if you check closely, what looks like tickling and patting may really be pinching and hitting. (Lots of nonverbal messages!)

Maybe you remember doing some of this yourself. Maybe you're still doing it.

Fights and Feelings

Some brothers and sisters hardly ever fight. They have strong feelings of love for each other and show it in many ways. They look out for each other and are quick to take each other's side if someone tries to be harmful in any way. They're very good friends and aren't jealous if one gets something and the other one doesn't.

Sheilagh, age thirty-two, has always been close to her twin brother. She has always been very protective of him. When he was sent upstairs without dinner, she made sure to sneak him a peanut butter sandwich, so he wouldn't go hungry. Today they're as close as they've ever been and are still looking out for each other.

Kent, age fourteen, said, "I've never fought with my sister. She's always been very small for her age. I'm very tall and I think she'd never get up if I hit her. I never would. Besides, my parents would kill me if I did."

Some Fighting Is Natural

Other brothers and sisters love each other but fight anyway (just as friends and parents do). Unless the fights are very violent and harmful, day-to-day arguments are pretty natural. In fact, there are parents who have told me they'd be concerned if their children didn't fight at least a little.

Allen, age thirteen, remembers a time when his younger sister "got me to the boiling point. I chased her into her room. She slammed the door and locked it. I started banging into it with my shoulder, screaming, and daring her to come out and play. She was hysterically crying. My dad came in, took me downstairs, and told me to wash my face. I was so mad that as I was washing, I broke a piece of soap in my hands without even realizing it. My mom went upstairs and brought my sister down from her room, holding her hand. I could have killed her (my sister)! But when I saw her face, all my anger drained out of me and I gave her a hug."

Bonnie, age eleven, said, "Even though I always say I hate my sister and wish she wasn't around—sometimes I even say I wish she were dead—I really love her. Because when she was in the hospital, I was really scared she was going to die."

Samantha's "shark story": Samantha told me that when she was twelve, her middle sister was nine and her youngest sister was six. They all shared a room together. She and her middle sister used to make believe the carpeting in their bedroom was the ocean. They used to push their little sister off into the "ocean" on their carpet and say, "'There are sharks and the sharks are coming to eat you! Here they come. They're eating your leg. Now they're eating your arm.' We'd make big, shark-type chomping sounds. This would make our sister cry hysterically, and we thought it was so funny. She was a real pain, anyway. She was always crying.

"Now that we're all older, we're much closer. We haven't thrown her to the 'sharks' in at least fifteen years! But we look back and smile (though her smile is not quite as wide as mine and my middle sister's). No wonder she cried all the time."

No matter how much scratching, growling, "I hate you," and sharkeating goes on each day, most brothers and sisters have a secret supply of good feelings for each other. Underneath the hateful shouts, the slamming doors, and the "it's not fairs", the close feelings are usually there. But they may show themselves only at certain times, for example, when a brother or sister is bullied, or one of them is upset, or if something serious happens.

Close feelings may show themselves only after brothers and sisters have become much older. The age differences, which seem so great when you're little, usually become less of a concern when you're older.

Rob, age thirty-three, told me that he and his brother were worlds apart when they were younger. Said Rob, "It's hard to be close when you're seventeen and your brother's eight. While he was growing up and playing with his toys, I was trying to figure out where I wanted to go to college. But now that he's twenty-four, I think I understand what he's going through right now. In fact, he's coming to stay with me in a few days. He wants to interview me about my work and may be interested in the same type of thing. It may be the first time that we'll be able to talk about something that we're both interested in that's got more to it than cars or the beach."

No matter what the differences in age or anything else, the fact is that brothers and sisters share many personal experiences over their growing-up years. They are able to look back together and relate to things that no one else in the world can.

Maybe that's what makes those brothers and sisters who really do have the good feelings underneath try so hard to become closer, even if they have to wait until they're older. That's also what might make them feel upset when they can't relate to each other and see each other (because of differences, being far away, or perhaps marrying someone who doesn't like the brother or sister), even if they want to.

No Matter How Deep You Dig

Unfortunately, some brothers and sisters who sound like they can't stand each other really can't. The hateful or resentful feelings on the outside are also on the inside. No matter how deep you dig, no love can be uncovered underneath. There's jealousy, resentment, and lots of comparing.

The other person's piece of cake is always bigger. Sometimes parents are the ones who take sides and cut the slices unfairly. Sometimes even if the pieces were carefully measured with a ruler, kids will think and believe that theirs is the smallest. (That has very little to do with the cake and much more to do with those inside feelings.)

The following was described to me by Mimi, age fifty-three:

My parents brought up a monster. If my older sister didn't get her way, she would throw a tantrum. She'd actually throw herself on the floor and kick, scream, and yell, so she could get her way. She was so strong, my parents just didn't know how to handle her. My mother used to say, "Please, please, give it to her. Give it to her. Give her whatever she wants." I remember when I was a little child, she pushed and pushed until she got her way.

I'll never forget the time I had gotten a new coat as a gift from my aunt. My aunt also got one for my sister. She picked a tan coat and I picked black. I hadn't worn it yet and my family was getting ready to go out to a religious service together. My sister decided that she wanted to wear my new black coat. When she started raising her voice, my mother said that black was an older color, and she's the older sister, so I should let her wear my coat. So I never got a chance to wear it for the first time. She did. And I've never forgotten it.

It's funny. I don't ever remember resenting my mother, even though I felt awful that I had to give up my brand-new coat. I think I felt so sorry for my parents that they had to deal with my sister. And yet, even though our childhood was so difficult, I kept up a decent relationship with her for years and years. Until we reached a point where nothing was enough for her. She was jealous of everything. It was too painful to try anymore. We haven't spoken to each other in several years.

Maybe Mimi and her sister would have been closer if their parents could have been stronger and handled her sister differently. No one will ever know.

If the underneath feelings are good, time and maturity will probably make them even better. If they're not good, as with Mimi and her sister, all the sharing and all the years together may not be enough to prevent a brother or sister from becoming the most distant strangers to each other, even enemies.

Why Isn't My Lollipop the Same as Theirs? and Other Jealousies

Think about your own family life and try to figure out the many ways in which each family member compares and competes with the other. What jealousies and resentments do you feel? What areas of competition actually encourage you to strive to advance yourself in a challenging, positive way?

- "He's allowed to cook breakfast, and I'm not."
- "He's allowed to stay up later than I am. It's not fair!"
- "How come she can go with you, and I can't?"
- "Why do I have to stay home and do chores when they can just go out and play with their friends?"
- "My older sister always gets real good grades and I don't."
- "Everyone always tell her how pretty she is, but they never say anything about me."
- "My younger sister always gets away with everything."
- "My older brother always gets away with everything."
- "Everyone else's piece of cake is bigger than mine."
- "I'm so jealous of my sister. She's so popular, and I hardly have any friends."
- "All the relatives pay more attention to her than to me."
- "My brother knows how to bake and I don't."
- "How come my sister is such a good athlete, and I can't even throw a ball? The guys tease me that I should take lessons from my younger sister."
- "Why did my brother get the looks and the brains?"
- "My younger sister is more developed than I am."
- "You only buy what he likes and not what I like."
- "You only make her favorite cake and not mine."
- "Why does Uncle M. only take her out to play tennis and not me?"
- "How come I always have to be the one to get hand-me-downs?"
- "He always gets away with things, and I always get blamed."
- "You only make time for him, never for me."
- "You don't love me as much . . ."
- "You listen to her, but you never listen to me."
- "He always hogs the talking during dinner."

Do any of these things sound familiar? What else would you include on your own list? You may be surprised to realize how much comparing you really do.

But remember, not all competition is bad. In fact, it can be fun, healthy, and make you strive to be better in a very positive way. It's only bad when you don't realize, accept, and respect that each person is different. And it's bad when you don't let your parent, brother, sister, or anyone else know when competition doesn't make you feel good.

One more thing: Many problems on the list of comparisons can be changed, if you just talk with your family about how you feel. For example, if you want to cook breakfast, talk about it with your mom or dad. You may just need to prove to them that you know the safety rules and maybe they'll let you—or teach you.

If You Think You're Not as Good as Your Brother or Sister

It may be that your parents always say to you, "Look what Beth [make believe your older sister is Beth!] got on her test. She got another ninety-five. I don't understand why you're having such a hard time with your studying. No child in our family is stupid. It should be easy for you, if you would only work a little harder."

Those kinds of comparisons can kill. They can kill the confidence that comes from knowing your parents accept you for who you are, for your own abilities. They can kill your strength to accept yourself as you are, because you're always believing you should be better; you're always believing you're not good enough; you're always believing you should be like your sister. Comparisons can kill any chance that you will relax and be able to concentrate when you take your next test, because you're so worried about doing at least as well as Beth (you may even feel pressured to cheat).

And, such comparisons can also make you want to "kill" Beth. Not really kill her but just not have her around. (Things might be a lot easier for you.) Even if you and Beth really love each other, these kinds of comparisons can interfere with close feelings between you. The sad thing is that it's not Beth's fault that your parents always compare you to her.

Because you're angry, you may purposely forget to give her telephone messages, spill her perfume, stick her brush in the toilet (only kidding), hide her stationery, or even try to embarrass her in front of her friends. But doing those kinds of things will only make the feelings worse between you and Beth.

Because you're frustrated, you might decide that since there's just no way you can get those high Beth-type grades, you might as well stop trying. You might think it's not worth trying so hard, knowing that your parents will never think what you get is good enough. That may be too painful. You may start talking and fooling around more in class, because you feel there's no point to paying attention. At least if your grades are really low, there's not even a chance they'll get close to Beth's. So maybe your parents will leave you alone.

What can you do? Since you're the one who feels resentful and frustrated, it's important to let your parents know how you feel when they compare you. (Even if they don't say anything out loud, if you *feel* they compare, it's still important to let them know.) Look back to the beginning of Chapter 19, "Your Parents," if you're not sure how to turn your feelings into words.

Since you're the one who might not think very much of yourself because you don't think you measure up, you can begin to work harder at accepting and valuing yourself for who you are, whether you get a 70, a 75, an 80 or a 95 (just like Beth). You can also work to improve your grades or at least keep them at a point where you're satisfied with them. You can decide to try harder.

Maybe instead of spending so much time comparing, your parents would be more helpful if they sat down with you and talked about study habits and ways to organize your work so you can improve. Then maybe on the next test you'll be able to get a 73 instead of a 70. The truth is maybe you'll never get a 95, no matter how hard you work. Maybe that's just not realistic for you to expect. But by comparing yourself to yourself, you'll be able to go as far as you can and not be so pressured to be like anyone else. You'll probably be amazed at how much better you'll start to feel about yourself.

And since you're the one who now realizes that Beth has little to do with this (if it's really because of your parents' unfair expectations—or your own), then maybe you and Beth can have a private talk. Maybe you can give her a chance to be the friend she might already be. Until now, it's possible that neither of you has been free enough to let those underneath feelings come out.

You have your own things that you can do, and you have a right to do them in your own way. If you always try to be like your sister, you may be disappointed for the rest of your life. How sad to spend all that time wishing you were someone else. You can't be like your sister or anyone else. You can only be yourself.

That goes for comparing how good you are at sports or how well you can bake, sew, sing, play the piano, or how many friends you have, or whether or not you're popular, or comparing your looks, hair, or if you're interested in a boyfriend or girlfriend. You can only be you. It's important for your parents to learn that, if they haven't already. And it's certainly important for you.

If It's Hard to Talk with Your Parents About Their Comparisons

If you're finding it hard to tell your parents how pressured and resentful you feel because of their comparisons, you might ask them to read this section and say you're feeling a lot like Beth's sibling.

If you really don't think you can say even that, you might leave this book on their pillows, opened to the section about Beth with a little note attached, "Please read. Maybe we can talk about this later."

Remember, you may not always be comfortable with what you want to say, but that doesn't mean you shouldn't say it. It's very important for your parents to realize how much their comparisons hurt you and how much they interfere with good feelings for your brother or sister. They may never know unless you tell them.

Sometimes It's Not the Parents Who Pressure and Compare

Some boys and girls just love competition. They compete whenever they can with their friends and classmates, so it's natural for them to compete with their brothers and sisters (and their brothers and sisters may compete back with them). Sometimes the competition is healthy. Other times it may cause bad feelings and pressures at home.

Even if parents don't say a word, kids might think their parents are comparing them. They feel their parents' pressure; they feel the competition, and they act in response to it. Bobby, age thirteen, told me, "My brother always gets hundreds. And even though my mother never says anything, I know she's comparing me. And I hate that!"

These feelings might make kids feel better or worse about themselves. These kids often continue to believe that their parents are comparing them even when they haven't checked to find out if their parents feel that way.

Sometimes it may be your relatives or the kids at school who do the comparing. If you find you are aware of a pulling or tugging at your insides because you think your sister or brother is better than you are, or that your parents, relatives, or friends think they're better—it's time to catch those feelings before they go any further and take a good, hard look at what those comparisons are doing to how you feel about yourself.

If you think your parents are comparing you, even if they don't talk about comparing out loud, ask them. Also be careful about pressuring yourself even more than anyone else might: those inside feelings in the pit of your stomach might be a signal that you have to work harder at accepting yourself.

What If You're Older, Younger, or in the Middle?

Many oldest children in their family have told me they feel they get blamed the most (because they should know better), have the most responsibility, have to live up to high expectations, have to set the example, and generally are very pressured.

But not all oldest children feel that way. I know I loved being the oldest. I felt special, don't remember any competition pressure, and felt that my younger brothers and sister looked up to me (most of the time). I don't remember being resentful of them and feel my parents must have worked very hard at making us understand that each one of us was (and is) special but different. Sometimes they got; sometimes I got. But the getting was always fair. I owe my parents a lifetime thank-you for their love and for teaching us to love and appreciate each other.

I think how parents handle their kids and what kind of feelings there are in the home really can affect how kids relate to each other. Just as with Mimi and her sister. Who knows, with different parents, things could have been different between them.

As much as I'd like to think otherwise, not all parents treat their children fairly. Some really do have favorites and don't try to hide their feelings. It's got to hurt a child who feels that a parent really doesn't love him or her as much as the others. That can also cause resentment of brothers or sisters.

But sometimes resentment has nothing to do with how parents deal with their children. Even when parents love each child and try hard to show it, sometimes the resentments that are inside a child are too deep for a parent or even a child to handle and get rid of. Sometimes help from a trained professional (for example, a school counselor or psychologist) will offer understanding and guidance in how to ease the anger and reduce the competition.

One mother of two teenage sons said, "The younger one would love to be friends with the older one. But the older one only 'saw red,' only reacted with a lot of anger and resentment toward the younger one. The anger seemed always to be there and had come out in many different ways."

Some younger children have told me that they resent the fact that the oldest gets more privileges. They sometimes think their older sister or brother gets more attention, gets to spend more time with their parents, seems more important, and is the favorite. Other younger children look up to their older brother or sister, miss them when they're off with their friends and especially if they go off to college or get married and move away, and almost regard them as another parent. The question of favorites doesn't even enter their minds.

Many middle children have shared that they think they're always blamed and that the oldest and the youngest are more special than they are. One parent, now in her forties, told me, "No matter how I try to convince my daughter that I'm not playing favorites, she won't believe me. She's our middle child and thinks that we treat her differently than her older sister and younger brother. No matter how equally we treat them, she will always see her portion as less than theirs or her present as not as nice. I hope one day she realizes we feel she's just as precious as they are."

Also, many younger sisters and brothers have talked with me about feeling left out if their older brothers or sisters seem closer to each other and do more things together. It may help to understand that it doesn't have to mean they love you less, just that they have more in common at this point in their lives. Let them know how much it would mean if they could spend more time with you. But also, it will help you to understand that it's natural for them to "hang out" together. As you grow older, you'll find that the age difference between you will seem less and less. It's natural to feel that it's hard to wait for that day to come.

If they're away at college or live away from home in another town, you can write or call and tell them how much you miss them, how much it would mean if they would write to you. If you don't let them know how you feel, they may never realize how much they mean to you.

From family to family, the feelings between sisters and brothers can be very different. Even in the same family, some brothers and sisters can be closer than others.

Sharing Your Room

If you're sharing a room with your brother or sister right now, and you're thinking, "What a pain!" maybe you'll smile and think it could be worse if you were Ann. Ann, who is now seventy-three, told me stories about how she and her two sisters not only shared a room when they were growing up, but had to share the same bed! (Are you smiling?)

The following stories will give you an idea of what can bother brothers and sisters, as well as what can feel good, when they share a room. Betty, age thirty-seven, told me:

I had no privacy when I was growing up. I would clean my room and my sisters would mess it up. I wanted them out when my friends were over, but I couldn't get rid of them. I never had moments alone for my own thoughts. I couldn't listen to records when I wanted to. When their friends did come over, they touched my things and spilled my perfume bottles. The worst was when I walked into our closet and stepped on my sister's turtle because she was playing with the turtle in the closet and left it in there.

Meredith, age thirteen, said:

> I feel like I don't have much privacy. If my sister and I would have our own rooms, maybe we wouldn't fight as much. We're constantly using each other's clothes and stationery. Sometimes I really get mad at her and I'll write signs on everything that's mine and say, "Do Not Touch. This is Meredith's."
>
> Sometimes it's good. If I get scared at night, my sister is always there. She comes over and stays with me until I fall asleep. If I have trouble with my friends, she gives me good advice.
>
> I feel like we have a very close relationship because we share our room. She can see how I feel. We can read each other's emotions better because we see each other more often.
>
> We're not that far apart in age, but the years still make a difference. Sometimes she comes to me with problems that didn't happen to me yet, so I don't know how to answer her.

Beth, age sixteen, shared:

> I really need to be by myself a lot. But there's no place for me to be alone. My sister sometimes doesn't understand. One time I was on the telephone and she heard something very private. That friend was over one day and my sister said something. I don't think that friend has ever forgiven me.
>
> Sometimes when I tell her something, I don't think she wants to know. She judges me. I just want her to accept what I say. We're very different. We have really different relationships with our parents. I think sometimes she's really jealous of mine, and I'm jealous of hers.
>
> With our beds together, I guess she sees me at my worst times. I don't think we're closer because we share a room. Maybe it's good in a way that we share. Except for wanting to be alone sometimes, she's pretty good about it most of the time.

Jim, age nineteen, said:

> It stinks! I have no privacy. He's older, so he thinks he runs the room. And he comes first, so he gets to put the stereo on, and he gets to listen to what he wants first. If I'm not in bed at a certain time and I wake him up, he gets ticked off. You know, things like that. It doesn't seem like I have many rights. But now he only

comes home on weekends, because he goes to college. So weekdays I have the room all to myself, which is good. It's better than before he went to college. There was just no privacy. He still acts like it's his room.

I think we're less close because we share a room. He's extremely different from me. He's very conservative. He's into boring music, I'm not.

Feeling good about sharing a room seems to be influenced by many things, such as the difference in your ages, your interests, your respect for each other's things, how you treat each other's friends, how much privacy you can have, your study habits, what time you go to bed, what time you wake up, and how neat or messy you are.

Now that you've read about other people's feelings, it's a good time to write down your own (if you share a room). Make a column for what bothers you and a column for what feels good. Put down everything you can think of, and then at the right private time, give your brother or sister the list to read.

Blaming won't help as much as just plain talking about what you'd like to change. Blaming can make the other person not want to listen. For example, if you're bothered by something, it would be better to start with: "When you do this in front of my friends, I really feel embarrassed. I'm not saying you're trying to make me feel that way on purpose. But that's how I feel . . . please don't do that anymore." Instead of: "How could you embarrass me like that in front of my friends? You are so horrible! You're such a loser!" So, the idea is to say what you feel and not approach them in an attacking way.

You might even ask your sister or brother to write his or her own list for you to read. This way, both of you can deal more openly with your feelings and try to work out any differences. That can help you figure out what each of you can do to make living together more positive and fun.

It's Better to Slam Your Pillow than Your Brother or Sister

Depending on how angry you are, you may have a hard time controlling how you let it out. Some kids slam doors; others stomp around on the floor as loudly as they can; others curse and yell; still others smash their sister or brother.

The only problem is that if you hit your sister or brother in the wrong place, it can be dangerous. As much as you might be saying to yourself that some action is deserved, I'm not so sure you'd be happy breaking an arm, busting a nose, or making a bruise that they'll remember for too long.

It's natural for you to get angry every once in a while. The only concern is how you get angry and what you do with your anger. Next time you're about to wind up and sock your sister or brother, think again. Especially think twice if you were about to hit your sister or brother in the face.

Here are some other things you might do that won't put them in the hospital:

- Yell as loud as you can, "I'm so angry at you! I feel like smashing you in the face!"
- Smash your pillow as hard as you can at least twenty times (you can make believe the pillow is her or his face, as long as your sister or brother's face is not on the pillow when you're smashing!).
- Tear up paper into as many little pieces as you can.
- Run around the block.
- Go out and shoot baskets or throw a ball against a wall.
- Go outside and throw a ball up into the air as high as you can. Do that at least ten times.
- Take a shower.
- Slam your fist into a punching bag.
- Take out a piece of paper and just start writing about how you feel.

If you want to settle your argument, remember to wait a little while until everyone is more calm. It's almost impossible to talk things out when you're in a rage. (That's good to remember when you're dealing with your parents, friends, and teachers, too.)

Feelings About Being Twins

In case you're wondering how twins become twins: *Fraternal twins* can be two boys, two girls, or one boy and one girl. They're not identical and often don't even look alike. That's because two separate egg cells are released by a woman's ovaries, instead of one. Both eggs are fertilized separately (only one sperm can enter each egg), and both fertilized eggs plant themselves separately on the wall of the uterus and each of them will develop into a baby.

Identical twins must either be two girls or two boys. They result when a single egg cell is released and fertilized. That single fertilized egg separates into two separate, identical egg cells that plant themselves on the wall of the uterus and develop into two babies who will look exactly alike.

Conjoined twins must either be two girls or two boys. Everything starts the same as with identical twins, but when the one fertilized egg cell separates, it doesn't completely separate. That's why conjoined twins are attached, when born, at some point on their bodies. They develop in the uterus from two identical egg cells that are not quite separated. Depending on where the babies are attached, doctors may or may not be able to separate them after birth (for instance, if they're sharing an organ and each needs it to live).

Triplets (three), *quadruplets* (four) and more: Just increase the numbers I gave you describing twins. For example, if triplets are born, there could be three separate eggs released at about the same time, fertilized separately and planted separately on the wall of the uterus, and you know the rest. Identical triplets are the result of a single fertilized egg cell dividing and separating more than once. If three of those cells attach to the wall of the uterus, three identical babies will develop. There could also be two egg cells that are fertilized. If one divides and the other doesn't, that would also result in having triplets (two will be identical).

Barry, age forty, father of identical twin girls, said, "It always annoys me when people hear you have twins and say, 'Oh double trouble.' I always answer them, 'No, double love.'"

If you aren't a twin, it will be hard to imagine what it would be like having a "double," someone who looks exactly like you or at least someone who was born at the same time as you, even if you don't look alike.

David, age fourteen (an identical twin), said, "I think it's good being a twin. You always have a playmate. There's always a friend there. I always have a person to study with. We play against each other in sports and help each other out if we're not doing something right. Michael's my best friend. But it bothers me when people make mistakes about who is who all the time. It's pain in the neck, and that's frustrating."

Michael, his twin brother, said, "We're very much alike. We have the same feelings. Sometimes we ask each other, 'What are you think-ing,' and very often we're thinking about the same thing. People always try to find ways to tell us apart. Kids at school ask us who we are in the beginning of the day, so they can tell us apart by the clothes we're wear-ing. But I don't think that we look so much alike. When I think of myself, I don't think of myself as a twin. I think of myself as my own person. I don't see that I look like David, I just look like myself. We look so different. We are different."

It might interest you to know that Michael and David also said their grandparents have trouble telling them apart, "and they've known us all our lives."

Rachel, age ten, is an identical twin. She told me, "Sometimes we dress the same, usually we don't. But we feel the same whether dressed like each other or not. When we dress alike, people say it's cute. But when we're not, we're just regular people."

Besides the frustration that's often felt when other people aren't able to tell identical twins apart, there are too many people who think they're just the same. So they relate to them as if they're one person.

Linda, age forty, mother of identical twin girls, said, "I don't think of them as twins. To me, they're two separate people. The only time I get reminded that they're twins is when they dress alike or if someone makes a comment to me."

Like everyone else, twins have their own feelings (even though many of them may be very much alike), their own personalities (though some-times they're similar), and their own dreams (though sometimes they're also the same). That's not unlike the way brothers and sisters who aren't twins might be. It just happens that twins were born at almost the same time, but they're different people.

Yet, there's a specialness about being a twin that I heard of from each twin I've spoken to. Sheilagh, age thirty-two, has a twin brother. (She was the one who snuck peanut-butter sandwiches up to her brother when he was punished.) She told me, "Just being with each other for those nine months, something must have clicked. There's absolutely a bond between us. I often think if I'm sad, *I wonder if he's sad.* Or if I'm troubled, I won-der if he must be troubled, too. I don't stop what I'm doing to call him and find out, but I do think about it. I truly believe it's a miracle when you have two individuals born at the same time. It's magical."

A mother of identical twin boys said, "The boys are special people. It's hard to say how much of that comes from the experience of being twins. It's such a unique experience. As close as we ever feel to them, it's interesting as a parent to know that you're not the closest. They're depending more on each other than on you."

What about competition? Of course, each set of twins (or triplets, or more) will have different feelings, just as brothers and sisters who are not twins will have their own feelings.

Sheilagh remembers identical twin girls who went to high school with her. She said, "I was friends with one of them. They fought over clothes, fought if one of them got something extra. They were vicious with each other. They'd fight if one got a date before the other, if one got her period before the other. I think I would have died if I had to deal with that all the time."

Sheilagh didn't have that with her brother. They were very close, hung around with the same friends, and there was very little competition between them. The only thing she remembers that was hard for her brother was when she passed her driving test before he did. Said Sheilagh, "Imagine, gosh, you're a boy and your twin sister gets her license before you! And she has to drive you around."

Dana, age forty, is an identical twin. She said, "There were never any competition issues that I remember. We were a little bit different; our personalities were different. We had no boyfriend competition. I don't think we ever liked the same boy. We dressed alike up until the sixth grade but in different colors. (I guess then we got smart and realized if we had different clothes, we could have a much bigger wardrobe.) We were always in different classes. My parents never brought us up to compete. I have to credit my parents for that. They never showed any favoritism while we were growing up."

Fourteen-year-old Michael said, "I don't like it when people say to you, 'Who's the better athlete?' 'Who's smarter?' 'Who's stronger?' What do they expect us to say?"

Ten-year-old Lysee (Rachel's twin) shared, "My parents treat us equally. Some of my friends are her friends, and some of her friends are my friends. The only time I feel yuck is if she gets a better mark in school." (Lysee, maybe you would feel better knowing that Rachel told me you have a harder teacher and she has an easier one.)

Besides the natural competition between twins, a lot seems to have to do with parents—what they expect, how much they try to teach each twin and the other children in the family that each is an individual. Each person is different. If parents expect the same things just because children are twins, that's just as unfair as expecting it from any other child in the family.

If you're a twin and feel people are treating the two of you together instead of as individuals, then it's time for you to have one of those private talks. Whether it be your relatives, friends, teachers, or your other brothers and sisters, they may not realize they're treating you that way unless you let them know.

But most of all, you're the one who needs to remember that you are you. You're not your twin, just as you're not any other sister, brother, or anyone else in this world.

One more thing. Though the twins I've spoken with happen to be very close, I'm sure there are twins who are very, very different and may not be close at all. If you are a twin and wish you could be closer to your twin brother or sister, no matter how old you are, it's never too late to try. Just start by turning your feelings into words (out loud or in writing) and hope they'll care enough to listen.

If you're a friend of a twin and are having a hard time separating being friends with one and not so much with the other, then it might also help to talk about your feelings. You don't have to feel the same way about them both; they're not the same person. But it's important for you to deal with your feelings, so you can at least enjoy the relationship you want to enjoy.

And if you're the brother or sister of twins and you feel your parents are playing favorites, it is important to talk with your parents. Or, if you'd like to have a better friendship with one or both of the twins, then talk with them about your feelings. Maybe you can all try harder.

It would also help to realize that—no matter how close you might be with your brothers or sisters who are twins—it may have nothing to do with their lack of love for you if they seem so close to each other. They may really love you very much. But what you might see between them—which makes you think they never feel that way about you—may be that special bond that seems to come from the miracle of being twins.

Feelings About Being an Only Child

Jennifer, age twelve, said:

> I think since my mom and dad are really great, I have a better time
> with my parents. But sometimes, like on weekends, when
> everybody's gone away, then it can get kind of boring.
>
> Some of my friends have older or younger brothers and sisters.
> I see how they really have fun with them, and then I feel kind
> of sad because I don't have any. But then I think of all the other
> things and I'm not sad anymore. Like, I think of how much fun
> I have with my parents. Sometimes I hear my friends saying that
> their moms are kind of boring, or their dads only play with
> them sometimes when they come home from work. So I feel
> happy with my family because my parents spend a lot of time
> with me.
>
> If I had the choice of having a brother or sister now or not, I
> think I'd stay being an only child.

A fourteen-year-old boy told me:

> I guess it seems that only children want to have brothers and
> sisters, and people with brothers and sisters want to be an only
> child! When I talk about this with my friends, they envy me
> because I'm by myself. I don't see why. They're not lonely
> sometimes, like me. I only have a dog to keep me company.
>
> My aunt and uncle have three kids. They're all younger than
> me. I guess I feel like they're my brothers and sisters. I always like
> to play with them. I'm going to sleep over there this weekend.
> Sometimes I envy my cousins. They seem to have everything . . .
> happiness, a nice home, a great family. I feel that they do more
> with their parents than I do with mine.

John, age thirty-three, said:

> Maybe there was a time or several times when I had a desire for
> another sibling [brother or sister]. In the long run, it hasn't made a
> difference. It would have been nice to have a live-in playmate. I
> was lucky enough to have two very intelligent parents who always
> gave me a lot of reading material and spent much time with me. I

went shopping with my mother, played ball with my father, and they never smothered me or overburdened me with attention.

I read huge amounts, and I guess my imagination was running full swing when I was little. I could turn anything into a game, like a cardboard box from a grocery store. It became necessary to be creative. I had to make up my own fun.

Ten-year-old Ken said, "I wish I had a brother or sister. Even if we fought, it would be better to fight than not have anyone around at all."

One thirty-year-old woman told me, "I learned how to keep myself busy when I couldn't see my friends, so I didn't miss having a brother or a sister. But I did always feel as though I was in the middle between my parents, and that keeping peace in the house was my responsibility."

Ellen, age forty, said:

Being an adopted only child, I wish I had a brother or sister. I was told that when I was three years old, my parents were offered a chance to adopt another child. It turned out that it was a boy. My father didn't want a boy, only another girl. So they said no. I asked them, 'Why didn't you adopt whatever you got?' A boy or girl would have given me a brother or sister. I can't understand why my father couldn't see past "girl." I feel terrible that I don't have a brother or sister.

I don't have a real family. That part of it is really hard. Maybe that's why I relied so much on my parents. I couldn't ever say, 'I hate that little kid' or, 'I wish I were my older sister.' I wish I had the choice to love or hate. If I had a brother or sister, maybe I would have hated it. But not having one, I wish I had.

I can only tell you what I miss. Two years ago, I was with a friend of mine when she got a call telling her that her brother's wife had their first child. She said, 'I'm an aunt!' A little while later I started crying. I realized I would never be an aunt. I hope I'm a grandmother someday.

Maybe you share some of these feelings. What would you add?

If you're an only child and are sad because you want a brother or sister and know you probably won't ever have one, all you can do is tell your parents how you feel and hope they'll seriously consider what you say.

Adding children to your family is up to your parents. If they've decided not to, or weren't able to, there must be a reason. You might feel better if you asked them to explain. (It might help to remember that just because you have a brother or sister around doesn't mean you will definitely feel good and be less lonely. There are no guarantees.)

In John's case, being alone forced him to become creative. He was always able to figure out something to do. Just because you're an only child and you're alone doesn't mean you have to be lonely. They're two different things. If you find yourself lonely, you can decide to do something about it. Invite a friend over, curl up with a good book, write a story, ask if you can stay overnight with your cousins, listen to music, watch a movie, bake something yummy. Try asking your parents if they can get you a pet.

Being your parents' only child makes you a most precious gift to them. If you don't already feel special, you deserve to start.

Feelings About Being Adopted

Kevin, age nineteen, shared:

> I was adopted before I was a year old. You know how kids have birthday parties? Well, the first thing I remember was that I always had two birthday parties. One on my birthday and one on the day they got me.
>
> My first blanket was the one I had in the orphan home. My first squeeze toy was also from before I was adopted. They brought those things home with me and always told me, "Oh yeah, you brought those home with you when we got you." They made me feel special. It didn't make me feel weird. It wasn't like, wow, I'm so different from the other kids. It was more that I was special.
>
> My parents read me all the children's books they could find for kids who were adopted. That made me feel special when I was a little kid. I have a younger brother who was also adopted. My mother is Irish Catholic and his parents were probably Eastern European. When people look at my brother and me they often say, "You don't look alike. Are you really brothers?"

I wanted to know what my real mom called me. Was it Baby X or Fido or what? But my new parents told me they kept the name my mother gave me because they were so grateful to whoever she was.

I didn't really think about being adopted until I was a teenager. I didn't know how kids are born until I was older. I didn't know what sex was. Then I'd think about it and wonder, who was my mother, who was my father? Didn't they like me? I tried to explain it to myself and make excuses because there were so many unanswered questions.

I don't ever want to look for them. My parents really love me.

John, age thirty-three, said:

My parents first told me I was adopted when I was about three years old. Their way of dealing with it was telling me that I was specially chosen, and that they went to a place where there were so many babies all over the place. But they wanted a special baby. And that was me. Throughout my life, I really haven't given it a second thought.

I guess if you're getting a lot of love and support, it really doesn't make a whole lot of difference as to who your parents were and why they didn't keep you. I feel it would be no more different for a child to be adopted than to take a puppy away from its mother and raise it and love it in someone else's home.

I'm very happy with the way I've been raised and the way I was taken in and welcomed by everyone. They were my family. They were my relatives from the start. Nothing was ever said or hinted at that it was otherwise.

I can't even remember anyone making a crack about my being adopted when I was in elementary school. If someone said to me, "If you could have lived with your real parents, would you have wanted to?" I could never say yes to that. What's real is the family that I have always known—my now family.

Maybe the reason so many adopted children search for their biological parents is that they want to find their roots. They're searching for their identity, where they came from. They also may be curious. They may get information that they've always been searching for and one day go knocking on their biological (birth) parents' door. I imagine that would come as a great shock for the parent(s). I would guess there might be an overflowing of emotions at that moment. Maybe a great sigh of relief from the child who's been searching. (Sometimes the parent who has given the child up for adoption is the one who searches for the child). There's no telling where the relationship will go from there. There's no telling if the parent(s) really will even want an active relationship with their child, after so many years of not having them as part of their lives. There's no telling if the child will feel good with his or her biological parent(s).

Some children want to know about their biological parents. Others, like John and Kevin, never want to know. This is so personal. But perhaps the most important, wonderful thing is that children can be adopted in the first place. Adopted children can have special, warm, close family feelings the same as children brought into that family by actual birth. In fact, many babies are brought to their new homes shortly after birth. Others are adopted much later.

But no matter when a child is adopted, adoption is a blessing. It gives adults a chance to be parents—and gives a boy or girl a home and a family they may never have had otherwise.

Grandparents and Other Relatives

An uncle you think is wonderful may seem like an old fogey to your brother or sister. Your elderly aunt may have a twinkle in her eyes when she looks at you that gives you the message that you're special. You may think your mother's sister understands you even better than your mother does.

Your cousins may be a real treat to be with one day and real pains another. Sometimes the comparisons people make between you and your cousins may seem worse to you than being compared with your sister or brother or your friends. You may think your aunt cooks meat like shoe leather, or that your uncle's cigar smells gross.

You may live near your relatives, far away, or anywhere in between. You may think you see your relatives too often or not enough. It just depends. It depends upon so many things.

As you read through the many feelings about relatives that were shared with me, think about your own feelings for your own relatives.

Jennifer, age twelve, said, "The only aunt who I really ever see is my aunt Dorothy. She's really great! She takes me places, and I always feel like she's spending too much on me. I really love her."

Marlene, age eighteen, said, "I love visiting my aunt Sylvia and I am sorry I only get to see her about three times a year. The last time I saw her, she took me shopping for my college clothes. We had so much fun. We ran around from one place to another and got so much done in such a little time. I wish my mother had that kind of energy. I feel cheated. Sometimes I wish my aunt was my mother."

Michael, age eleven, told me that he loves to visit his cousin. Since he has only younger sisters, it's great when he can spend time with a boy cousin who's almost his age.

Will, age twelve, told me, "For a while lately we thought my aunt and uncle would get divorced. They've been having a lot of problems. He's the laid-back macho kind of man who doesn't want to be seen at a counselor or anything like that. My aunt saw a counselor and took her children. They had to do it in secret because my uncle was against their going. But then they got him to go. I think it helped a little."

Hank, age twenty-two, said, "My father's brother, Ed, has been more like a father to me than an uncle. I have always felt I could talk with him about personal things, and he always made time for me. When it came time to decide if I could go to college, since no one in my family ever did, Uncle Ed was the one who encouraged me to try."

Leslie, age ten, told me that she loves to go shopping with her grandmother but she hates when her grandmother buys her cousin the same clothes that she buys for Leslie.

Elaine, now thirty-five, remembers her favorite uncle with love and sadness. She said, "I always called him Unk. He gave me my first tennis racket when I was eight and spent hours teaching me how to play. He taught me about music, took long walks with me, and called me funny nicknames. I loved him so much and we were very close. The sad part is that he moved far away after his divorce. He hasn't contacted our family or written me in years. I can't understand where all that love could have gone."

Nicole, age nine, said, "I love visiting my cousins. They live in a big house in the country, and I get to ride horses."

Peter, age fifteen, said, "I hate it when my relatives come. My father has never liked my aunt Betty, and every time we have another holiday to plan, my parents fight for hours about how much my mother wants to see her family and how much my father hates them."

Jeanne, age ten, said, "It's not fair that I always have to invite my cousin to my birthday parties with my friends."

Martin, age fourteen, said, "I love to have dinners at my aunt's house. She's such a super cook and my mom's cooking is a disaster. My mom is great at heating up frozen dinners. That's about all. I love her, but I can't stand her food. At least at my aunt's we can have a feast."

So many different feelings for so many different relatives. This is probably a good time for you to grab a piece of paper (if you haven't already) and make your own list of favorites. Think about who's at the top of your list and who you'd like to scratch off if you could.

Also think about all the things that might make you feel the way you do. Are there any relatives whom you have disliked for things that you realize are not their fault? Are you making unfair judgments or comparisons?

For example, do you think your cousin is a wimp because he or she can't play ball the way you do? Are your cousins no fun to visit? Do they embarrass you every time they come to your home and you have to include them in games with your friends? It can make a big difference if you accept that your cousins are just not athletic. Then, you can still play, but not expect them to be better than they are. Or, perhaps you can think of something else to do while you're together.

If you're lucky enough to have grandparents that you know, you probably already know how special they can be. Grandparents just seem to understand even when parents don't. Grandparents will often have time to listen, when parents don't. Grandparents just love to go fishing, to ball games, and to the zoo.

Sometimes, even if parents are old-fashioned, grandparents can be "with it." When you least expect it, your grandparent may slip you a dollar or two. Grandparents have been known to lend or just plain give large sums of money so their grandchildren can go to college or start a business or follow any other dream.

Most grandparents are wonderful, but there are always a few who are grouchy, nosy, or just not interested. Some are overprotective and don't let their grandchildren do things for themselves, even when they can, and even when their parents allow them.

Some live close by and can see you often; others live farther away and may come for a week or two to visit several times each year. Still others may live with you all the time. (That can be wonderful. You may also find at times you feel it's tough on privacy, since they're always around. As much as you may love them, every once in a while, you may wish you could be alone with your parents and brothers or sisters. That's a natural wish.)

Grandparents come in all different ages, shapes, and sizes. Some are healthy, some frail, some ill. Some grandparents are forgetful. But most, if not all, are lovable and to be treasured.

Here are some ways you can get to know your grandmother or grandfather even better. If your grandparents are no longer alive, you can still ask these questions about them, so when you look at their pictures, your smile can be a little wider and you'll feel you know them better.

This list can also be used for parents, aunts, uncles, friends' parents, teachers, and other adults.

> *Ask them to tell you about when they were growing up (be sure to add your own questions, too):*
> - Where did they grow up?
> - What were their parents and family like when they were young?
> - What about their family feelings?
> - What was it like living where they did?
> - If they went to school, what was it like?
> - What subjects were their favorites? Which didn't they like?
> - If they went to church or synagogue or another house of worship, what was it like? How did they observe religious holidays?
> - What was the world like then? Was there peace? What about the wars? How did what was going on affect their everyday life?
> - What did they dream about? Did they have any secret wishes?
> - What were their hobbies? Did they play any sport?

- What things were invented when they were younger?
- How did these inventions change their life?
- Were they ever lonely? When?
- Do they remember their first girlfriend or boyfriend?
- What was dating like?
- What was it like to talk with their parents about dating and sex and other personal things? (Did they ever talk about these things?)
- What are their feelings about the way they have lived their life?
- What would they change? How could they live their life differently if they could?
- What kind of things make them happy? What are their fears?
- What's their favorite flavor of ice cream?
- What's their favorite food?
- What's their favorite book? Now and when they were little?
- What about music?
- Have them tell you stories about your mother or father when they were growing up.

Share your experiences with them.
- Tell them about school.
- Let them in on a few secrets.
- Tell them about your friends.
- Talk about what bothers you, what scares you, and what you love.
- Talk about family feelings.
- Share your dreams.

Have your grandmother (or your grandfather) write down some of their favorite recipes for you. Take pictures of your grandparents every so often and make sure to have someone take several of you and your grandparents together.

Remember to tell them, "I love you." No matter how many times they hear it, they'll love to hear it again.

As I told you at the end of Chapter 19, it can mean so much to try to share your life with the people you love as much as you can and make an extra effort to show them you care.

Jamie, age sixteen, told me that she and her brother asked their grandparents to speak into a video camera and tell the story of their lives. It's something they'll always have.

Just because you're together with your grandparent doesn't mean you'll want to have long conversations every time. Maybe on some visits you'll get to speak for hours. On others, you might only have time for one or two questions. And sometimes, you may just feel like sitting together silently, feeling the closeness you have in a nonverbal way.

Lots of people mistakenly think they're supposed to talk every minute they're together. Sometimes it's just nice to be together in silence. But at least if you wish to talk, you now have lots of things to talk about.

Since it's not always so easy to get private time, this can be great table conversation for the whole family. You and any brothers or sisters would probably be fascinated to hear the story of your grandparent's life. Your parents would, too. (Remember, you can ask your parents to tell you about their life stories, too.)

As you continue to grow up, and all through your life, I hope you'll be blessed with the chance to share family feelings that feel good to you. If they don't feel good, perhaps now you'll be better able to talk about what doesn't feel good and realize if both people care enough, you can try to work together to make the feelings better.

But if the feelings are bad and you're the only one who wants them to improve, I also hope you'll find the strength to accept that you cannot change or force anyone to care about you if the feeling is not within them—or if they don't want to. Even if the bad feelings are from parents, grandparents, brothers, sisters, aunts, uncles, or cousins. Those bad feelings don't mean that you're not important . . . just that the relationship isn't working, isn't meaningful, isn't meant to be—unless the feelings change.

When there's nothing there—no matter how deeply you dig—then as painful as it may be to walk away, you can and must try to create new family feelings elsewhere, with friends and other family members.

Chapter 22

DEALING WITH DEATH

Maybe you're wondering if you should read this chapter or not. After all, death is not something that's very pleasant. It may make you sad or scared even to think about it. Those feelings are very natural.

So why should you choose to read about death? Well, the fact is, death is a part of each person's life. Yours, mine, and everyone's. Maybe you've already experienced someone's death and have felt the feelings that are part of losing someone you love very much. Or maybe a dog, cat, bird, hamster, goldfish, calf, or horse of yours died.

Maybe you've never talked about death with anyone. Many people keep feelings about death to themselves (adults as well as kids). That's why they may not realize that other people have similar feelings.

Many kids have talked with me about not knowing what to say or how to act with a close relative or friend who is very seriously ill and is expected to die very soon. They want to know what they might say to comfort a friend when a person in their friend's family has died. They want to know how to deal with their feelings if this loss happens to them.

They're not sure how to make themselves or anyone else feel better if their pet has been hit by a car or has to be put to sleep when a veterinarian (an animal doctor) has to inject an animal that is too ill to live with medicine that causes them to die.

This chapter will help you deal with death in a kind, comforting, honest way. You'll find that here, too, you can turn your feelings into words. I hope it will help you to understand how death is another thing all of us must try hard to accept, since we don't have the power to change it.

Death Is Forever

This is one of the things that's so hard to accept and understand, no matter how old you are. Some parents think that their kids will be too sad if they know the truth, so they tell them Grandma has "gone to sleep" or Uncle Ned has "gone away." But these well-meaning parents somehow can't bring themselves to say that these relatives and friends are never coming back.

If your parent told you that about someone you loved, you may have spent many years watching out the window, checking the mail, and running to answer the telephone, hoping and expecting your Uncle Ned would return. Each time the doorbell rang at holiday time, you might have imagined it was your Uncle Ned finally coming back to surprise you. Or you may have been afraid to go to sleep at night, thinking that if Grandma went to sleep and never came back, you didn't want the same thing to happen to you.

Cartoons on television sometimes show steamrollers flattening out funny characters so they can't move, only to have them spring back to life the next minute. Cartoon animals and cartoon people that get pushed off cliffs always seem to appear moments later, fine as can be, ready for their next adventure. Cartoon people that get shot dead seem magically able to recover. They always come back.

But those are cartoons—not real life. Death in real life is forever. It's not sleeping, even though a dead person's eyes may be closed. Death is more like a peaceful stillness, a quieting.

When people die, their hearts stop beating, their brains stop working, and all the organs of their bodies stop functioning (working). They no longer have the supply of blood and oxygen needed to stay alive.

But when people sleep, their hearts still beat, their brains still work, and all their organs are getting the food, blood, and oxygen needed to remain healthy. That's a very big difference. So during sleep you are resting and giving your body a rest, but your body never stops working. In death, you and your body stop working forever. There's no returning.

What About Losing Your Pet?

When an animal dies, it is also forever.

Neal, age thirteen, shared his feelings about when his dog had to be put to sleep last year:

> I was talking to my mom on the back porch. I don't exactly remember what we were talking about. But I had a funny feeling, and I said to her, "You're not putting the dog to sleep, are you?"
>
> She wasn't really saying anything like that, but I just had feelings about it. She went in to talk with my dad and when she came out, she said they were thinking about it, that the dog was very old and very sick, and they thought it was time. I started crying.
>
> My mom said we were going to do it in a week. So I spent a lot of time with my dog that week. I let her do anything she wanted. When we had to take the dog to the vet to be put to sleep, that was traumatic.
>
> When we had gone to the vet before, she never liked it. So as soon as we brought her there, she didn't want to go in. It was like she didn't want to die. The vet told us she would probably be gone by the time we got home.
>
> It took me a while to accept it. I think probably I was kind of like in shock for a while, almost like I didn't feel any feelings about it. I'd say that after three or four months, I kind of started to accept it. But a year from the day she died, I was still crying about it. Not every day. But maybe once a month or something. I think the last time I felt so bad and felt like crying was about two months ago.
>
> I used to come home and expect to have to walk her. Then I'd realize she wasn't there any more. My parents didn't really say too much. They were basically just there for me. I had a friend who had just gone through the same thing, so that helped a lot.

Pets are almost like people in so many homes. They're loved, cared for, and often spend more time with kids than real people do. Pets can fill the gap of loneliness; pets won't tell your secrets; pets can be best friends. No matter what kind of pet you have, the feelings of closeness, the attachment, and the love, can be very special.

Even a year after Neal's dog was put to sleep, he shed tears from knowing that he won't ever be able to be with his dog again. Even if he gets another dog, it will never be the same as that one.

In the same house with the same pet, each person has his or her own feelings. Jeremy, age twelve, told me:

> We had a little cat. She was just a kitten, and she was run over by a car. We were on a trip. And when we got home, my mother and sister just sat on the couch and cried. I just couldn't really figure out why they were doing that. Sure you can be sad, but . . . Now I understand, but it just didn't seem like they needed to cry. They cried for about an hour. It was weird because I didn't feel like crying. So I sat at the other end of the couch and just watched them and thought, "What are they doing?"
>
> I don't think I was as close to the cat as my mom. My mom let me pet her every once in a while. But unless we sneaked and quickly petted her, she was really shy and ran away. It was hard to get near her because my mom was the only one who fed her. They had our neighbors bury her. I asked if I could go down and ask them where they buried her, and they wouldn't let me go down. I couldn't see why. They said they just didn't want to know.

Just like with people, each pet is different, and each relationship is different. One pet may prefer to sit on your lap rather than on your brother's. Another will run to your sister before anyone else. It often depends on who spends the time, who feeds, and who really goes out of his or her way to show the pet love. It's not so different with people, is it?

If Neal ever gets a new dog, his parents will be replacing a pet but never the actual dog. No living being can exactly replace another, be it a person or an animal. They can only be themselves and create their own place.

That's why, when parents think they can just switch one new goldfish for the dead one that they had to flush down the toilet while their child was at school, many little kids will be smart enough to notice that they shwoosh their tails a little differently or the spot that was on the fin is no longer there.

Even though parents may be trying to protect their child from sad, hurt feelings, I question whether they're really doing their child a favor. Some parents don't want to deal with it themselves, because they don't know how to handle the feelings with their child.

Maybe besides buying a new goldfish, which can be fun to shop for together, parents could give their children a far greater gift if they allowed them, starting from an early age, to learn to deal with all the kinds of feelings that are so much a part of life, even if it meant that they'd be sad for a while. And that includes dealing honestly with death.

Kids have told me about special canary burials in shoe boxes with candle ceremonies and speeches. They've talked about the funeral service they held before flushing their last goldfish into "fish heaven."

Somehow, when you're included and are even allowed to plan for the funeral, it not only gives you the chance to be at peace with your loss, it gives you practice for when people you care about die, too.

Death Knows No Age

One of my students just told me that his sister was killed a few weeks ago. She was seven years old and was hit by a car when she ran out into the street in front of their house so she could get ice cream.

Robin, age eleven, told me, "My friend's mother died when she was five. Now she has another mother and acts like nothing ever happened. When we had parents visit school, she just said, 'Well, my mother's coming, too.' I don't think I would be able to adjust the way she did."

Ben, age eighteen, talked about his brother's death two years ago. He was twenty-eight years old when he became ill and died. He had a wife and two-year-old son. Ben said, "It just doesn't seem fair."

Sharon, age twelve, shared how good she felt that she was able to know her great-grandma for so long. Said Sharon, "When she died in the beginning of this year, she was ninety-three years old. I was very sad, but I knew I was lucky to even be able to know her at all."

Fred, age thirty-one, said, "I think one of the most difficult times while I was growing up was when my friend died. We were in tenth grade and it was during the summer. A lot of us spent hours each day practicing our diving in a nearby swimming pool. One afternoon my friend cut his dive a little close and hit his head on the side of the pool. The emergency squad took care of him really fast, but he had damaged his brain and died three days later. We were all in shock. He was only sixteen years old."

Some kids probably still think that death is only for those who are old. But death knows no age. Death will take infants, children, teenagers, parents, grandparents, and all others. Death will take friends. Death will take the rich as well as the poor, the popular and famous as well as the lonely. Death will take one person, two, whole families, or entire cities of people all at once. Death is not choosy.

Though We Can't Prevent Death, We at Least Can Try to Live Longer

Though it's not within our power to prevent death, we can try not to put ourselves in risky situations that play games with death. Unfortunately, too many people die long before they would have otherwise, because they were careless, took chances, or had poor health habits and didn't get proper health care.

Paying more attention to what you're allowing yourself to do can help you in your efforts to live a longer life. You can be careful crossing the street, not run out between two parked cars, not drive with someone who has been drinking, not swing a baseball bat too close to someone's head, not run down the stairs holding scissors, not go swimming alone, not play with guns. Being careful might add years to your life, as well as to the lives of those you love, and those you don't even know.

Making sure you're healthy is very important now and all through your life. Try to have breakfast each morning, eat foods that are good for you, and get enough rest and exercise. Be sure to get regular check-ups with your family doctor or health clinic. Don't forget to have your teeth and eyes examined, too. If there's anything at all that doesn't feel right to you, even if you think it's silly and will probably go away by itself, say something about it. It may be nothing. But if it's something, usually the earlier you check it out and get the right medicine or treatment, the better off you are. You deserve to give yourself the proper care.

Death Teaches Us a Lot

As much as you may be saying to yourself, "Why do I even have to think of these things? It doesn't make me feel very good," knowing about death is as important as knowing about life. Death is a part of life. In fact, death is probably the only thing in life that you can be sure of.

Knowing about death teaches us that we shouldn't waste time. Death teaches us to appreciate the little things, as well as the big, and not take the people we love for granted.

A fourteen-year-old boy said, "I've been thinking about my grandfather dying. I don't know if I could go on living without him. I've been seeing that he's getting older, a little more forgetful. I love him so much. He just went away on a trip. I've been thinking, what if he never comes back? When he does come back, I want to spend as much time as possible with him."

Death challenges us to live, to share, and to love as fully as we can each day.

If Someone Is Very Sick and You Know They Will Probably Die Soon

Dealing with this is not easy. It can be painful and sad. You might feel cheated that you didn't have more time with that person. You might be very angry. You might say to yourself, "Why him?" Or, "Why does she have to suffer so much? It's just not fair."

No, it's probably not! But, as I've said before, life isn't fair all the time. This is one of the times it isn't. So, since you don't have the power to change the illness, the only thing to try to figure out is what you *can* do.

If the ill person is at home (sometimes they may even be at your home), you don't have to be concerned with visiting rules, such as at a hospital. You can see him or her as much as you wish. Remember, though, that they might be tired. So you may want to make more short visits rather than fewer long visits.

You can make pictures for the ill person, write him or her poems, play music, read aloud, or just sit quietly together, feeling close. You can go back to the list at the end of the chapter titled "Family Feelings" and ask about their childhood and how they feel about different times of their life. You can talk about yourself, your family, your friends, school, what you hope to do in the summer, and so many more things.

You can also talk about your feelings about their illness. If you're very sad, you can say, "I'm very sad you're so sick." If you're thinking you're going to miss them, you might want to ask your mom, dad, or someone else close if it's okay to say that. (Sometimes, people who are very sick aren't told how sick they are. So you need to find out how much they know.) If it's okay to tell them, you can say, "I'm really going to miss you."

Ronnie, age thirty, shared, "I had a very close friend who was sick for several years. Last year her illness became worse and she reached a point where the doctors said she only had a few weeks to live. I was having a lot of trouble with my feelings, mainly because I kept them inside. I realized that I hadn't told her how much I loved her, and I didn't know if I should say anything because I knew if I started talking, I would probably start crying and never stop. I spoke with another friend, who suggested that I write my feelings down and give them to her. Finally, I did. In my letter, I told her I loved her. I will always be grateful that I did. She died two weeks later. I think if I never told her, I would have felt sorry for the rest of my life."

Ronnie's sharing of what she felt helped her not to look back and feel guilty or sorry. She was at peace with herself for taking the chance to share her feelings, as hard as that might have been.

If the person is in the hospital, you can ask if your parents or other relatives will take you to visit. If you don't like the smell of hospitals or the look of the tubes and things like that, tell your family your feelings. You might have to try harder to overlook the tubes (if you can) so you can realize that behind the tubes is a person you love very much who will feel so good to see you.

Even if that person only opens his or her eyes every once in a while, if you are there at that moment, it will mean so much. (You might even notice smile wrinkles around the corners of the person's eyes. You also might notice a few tears because they're so happy you're with them.)

Sometimes when a person is too sick to open his or her eyes, you can just sit close by and maybe touch an arm or hold a hand.

It may be hard seeing someone you remember as being healthy lying in bed with hardly any energy or strength. The sick person may not even be able to sit up, seeming to waste away because he or she lost so many pounds from the illness. It's hard seeing someone you love suffer.

In fact, that's why there are so many cases in the newspaper of families who want to "pull the plug" on the machines that are keeping their relatives alive. They often feel they would rather allow their relative to die sooner, but with dignity and a sense of respect, than to be kept alive by being attached to so many tubes and machines. There are lots of feelings about this, both for and against a person's or family's right to decide to stop the treatments or machines.

If you really don't like to go to hospitals and think you'll be too upset to go, then you can write a letter, card, poem, or story and have your mom, dad, or someone else read it to the sick person. You can also speak into an audiocassette tape that can be played for the ill person to hear.

If Your Friend Is Sad Because Someone He or She Loves Is Very Ill or Dies

Eleven-year-old Danielle said, "My friend's mother is very sick and is going to die. I don't know what to say. When I say something, I always feel it's the wrong thing. How should I act around her, because I can't forget that her mother's dying?"

First of all, you can suggest some of the ideas I just gave you. Maybe that will give your friend a better idea of how she can share her feelings with her mother. As a good friend, you might also tell her how sorry you are about her mother. If you're not sure what to say, you can tell her, "I just never know if I'm saying the right thing." Or, "I wish I could help."

Your friend may feel comforted if you let her know it's okay to come to you if she feels like talking. You can also tell her it's fine if she just wants to be together with you—silently. She doesn't have to worry about talking.

Neal, age thirteen, shared:

Just recently my friend's father died. He's had a couple of other experiences with death. A dog and a couple of birds of his died. His father was in the hospital for about four months and then he died. So it wasn't a great surprise or anything. He died two weeks later than they thought he would. I think his relatives gave him support. They talk to him a lot and are really open. Many of the friends he feels open with have gone through or are going through things like divorces or deaths.

I think it's becoming a little more common to see these topics on TV and in real life. We're kind of introduced to them earlier, so we're more prepared and can accept it more easily. But for some people, if they're very dependent on the person who died, it can really take a toll on them.

When Death Comes Suddenly, Without Warning

While Neal might have been more prepared for his friend's father's death because he was sick for several months, there are other situations that can come as a shock. If parents or other loved ones die from a sudden illness or in a car accident, there's no warning, no preparation, no time even to think about saying good-bye.

This is particularly hard to imagine and even harder to accept—for adults as well as kids. It's scary to know that from one day to another, there's very little control over many things, like accidents, that could take us by surprise and change—or end—our lives.

Instead of walking around worrying that something terrible will happen at any moment, we're much better off directing our energies to all that we *can* control. That is, we can work at appreciating those we love and showing our appreciation, sharing ourselves, getting to know our loved ones, and actively living our lives as fully as possible. Then, if someone we love is taken from us suddenly, or even after long suffering, we at least can find strength in knowing that we made the most of the time that we *did* have.

If Someone You Love Dies

When someone you love dies, you may have many different emotions, including surprise, shock, disbelief, anger, and sadness, until you are able to reach the point where you can really accept that the person is physically no longer with you.

Even when you know the illness has gotten worse and there's little time left to share, it's so hard to be prepared for such a loss. That's probably because you can't fully anticipate or feel the feelings of loss until the person dies. Until then, you only can imagine how losing someone feels. Only after their death will the loss be final.

In the weeks or months after the death, it may take a while before you stop saving reports to show them, stop expecting them to come home for dinner, stop planning to tell them something only to realize you can no longer do that. Holiday and birthday time may make you especially sad because of relatives (and others) who have died and can't physically be with you.

Each person will react to news of death in his or her own way. Some will cry. Some might scream. Some will just get very quiet and go off by themselves. Some people may not cry until weeks later, when the death begins to become real to them. Kids have talked with me about trying to cry at funerals. They thought that their relatives would think they didn't love the person as much if they didn't cry. Some kids even questioned their own love, confused about why they didn't feel like crying (when most other people were).

But crying, whether right away or later, is not a measure of love. It's simply a good way to get out your emotions. Some people let themselves cry in front of people, some cry privately. Some don't cry at all. Crying is very personal.

In 1936 my mother wrote down her reaction to her grandfather's death in her diary:

October 22: While doing my homework about ten thirty, Daddy

walked in and said that Grandpa had died. I can't believe it yet. He was sick for nine weeks, poor thing. We stayed over at my aunt's, and everyone cried terribly. Dear Grandpa. Tomorrow is the funeral. I can't imagine him buried.

October 23: We didn't sleep all night because mother was coming home from upstate with the undertaker. [They brought her grandfather home to be buried.] Grandma and all the family came to my house. We all carried on terribly. Then we went to the chapel. I couldn't help but cry because I couldn't believe that Grandpa died. We then went to cemetery, and they put Grandpa in the ground. I'll never see him again. I still can't believe it.

Death Can Be a Blessing

As much as we might wish that the people we love could live forever, those dreams of forever can fade when serious illness strikes. Especially if there's a lot of suffering, those who are watching it from the sidelines might begin to feel that death would be a blessing. In fact, the person who is ill might think that, too.

In such instances, as hard as it is to say death's final good-bye, the people who live on are almost relieved, because they know in their hearts that death has taken that person out of his or her suffering and finally put him or her at peace.

Illness always takes its toll. The longer the illness, the more likely it is to drain the emotions of other family members who have to sit by and watch the suffering. Illness often requires a lot of attention, discussions with doctors, painful decisions, visits back and forth. Sometimes relatives live close by; other times, they're thousands of miles—even continents—away. The knowledge that someone close is ill is always on your mind. Besides everything else, medical care over long periods of time can cost a lot of money.

So, if someone close is breathing only because he or she is attached to a machine, or is in a coma, or has trouble eating, or seems to have become "half of themselves" because of all the lost weight, or is in pain most of the time, try not to be too hard on yourself if you find yourself feeling that death would be a blessing. The person who is ill may just be feeling the same thing.

Funerals

When a person dies, the family usually arranges for a funeral service. Each religion has its own customs, laws, and beliefs about when to schedule the service and how soon after death the person must be buried (lowered into a grave, usually at a cemetery) or cremated (turned into ashes).

The funeral service can be a source of great comfort, as well as a beautiful chance to talk about how much that person meant to his or her family and friends. It's like saying good-bye in public in front of relatives, friends, and all others who wish to attend so they can pay their respects.

If someone close died in your family, did your parents allow you to attend the funeral service? Some parents think their children won't be able to handle the service, so they don't let them come. Other parents may think it's fine for you to attend the service but not the burial (at the cemetery). Some parents try to make their children go to the service even if the child feels strongly about not wanting to go. Still other parents give their children a choice.

Parents have many different feelings about letting their children be part of a funeral. Their reaction often has to do with how comfortable or uncomfortable they are themselves.

My mother was allowed to attend the service and the burial for her grandmother. Once again, her feelings were saved all these years in her diary. This time it's from Wednesday, May 5, 1937:

> Early in the morning we prepared for the funeral. I went with the family to the chapel. We cried so much, because it was so awful— just losing Grandpa six months ago. I saw her in the casket and she looked lovely, as if she was just sleeping. My friend and her mother were so nice, they watched over me and couldn't refrain from crying, too. They felt the same way I did.
>
> We went to the cemetery. It was a horrible sight as Grandma was lowered. It didn't take long and we went home never to see her again. I'll always remember her, she was so sweet to me.

As my mother shared, it can be very difficult to watch a loved one be lowered into a grave. Perhaps that's the part that parents try to protect their children from, by telling them they can't go to the cemetery.

That's a very personal decision, and of course, parents need to know their own child to help them make the decision that will be best for him or her at the time.

But just because it's sad and you may cry doesn't mean you should stay away from saying a final good-bye to someone you love. It's important to learn that you can deal with sadness, as well as be able to enjoy all the happy things. Just because the experience might upset you doesn't mean it is the wrong decision to go. As long as you understand what the experience will be like, what you can expect to see, and what you can do if you don't feel like staying to watch, you should be able to handle it. For example, parents might tell their child if they feel too uncomfortable or it's too upsetting to stay at the service or the burial, he or she can hold on to their parent's hand even tighter, or walk out of the room, or walk away from the grave site. The parent can promise to walk with them so they know they won't have to deal with this alone.

Chances are, you'll always be thankful you pushed yourself to go, if deep down you want to and your parents will let you. If you don't want to go, and your parents are giving you the choice, try to talk about your feelings with them, so they can help you understand whatever decision you wish to choose. It's natural to feel that funerals are tough to handle. Adults often feel this way, too. Whether or not you attend, you can still say private prayers.

Death can teach you to appreciate life. My own son had never gone to a cemetery until he was thirteen years old, when he went to his closest friend's grandmother's funeral. At the grave site in the cemetery, my son watched as the casket was lowered into the ground. The men began to shovel dirt over the casket. And as the casket was almost covered, my son started crying hysterically. I held him close as he continued to watch through his tears. Soon he stopped crying and just stood there watching in disbelief. He whispered to me, "She's gone!"

After that he said it had never been so clear to him before—that when a person dies, he or she is never coming back. Though it was a painful lesson, no book or talk could have given him the understanding he felt from being there. He told me afterward that he wanted to start seeing his own grandparents more.

If you want to be part of the funeral and your parents won't let you, it is important to let them know. You can say, "I know you don't think I'm old enough, but I really want to be there." Or, "Maybe you think

I can't handle it, but please don't keep me away. It means a lot to me. If I get upset, I'll walk away or get back into the car. I want to try to handle it."

It may help to remind your parents that a funeral is an experience that happens only once for each person. There's no second chance to go if they keep you away. Especially if you're very close with the relative or friend who died, keeping away would be hard and you might not ever forget that you couldn't go. If you're old enough to be reading this right now, you're old enough to talk with your parents about what choice you want to make.

If your parent is pushing you to attend and you feel very strongly about not going, you might say: "Please, this is too uncomfortable for me. I love _____ very much. But I just don't think I can handle being there. Please understand."

Again, not wanting to be at a funeral doesn't mean you love that person less, just as crying is not a measure of love. It may be hard for your parents to think about this clearly because they might very much want you to go. They may feel hurt, think that you're not being respectful, think that "if you loved" that person, you would want to be there—no matter what. They may also feel they need your support and want you by their side.

There are many feelings to consider and try to understand. The decision to attend a funeral is very personal. The more you talk about and explore your feelings with the people who are close with you (especially your parents), the more clearly you'll be able to decide what is best for you to do.

A Time for Grief

Usually after someone dies, family and friends gather together so they can give each other support and strength, and offer comfort to each other. Neighbors and relatives often bring cookies, cakes, and even whole meals to help out during this difficult time. This is considered a period of grief or mourning or sorrow.

It's very hard to get used to the idea that someone with whom you have always shared your life is suddenly just not physically there. Getting used to living without that person will take time. Many people find comfort, during this difficult time, through prayer and their relationship with God—whether they attend services at their church or synagogue, or pray privately on their own.

A close friend of mine, whom I have known since elementary school, wrote this to me in a letter after the death of her mother last year: "I'm trying to live and do things as usual, but they really aren't the same. Yes, time does help, and I am slowly coming to grips with the reality. But the hardest part is when something happens and I can't share it with my mom. There are so many small things that occur that only she would really enjoy, appreciate, and want to hear all the details about. We kept her very well informed on what was happening in our lives, and now there's no one else to share it with in the same way, no one else's life centered about our family. But, certainly, she had to make the same adjustment in her life, and I will, too."

Each person's grief is felt differently. Even in the same family, one person may feel ready to go back to work or school, another may feel the need to stay home a bit longer. It has nothing to do with how much they loved the person who died, only how they need to handle their feelings.

Remember that the amount of tears is not proof of how much someone cares. Nor does it mean that the person who cries is weak. And, how quickly someone starts doing things that seem quite normal doesn't mean that the hurt isn't inside or that they loved the person any less.

While many people think they should be careful during the mourning period and not mention the name of the person who died, his or her relatives might feel very good thinking back to old memories. Such talk might even make them laugh. They would probably appreciate hearing how much the person they mourn for meant to you. Joan, whose son committed suicide when he was nineteen, shared: "Going on with grief is very personal and very individual . . . and everybody brings their own personality into it. No one should ever sit in judgment or criticism of someone else's grief or how they proceed forward."

Don't be surprised if it takes many, many months (or longer) before things begin to get back to normal. If you find yourself saying, "I should feel better by now" or, "I shouldn't feel so sad," remind yourself that it's not helpful to deal with "shoulds" when you're dealing with your feelings. It's not a matter of what you "should" feel, but rather what you *are* feeling. The fact is, you do feel sad; you don't feel better. You can only get stronger on your own time schedule, no one else's.

Death takes time to get used to.

Remembering

My grandmother died about ten years ago and I still cry sometimes about missing her. Every time I pass the apartment where she lived, I can just see her leaning out the window, waving good-bye to me and my children. Recently I was in a department store with my daughter and saw an older woman who reminded me of her. I started to cry. I don't think that any number of years will erase how much I love her and how much I miss her.

A girl in the sixth grade told me, "My father died when I was very, very young. And when somebody mentions anything about it, it hurts. When I see my friend's father playing with her, I really feel bad."

It's natural to feel sad, natural to continue to miss someone you loved very much and will always love, even if they're no longer physically here. Boys and girls continually share their confusion with me about whether it's okay to talk about the grandparent, brother, sister, parent, or friend who has died—even if that person died before that boy or girl was born. They worry that if they bring up the subject, their other family members will be upset, very sad, or possibly angry. And so, too often, they keep their feelings silent. Sometimes for years.

Turning feelings into words will help you talk about the grandparent—or anyone else—you miss. If it's hard to be in your grandparent's home, you can say: "It's hard being here. I get so sad thinking about all the times Grandpa sat in that chair or played cards with me at that table." Or you might say, "I never know if it's okay to talk about Grandpa. I'm afraid to get you sad, but I really want to know more about him. Do you have any picture albums?" If it's too uncomfortable to be at the park where you and your brother used to play ball, you can tell your friend, "It's really too hard for me to be here right now; _____ and I used to come here together. It makes me too upset to be here. I keep thinking he's going to come around that path on his bicycle. Let's get out of here, okay?"

It's natural to remember.

Yet, Life Goes On

Robert, age twenty-nine, said:

> No matter how close the person is, ultimately life goes on. You're shattered for a period of time, but life goes on. Death is a life experience. It's kind of strange.
>
> Every once in a while, we'll stop and remember, but there's no time while living to stop for the dead. We mourn for a period and it hurts. And we can't believe someone so close to us has died—or someone our age, a peer, has died. When I was younger and my friend died in the ninth grade, I was totally blown away.
>
> Recently I got a letter from the mother of a girl whom I had dated, telling me that she had died. My mouth dropped. Now it's two months later and I passed her name in my phone book the other day. I stopped for a second and I thought about it. But I moved on.
>
> No matter what goes away, what is lost, or how much pain is involved at the time, we have to move on.

Even my mother was amazed to look back in her diary and find that after the death of her grandmother, whom she loved so dearly, she went right on with what she had to do.

On Friday, May 7, 1937, the day after her grandmother's funeral, she wrote, "The family is sitting together again today. Went to school and rehearsed my speech all afternoon. It's going to be a hard fight."

On Saturday, May 8, 1937, she wrote: "Stayed up at Grandma's house, and then went to Sonia's store. At night, Martin, Lenny, Shirley, Harvey, Marvin, and I made posters for my campaign."

Life has to go on.

Suicide: When People Take Their Own Lives—or Try To

When someone takes his or her own life, it's called committing *suicide*. If they try to kill themselves and don't succeed, that is referred to as a suicide attempt. It's incredibly painful to imagine how desperate people must be who turn to suicide, thinking it's their only answer.

You might be sitting at your lunch table in school one day and hear someone say, "I just feel like killing myself!" If a boyfriend or girlfriend has broken up with that person, or the person thinks that he or she is going to get a failing grade, or there are family troubles at home, it may seem like a natural thing to say. You might think nothing of that remark. Many people would let it pass right by.

Although it's common for kids to think about suicide, the problem is some people really mean it. They may seriously want to kill themselves or at least may be seriously thinking about it. Those remarks are really their cry for help, but all too often no one takes them seriously.

I spoke with Jeff, now twenty-three, whose older brother, Doug, committed suicide five years ago. He shared:

I guess what strikes me most is that suicide could just absolutely happen to anyone, especially someone that you don't expect. Because if you expect it, a lot of people usually react to it. If you think someone might be suicidal, people will pay attention to what that person says. But if someone who you would never expect it from mentions it out of the blue, a lot of people wouldn't think anything of it. And you have to. Because it can be serious. It can be a crying out for help.

I knew Doug for my entire seventeen years until he killed himself. When he said to me, "I was thinking about hanging myself," it was the farthest thing in my mind that he was serious. It's something I never would have in a million years pictured him saying and meaning. I thought that he was just saying it as an expression.

I guess probably one of the other most important things is that at the time that you do hear it, at that moment, push on, try not to let that person get off the phone. With Doug, I kind of got off the phone with him and I hadn't really pushed the matter with him at all because it didn't strike me at first as meaning anything. And when I started thinking about it, I called him back the next day and it was too late. What he said was bothering me, it was kind of echoing in my mind. And when I called him back, he said, "Oh don't worry about it. I didn't mean it."

And that was the last chance I had to talk with him. He killed himself two days later. I guess actually I do believe it now, but I never would have guessed it.

I think if I had any idea . . . if I had ever read something that said to me that someone had lost a brother through suicide, even though it was the last thing they could ever imagine would happen, I think that would have been the one thing that might have made a difference in my taking what Doug said seriously. I think if you can get one thing through to every single person who reads this it should be to help them know that it could be them. Their family, their friend, or anyone, no matter what their age.

I don't know what I would have done. What I should have done is stay on the phone. And talk with him about whether or not he was serious about what he was saying, while whatever it was still was on his mind—instead of waiting to talk with him about it the next day. And hopefully, I would have told my parents that he was serious. And possibly we could have helped to save his life.

It's important to realize that even if Jeff had kept Doug on the phone, even if he had told his parents, even if they traveled to where Doug was at college—they might not have been able to save him. No one can live anyone else's life for them. And while it's critical to take people seriously—and do everything that might help them—sometimes, it's not possible to stop a person from committing suicide if they're so completely determined to kill themselves.

Doug and Jeff's mother, Joan, shared:

Some of the things that have helped me personally are trying to get some short- and long-term goals, always something to look forward to. And I try real hard not to subject myself to difficult situations, if possible. For example, certain conversations that people are having that are so hard to listen to, I've learned I can walk away from them without feeling I have to be embarrassed or uncomfortable . . . that it's okay.

You really need to let people you're close to—friends and family—know that you still want to talk about it. That you still want the name of the person who you've lost to be brought up in conversations. . . . So you set the guidelines for other people, to let them know that it's okay. There are times when you really don't want to mention it and times when you need to unburden yourself. You really need to let them know, because many people just don't know what to say. They're so afraid to bring that person up in conversation.

Doug always came across as someone who was never scared, [with an] "I'm invincible" kind of personality . . . and I think that comes with youth.

But he was a chance-taker. I think that with the drugs that he was doing, especially the LSD, and smoking pot and other things, that he always thought he was in control—so we always thought he was in control. But with the drugs that he was doing—he didn't even know what was happening to his own personality, and that is probably why he sent Jeff these mixed messages.

And from his suicide note, it showed us that his personality had turned around completely. And we, as the survivors, we can ask *why* forever, and we'll never truly understand.

But the one thing that I have learned was that he was sick . . . which is a very hard thing for a parent to say. Whether it was because of the chemicals in the drugs—which throws your whole thinking out of whack—or not, I feel I can accept it better, feeling it was a form of sickness. It helps us accept it better to understand that he lost the control to be able to allow himself to go on living.

Ron, Jeff and Doug's father, adds:

Knowing that we can't change what has already happened, we find strength in each other—Joan, Jeff, and I—to move forward and make the best of life that we can.

As much as I hurt every day, as much as I deal with the Douglas situation every day, we just can't allow the past to take away all the good things that are left to do.

As hard as it is to move forward, we do move forward, because unfortunately, none of us knows how to go back. If we did, we'd try to change things. But that's not possible.

In the last five years, my business life has taken a tremendous positive turn. Yet, when I evaluate what that really means and what it means to me, obviously I would trade it in a minute if I had the opportunity to keep Douglas as part of my life.

We must go on with our lives, especially when there's a suicide. . . . The pain of those who have died, however they died . . . is gone. Those of us who survive must live with a different pain. . . . But we must choose to go on.

Suicide attempts: Sometimes people really don't want to end up dead Sometimes, people don't really want to end up dead when they attempt suicide, so they may make only a slight cut on their wrists instead of a deep one. Or they may take only some of the pills in the medicine bottle instead of all of them. Just two weeks ago, a girl in the eighth grade in my town was found unconscious in the girls' bathroom at school. The teacher felt she had been out of class too long and sent someone out to look for her. It turned out she had taken several pills from a medicine bottle but not enough to kill her. Just enough to make her pass out and get the message across. Everything about what she did said, "Help me! I'm troubled!"

Some people who plan to make an unsuccessful attempt at suicide, hoping that someone will find them, accidentally end up dead. For example, if the knife slips and they accidentally cut their wrists too deeply, or if they didn't realize how strong even the few pills would be, or if no one showed up in time to help them, as they planned.

If you ever hear someone say that they would rather be dead, listen very seriously—whether they are the most popular person in school, are on the high honor roll, are a super athlete, seem to have close family relationships, are going out with someone they seem to like, or seem to "have it all." It just may be they're crying out for help. Remember not to be fooled by what looks like confidence on the outside. Even if they're smiling, inside they could be very seriously thinking about "ending it all." Any remark—*from anyone*—that even hints of suicide needs to be taken very seriously.

Warning signals for suicide Other warning signals, besides an actual suicide attempt and the fact that someone is talking about suicide, might include:

- if someone starts staying to themselves a lot
- if they start to look very sloppy (not grooming themselves)

- if they don't care about their schoolwork or school activities anymore, and are cutting classes
- if they're just not hungry each day at lunch (changes in eating patterns)
- if they're sleeping a lot
- if their behavior seems to be different, or if they're taking risks
- if they're drinking alcohol or using other drugs
- if something very troubling has happened to them or someone close

They might also talk a lot about death or give away something of theirs that you know is very important to them. If someone close to them has recently committed suicide or if you know they have tried suicide before, be extra aware of what they share and how they act. The problem is, there aren't always signals. A phone call to each of their friends might represent a final good-bye.

You also need to realize that any one of these signals or even a combination doesn't definitely mean the particular person is considering suicide. The concern is that we all be extra aware and serious about the fact that it's possible.

If you're worried that a friend will commit suicide One very important thing to remember is that it's an unfair, much too heavy burden for you (or anyone) to be responsible for someone else's suicide threats. You can let them know you're concerned, be there for them, offer support, try to get them to get to go for help, and even offer to keep them company when they go. But, just as with any other area of concern (problems with alcohol or other drugs or pregnancy), you can't get help *for* them if they're not choosing to get help themselves. But you can seek out help yourself and let an adult know you're worried about that person. Even if you aren't positive that your friend seriously needs help, let an adult know. This is not a time to take a chance—your friend could be serious.

A boy in the eighth grade talked with me about how scared he is that his girlfriend might commit suicide. He told me that her parents just split up and she really likes him a lot. He had been thinking of breaking up with her. But he felt if he broke up with her, then it would be too much for her to handle on top of everything else she's dealing with. He didn't know what to do and was very sad for her. He told me he really cares about her but didn't want to go out with her anymore. Because she was talking about suicide, he felt trapped in the relationship.

What if he stayed in the relationship and then she committed suicide anyway? Would he always wonder what he could have said or done that would have made a difference? If he broke up with her and she ended up committing suicide, would he carry around the belief for the rest of his life that her suicide might have been his fault? It's a tremendous burden for him to believe he is responsible for her staying alive.

Besides urging her to talk with an adult who is trained to help her, it would be important for him to seek out his own adult advice in order to deal with this situation as well as possible. It could be a tremendous relief for him to talk openly about this with his parents or a school counselor, school psychologist, or Suicide Hotline.

It might help if he could get across to his girlfriend that he cares about her very much, even though he no longer wants to be her boyfriend. He won't be ending his relationship with her just because they stop "going out." He can say that he still wants to be involved in her life, spend time with her, and be there for her. It's just that he just doesn't want to be going out with her in the same way.

Even as I'm writing this, I know in my heart that all the understanding in the world probably won't be able to take away how scared he is about what his girlfriend might do to herself. The difference needs to be that he won't feel personally responsible. . . . That doesn't mean he shouldn't care and shouldn't try to help in every way possible. That only means he isn't *her*. He can't live life for—or be responsible for—anyone else but himself.

If you're the one who feels life isn't worth living If you're the one who feels that life isn't worth living, I hope you've learned that *you* can make a decision to help yourself. Even if it seems that there's nobody else in the world who cares about you, you can be the one to start caring about yourself. You can remind yourself that somewhere inside of you is what makes you so special. And no one—nothing—no situation—not failing grades, losing a boyfriend or girlfriend, low self-esteem, the death of someone you love, parents splitting up, money problems at home, being rejected from a certain college, not making the team, not measuring up to a brother or sister, not having any friends, rape, being "busted" for drugs, being kicked out of your home, having to go to jail—is worth enough to take away from your right to live your life as fully as possible. *Nothing* has a right to take away from your belief that you're worth it—and you have a right to live, no matter what.

Don't try to handle alone whatever it is that's weighing so heavily on you. If you're having suicidal thoughts, you need to speak with someone who is trained to help you—immediately. Even if you can't imagine admitting what you're feeling to anyone. Even if you don't believe you're worth it anymore, even if you don't think anything could ever change for the better. Push yourself and let someone know that you're hurting so badly and are so desperate.

And understand that if you reached a point where you no longer think you're worth it, that doesn't mean you're not. It just means you're too upset and down on yourself to be able to understand that you are. And if you are so desperate and so depressed that you're not capable of believing that your life can take a more positive direction, that doesn't mean it can't. It just means that because you feel so hopeless, it's hard to be able to believe that it can.

It would be tragic for you to commit such a final act as taking your own life, never giving yourself the chance to learn that things don't have to stay the way they are. And never giving yourself the chance to learn that in time, with help—however slowly—you can feel better. And that you can get past whatever it is you're dealing with.

No matter how big a mistake you might have made or how alone in this world you think you are, you have the power to decide to live. You can begin to take steps to make your life better, to learn from your mistakes, to make a "fresh" start. *You* have the power to decide to hold on. Even if you're scared, you can ask for help. If you don't know what to say, you can start with, "I don't really know what to say to you. I'm having a lot of trouble. And I want to kill myself . . ." Or, "I'm thinking about suicide. And I'm very scared. I need your help."

You have the power to break your own silence and not deal with your pain alone. You're worth it. If only you would believe it.

Even if something happens that is the very worst thing you could ever imagine, you'll figure out a way to deal with it somehow, solve it somehow. Or you may come to understand that nothing you can do will change what happened, so you can try to accept it and move on. And as time passes, so, too, will the terrible feelings. You'll find you'll be able to become less and less depressed. Your situation will seem less and less desperate. Eventually the hurt will fade and will become history. It's natural to think that you'll never get over it. But you can. Trust that you will be able to—in time.

For each one of us, life will have its ups and its downs, its joys and its pain. Some days will be great, some awful. Some will be exciting, some boring. Some will seem smooth, some filled with problems. Some problems can be solved. Some can't. Some mistakes will be more serious, some less. Everyone makes mistakes, everyone must deal with efforts that fail, everyone has his or her breaking point.

And if it's not a particular mistake or situation that's making you consider suicide, but deep feelings about not being "worth it" or not measuring up to who your parents (or anyone else) expect you to be, remind yourself that you can only be you. It's time you realize that it's just fine to be you. You can't be anyone else.

Think back over the years and try to remember a time when you had a terrible problem that made you think the whole world was caving in on you. Do you remember thinking that it would never pass, that you would never get over it? How long did it take before it started to ease and become less terrible? How long was it before you were able to "let it go" and move on to other things? The fact that you're able to remember that you did get through it will help prove to you that you can again.

If you're thinking, "But that was a different situation—this is much worse . . . " It's *okay*. You can deal with anything if you allow yourself to try. Those problems that can't be solved or set right simply have to be accepted, learned from, and put in the past. Some will take longer to get over, some not as long. Most things work themselves out in one way or another. You don't have to let yourself give in to whatever difficulty is taking place at this moment in your life. You have a choice. You can choose life.

There are some kids who think that drugs are the answer when things are hard to handle and they feel hopeless. Although drugs may help a person escape reality, reality still stays the same. When the alcohol or other drugs wear off, the problem is still there. And drugs can make bad feelings even worse. Drugs can be just the thing to push you to commit suicide. Escaping from problems doesn't work. You need to be clearheaded to somehow work them out.

There are so many people around who are waiting to help you. Don't expect them to guess that you're hurting just by looking at you. Some kids think that, if people really cared, they'd notice. But it just may be they don't realize how deeply you're hurting. You need to let them know, out loud or in writing.

Make a list of those around you who can help (parents and family, school counselor or psychologist, coach, teacher, principal, religious youth services, local hospital or clinic). You can also look up local crisis or suicide hotline phone numbers or even see if there's a suicide prevention center in or near your town. A helpful number is the Boys Town National Hotline (1-800-448-3000) for boys, girls, and family, where someone will be available to help you twenty-four hours a day and the Crisis Helpline (1-800-444-9999). If either of these numbers changes, dial 1-800-555-1212 for new information. Remember, if the first person doesn't work out, go on to the next, and the next, until you find someone who can help you.

When you feel so awful and life doesn't seem to be worth living, try getting up early enough to see the sunrise. Try to appreciate that there is still beauty around you, peace to be found. Make some private time for yourself. Also reach out and ask to spend some time with a close friend or someone in your family. Take lots of slow, deep breaths. Take a long walk. Go to the beach, a lake, a mountainside, a park, and just sit to collect your thoughts. Try to take a step back from all the agony, all the pressure, all the pain.

Think of what you wish could happen in your life—all your plans, all your hopes, all your dreams. If nothing else, get angry enough to say to yourself, "Why me? It's not fair! I deserve a chance to live just like anyone else does." You're right, you do. Just hold on. You can *decide* to hold on.

Steps to holding on and going forward: Steps to preventing suicide

The first step in holding on is to:
- admit that you're having dangerous thoughts and admit that you can't handle these feelings alone.

The second step in holding on is to:
- identify the "helping" people in your area and choose one person to approach.

The third step in holding on is to:
- Let that person know you're in trouble, and
- trust that if the first person doesn't seem to relate to you, doesn't seem quite as helpful as you hoped, you can try the next person, and the next.

The fourth step in holding on is to:
- be as patient with yourself as possible. Learning how to cope, understanding your emotions, being able to handle your reactions, takes time. Working through hurts and problems is a process that may take weeks, months, maybe years. But once you take that first step, you can at least appreciate that you cared enough to help yourself.
- realize the important thing is that you're moving forward, taking steps to feel better. If every once in a while it seems you're taking a few steps backward, that's natural. It's not so easy to work at understanding difficult feelings.
- trust that if you not only learn to understand yourself and your situation better—but also learn the skills and tools to cope with what you're dealing with in your life—you'll begin to see a positive change within you. Step by step, taking one day at a time.

So if you find that your growing-up years are filled with pain from tough family feelings, loneliness, pressures that are so hard to handle in school, or anything else that may make you wonder if it's worth holding on, know that it's worth it. And know that you can. You deserve to survive. You deserve to want to.

CHAPTER 23

HAVING A DISABILITY

I like to think of our bodies as "packages." Each package is like a wrapper for the person who's inside. Just as people compare clothes, grades, and labels on their jeans, they also compare body packages.

It's amazing to me how much people depend upon someone's package to judge whether or not they even want to say hello. Think about the "body packages" that you see every day. Imagine your class at school. Can you think of anyone (be honest) you have never approached simply because you didn't like something about their outside appearance? What was it that turned you off? Who have you gone up to just because you liked what they looked like, knowing nothing else about them? Did you end up liking who that person was when you got to know them?

The appearance of someone's body can create different feelings, both for the person inside that body and for those around them. That's true for everyone, and especially can make a difference if someone has a disability.

There are times that a disability has a lot of power. Imagine that a person's disability can make some people cross the street when they never planned to go that way. Imagine a disability being able to make people laugh and tease. Imagine a disability having the power to fool people into thinking the person inside doesn't have the ability to love and be a good friend or feel the need to be loved.

Whether someone has a disability or not, all outside appearances seem to have the power to influence people to feel good or bad about themselves. Too many people don't realize it's up to each person to keep reminding themselves that no matter what their outside looks like, no matter how badly any part of their body is deformed or "damaged," they are whole people inside. Each person can decide to feel good. Feeling good comes from each person's mind and heart, not from their "package."

It would help if everyone would understand that people are not their arms, not their legs, not their crutch or their wheelchair—they are who they are inside. As I said in Chapter 17, what makes a person beautiful is something you can't see!

While a disability might affect outside appearance, it doesn't have to affect that person's personality on the inside. You can't know who a person is or how amazing they could be in your life just by looking. Too many people are fooled by packages.

Feelings About Having a Disability

Lisa, age seventeen, shared:

I have a mild case of cerebral palsy. When I was born, there was not enough oxygen being supplied to my brain, so part of the brain cells are not functioning; they kind of died. I have it on my right side mostly. My left side is pretty good. [Lisa gets around in a wheelchair.]

I have my ups and downs. Sometimes I get depressed because of my disability. I used to feel like I was totally different, like I was really weird. Though I know there are other people worse off than me, sometimes I do get the feelings, Why me? Why am I like this? Why can't I be like anybody else?

But then I think that there's a reason for me being like this. Maybe God saw me as an individual who was strong, that I could handle what He was going to put me through. Sometimes I feel privileged, because I can now understand what other people feel and what they're going through. So I'll never make fun.

There are still times when I don't feel able to accept my disability. Sometimes I feel like I could dig a little hole and could hide in there. I especially get upset with guys. I really get annoyed when they just look at my wheelchair and then they don't say anything to me. I feel really bad because I want to be like anybody else. I go home and I look in the mirror and wonder, what was he looking at? My face? My chair?

I still have a hard time. Some days are worse than others. But isn't it that way with people who are not disabled, too?

When Lawrence was growing up, he didn't do well in school. His parents kept having him tested, but the tests didn't prove anything. So, the more he tried, the more frustrated he got. His mother told me, "Nobody discovered he had a learning disability. I kept being told that he didn't want to do schoolwork and he was a troublemaker. We were told he should have been doing better.

"As his friends passed him in their learning and as the years kept passing by, everyone got smarter and he felt dumber and dumber and dumber. My son felt he was stupid. 'I can't read' turned into 'I don't want to read.' This was then taken as not obeying or a mental attitude rather than a physical problem."

Lawrence was later found to have *dyslexia* (dis-LEX-ee-uh), a learning disability that causes him to read certain letters and numbers backward. Nobody noticed he was doing that.

Is it any wonder he had trouble reading and doing his work? How sad that he felt so frustrated and bad about himself all those years, when it was really a physical problem that prevented him from learning.

After his disability was discovered, specially trained teachers helped Lawrence catch up in his reading and learning in a way that he could finally understand. His mom told me that he began to feel much more confident about himself and became happier in school.

Michael, age thirty-one, is paralyzed from the waist down. That is called being a *paraplegic* (par-uh-PLEE-jik). Before the car accident that left him in a wheelchair, his nickname was Shorty. He felt he wanted to keep on being called Shorty, figuring that anyone who meets someone called Shorty in a wheelchair will never forget him. He said:

I can't speak for people who have been handicapped since birth. I know that when I first got hurt, I was seventeen. I was Mr. Popularity and was into sports and everything.

At first I didn't want to go out in public, didn't want to go to restaurants, or even back to school. I felt like kind of a freak. People would stare at me, especially little kids. But they were just being honest. It took me a while before I realized it was just human nature for them to be curious and I might have stared, too.

I might have stayed by myself a little longer if I didn't have to go back to school. Being in school forced me to be with a lot of people. I got a lot of support from my family and friends, which helped.

I felt like I was the only one when I was first hurt. All I saw was this long, long road ahead of me. But it's like if someone just throws you in the desert, do you just lie down and die and let it happen to you? A person has no choice but to try to live.

I started getting over my injury when I went to the rehabilitation center and met other people who were handicapped. As soon as I met someone who had a more severe disability than I had, I realized I have a lot to be thankful for. That's when I started to quit feeling sorry for myself.

After I learned that important lesson and was starting to appreciate what I had instead of being upset about what I didn't have, that's when my life changed and I became valuable to society. My personality also changed back to my normal, fun-loving self. I still seemed to be fairly popular, even though I had a different deck of cards to deal with. It just took more effort on my part to get someone to realize that they might want to be my friend. Now I'm married and I'm getting on with my life.

A woman who worked with physically disabled children said, "There was a very attractive fourteen-year-old girl with cerebral palsy. Her legs were a problem more than her arms. She was mainstreamed [that means that she attended regular academic classes with the other kids who did not have a disability] in our junior high. There was an eighth grade dance and she really wanted to go. We talked to her about it for a long time. Finally, she decided that she wanted to go in her wheelchair. So she went.

"At the dance she stood up from her wheelchair and moved in place to the music, holding onto somebody who had come over to her, who was one of the chaperones or people in charge. She was in her glory."

Shirley, age sixty-two, said:

I was a year old when I became ill and lost my sight in one eye. I have learned to live with it. My uncles used to call me the cockeyed kid.

This has really been a hidden disability. Nobody really knew about it but me. Because I had a popular childhood, it never was a problem for me, except when I wanted to go swimming at camp. If I took off my glasses, my eyes crossed. I was upset that anyone would see them.

Also, when I was fifteen, I went out with a boy who complained about my glasses, because our glasses clacked when he tried to get close to me. I think I wore them on purpose just so he wouldn't kiss me.

The only scary thing is getting older. My glasses are getting stronger and stronger. I have heavier and stronger lenses. And if anything happens to my other eye, then I'll be blind. I've been fortunate so far, and have always had an active life. So, I'm only going to think positively about it. So I cope.

Bobby, who was paralyzed from the waist down because of a bullet that wounded him in the Vietnam War, shared, "I've stopped thinking of myself as disabled. It's been so long since I've thought about my disability. . . ."

Bobby, maybe that's the whole point. To have stopped thinking of your disability, you can't be allowing the injustice, the anger, and the resentment of what the war did to you get in the way of continuing with the rest of your life in a positive way. It means that you've come to accept yourself as you are, even though your body is no longer the same.

The bullet may have injured your spine, but it couldn't get deep enough to scar who you are—unless you let it. You are still the person that you always were when you were able to run around without your wheelchair.

I guess the main difference is that you have to do things in a different way. So, instead of walking, you move in your chair. But you still drive a car; you still get out and go where you want to go. Even if you go a little slower (which I understand that you don't!), you still get there with your wheelchair. You still have the same need for people who are important in your life, and you still have your dreams. If your old dreams are no longer possible, you've got the power to create new ones. And you can love and relate to people as you always did.

Shorty, too, was able to accept his car accident and resulting disability as something that can't be changed. Since he doesn't have the power to put the feeling back into his legs, he concentrates on putting all the feeling he can into life; not only for himself, his wife, and other family members, but for many children and adults who also have disabilities in one form or another. He's teaching them how they can go on camping trips, travel down rivers, or even climb mountains if they allow themselves to.

Ann, now in her thirties, used to be a marathon jogger before her car accident. She is now paralyzed from the middle of her back down and works in the physical education department of a college. She plays racketball in her chair, mountain climbs in her chair, goes disco dancing in her chair (and even banged her nose a few weeks ago while dancing because she fell out of her chair), and doesn't see her disability as an obstacle to anything she wants to do.

Lisa, sixteen, has only known herself with a disability (she has had cerebral palsy since birth). She, too, has had to work at accepting herself and has tried to do as much as she can to live each day fully. She's on the student council and home economics club, and plays on the hockey team at her school. She'd like to be an actress, a model, or a lawyer.

More and more people who have a physical disability are doing physical activities that they themselves and their families and friends might never have thought possible. When they get *disabled* out of their heads, so many things are possible.

Accepting Yourself and Your Disability

Whether someone has a disability since birth or because of an accident or illness at an older or younger age, the key seems to be the ability to accept themselves and their disability. Lisa, Shorty, Bobby, and Ann have clearly come to accept their disabilities, each in her or his own way. Their personal strength continues to prove that, no matter what, you go on.

According to Bobby:

Not everybody adjusts to disability well. Some people find it a devastating blow from which they really don't fully recover. Others find it the kind of blow that consistently hampers [continues to get in the way of] their pursuit of a happy and rewarding life. And others basically take it as just one of the many different kinds of problems that you encounter in life.

I don't know what the trick is in trying to figure out who will or who will not be able to adjust well to various types of disabilities. I've seen some of my friends who I would have thought would be the strongest become disabled and commit suicide because they couldn't handle it. I've seen people who seemed like they'd never get it together become the best adjusted of all. Even with those who adjusted very well, it's important to realize that this doesn't happen overnight.

Support, lots of love, understanding, and acceptance from family and friends are very important in helping a person overcome his or her disability. Michael shared, "It's really important to force yourself to be with other people."

Said Bobby, "Family support needs to be balanced. You need a family to assist you when you need help, but you also need a family that's there to give you a little kick in the pants when you need that, too. The most damaging factor can sometimes be those that are overly protective and those that respond with pity and sympathy. They're well-meaning but they can kill you with their kindness."

It's important for family and friends to realize that the person who must adjust to having a disability (or any kind of life change) needs an outlet for feelings. They need to be able to talk openly with people who care enough to listen. And, if he or she screams and yells more than usual, it would help for others to realize that may be their way to get anger and frustration out. As Shorty told me, "It's like a teakettle that you can't hold in. You've got to let off the steam. It's good to cry sometimes."

Bobby shared, "I think in the end, what helps an awful lot is just to realize what you are, what you're capable of, stop dwelling on what's beyond your reach, and to relieve some of the frustration in life by making goals that you can obtain."

Feelings About Having a Disability Shared by Those Who Do Not

Jen, age twelve, said, "There was a girl with a disability in my second- and third-grade class. I don't remember her too well, but when other people made fun of her, sometimes I'd try to be friends. And then people would make fun of me because I was being her friend. Then I'd try to avoid her and I'd always feel guilty about this."

Isn't it interesting that having a friendship with someone who has a disability can create the same type of peer pressure situation as being friendly with someone unpopular who does not have a disability? The difference is that there are times when the person who has a disability doesn't even have to do anything to become unpopular. All they have to do is appear.

Fran, age ten, said, "I saw a guy with one leg using one crutch who was dancing with this girl right in the middle of the dance floor. I thought it was great that he could dance and everything. It was kind of gross to look at his pants hanging, but . . ."

Christina, age eighteen, shared, "Because my sister is handicapped, my mother always used to take her side when we were having a fight."

Timmy, age twelve, said, "Well, the people with artificial arms, like plastic arms, at least they could use it like their fake arm was a regular one. As long as you're alive, that's what's important."

Barry, age fourteen, told me, "I can't stand looking at retarded people. It gets me sick."

Sean, age twelve, said, "My sister has cerebral palsy. I help take care of her when my parents aren't home. I have to watch out for her when she's sitting in her wheelchair in front of the house because sometimes the kids are mean.

"She says some very funny things, but it's hard to listen to her because the words sound like she's speaking in a space tunnel. It takes so long for her to say something, but I can understand her. The only thing that bothers me is when saliva runs down the side of her mouth."

Andrea, age eleven, said:

When I was in the fourth grade, a girl in my class had a learning disability. My teacher favored her. She wasn't crippled or anything. She was a normal person but she needed help in talking. She just talked and slurred. So she was normal except for that.

On the playground, she would kick people and call them names and then run to the teacher and tell and lie and get the other kids in trouble.

When I was at a pancake restaurant with another friend and her family, we saw D. there. We didn't look at her because we hated her. So, on Monday in school she told the teacher that we weren't talking to her over the weekend, and we got in trouble.

Then, five girls asked to talk to the teacher. We told her about this girl and how she acts. The teacher said, "Well, she has a problem. And we just have to help her and try to ignore it." And it was really annoying because D. would stand there smiling.

I think she used her handicap to get whatever she wanted.

David, age nine, talked with me about a boy who has a speech problem. He said, "Everybody knows this boy is very smart. Sometimes we talk about how smart he is. People don't like him because he always acts funny in class and laughs at everything. And he talks out loud when he's not supposed to. But everyone knows he's very smart.

"Whenever he slurs or stutters and someone laughs, everyone tells them to shut up and that he can't help it. Everyone knows how he acts and tries not to let the other kids make fun of him, because he can't help it. One time no one made fun of him. But it took him about twenty minutes to read one or two pages."

Neal, age thirteen, said:

There are certain people who are physically disabled. Some of them have become friends with kids who aren't disabled, and they're recognized as being nice. They're just normal and accepted.

In terms of mental disability, there's a boy at our school who is really treated like dirt. He's very close to his family, I feel, because he doesn't have too many friends. When you don't have too many friends, you turn to your family. He has a very understanding, nice family.

Many people ridicule [RID-ih-kyul, make fun of] him. Because of this, he isn't athletic; he's not in any sports, and he's really not recognized as a nice person, even though he is really kind.

Maybe you or someone you know has had many of these feelings. It may be more or less comfortable for you to look at and be near a person, depending upon his or her disability. But perhaps a change of approach would help. Maybe, instead of looking at what seems to be wrong with their body, try looking with a positive attitude toward learning who they are as a person.

For example, instead of dwelling on the leg that's not there, or the pant leg that's swaying empty in the air, why not concentrate on all the rest of that person that's "filled in." Instead of being turned away by saliva, look past the saliva to the expression in their eyes. Try to concentrate on the person, not the person's body.

I don't pretend that changing your approach will always be easy. But just keep reminding yourself there's a person inside each body, no matter what their body looks like. Their body isn't who they are.

George, age thirty-four, said, "Last year I met someone who was a paraplegic (paralyzed from his waist down). It was the first time I had any real contact with someone who had to stay in a wheelchair. It was very strange for me because I love to jog. I had to catch myself from saying, 'Last night when I was running,' or 'After I leave here, I'm going to run,' or making any mention at all about what I took for granted. As it turned out, the hang-up was mine and not his. And as we got more friendly, I found out it was okay to talk about anything I wanted, and now he's a very valued friend."

A word about guilt: maybe sometimes we feel so guilty that we're physically okay and they're not that we hold ourselves back from talking about activities that we think the person who has a disability can't do or might have difficulty doing. We think they might feel upset, hurt, pity for themselves, or even rejected.

If you don't tell the person the truth about your feelings, they may sense (from your nonverbal communication) that you're not telling them the truth, that you're holding back. That's when they may feel hurt, rejection and that they're being pitied. It would be better not to censor your conversation. Say what you would say anyway. You can be a lot closer for it.

One more thing: Some people have more than one disability. But just because, for example, they appear not to be able to control their muscles, it doesn't mean that they can't hear or answer a question— even if you'll have to be patient as the sounds very slowly, sometimes with great difficulty, form words.

As Lisa said, "I hate it when people ask 'How's Nancy?' and she'll be sitting right there." Henry said, "When people see my crutches, they yell in my ear and think I'm deaf!"

Having a Disability Doesn't Mean Mentally Retarded

Though a body may appear twisted, shaky, and have to remain in a wheelchair, and lets out grunts instead of words, the person inside can be beautiful and bright. Too many people think that a twisted body or a body that doesn't function in a normal way means the person inside is mentally retarded. Very often that's just not true.

If a person is mentally retarded, he or she also needs love and friendship, is able to share love with others, and is special just like anyone else. While I'm not going to concentrate here on mental retardation, my point is simply to make sure you understand that you can't make judgments about people because of what they look like.

Too many people are so quick to judge, and quick to stay away. They're quick to decide that their normal body means they're better. They can't imagine that someone whose body isn't as normal has any feelings or need for love. And they can't imagine that someone so crippled could possibly give love and enjoy sex. They imagine wrong.

What did you do and how did you feel the last time you saw someone who has a disability? If you have a disability yourself, what feelings do you get from people when they're with you?

Disability Isn't Catching—Feelings and Attitudes Are

Said Henry, an actor and comedian, who contracted polio when he was four (he walks with leg braces and uses crutches): "Attitudes are the real disability. Nobody wants to be around a disabled person. Society will take care of us, but they don't want us. They need to understand that disability isn't a disease. It's not catching. People who are disabled are not considered sick."

Where do these attitudes and feelings come from? They come from parents, the media (television, movies, newspapers, radio), friends, school. We also get messages from the people who have a disability.

Depending on how withdrawn, angry, accepting, or full of life they are, their message may be negative or positive, weak or strong, or somewhere in between.

Starting when children are very young, they get messages about people who have a disability. They're often taught that the person with a disability is different and they need to stay away.

When you were little, do you remember seeing someone in a wheelchair, or on crutches, with one leg, or with only part of an arm? If you said to your parents, "Oh, look, Mommy and Daddy, that woman has only half an arm!" they could have said, "Yes, she might have been sick or had an accident. Or maybe she was just born that way. But her arm has nothing to do with how nice a person she is. You'd have to get to know her to find that out. After all, people don't need arms to be friendly!"

Or did they say, "Come along, we don't want to get too close. You'd better not talk to her. Leave her alone"? Message: she's different. If your parents are uncomfortable or have negative feelings about any disability, they might have passed those feelings on to you.

Said Henry, "People are so aware of what we can't do. They should look at what we can do! People with disabilities can adapt; they can adjust. They must adapt if they want to live." Henry plays baseball, flies airplanes, goes bowling, and swims a mile every day. He does all this, and more, with his legs in braces and using crutches. He's comfortable with himself. He's stopped wishing that he'll get better every time he blows out his birthday candles. He accepts himself and is very independent. How sad that some people can look at him and only think of him as a cripple.

Shorty, too, feels, "Most people are unaware of what people with handicaps can do. They have a conception [image, idea] that people who are handicapped need help with every curb, help with every door."

The problem is, too many people with disabilities actually believe the weak and helpless image. An eight-year-old girl who walks with crutches went up to Henry and said, "Do you feel handicapped? I don't!" How wonderful that she can realize at an early age that just because she has a disability doesn't mean she has to feel helpless or set apart from society.

If you have a disability (or know someone who does) and are not feeling very good about yourself and your life, you can check my usual list of helpers (parents, school counselors and psychologists, teachers and coaches, religious leaders, youth services) and add to it local chapters of organizations and centers that deal especially with certain kinds of disabilities, such as cerebral palsy.

If you can't find a chapter near you, have someone at your school, perhaps the librarian, help you find the address and telephone number of a chapter in the nearest city or the national chapter. You can call or write a letter there for more information about your disability. You can also dial 0 for the operator and ask how you can get this information.

It's normal to be scared or confused or angry or resentful about having a disability. It's also normal to feel that you might not be so useful to yourself, your family, and society in general. But you don't have to stay with those feelings. And you don't have to handle them alone. There are things you can do and many people you can talk with who can help you if you just push yourself to find them. You can choose not to let your disability limit you more than you must. Besides school counselors or those related to mental health service, there are also specially trained career counselors who can help someone who has a disability learn about the many opportunities and activities that are possible.

If you're calling for help, try not to be frustrated if you're told to call several different phone numbers. One phone call can often lead to another and another until you get the right person in the right place. Remember once again, if it doesn't feel good to speak with one person, go on to the next. Let them know what you're feeling so they can learn to be more sensitive to your needs.

Push yourself not to give up. You're worth it!

Another Attitude to Clear Up—About Sexual Sharing

Many people feel that because someone has a disability, he or she does not have the ability to enjoy and share sexual feelings. That's not true. Some even believe that having a disability prevents you from being able to have a child. Though certain people cannot, there are many people who have a disability who can, even if they're paralyzed. Also, many boys and men who have a disability are able to have erections or partial erections. Many girls and women who have a disability can feel genital sensations on the vulva and in the vaginal canal, and many can reach orgasm.

As you already know, there are different ways to express and share sexual feelings. A couple may choose to kiss, hold hands, hug, and touch in more intimate ways.

Whether people have a disability or not, each touch, each feeling, each kiss, is going to be different for each person. There is no one way to do any of these things. And there's certainly no right way. It's up to each person to decide if what they share seems right and feels good to them. And if what's shared doesn't feel so wonderful one time, people can teach each other what might feel better the next time. It is important to talk about those feelings.

Perhaps the attitude that people with a disability don't need or want such closeness comes from false messages other people get from just looking at the disability. To look at certain people's bodies might make someone wonder not only if that person has such feelings, but also how they could possibly share them if they wanted to. Fair question.

Even if parts of a person's body have no feeling, a person never stops feeling inside, no matter how they're born or what accident or illness strikes. Inside needs are the same for everybody, no matter what the outside package.

I'll never forget a program I saw when I was a child. A man had been in an accident and could not move any part of his body. He was completely paralyzed. As a close relative of his was sitting next to his bed, crying and feeling very pained by what had happened to him, the camera zoomed close to his face and showed that a tear had dropped out of his eye. He couldn't speak, he couldn't move, his body couldn't feel, but he could feel inside. And he cried.

So how can that inside feeling be expressed when someone is paralyzed, has lost a limb, has hands that are always in a fist, or cannot see? If people can't move one limb, they'll move another. If they can't touch with their hands, they'll feel with their feet, their arms, or just their elbows. If they can't see with their eyes, they'll "see" with their hands. If there's no hand to touch, they'll touch whatever part of their body there is to touch. If they can't share sexually with their sexual organs, they'll share sexually with their hands or whatever is possible.

Sex is not just "penis meets vagina." Sex can be the most special, close sharing of feelings between people. Just to be able to crawl out of a wheelchair or take off braces, hug someone very close, touch them with any part that feels, and have their lips meet—can be a sexual sharing. Sexual desires stir from inside. The ability to feel love and closeness (also called intimacy) is always able to be felt inside.

Be careful how you judge people who have a disability. Even though their outside may be different from yours, their inside feelings and needs are the same.

When a Child Has a Disability, Parents Often Overprotect

According to Ruth, mother of two children who have a disability, "There's a human part of the breast that reaches out for the ones who can't do things for themselves." She talked about the frustrations, the pain, the overwhelming burdens, tremendous needs, and always the affection and love for her children.

So often parents of a child who has a disability have the tendency to be overprotective. Ruth talked with me about this and was very aware of not being that way. But she agreed that too many parents are. It's almost a natural tendency because, as a parent, the concern is to take care of your child, no matter what. If parents see a child's disability as a weakness, then it's possible they'll smother the child with care. And as much as the smothering might feel safe for the moment, eventually children who have a disability become adults. If they've never had practice being independent, then what?

Sometimes parents are overprotective because they feel guilty. They may think the disability was their fault. But also, a parent might be truly afraid that his or her child will get lost, just not know how to get on a bus, or be taken advantage of or abused.

According to Jane, who teaches children with learning disabilities, "Parents also deny. They'll do as much denying as the children sometimes. For whatever reasons, they'll often say, 'My child doesn't really have a problem. They're just lazy.' That puts a great burden on the child who is trying very, very hard but finds it difficult to do better."

Jane also feels that parents need to allow children to make mistakes, even if they fall on their faces, to prove to themselves that they can get back up again. Ruth agrees. She said, "Only if children are permitted to make the errors, can they begin to learn the skills that will make them independent, eventually . . . at least to the extent that they can be."

Parents, too, must work harder at accepting what they know they cannot change. If your parents are being overprotective (whether you have a disability or not), it is very important for you to first, recognize that they are being overprotective; second, understand it's out of love, or perhaps guilt or the fear that you can't do something for yourself; third, find some private time so that you can talk with them about all these feelings and your need to try, however slowly, to learn to rely on yourself as much as possible.

Henry said, "Parents have to give a disabled child more so that child will be able to compete. If the child can't use his or her legs, they should be encouraged to develop their arms.

"When I was sixteen, I traveled by plane to Mexico by myself. I went to school for the summer. I wouldn't be as independent as I am today without my parents being the way they are."

Shared Lisa, "When I come home, it's just me and my mom. If it wasn't for her, I wouldn't be physically where I am now. She's the one who said, 'You got to do this. You got to do that.' "

And Michael:

Overprotection from parents is the worst. It's the reason that many handicapped kids grow up immature and unaware. It's easy for parents to protect them to such an extent that they never leave their mother's apron.

One of the best things that can happen is that parents get tired of dealing with their child's attitude [being spoiled or expecting the world to treat you like family] and allow them to grow and learn on their own. You have to get in the street and have to learn how to live.

You have to learn who to trust and who not to trust, what is real, what is phony, what is the truth, what is false, what is love, and what is pity. There are a lot of lessons to be learned in the street. And it's too easy to retreat back to your mother or father's open arms.

Having a Disability, Being Challenged

After people accept themselves and their disabilities, then the only disability left to deal with is in their minds.

It all boils down to attitude, beliefs, self-confidence, not allowing your disability to beat you, and accepting what you cannot change. It's realizing that if you can't paint by holding a brush in your hands, you can hold it in your teeth or in your toes. And it doesn't matter what your sisters, brothers, and friends are capable of doing. They're not you!

If you can't learn as you'd wish, then you can go as far as you can go, understanding and accepting your own limits and not hating yourself for something you can't control. You can learn to make lists and get things ready the night before school to help you organize your thoughts and remember what you have to do. You can learn to communicate how you feel when your parents, teachers, or friends compare you to anyone but yourself.

If you can't walk on your feet, you can walk on your crutches or "walk" in your wheelchair. If you can't express yourself in words, you can press one key at a time on a typewriter or learn sign language.

People who have a disability can do many of the same things as anyone else; they just have to do them differently. Henry doesn't even like referring to himself as disabled. He'd rather say he's "differently able!"

It will help to understand that your parents, friends, and teachers may try to prevent you from following your dreams. Think carefully about what they advise, talk with them about any concerns, and begin to separate their imagined fears from what could be real.

Lisa (remember, she wants to be an actress, model, or lawyer) told me:

> What gets me the most is when people will tell me, "Oh, you can't do that; you're in a wheelchair. What actress do you know who's in a wheelchair? What model do you know?"
>
> A guy who talked at our school was from a place where they give jobs to the handicapped. He said, "You just got to make people see the way you are." I was asking him about being a lawyer because he went to law school at one point. He told me not to be

surprised if people tell me I can't even reach the books! He said not to get hung up on those people who don't feel you can do it.

When people tell me I can't do it, that makes me want to do it ten times as hard.

Shorty said:

I'm trying to change the attitudes of the public and also the attitudes of those people who are handicapped. This is no small job. I like challenges. I like to do activities in the outdoors, like camping, scuba diving, and boating. To me, it's a real adventure.

That's why I'm putting all my efforts into sharing these adventures with other people who have physical disabilities. The outdoors opens up a whole new world for the handicapped.

I have told other people, "What's a city curb when you've crawled through the swamp?" If you've been through the woods crawling on your butt trying to get over a creek, the city curbs are not that frustrating anymore.

On the other hand, it's confusing to me why city curbs and other barriers were ever built by man in the first place. There are moments when I think the nondisabled are plotting against us!

But the laws are slowly changing. As days go by, more bathrooms are being built that are easier for the disabled to get to, more buildings have ramps for our wheelchairs and crutches, and more parking lots have wider spaces. There are all sorts of changes taking place in the buildings of our country, so that we can be part of society instead of outside society.

CHAPTER 24
SCHOOL

School can mean friendship, rushing to your locker between classes, "Hey, what's up?" in the halls, learning about worlds you didn't even know existed, football games, homework, meeting in the bathroom seventh period, lunch lines, after-school sports, sitting next to your best friend in English, and checking to see who gets breasts first.

School can mean bake sales, class trips, detention, locker rooms, new math examples, passing notes, pom-poms, concerts, having a crush on the new art teacher, late passes, election campaigns, exams, track meets, and going down to the nurse.

But it can also mean being teased every time you get on the school bus, standing alone at recess, being yelled at for something you really didn't do, cutting classes, loneliness, being sent to the principal's office, hearing a rumor spread about you in the halls, being suspended, being put down for how you dress, being told, "Me and my friends will be waiting to kick your butt after school," being picked on by your teacher, failing. It just depends. . . .

School is a blending of so many things. Besides teaching facts, school teaches you about responsibility, about your ability to achieve, how you relate to teachers (adults) and make friendships. School also has a lot to do with how you feel about yourself: whether you feel confident, shy, afraid to try, smart, or stupid.

This chapter will give you the chance to think about the feelings that you have about you, your teachers, and the many different parts of your life at school.

You might want to grab a piece of paper so that you can write down past school experiences that you remember made you feel good, as well as those you wish you could forget. After taking a good look at your list, you can begin to see more clearly how your early school history might have influenced the attitudes and feelings you have today. Here are some questions that will help you remember some of your feelings:

- Did you like school? Dislike school? Not care one way or another?
- Were you praised a lot? Punished a lot? Teased?
- Did you like your schoolwork?
- Did you find you could learn easily, or was learning a struggle?
- Did your teachers think you were smart, average, or maybe a little below the rest of the class?
- Did you ever read from the blue book while everyone else was on the red?
- Did you feel the teachers liked you?
- Did you have friends at school?
- Did your teachers put gold stars and "Good Try!" on your work?
- Did they crumple up your papers a lot and say you should do them over?
- How do you feel about school now?

If you still have your family feelings list (if not, you might want to make a new one), see whether your feelings at home were similar to your school feelings during the same years. We really can't talk about school feelings without mentioning family feelings. I'd also like to make sure you realize that if your family feelings aren't good, you can still have good school feelings.

Family Feelings Can Influence School Feelings

There are many ways in which your school feelings might be influenced by your family feelings. For example:

- If your parents always expect you to get high grades, you might always feel pressured in school.
- If your parents and grandparents didn't go to or didn't finish school, and you're the first one in your family to be able to attend, you might feel a lot of pressure because you want them to be proud and may feel like you'd be letting them down if you don't do well.
- If your family is having troubles, it can be hard to concentrate in school.
- If there's a lot of competition within your family about how well you do and how well your sister or brother has done, you may end up working harder, or may resent all the pressure and just decide to stop trying.
- If you have to take on a lot of responsibilities at home, as much as you care about school, it may be very hard to spend time on your work.
- If you have no (or very little) privacy at home, it may be very hard to concentrate on your work.
- If . . .

You can add your own experiences and feelings to this list. The main thing is to realize that there is a connection.

When your family feelings are good, and you know they'll give you support and love—even if you mess up on your report card—then you'll likely have much more freedom to try. If your family puts pressure on you, doesn't feel what you're trying to do is important, or is just not there, then it can be harder.

But no matter what, you are the one who will walk through those school doors in the morning. You are the one who will sit in your classes. You are the one who has the chance to speak with teachers, nurses, guidance counselors, school social workers, or school psychologists, if need be, in order to go forward in a way that feels good to you. You need not be held back by a family who's insensitive to how much school can mean or how important it is to be free to achieve at your own level.

I'm not saying that any of this is easy. I'm only suggesting that you have more control than perhaps you think you have. You have more choices. You don't have to sit back and be miserable and say, "Look what everyone is doing to me. I can't help it! How can I work? How can you expect me to try?"

First you have to make the decision that you care enough about yourself to want to take the first step. Let people who can help you know you want to try.

All Different Kinds of Teachers

One of the most important parts of school is being able to get along with all kinds of teachers. You never know who you're going to get and how they'll act with you, no matter what kind of stories you've heard.

I will never forget how nervous I was on the first day of school in the eighth grade. Everyone had told me what a horrible, scary person my homeroom teacher was. So I walked in expecting to see a monster! Well, she wasn't warm and wonderful, but she wasn't a monster. She was at least fair and didn't really bother me. She just wasn't the kind of teacher you felt like hugging. But she also wasn't as awful as everyone told me she would be.

It really boils down to how *you* relate to your teacher. The person who tells you how rotten he or she is might have really misbehaved in class, been rude, not worked very hard. Or the teacher might really be rotten, but you're better off deciding that for yourself.

Throughout your years in school, you'll have so many different teachers, all with their own personalities, their own styles of teaching, their own rules, their own ways of getting you to work harder. Some will be exciting, some will be okay, some will be boring.

Though it can be wonderful to be fond of your teacher, it's more important to realize that you are in class to learn—about the subject, as well as about yourself. While teachers aren't hired to entertain or love you, it's nicer to be in a class that feels good.

Just because a teacher is strict doesn't mean he or she can't also be nice. No matter what a teacher looks like, what style of clothes he or she wears, how big or small, old or young—the only way to learn who they are is to give them a chance. Some teachers will have warmth, some won't. Some will seem to care more than others. Sometimes you may not realize how much they really cared until many years later. And true, some teachers seem to care more about their subjects than about the students in their class. But that doesn't have to mean they wouldn't respond to you if you make the extra effort. If they don't, at least you'll know you tried.

But, no matter how little control you have over who your teacher is or what he or she is like, you *do* have control over your behavior and work effort in each of your classes. It will help you a lot if you can try to do the best you can, even if you are not as happy as you might be with a particular teacher. It will help if you try to deal with each teacher as he or she *is* rather than waste your time and energy expecting or wishing them to be who they are not.

If you feel that a teacher is not treating you fairly, it's important to speak up! Your teacher may not even realize how his or her actions are affecting you, unless you share your feelings honestly.

If your teacher won't listen or continues to treat you in a way that doesn't feel good—and may even cause you to have bad feelings about coming to school—it's important to talk about this with your parents. They can try to discuss these feelings with your teacher (with or without you present). If there is still no change, they can approach the guidance counselor or the principal of your school for help in the hopes that changes will be made for the better.

Teacher Power

Teachers have an incredible amount of power. Some teachers have the power to make a child believe in himself or herself for the first time. Some teachers have the power to make a child trust that somebody really cares when it seems like nobody else does. Some teachers have the power to make a child feel comfortable and safe. Some teachers have the power to stimulate, to challenge, to encourage a child to learn and achieve in a most exciting way. It's no wonder that teachers who can make such a positive difference in the lives of their students are considered so special.

But there are some teachers who have the power to keep a child from opening his or her mouth for a whole school year. And some teachers who have the power to make a child have stomachaches almost every morning. And some teachers who have the power to rob a child of his or her confidence and self-respect. Sometimes these teachers don't even realize how their power is affecting their students.

A woman who wanted me to be sure to let everyone know she's now a senior citizen—and *still* remembers—told me about her seventh grade teacher. It seems that this teacher also taught her older brother and sister, who always earned excellent grades. She found studying to be a struggle and didn't do nearly as well as her brother and sister did in that class. One day the teacher said to her, "I guess, when it came to you, they ran out of brains!" That really hurt. And she never forgot.

Teachers have the power to question ability, reduce confidence, and make students feel they don't measure up.

Diane works part time in a fast-food restaurant so that she can help pay for college. She and one of the guys were preparing food and singing. She turned to him and said, "Hey, you have a nice voice! Do you want to come Christmas caroling with a group of us after work?" He told her, "No, thanks. I never sing in public or with groups, ever since my third-grade teacher told me that my voice was too loud when the class sang."

Teachers have the power to silence.

Hal, age fifteen, said, "We have this one teacher who is really great. Any time we have a problem, we know he'll listen. We can go to him after school and talk for hours. A few weeks ago, my girlfriend's group of friends had a huge fight. Everyone decided that they should go to this teacher so he could help them settle it. They stayed talking for about three hours after school and everyone felt better."

Teachers have the power to listen, offer guidance, and to be there and show they care.

George, age thirty-four, told me about a language teacher he had in high school. Said George, "He would totally try to intimidate [threaten, scare] people. He made me scared to even ask a question because he'd yell at anybody who didn't know the answer and would make that person feel stupid.

"He had a profound impact [big influence] on my learning ability for foreign languages. He was such a bad teacher. He was more like a clown in a show. Instead of encouraging me to learn, he instilled fear. He definitely turned me off foreign languages."

Teachers have the power to turn off. (Sometimes, it's the teacher who turns a student off, not the topic. It's too bad that the student doesn't always realize this difference at the time.)

Maggie, age thirty-three, told me that she'll never forget her seventh grade gym teacher. She said, "In class, when I tried to serve, I couldn't even hit the volleyball over my side of the net. Kids laughed and made fun of me. Although the teacher told them not to do that anymore, I knew what they were thinking and I tried to figure out any excuse to get out of playing in class. My teacher offered to spend extra time with me to help me with my volleyball skills. She came to school early for about two weeks, just to help me. The kids in class were amazed at how well I started serving. They probably couldn't imagine how that happened. The teacher told me that her early morning helping sessions were our secret. Her caring meant a lot to me. She didn't have to do that."

Teachers have the power to give of themselves in an extra special way, to help build confidence and skills that can make a difference.

Lisa, age thirteen, told me: "I have this teacher who goes out of his way to bust on you [make jokes on you]. He usually chooses one person every year who he picks on the most. This year it's me and one other girl.

"There are some people who don't have to work hard to get good grades. I work my butt off. I spent the whole weekend at the library, was up working until one o'clock one night, and when I turned in my paper, he said, 'I'm surprised you had time to do it because you're always so busy with your friends.' "

Teachers have the power to frustrate.

Paul, age twenty-three, said, "My English teacher in college really cared so much. She gave so much of herself, was so patient. I really struggled and stretched myself to do as well as I could. It was a real positive experience. She was the first teacher who took that kind of time to teach. She was very happy when I did well."

Teachers have the power to encourage, to strengthen confidence, to motivate [stimulate you to want to learn].

A seventeen-year-old girl shared:

This is something that's not easy for me to say. I quit school. I I had a lot of problems in high school. Teachers were always trying to tell me something was wrong with me. I never was interested in what they were teaching.

The teachers sat up there like they were kings and queens and would treat me like I was dirt. The kids that were interested in school and were looked at as smart, were treated better. But the kids that were not as school-oriented [not as inclined toward school, didn't like it as much, weren't interested] were shunned and shut off. I felt I was treated so badly during high school. That's why I quit.

The school was trying to tell my father that I needed psychiatric help. Anything I did, even the slightest thing, they would kick me out and suspend me. They didn't handle me right. They said all these things about me that weren't true.

The best thing I did was drop out. I recently got my high school equivalency diploma [diploma that's equal to a high school diploma, but earned at home, not by going to school] and I'm doing well now. I'm going to start going to college soon.

I like doing things slowly. The slower I do it, the more I've realized everything can be better. Even my friends are saying, "Why don't you go to college now? Why aren't you going?" What they're going for now is something I may decide to do five or ten years from now. I realize I can do it and I'm going to take my own time.

Teachers have the power to ignore, to disregard, to misunderstand, to turn away.

Said V., now a teacher and counselor, "No one really took the time for me. If I had a few teachers who adored me, loved me, nurtured me, 'watered me,' and took the time for me, they would have gotten everything from me and more. All you need is that one special teacher who helps you see the world differently.

"So I decided to become a teacher myself . . . so that I could give to students what I never got."

I'd like to believe that somewhere inside all teachers is the power to care about their students. How special those teachers are who do reach out and give of themselves in order to make a difference.

This might be a perfect time to consider the special teachers who have cared about you, helped you, and made you feel more positive about yourself and your learning.

Many times, people make sure to tell others when they're upset or unhappy with someone, but don't always let people know they're appreciated. You don't have to wait until a holiday or the last day of school to write a note or tell a teacher how much he or she has meant to you.

Talking with Your Teachers

Have you ever been bursting to say something but just were too afraid, too embarrassed, or too concerned that your teacher or classmates would think you were stupid?

Many kids would like to say much more to their teachers, both in class and privately. But often that's not so easy to do. Sometimes your teacher just might not seem like the type who would listen.

Try not to be held back by what your teacher looks like. Even if he or she is six feet tall, has a gruff voice, doesn't like ice cream, and works as a part-time troll that eats billy goats, you owe it to yourself to say what you need to say to your teacher. Speak softly, respectfully, honestly, but speak—even if you're scared, even if you think they'll believe you weren't paying attention. In fact, that's just what you can start with (turning feelings into words): "Please don't think I wasn't paying attention. I really was. But I'm just not sure about something. Would you please explain it to me?"

If you don't ask questions, how will you learn? How else will your teacher be able to know what you don't understand? It's your right to speak freely and say what you need to say. It's often more comfortable to talk privately. You deserve to get answers and explanations for your questions. That's what teachers owe you, because teaching you is their job. But they can't look at you and magically guess what your question is or if you have a question, unless you ask.

Sometimes your teacher may be too busy to make himself or herself available for you. If they seem hard to find or won't give you time, tell them you need to speak with them very badly and perhaps the two of you could meet before or after school. Sometimes it's a good idea to ask them if they have a free period during the day. If so, perhaps you can get a special pass to see them at that time, or see them during lunch or study periods.

Finding the Right Words

It might be helpful to turn to the beginning of Chapter 19, "Your Parents," where I have suggested different ways you can express your feelings in a clear, honest way. The same idea for communicating how you feel can be put to good use with teachers.

Here are some more examples of how you can turn your feelings into words:

- If you weren't the one who was really talking, you can say, "I just want you to know that it really wasn't me who was talking."
- If you find something hard to understand, say, "I'm finding this hard to understand."
- If you don't know the answer, you can say, "I'm sorry, I don't know the answer."
- If you think you're being blamed unfairly, say so.
- If you feel it would make a difference in your ability to concentrate if you changed your seat, ask.
- If you're sorry you talked out of turn, say so.
- If you think your teachers are expecting too much of you, tell them in exactly that way.
- If you think they're pressuring you, tell them that you feel pressured.

- If you did something wrong, all you can do is apologize, say you're sorry, say you didn't mean to break the rules (or whatever) and you won't do it again in the future.
- If you think they're comparing you unfairly with an older sister or brother, let them know that makes you feel uncomfortable and upset when they compare you. (You can also remind them that you're not your sister or brother, you're *you*.)

If you can just remember to turn your feelings into words, you'll never have to wonder what to say to your teachers, your parents, your friends or anyone.

Remember, too, that you may not always be comfortable speaking with your teacher. Even if you know what you need to say, it may be hard to get the words out. In fact, as you were reading through the list of ways you can express your feelings, you might have been thinking that you can't imagine saying any of those things to your teachers. Most kids would probably feel the same way.

But even if you're uncomfortable, that doesn't mean you should hold back your feelings and not talk. Keep in mind that how you say what you say can make a big difference. If you're respectful and private, you have a better chance that your teacher will give you respect and care enough to listen to your concerns. Sometimes you'll just have to push yourself to get the words out. After that, each time will get easier.

And remember that you don't have to have all the answers. If you're honest, that will usually count and be appreciated. Instead of making up something that's not true, you can say: "I don't know"; "I'm not sure"; or "I'm sorry but I'm just not prepared. Can I speak with you later?"

The expression on their face, how they move and react, will help give you a clue as to whether they seem to be relaxed, tired, tense, pressured, grouchy, or in a good mood. Sometimes bulging veins in the neck can be a sign of tension. (Unless, of course, their veins always bulge!) Let your teacher know you'd like to talk, and if he or she seems tense, you might be wiser setting your meeting for the next day. If you're not sure, ask if they would mind speaking at that time.

One more thing: There's usually a favorite teacher or two in every school, the kind of teacher everybody talks to when they have a problem.

Don't take it personally and think they care about everyone else and not you if they don't talk with you on the spot and take care of your problem immediately. Sometimes, because everyone wants their time and they like giving their time, it's hard for them to be there for everybody.

Teachers' Pets

Jennifer, age twelve, told me, "Sometimes the teachers of my cluster seem to pay more attention to one girl. She's always going down to get messages, and she gets special privileges. She's pretty intelligent. I can't really think of any other reason. I don't really care. I just notice."

Probably each teacher has a few favorites. I guess that's natural. But very often you won't even know who the favorites are.

Other times, a few boys or girls might be singled out. They seem to be the ones who are asked to do the errands and have other privileges. Other students may become resentful or jealous of those classmates. Yet, it's often not the student's fault that the teacher is playing favorites.

Kevin, age fourteen, said, "I feel I get along with my teachers well, no matter who the teacher is. I think they like my attitude because they seem to show it with their comments on my report card. I don't try to be a favorite. If they like me, that's their choice. But I don't try to be the teacher's pet."

One teacher said that many of the teachers he knows end up calling on the kids who raise their hands the most. If you feel your teacher is overlooking your raised hand, let him or her know you'd like to be called on more.

You can also try to be more friendly with your teachers. Say hello to them in the halls, smile, ask them how they are when you walk into class. You might be pleasantly surprised that they'll pay more attention to you, too. Not as a pet, but as a person.

Homework

Do it.

When it's assigned. Complete it on time. Be organized. Keep a little notebook or daily planner for your assignments. Check off your work for each day before closing your locker at the end of the day. That way you can be sure to bring the books home that you need.

Try to be up to date and hand in work on time.

If you know in advance that you have a book to read or paper to write, then try to pace yourself, doing a little each day, so you won't be faced with doing it all at the last minute. Be sure to write on your calendar when papers and book reports are due or when tests are scheduled. It can also help to figure out how much time you might need to do your work—then actually write in your planner, "Start studying for the test" or, "Start the outline for the term paper."

If you're confused, you can contact a friend. But it is better to try to see your teacher before school or before class the next day. That way you can show you're interested and get an explanation at the same time. You can also ask your parents for guidance.

If you have tons of work and it seems you'll never finish and it's all just too much, try taking one assignment at a time, one paper, one book. And as soon as you finish one, go on to the next. You may be happily surprised at how you can just keep crossing things off your assignment list.

If you are overwhelmed by the burden of having so much to get done, you may sit back and say, "It's just too much, how can my teachers do that to me? Don't they know I have other subjects, too?" Since you don't have the power to change your assignments, you *can* decide to concentrate on getting them done. Instead of spending time and energy complaining about what you think you can't possibly do (and probably don't want to do!), just get it done. Start with one assignment, then the next, and the next.

Don't do:
- Last-minute work (if you can help it). If you rush your assignments, you won't have the full chance of testing out what you know and what you don't.
- Your homework on the bus (or leave it on the bus, either), in homeroom, or while the teacher is going over it in class.
- Your homework during lunch. While lunch offers extra time to study or do work, it is not a good idea to make a

habit of saving all your work until then. You're likely to be more rushed, as you'll only have a limited amount of time. And wouldn't it be nice to relax and take a break from the day's schedule? Doing your homework at lunch may even cause you indigestion!

- Your homework all over your home. Try, if possible, to keep your books and papers in one area. That way you can find things as you need them and won't have to go around searching.

Taking Tests

Many people hate to take tests. But, like them or not, they're a fact of life. Think about how you feel about tests. Are you one of those people who does very well in class and then does poorly on each test? Lots of people seem to have difficulty taking tests. Besides the preparation, the amount of pressure you feel is an important thing to consider.

Pressure is not always negative (bad). It can challenge you and push you to do better and better. But if the pressure is too strong, you may have a great deal of trouble concentrating.

There are several things you can do (besides studying) to help yourself be more prepared and organized while taking a test. These ideas can help you approach your test with more confidence:

Remember to bring with you any essential items such as pencils, erasers, or tissues. Be sure you either have a watch, or can see the clock, or can ask the teacher to keep you aware of how much time you have left.

Reading test instructions is very important. Right at the beginning, check if you have all the pages of the test, see how many questions there are, and read the instructions carefully. Ask questions, if you're not sure what to do (even if no one else has a question).

Work carefully and steadily. Try not to spend too much time if you're having difficulty with a particular question. Put a mark next to it so you know to come back to it later, and go on. You may find that other questions will remind you of what you couldn't think of before.

Again, be aware of how much time you have left so you can get to all, or at least most, of the questions.

Don't be concerned about what anyone else is writing. Everybody is different. Everybody works at his or her own pace. If some people seem to whiz through the exam and finish before you've even gone on to the third question, just remember that speed doesn't always mean accuracy. They could finish very quickly and get everything wrong! And just because someone else is writing a lot, it doesn't make what he or she is saying correct.

So, rather than concerning yourself with everyone else's pace, you need to set your own. Make sure to check that you've answered every question before turning in your paper.

Also know that some teachers will think you've cheated if you even look a tiny bit away from your paper, stretch, drop your pencil, drop your paper, or suddenly have a great need to tie your shoe. Know who is watching you and play by that person's rules!

Sandy, age fourteen, said, "I do well in class, but I never seem to do well on tests. I panic!"

Gail, age fifty-eight, said, "I was always slow taking tests because I was a slow reader. My grades were very good, but it just took me longer than most of the other students to finish. Even though I knew what my problem was, I remember being embarrassed that I was still sitting there when just about everyone else was ready to leave."

Marilyn, age forty-two, told me, "I always hated taking essay tests. There was nothing worse than sitting down to take an exam and having your mind go blank while everyone around you was scribbling their answers."

Allen, age thirteen, said, "I love taking tests! They usually take up the whole period. Tests are easy for me."

Just as with everything else, there are so many feelings about tests, so many different kinds of pressures. If kids come into a test thinking that their parent(s) will "kill" them if they don't do well, or that this grade will make them pass or fail for the whole year, or even just the marking period, how well do you think they will be able to concentrate?

My guess is that the panic, worry, and tremendous need to do well might interfere with their thinking. It can also force them to feel they have to cheat.

Cheating

Jennifer, age twelve, said, "Sometimes when kids don't get an assignment done, they ask someone else if they can copy theirs. I don't think I'd give them my assignment to copy. But I wouldn't report them or anything. I'd just let them do what they want. But not with my paper. I don't think it would be hard to say no, even to a friend."

If you think someone is trying to cheat, you can cover your paper or ask the teacher to change your seat.

Kevin, age fourteen, told me, "There's a lot of cheating in the classes. If the teacher walks out for one second, the kids start asking for answers. Or if we're doing classwork, some of the kids will just wait for me to finish so they can get the answers. I won't give answers to them. I can't stand that! Just that they would even think that I would give them the answer because they neglected to do their work and I didn't."

Bob, age twenty-eight, said, "I was great at cheating! I was a master cheater! I think probably the worst part about it was that I really studied hard. But still I made sure to sit next to a kid who was smart, because I couldn't take a chance that I would fail. Even after staying up sometimes until two in the morning studying, I couldn't allow myself to try to do the work on my own. I couldn't take a chance on myself. Because of the way I was brought up, I was never allowed to make mistakes. So even though I really studied, I was too scared not to cheat."

Neal, age thirteen, said, "I think some teachers are very strict and make it hard to cheat. But in certain classes, cheating on tests is very easy. You'll never get caught. Personally, I don't really cheat. But I don't like to have a teacher watching over me when I look up at the clock.

"I would say that the majority of students don't cheat. But those that do cheat, cheat a lot. I don't think it's really fair. It's the person's responsibility to do their own work and not take it from other people."

Kim, age eleven, said, "It's not cheating when someone asks you a question on a test. . . . It's just asking."

According to one teacher, "Kids don't like it when another kid gets away with cheating. Someone who has gotten a 90 and hasn't cheated would probably feel their 90 is worth more if someone else gets it and doesn't deserve it."

As a teacher, I am always amazed at how many students think I can't see their eyeballs looking sideways, while their bodies seem perfectly straight in their chairs. As you have seen, the need to cheat is a little different for each person who chooses to do so. Some people just aren't prepared; some, like Robert, are too afraid to be wrong, too afraid to allow themselves to be truly tested; others are lazy.

There are several concerns about cheating. One very important one is what might be the consequences if you get caught? At some schools, you get kicked out, and that's that. The fact that you cheated may go on your permanent record. Will your teacher tear up your paper if he or she sees you cheat? Will your teacher also tear up the paper of the person from whom you are cheating, even if that person doesn't know you are?

Sometimes a teacher may not tear up a paper; he or she will say something to you about it in front of the whole class. That kind of embarrassment can often be much worse than one low grade.

As much as your parents might be pressuring you to get good grades, how would they feel if you got them by cheating? If you haven't talked with them about how pressured you feel—and how the pressure has caused you to cheat—it's important to let them know.

Still another concern is just how long you intend to keep up your cheating. If, for example, you are able to get into a certain college because of the high grades that you got from cheating, will that mean you'll have to keep cheating in order to keep up with the work and be able to stay there? How much pressure do you think you'd feel then? When do you call it quits? When do you stop trying to be someone you're not?

If you do your own work and strive to do as well as you can, learning can be much more satisfying and enjoyable. You won't have to pretend or deal with grades that you know are not honestly yours. And you won't set yourself up for unfair expectations from parents, teachers, friends—and yourself.

Passing Notes

How could I write a chapter on school without including note passing? I'll never forget the time in the sixth grade when my teacher caught me writing down all her sayings so that I could imitate her with my friends after school. I nearly "died" when she came over and picked up those pages! I thought she was going to read them aloud to the class, but she didn't. It was enough that she knew I was doing that to her. I think I might still have my composition somewhere, promising to be a better person and never do that again.

According to Hilary, age eleven, "Passing notes is a part of school. Classes would be so boring without notes! They're a new way of talking."

I suppose, without notes, some girls and boys wouldn't be able to find out who likes whom, who just got her period, who smells, who's cute, who's coming to the party on Friday night, where everyone is going to meet after school, who's finally wearing a bra, whose parents are getting a divorce, or who's bored.

Just beware that you might be caught! If you're comfortable with what you say in your note, then you have little to be concerned about, even if you're caught. But notes can sometimes be very embarrassing. If you're telling secrets, you'd be wise to remember that some kids might just open up your note and pass it around the school instead of to the person in the blue sweater.

Some teachers have very creative ways of dealing with notes. I was told about one teacher who takes every note he captures, makes copies, and hands one out to each person in the class!

A note about notes: If you're spending much of your class time writing notes, as much as you might love to pass notes, it would help for you to think about how distracting those notes can be to other classmates, your teacher, and—believe it or not—yourself.

If you're concentrating on notes, you're probably not concentrating on the lesson. If the reason is you're bored, and you feel notes are the best way to pass the time, then I suggest you speak with your teacher. Several of you might want to get together with your teacher and share ideas as to how the class can be more interesting and challenging. Some suggestions are creative projects and assignments, debates, different kinds of research papers, or role playing (that's when classmates act out a certain situation).

Although I can't speak for all teachers, I could say that many would appreciate knowing how students feel in their class—as long as the feelings were presented in a respectful, positive way. Teachers can't be sure how their students feel unless they're told.

The Locker Room

While many kids can't wait to get into the locker room to talk about who they're going out with, after school plans, what they just did in class, or the cute boy or girl who just moved in, there are other kids who wish the locker room had never been invented. This is often because they may feel left out (as they might feel at recess), or may just not be happy about having to get ready for gym class. Others may hate the idea of having to change clothes in front of everyone else, especially if they're much more or much less developed.

It can help to remember that growing at different rates is just part of growing up. With or without a bra, with or without pubic hair—each person is going to be at their own stage of growth. So it's important for everyone to respect each other and not call attention to anyone else's differences. (Since locker rooms usually mean changing for gym class, it's also important to respect athletic differences.)

Locker rooms can actually be more fun than you may realize. It's a chance to talk to people in your class and get to know them better. If no one seems to approach you, you now know that you can take the first step. If you enter the locker room together with someone and start talking, you can continue talking while you change.

Moving to a New School

Moving to a new school in a new town can be exciting. You get to meet new friends, do things in a slightly different way, maybe get to see a different part of your country. But it can also be a bit scary and lonely until you get to meet some people you feel comfortable with who'll take you around and show you everything.

You might meet one person who you "click" with immediately who will show you around, or you might want to observe and watch the different groups at school and see which kids appeal to you the most. Or you might wait and see who extends themselves to you. You can also join a club. This way you can meet friends through enjoying a common activity. Any one of these choices or any combination of choices is fine.

It will help to remember that you don't have to wait for someone to come up to you. You've got the ability to walk up to someone else and say hi. You can ask other kids where certain classrooms are, to show you where the lunchroom is, or to help you find the gym. Go easy with new friendships and take your time looking around.

Keith, age fourteen, said, "When I was younger, I used to say hello and act nice to a new person. I tried to show them around and tried to make friends with them. There was a new kid who came into school this year. I said hello and tried to be nice to him, but other people influenced him away from me. They said something to the new kid behind my back so he wouldn't associate with me."

Debby, age twelve, said, "I was really nervous the first day I went to my new school. I didn't know if the kids would like me. I missed my friends. I didn't know what the teachers were like and how hard the work was going to be."

L., age thirteen, talked about her friend who moved to a nearby town. Said L., "When I first talked with her, she said all the kids were drinking and she would never do anything like that. Then I saw her a few weeks ago, and she talked about how she went drinking with her new boyfriend. She changed so much. If you don't smoke or don't drink in that town, you're a priss. She used to be a really good student, really smart. Now she doesn't even care about her grades anymore."

Sometimes, in order to be accepted, people will do things they never expected to do. All the more reason to always be aware of your feelings and choices—and to remember that you don't have to compromise who you are just to get others to include you.

Jeff, age fourteen, said, "When I moved in the third grade, there was one boy who came up to me and said hi, and that made it all okay. He took me around and introduced me to the other kids. We're still really good friends."

H. moved into her new neighborhood when she was eleven. A girl came over very quickly and acted very nice. She started introducing her to people but then would take them off to the side and tell them she was a loser because of what she wore. Said H., "I found out she did this each time she introduced me, and while everyone would laugh, I would stand there like an idiot. I trusted her, that's what hurt so much."

If your grade is moving on to a new school, at least you know you've got company dealing with a new situation. So if you're scared and think you'll get lost, at least you know you can all be lost together. But sometimes because a school district is quite large, your group of friends might be split up. In that case, moving to a new school might seem like its also moving to a new town.

Be patient. Understand that any scary feelings you might have are normal. Just go slowly, learning as much as you can about the new people you meet, the rules, and the opportunities that are there for you to make your move feel as good as possible.

New schools will probably seem huge for the first days. But after a week or so, you most likely won't be able to imagine that you went to that small elementary or middle school. Your high school will probably be larger than your middle school or junior high, and if you go to college, that may be larger still, with many different buildings instead of just one. (Some high schools have campuses, too.)

If you change from a public school to a private school, you may need to adjust to wearing certain clothes (a uniform) that other kids must also wear. Or you may be moving from a school where you live at home to a boarding school in another state or even another country. Aside from meeting new people and getting used to new surroundings, your adjustment will include living together (away from home) with other students who attend that school.

Keep in mind that every change takes time. Each new step takes adjusting. And once you adjust, you'll know for sure that you were ready to arrive. Most kids find they wouldn't want to go back.

If you're having trouble getting used to your new situation, you can check your school list of "helping" adults (teachers, coaches, counselors, and so forth) in order to talk with them about what you feel, and learn what you can do to try to make things more positive.

Advanced Classes, "Regular" Classes, and Special Education

Often students are put into what is known as "tracks," a term that teachers use to group students together by their ability to learn.

There's usually a group of students who are placed in either an accelerated or an advanced class. Those placed in an accelerated class are the students who may complete a program in two years instead of three or in one year instead of two. Those students who are placed in an advanced class will usually be offered more difficult or enriched subject matter. While many students in these accelerated or advanced classes are happy about the chance to work at higher levels, some feel pressured.

Although some of the pressure is quite positive and can help push students to achieve in a very exciting way, the pressure can also be negative and destructive.

John was placed in the advanced class in seventh grade. All his friends were also in the advanced class. He had a difficult time keeping up with the work, so his teacher wanted to place him in the regular class the next year. But John insisted that he would do everything in his power to keep up with the work. He was really concerned that people would say he wasn't good enough for the fast class.

Other students are grouped together in "regular" classes. Because most students in these classes are able to do the work at that level, there is often less competition within these classes. But, as a group, they may feel they're not quite as "good" as the advanced class. Some kids who could be placed in advanced classes are relieved to be in the "regular" level because they don't want the added pressure. There are lots of different feelings about this.

Some kids get placed in special education classes or resource rooms for all or some of their subjects because that's where they can best learn, according to their special needs. Some students in the special education classes may have a learning disability, some may not. Many kids really work well in these classes and find that the teachers' special training to help them is exactly what they need to be able to understand the subject.

Because many students are quick to judge kids in special education classes as inferior, being in this class may make someone feel bad about themselves and not think they're as important or as good as those in the regular and advanced classes. The same feelings have been expressed by those in remedial classes (such as reading workshops and speech).

It's just not true that some kids are better than others because of what class they're in, what grades they earn, or for any other reason. Each person is as good as anyone else—no matter what. All kids can be good students, no matter what class they're in.

It really is important that there are different classes to meet special needs. Being in any type of class has nothing to do with whether someone in that class could be a good friend. It just has to do with how that person needs to learn. It's time for kids to stop the negative comments that can be so hurtful and start appreciating how positive it is that kids have the chance to learn according to their needs.

Very often being placed in a special class is just the experience that can cause you to have more confidence and feel better about yourself. F.'s story is an example of how that can happen. When F. was in junior high, she could never learn math. She had a social studies teacher teaching her algebra and, as a consequence, got off to a wrong math start. As a result of having a rotten math experience in the ninth grade, all her math classes became a nightmare.

She barely passed tenth grade math and then was asked to take a special education class for eleventh grade math. Instead of doing eleventh grade math in a year, she now had to complete it in a year and a half.

At first she was embarrassed and ashamed for being placed in what the kids called "dummy math." But the class was slow enough to give her the opportunity to finally learn math the way she should have in the ninth grade. She got 95s in math on all her report cards and felt great.

Repeating a Grade or Skipping a Grade

The same need for understanding applies to those who repeat a grade. Students who are "left back" are being given an important chance to learn information and strengthen skills in order to move on. Just imagine how it would feel to be placed in the next grade if you really were not prepared to handle the challenges and pressures of new work.

Even though, deep down, kids might find it a relief to repeat a grade, because the extra year can help them feel more confident and ready to move forward in a better way—it still can be tough getting used to it. Their adjustment often has to do with how other kids react—if they're understanding or if they tease and give them a hard time. Some kids may feel awkward if repeating the grade puts them in the same class as their younger sister or brother. Some have difficulty because their closest friends have moved on to the next grade. Some feel that repeating a grade makes them a failure. That's not true.

It would help for everyone to understand if someone fails a test or fails a course, that doesn't make the person a failure. It means that whatever they did to approach their learning didn't work as it needed to for them. And they must now get extra help (from teachers, tutors, parents, or anyone else) in order to approach their work in a way that will give them better results. Sometimes the extra help means repeating a grade.

Students who are "extra advanced" in their ability to learn may be given the opportunity to "skip" a grade or move ahead to a grade beyond where they would normally be. Here, too, while a student might feel very positive about this move, it may be hard to adjust to no longer being in the same grade as close friends. Allison, an eleventh grade student, told me, "One of the hardest things about skipping a grade for me was that all my friends were able to get their driver's license a year ahead of me! I'm the youngest in my grade."

Lee, age fifty-one, told me he was suddenly put two years ahead when he was in the ninth grade. Looking back on it, he said, "More than anything, I just wanted to be with other kids my own age. It was hard feeling like I had to 'act older' than I really was, or felt, or knew how to be. So, I graduated ninth grade at age twelve and graduated high school before my sixteenth birthday. I had no friends my own age until I was about twenty-three or so. As much as I liked and was ready to be challenged by the work, it was really hard, socially."

Whether repeating a grade or moving forward, there will probably be many adjustments to be made, not only with work but with friends and classmates. Teasing, judging, and cruel remarks about achievement levels can cause other kids to feel like crawling into a corner and hiding. And although each person needs to find their own strength to feel important, to accept themselves for who they are and where they're at (no matter which class they're in), other people's positive and accepting attitudes *can* make a difference.

School Violence

Throughout this book, I've encouraged you to respect and accept others. Teasing and bullying must stop. Abuse in any form is unacceptable. Using fists and knives and guns instead of words is unacceptable. It's against the law. It also can be deadly.

There are many thousands of kids who bring weapons to school and many thousands who stop going to school because they're afraid of the violence. If school halls and grounds were safer, more kids would be able to take advantage of all that being in school has to offer.

It's time to put the guns down and learn to live with each other in peace. It's time for kids who think they need to act tough to give themselves a chance not only to survive their childhood but to be more challenged and productive and follow their dreams. With or without family encouragement, no matter what friends are doing, each kid can make the decision for himself or herself to end the violence and make a positive change. I'm not saying that this kind of change is easy—only that it's possible. And for survival, it's a must.

If a person doesn't like someone, even if it's brutal hatred, they can leave that person alone and have nothing to do with him or her. They can choose not to bully, not to be violent in any way—no matter what anyone around them is still doing.

I refuse to believe that any child is born with dreams of killing or being killed. I suppose that because life can be so tough, those who are violent have reached a point where they're so angry and so in need of lashing out. Perhaps they feel they don't have any other choice but to follow that destructive course. That's not true. They can choose to stop. They can ask for help. They can go forward differently, one step at a time.

Motivation

Motivation (moe-ti-VAY-shun) has to do with caring about and wanting to learn. Think about your own feelings about learning. Do you feel you're putting your best efforts into your work? If not, what do you think is causing you not to try?

Many kids want to do well but don't believe they can. Because they're afraid they won't do well, they may try to protect themselves from disappointment by not trying. Other kids may feel it's not cool to seem like you want to learn, especially if their closest friends don't care about learning. Still others don't know how to approach their work but don't let anyone know. Sometimes family problems, difficulty with friends or boyfriends and girlfriends can make it hard for kids to be able to concentrate. Sometimes kids spend more time with their friends and don't leave the time they need to do their work. And some kids really don't care.

Leslie, a ninth grader, told me:

> I used to feel awful about coming to school. I hated being there because I felt so stupid. Most of the time I didn't do my homework. I didn't care. I just tried to copy from people on the bus if I could.
>
> One of my teachers came up to me last year and said that he felt I seemed very unhappy. He asked if I'd mind if we talked for a little while after school. When I finished talking with him, I had the feeling of hope . . . and I never had that before. He said he'd help me. And he did. Not only with how to do my work in his class, but he also met with me and all my other teachers and they all worked with me so I could learn how to work better.
>
> I kept this a secret from my parents because I wanted to surprise them with how I was going to do better than I ever did. I now love going to school. I never thought I could do it.

If you know that you're in need of help with organizing your work and your time—or, if you're feeling that you can't do the work but don't know where to begin—let someone know. Talk with a parent or teacher and ask for help. It may make all the difference!

Chapter 25

GETTING PAST DIFFERENCES

I'm writing this chapter in the hopes that you, as a boy or girl, will be able to see what many adults are perhaps no longer able to. Perhaps you will be more able to look at new people and ask them such things as their name, what they like to do, what makes them feel good, what they feel strongly about, what hurts them, what their family life is like, whether or not they like to go camping or play sports, what music they like, if they like fajitas, if they've ever tried chocolate chip cookie batter, who they think will win the Super Bowl, what are their dreams . . . and listen to their answers to begin to learn about who they are instead of just judging their race, nationality, religion, how much money they have, or anything else.

We all need to work harder at understanding and accepting that outside appearances are only a covering, a wrapping. Maybe if people weren't so quick to judge, we wouldn't hear statements such as, "She's Mexican, why are you so surprised?" or, "He's white, he should have known better" or, "She's black, what do you expect?" Maybe you will be able to allow yourself to meet a *person* instead of a "package," learn his or her name, and say, for example, "Mom, Dad, this is Tommy."

If you introduce them to Tommy as just Tommy, maybe all of you will have a real chance to get to know each other. If you introduce him by saying, "This is Tommy, he's rich!" or, "This is Tommy, he's Catholic, or Jewish, or Moslem, or Mexican, or African American, or Latino, or Hispanic, Native American, or Asian, (or whatever)," then you may not have a full chance to let them know who he really is. They may concentrate on what his background is and what country his family is from instead of freely allowing themselves to get to know him — as Tommy, human-being-type person.

Racial Differences

A person's race (color) is something he or she is born with and keeps forever. It can affect the feelings of everyone who's close enough to see. When you look at a person, you know right away whether you're seeing reddish, yellowish, tan, black, white, or any other color skin.

The color of a person's skin has an amazing amount of power. Imagine a skin color having the power to make someone afraid. Imagine a skin color having the power to make someone feel they would never want the person inside that color to be in their home. Imagine a person's skin color having the power to make one or more people become violent and want to kill that person without ever having spoken to him or her. Imagine.

Kids who have gone to school all their lives with people who have different skin colors usually don't see those kids as being "colored." They just see the friends they've always gone to school with. They see the person inside.

However, when kids are forced into situations with kids whose skin color is different, it may be very clear to them that there are racial (RAY-shull) differences. If their parents are comfortable with racial differences, they'll probably be comfortable, too. If their parents are not comfortable, it may take a lot of work at trying to understand and accept that color is only a wrapper.

Depending on where you grew up, what your experiences have been so far, and especially what your parents have taught you, you will either have friends who are of different skin colors or you might prefer to stick with friends who are the same racial background as you are.

Feelings About Racial Differences

Neal, age thirteen, said, "I don't feel there's a racial problem at our school. I'm kind of glad it's integrated [mixed races]. I basically judge people on the way they feel about things, not where they're from."

Francis, a woman who devotes herself to spreading understanding among all people, has worked for years with African American youth and is a leader among African American people. She said:

> Usually, for the small children, there is little concept [idea] of hatred, except that which might be influenced by their parents. A mother or father might say, "You don't want to be like those people. You can't play with them. They're dirty." If left alone, black and white kids can play together. If they're strong enough, they can overcome the differences.
>
> I can always tell the attitude of a parent. I love children. And when I'm in an airport and see a mother with a baby, I very often smile and say something to the child. I don't care whether the mother is black, white, or a purple-people eater, I'll look long enough to try to see if I can get the child's attention. I'll say, "Hello, what's your name?"
>
> I can pretty much tell they're anti-black if they pull the child away. Or, if it's okay, they'll often say, "Tell the lady your name; talk to the lady," and so forth. Where the parents don't show negative vibes [feelings], the kids don't show any.

Patricia, age eleven, said about kids of different colors, "At parties, I don't like to kiss them."

Jonathan, age seventeen, said, "I don't understand why my parents are so upset. Just because my girlfriend is part Cherokee Indian and part Mexican, I don't know what all the fuss is about.

"She's still my girlfriend; she understands how I feel; she's pretty, and she means a lot to me. Is it ever possible that I could have a relationship with someone out of my race, where I could feel comfortable and not get hassled by my parents?"

Natalie, age fifteen, told me:

> Three other girls and I were really close. We went to Girl Scouts

together; we were a real foursome. You couldn't see one without the others. The only problem was that one of the girl's parents was really prejudiced.

All four of us had our birthdays four months in a row. Mine was the last month. The first two girls had parties, and we all went. Then came time for my other friend's party. Her parents objected to letting her invite me because I'm black. It really hurt because we were such good friends.

I have never set foot into her house. Her mom has calmed down a little. But her dad, forget it! I'm really happy that at least my friend is not prejudiced.

T., age fourteen, said, "The majority of my friends are white. All the other black kids used to look down on me. They used to call me names and make fun of me. I knew they just envied me because I could get along with just about anybody.

"You can have people turn on you even if they're your own color. It doesn't have to be that you're talking about someone of a different color."

Donna, age seventeen, said, "When I was fourteen, I had to leave my house because my father was getting sexual with me. I lived on the subways for a year with no one to talk to and no one to turn to, and a police officer took me into his home.

"My new family was black. They adored me, fed me, clothed me, and gave me a new life. Now I have a place of my own. My new sisters come to visit me from time to time. And people give us strange looks when I introduce them as my sisters. We get very amused at their reaction."

Lisa, age seventeen, said, "I have friends that are normal and friends that are handicapped. It doesn't matter to me. I have friends of all different religions and all different colors. It doesn't matter to me, and it doesn't matter to my mother. One good friend of mine—she's black and I'm white—and I go up to the people and say we're sisters. People say, 'What?' Then I just tell them that I fell in a bucket of bleach!"

A clergyman who lives in a small town in the Midwest and is one of the only Philippine families in the town shared his feelings with me about color. He told me that his daughter, who is now in kindergarten, has begun to notice that she's different from everyone else. He explained to her that many people spend hours in the sun during the summer, trying to get their skin to look as beautiful as hers does all year round. She seemed happy with that answer. His only fear is that she will grow up hating her color.

Some of the experiences shared with me are too painful and nasty to mention. You can probably make your own list of things that people who don't respect each other might say to each other. Too often, the words aren't pretty; the feelings aren't good.

I'd be guessing if I tried to figure out all the different reasons some people in one race might find it so hard to get along with people from another. There have been so many years of struggling, riots, fighting, and unfair laws. But for right now, maybe it would best to understand that we can't erase what has already taken place.

We can't undo old injustices or old ignorances that led to conflict between races. We *can* learn from the past and go forward with more respect, staying open to appreciating and sharing our differences— instead of fearing, fighting each other, and never giving each other a chance.

We can also keep in mind that bad feelings or bad behavior by one or a few people of a particular race (or any other background) doesn't mean that every person in that race is bad.

Kevin, age seventeen, told me, "In our school cafeteria, there are groups of kids who sit together, like the blacks with the blacks, the Latinos with the Latinos, the Asian kids with the Asian kids. It's really like there are invisible lines that no one crosses."

If, when you see someone in school or anywhere, you find yourself thinking that you can't relate to that person (or think you don't even want to) just because they're of a different racial background, stop and think again. Before passing that person by, you might consider for starters, at least saying hi. "Hi" can turn into a few sentences. A few sentences can turn into the beginning of the chance to let a new person in your life, one conversation at a time. You never know, he or she could turn out to be a most wonderful friend. You can never tell just by looking at their outside.

Besides, color is just that: color. We don't become friends with color. We don't become friends with skin. We become friends with the person inside that skin, no matter what his or her race might be.

Even if you understand this, I'm not suggesting that taking such a first step is easy. If you've never related to someone of a different background before, it may be very natural for you to feel uncomfortable. But you now know that it's okay to be uncomfortable. That's natural. It's just not okay to let the discomfort prevent you from pushing yourself to take the first step.

We can all learn from Sarah, age thirteen, who said, "I personally think that there is no color that's better than any other color. We all bleed the same blood. We're the same, everybody in the world—black, white, yellow, blue, dark, light—we all have something beautiful about us. Also, God doesn't make ugly! God doesn't put anybody on this earth who's not beautiful. And love sees no color."

Religious Differences

You can't look at someone on the outside and tell what religion that person is, unless the person is wearing special clothes that are a symbol (representation, sign) of his or her religion. You might say that a person's religious "package" is worn inside out. Only the person inside can see it. They have to choose to tell you what their beliefs are. Otherwise, you can't be sure.

Differences in religions seem to center around how each religion sees and worships God. Everybody sees God in his or her own way. Everybody worships in his or her own way.

I spoke with Yamilee, age fifteen, who shared:

"I am Christian. Episcopalian Christian. I go to church every Sunday. I've been going every Sunday since I was in nursery. I'm not like other people that pray every time something bad happens. I'm constantly praying. I read my Bible. I take my Bible everywhere I go. Like, I go to school and I read it on the train.

I'm in the choir and I'm an acolyte. In my church, we have crosses and candles being held down the aisle. So we carry one of the crosses or we'll be a candle bearer. We help the priest with the services. When I'm an acolyte, I feel much closer to God. We also have a youth group and we go lots of places. Every year we have retreats. We have fun, but we also talk about God and how He helps us and why people do what they do.

I strongly believe in God. I was taught from my parents and everyone never to say the Lord's name in vain. And never to judge anyone. But that's kind of hard to do. I was also taught to lay all my troubles on the Lord and He will help me out. I grew up depending on the Lord."

Danielle, age fourteen, shared:

Being a Jewish teenager, it's hard to be the minority around Christmas time and when all your Christian and Catholic friends are going to church. But on a day-to-day basis, my religion doesn't really affect what people think of me.

Although I'm not really religious, religion is a part of my life and I can see myself wanting to carry on tradition and raise my children as I've been raised religiously.

All religions are pulled together in my school. All the Presbyterian kids are friends with all the other Presbyterian kids. All the Jewish kids are closer with the Jewish kids. But basically, when people look for friendship, religion is not the first thing that you judge about a person. I think at our age, religion doesn't matter that much. You may be drawn to people more who are like you, but I don't think people our age discriminate that much. I don't think religion is a big problem.

When my grandmother died, I really had a hard time. And I needed some kind of backbone to fall back on, which was my religion. I had a hard time dealing with the situation. So I talked with my rabbi and members of my Jewish community. It helped me a lot. And it helped me in getting some structure in my life—something to believe in.

I also spoke with Everett, age twenty, who told me:

Having grown up exposed to a variety of different religions—in my childhood, I grew up within the Methodist religion, going to a Methodist Church, then attended an Evangelical Free Church throughout my high school years, and most recently, I've spent three years at different Catholic colleges—my beliefs come from a true relationship with an ultimate Being. Not necessarily even putting a label as "God," but with a definite establishment or identification of someone else, a higher Being, that I can call my own and communicate with on my own, at my own level. Whether it be through quiet time and reflection, a prayer while driving down the highway, or just different things in society that remind me of something or someone I care about and then saying a prayer for them, and communicating in a way I want to or feel like at the time (with "God").

More recently, with the loss of my uncle, my first instinct was to run to God. When I think of my uncle, I think of the joys in his life and what it meant to me and how that relates to him being in "heaven" or somewhere, in a place beyond our existence, in some form of eternal life—with his spirit and his being in my heart.

And I spoke with a women who talked with me about her granddaughter who is studying in Israel and the meaning of having faith. She read to me from her granddaughter's recent letter, "I went mountain climbing and I watched sunrise from the top of one. After you've seen what God has done in nature, it's easy to see that God can do anything."

Some people feel they have a very close relationship with God. Some people are not so close, and others have no relationship at all. Some people worship at home, attend religious services, and live a religious life according to their beliefs. Other people attend religious services and go through the motions of doing religious things, but they really don't feel it inside. For instance, they may just worship because their parents tell them to. Still others have religious feelings but worship only in a very private way. They never go to religious services, but they believe there is a God. There are also people who have no belief in God.

Sometimes people from other cultures worship in a way that may seem interesting and exciting. You can take some books out of your school or public library or have your parent check the Internet with you. If you've ever traveled to a foreign land or if you live in a big city, you might already have had a chance to learn about other religious differences.

When Religious Differences Get in the Way

The religious part of a person can be very powerful. Strong enough to break close friendships, strong enough to burn buildings, strong enough to burn people, strong enough to separate nations.

Some people are able to see past any differences and relate to the person for who he or she is. But there are others who taunt, tease, call names, and paint disrespectful symbols on houses of worship.

When people strike out at different religions, it's often because of ignorance and prejudice—just hating for the sake of hating, perhaps even feeling superior (better than others) or threatened—simply because the beliefs of others are different from their own. People may also strike out at others because they have tremendous anger at not being able to feel good about themselves and good about their lives. And they blame certain religious groups for their problems. This type of behavior is called *scapegoating*.

Some people scapegoat those of different racial backgrounds, religions, or nationalities; some scapegoat homosexuals.

If you ever feel the urge to lash out at people because of their differences from you it's important for you to stop, think, and ask yourself, "Who and what am I really angry at?" And, "Why?" I urge you to sit and talk with an adult who can help you deal with your feelings.

It's time for all people to learn to live with each other in peace, respecting each person's right to believe and to worship as he or she pleases.

Rich or Poor, and Where You Live

Seventeen-year-old Meghan said:

> There are some rich people that you'd never know are rich. Other rich people make it a point to talk about their boat and their big cars. They'll make it a point to say, "You're poor and I'm rich." When they throw it in your face, that's the worst!
>
> I just let them tell me all about their stuff. I don't say, "I have this," or "I have that, too." I just let them talk. I know I'm comfortable and I'm happy.
>
> I have a friend whose grandmother paid for everything so she could travel and go to college. She would dig that into me. She knew that every penny I worked for goes into the bank so I could save up for going someplace.

She would tell me that she toured Europe and all the other places where she's been, and I'd just say to her, "That's great. I'll have fun, too."

Sometimes the comparisons don't have to be that dramatic. It can simply be an excuse that you feel you have to make if your friends come home with you. "Oh, don't mind the empty room, my parents are fixing it up." "Oh, I hate my room."

Some kids are even embarrassed by being rich, because it makes them seem different. Vicki, age fourteen, was driven to school in a limousine. She told me she made the driver drop her off a block from school, so she could walk in like the rest of the kids.

Handling comparisons about clothes, homes, cars, jewelry, what vacations someone's going on, or where in town someone's home is located can be difficult for kids, whether they have more or less than other kids.

I spoke with Eric, age fifteen, who told me, "There's a big division in our school between kids who come from one side of town and kids who come from the other. I don't understand why everyone can't get along."

It would be great if people would only be concerned with who a person is—instead of judging them by where they live, how much money their family seems to have, or anything else. That way, everyone can be given a fair chance.

Where You Live Is Not Your Fault

First of all, do you feel it fair for any boy or girl to be put down for what his or her parents have or don't have? What kind of control do you think kids have over the home they live in, the vacations they take, or what clothes they can buy?

Some children who live in big mansions would do anything to be able to live in a tiny apartment or anywhere else as long as the family feelings could be there. Big houses can be warm and wonderful or they can be lonely. And small houses can be warm, joyful, and very rich.

It's not the money that's most important, it's the love.
All the money in the world can't buy love if it's not there.

Getting Past Differences

Many kids would not consider themselves or their family prejudiced. It's not that they walk around, looking at other people who are different, saying to themselves, "I wouldn't want to be their friend." Or, "I wouldn't want to have anything to do with them!" It's just that they would never consider that person in the first place.

How do you relate to those who are different from you in some way? It might help you better understand where your feelings come from if you take a few moments to think about:

- What messages have you gotten from your parents, relatives and friends about those who are different? Do you feel they are accepting or non-accepting, comfortable or uncomfortable about these differences? Do you feel you are more or less comfortable or accepting?
- Are you different from most of the kids in your school or neighborhood or more or less the same—and how does that make you feel?
- How much personal contact have you had with those who are different from you? Have you ever had a close friend who is of a different background?
- Have you ever been told that you couldn't invite someone to your home because of their differences? Have you ever been left out because of your own differences?
- Have you ever had a fight—whether with words or fists—because of differences?
- Have you ever teased or put down anyone because they were different? Have you ever laughed at jokes or rude remarks about someone because of their differences? Have you ever been the one others laughed at?
- Have you avoided anyone in your school or community because you didn't think you could relate to that person (or didn't think you wanted to) because of his or her differences?

Whatever your experiences have been, they have helped to bring you to where you are in your feelings today. Most important is that you realize you can stop and consider how you feel. And if you realize that you're not seeing people as people—but only as colors or religions or anything else—you can make a new decision to see others and treat others differently. You can start to give people a new chance.

You can begin to make a difference. For example, if the group at your lunch table starts making fun of someone because of their differences, you don't have to laugh. Your response can help begin to make an impact on those who did laugh.

You can decide to reach out more actively to the people around you, even if you never reached out before. You can start now. You can decide to start making a positive change.

Chapter 26

THE ROAD TO INDEPENDENCE

You'll probably find that the road to becoming an independent adult will be filled with cracks and gravel, rocks and detours. It may even be blocked up by a boulder or two. This is why the growing-up years are often thought of as a time of confusing choices.

I'm going to take the last few pages of this book to give you a chance to think about some choices that can add to your sense of independence, your good feelings about yourself, and how you can make a difference in the lives of others.

Earning and Saving Money

As I've said so many times, there are certain things you can control and other things you can't. It's important to be able to tell the difference.

Earning and saving money is on the "can control" list of things that affect your ability to be—and feel—more independent. You can't control what a parent is able to earn, but you can have some control over what you do for yourself.

Prices are often so high and there are so many basic family needs, that sometimes the only way kids can afford to have a new jacket—or go to the movies, or buy an extra program for the computer, or be able to go out with friends for pizza after school—is to earn some extra cash so they can pay for it themselves.

You may already get an allowance. If you don't and wish you did, this might be a good time to speak with your parent (or other adult you live with) about the possibility.

Whether or not you get an allowance, you might consider what else you can do to earn money. If you're under a certain age, you may not be able to be legally employed (for instance, at a store or factory) in your state, but that doesn't mean you can't work. Paper routes, baby-sitting, shoveling snow, walking dogs, helping with groceries, and mowing lawns are just some of the ways you can still earn money even if you're a bit younger.

You may already know how just putting in some extra effort can pay off in dollars. There are little kids who stand on street corners shouting, "Lemonade!" kids who collect worms that they sell to people who are going fishing, and those who find golf balls in the woods and sell them to passing golfers. All the pennies and nickels can add up. I just paid a high school student to help me type one of the final chapters of this book. There are so many ways to earn money if you're willing to put in the time.

Aside from earning money, you're never too young to start saving money. You might ask your parents if they can arrange with you to open your own bank account. You'd be amazed how savings can add up if you save regularly. That will help give you more freedom to buy and do things.

When you're old enough and find the need to have a checking account too, your parent(s), as well as your bank, will need to explain to you the importance of keeping careful, proper records of each check you write, how much you spend and where, how much money you put into your account—in order to always know your correct balance (the amount of money that is in your account). They'll also explain to you how you can keep the balance up-to-date when you get a monthly statement from the bank.

Along with the idea of earning and saving money is being able to budget (portion out) your spending. You may have already found that money seems to go very quickly if you're not careful about what you spend. Pizza, chocolate chip cookies, hero sandwiches, movies, CDs, ice cream, cosmetics, and anything else that would be on your own personal list—all can add up.

Some kids end up borrowing money from friends. That's fine to do once in a while but can get you deeper and deeper in debt if you do that often. Also, if you don't pay back, some friends find it awkward to ask you to. Even close friends can begin to feel resentful—and may or may not feel they can let you know. That can begin to affect your friendship.

If your friend asks you for money that you simply don't have, can't, or don't wish to lend, remember you can turn your feelings into words and say, "I'd really like to help you out, but I just can't." If your friend owes you money, you can say, "You probably just forgot, but I really could use the five dollars that I lent you last week . . ."

Caring—Making a Difference in the Lives of Others

Even if you have no money to give—you can give your time and make the effort to help people who are in need. Kids have said to me, "There's so much need in the world. I'm just one person. What can I do?" Or, "I'm just a kid. What can I do?" You can do more than you might imagine. It all starts with caring—and wanting to make a difference. The next step is to explore what ways you can give. Then, pick one. And get started. Isn't it great to know you can?

Amanda is now thirteen. She said:

> The first time I helped someone was when I was in the first grade and my first-grade teacher's daughter was dying of cancer. Her daughter didn't have health insurance, so my teacher was using her life savings to try to help pay for all the medical treatment to help save her daughter's life. I felt bad for her. That's when I began to realize that some people are not as fortunate as I was.
>
> So I made wooden reindeers and I raised a thousand dollars selling them for the holidays. I gave the thousand dollars to my teacher to help her pay for her daughter's medical bills. Her daughter did die. But when I gave her that money, it just gave me

that feeling. I was really proud that I was able to raise a thousand dollars for someone else. I mean, I was just a little kid and I raised a thousand dollars. It was such a special feeling.

In second grade, Amanda started collecting new stuffed animals to give to abused and neglected children who are represented by the court system. Amanda said:

I gave them stuffed animals because it's nice for kids to hold on to something warm and cuddly when they tell their sad story in court. And when you think that they don't even have something to comfort them, the stuffed animals are like having a little friend.

Since about third grade, I've been giving to the Children's Home Society. Since then, every Easter, I collect about 200 stuffed animals and give them out at an Easter Party. When I watch the kids get them, they're so happy and grateful. And they're immediately in love with the stuffed animals. It gives me a really good feeling.

I'm going to collect stuffed animals for that society again this year. And, hopefully, I'm going to continue that for a long time.

My parents helped me set up this program. I named it "To Have and to Hug." A friend of my parents designed a logo [a picture representing your company name], which is on my stationery. I have a letter that I give or send out to companies. It explains what I'm doing. If I was in charge of a company, it would probably melt my heart to see these kids and their reactions to these nice stuffed animals.

I ask them for one, two, or as many stuffed animals as they want to give—and tell them that the donation is greatly appreciated by me and the kids.

I also talked to Eric, Amanda's brother, who is seventeen years old. He said:

Once you start doing community service, you get hooked on it. I know that kids are kids and they may not know who to contact or how to get involved, but there are probably programs in each city around the country which offer some type of community service. And it's not something you can give up easily after you see the results.

Certainly, for me, after I started my project and I saw what just shoes—which I took for granted prior to starting this—could mean . . . I never realized shoes could mean so much to kids.

After handing the shoes out at an annual [AN-yoo-ul, once a year] Christmas Party and seeing the kids' reactions, I began to understand that these shoes did more than cover needy feet. They added a sense of pride that too often did not exist before. I've learned that new shoes actually add to these children's self-esteem. Truthfully—the shoes for some of them changed their whole personality around.

Like I said, it's not real easy to just walk away and say, "Okay, I did this community service and I don't need to do it anymore." Because there's always people out there that could use the help of others. And I think if more kids got involved, they would see the benefits of helping others and they, too, would want to participate. It's not only the benefits for who you're helping, but it's also a benefit for the person who is giving of themselves. Because you get such a good feeling inside of you and you want to do it again.

The first years I went around with my mom, I went into the shoe store by myself and asked to speak with the manager. I told him what I was doing and told about the project. And I simply asked, "Would you be able to donate?" That year, we got a big response. This is going to be the fifth year and with over a hundred shoe stores contributing, the project has really grown.

Now shoe stores that may have donated one or two pair the first couple of years are donating maybe four or five pairs. That has made a big difference. From the major shoe companies to local shoe stores, to podiatrist [foot doctor] organizations and individuals wanting to contribute, I have found that the sources are unlimited.

I asked Eric how he first got started. He explained:

At first, when I started—before I actually began the project, I was given the name of a family which had six boys. We (my parents and I) contacted them and arranged to take them out to lunch and then to a shoe store in the mall. When I told these boys they could pick out any pair of shoes that they wanted and I would buy it for them—you would not believe their reaction. I still can't get over their response. At the beginning of the day, when I first saw them, they were shy and very quiet. And by the end of the day, they were running up and down the mall, laughing, yelling, there was a dramatic change in their attitude. I never knew that shoes could do that.

So after I saw the reaction of these boys, I decided I wanted to do this for more kids. If I could make six kids so happy, why not sixty or six hundred, or maybe someday, six thousand.

Obviously there's some effort involved, there has to be. But for the effort that I put in, and the satisfaction that I get out, there's no comparison.

It was especially meaningful to me to learn that when Eric took those six boys for the shoes, he used some of his own money that he had received as a gift from his Bar Mitzvah (a special religious ceremony which ushers thirteen-year-old boys into adulthood in the Jewish religion; for girls, it's called a Bat Mitzvah). From that experience of giving on his own to those six boys, he started his "Stepp'n Up" project with the help of his parents. This project has already provided over a thousand pairs of donated new shoes to needy children. For his efforts, Eric was recently recognized through the Noxema Company's Extraordinary Teen Awards Program, as one of America's top five outstanding teenagers.

Emma, eleven years old, also has given of herself to make a special impact on the lives of others. She said:

When I was in fifth grade, I saw the movie *Philadelphia*. You know how some movies touch your heart? You have different emotions . . . well, that one was really sad and I cried. And I decided to raise money for AIDS.

So, we started a school store, called "Have a Heart Store" because it was around Valentine's Day. It sold school supplies and snacks and we made a thousand dollars. We had a big celebration with big checks. We gave part of the money to AMFAR (American AIDS Research Foundation), we gave part to VNS, the Visiting Nurse Service of New Mexico, and we gave the rest to the Whitney Project. In New Mexico, this project arranges for school classes to have a pen pal with someone who has AIDS. In the first year, one class raised enough money for a girl from Chicago, who was named Whitney, to fly out and visit with her Dad. Whitney has AIDS, and the project is named after her. And now it's a nationwide program.

Our class was very proud of what we did. We also went to Head Start and visited the little kids once a week, and now I'm a volunteer at the Nursing Home and the Salvation Army.

A few weeks ago, I was a finalist for the Amy Biehl Youth Spirit Award. Amy Biehl went to South Africa to try to help people and she was beaten to death. And so her family started a foundation called the Amy Biehl Foundation. Every time she saw something on the news, Amy had to help. And so my mother nominated me. Her family says that I reminded them of her.

I've also been walking AIDS walks since I'm six. This year, I had to do it on crutches because I had a foot operation.

You have to like yourself. You have to be confident in yourself. You have to let the world know that you want to do a good thing. And then you go do it. If you like yourself, you can like others. Caring makes the world go around.

I spoke with Amanda's and Eric's mother, who said:

My husband and I were parents for fourteen years, with three children, before we learned—through our six-year-old daughter's desire to help her teacher—that we had an obligation to educate our children about community servcies and how and what to do to help others.

Even when kids want to help, they often don't know how. Don't be afraid to ask someone, to get ideas from other people. Rabbis and priests and other religious figures are wonderful for giving suggestions. Call upon people in the community for assistance and ideas. They've been there. They deal with this all the time; they have the experience that we don't.

There's no question, it has to be very much of a family project. When Eric and Amanda were younger and went around for the shoes, we coached them on what to say, we discussed what they were going to wear when they went into the stores. We had stationery printed for each of our kids with a logo. The printing costs were donated by printing companies.

Every time the kids did something, we always sent out a press release [article to let the local newspapers know what they did]—not to give publicity to the kids, but when you ask a store owner to give you stuffed animals or shoes, and they see what you're doing is in the newspapers, they know their donations are going where they're supposed to go. Newspapers are always looking for articles like this. If you write it up and send in a description of what you're doing, they'll often print it.

We've told our kids "You have to do this [help others]." Did they fight us? Not one single bit. Are they getting the message that they can help? Absolutely. We, as parents, say, "We're the coaches. We have the football and we're going to throw it to you to get a touchdown." And when they cross that line—when they see what a difference they can make—there's such a feeling of "Oh my God." And when they get that feeling, they're going to want to do it again.

If your family hasn't ever been involved in working together to give to those who are in need, this is a wonderful time to start. You might even suggest having a special family meeting or talk about this at dinner. You might read this section with your parents to help figure out ideas about how you all can get involved with community service, if you haven't already.

You can contact local organizations, religious groups, agencies, hospitals, nursing homes, youth services, and other institutions in your area. You can look into what's being done for the homeless, if there's a nearby soup kitchen where you can volunteer to help out. Perhaps there are Big Brother or Big Sister–type programs or agencies that would appreciate your help in answering phones or actually being a Big Sister or Big Brother. Teachers are also good to contact. In many public and private schools (including colleges and universities), kids can't graduate without a certain number of hours of community service. So someone in your school system can also be a mentor (a leader, coach, or teacher) to assist you to set things up.

On a very personal level, you can offer to buy groceries for a sick neighbor. You can bake cookies and bring them to a senior citizen center. You can offer to keep someone company just to talk. Whether a person is younger or older, the list of ways to make a difference in the lives of others is endless. And if you have your own children some day, you'll be able to teach them what giving can mean.

Eric started by saying, "I'd like to help. What do you need? What can I do to help?" You, your family members, and friends can ask the same question. That can get you started.

Putting It All Together

I hope by now you realize that you have ability to make choices that can be creative, challenging, and rewarding. You also know that some choices will be harder than others. But no matter what, you have the ability to roll with whatever happens, keep a positive attitude, and try to stay in control of what you allow yourself to do.

If one path doesn't seem to be right, you can choose to try another. You even have the strength to build your own road when there seems to be no other way.

There may be many situations and people who will try to influence you to stray from the path that will lead you to independence. They may question your direction and tell you you're making your decisions the wrong way. If you find you're too afraid to make decisions because you think that you'll make a mistake, just remember that mistakes are a part of life. Everyone makes them. Remember also, that it's possible your decision could have very positive results. And if you take a chance on a decision and turn out to be wrong, you can learn from each experience and be wiser the next time. (Just try not to make the same mistake more than once!)

Remember that not everything will work out as you plan or hope. That's the way life is. Sometimes it's up, sometimes it's down. Some days will be easier than others.

Try not to get too stuck and frustrated about things you can't change. If you find yourself agonizing over what you feel you shouldn't have said, or should have known or shouldn't have done, take a break in the action. Take some deep breaths and call a time-out. Remind yourself that what's done is done. You can't go backwards. But you *can* accept what took place, learn from it, decide not to let it hold you back, and begin to move on from there.

So, for example, if you went to the movies with your girlfriend instead of studying for your exam, you can't turn back the clock. If you said something to your best friend that you're sorry you said, the words are already out. If you went further sexually than you realize is right for you, you can't change what you already did.

But you can learn from everything. You can leave more time for studying next time. You can say new words to deal with what you said to your friend. You can choose not to allow yourself to go as far sexually next time. You can go forward, and be wiser from your experience.

The more decisions you make, the more you'll be able to build confidence and learn to trust your senses. You don't have to worry about scheduling in "maturing" or "growing" at ten-thirty on Friday mornings. Your growth will happen naturally, in its own time.

Just remember to go easy. Take things one day at a time. And don't forget to have fun along the way!

Ellen Rosenberg may be contacted by writing to:

Growing Up Feeling Good
P.O. Box 1223
Long Beach, NY 11561-0798

TOLL-FREE HELPLINES

Times given are Eastern Standard Time. Central Standard Time is one hour earlier; Mountain Time is two hours earlier; and Pacific Standard Time is three hours earlier. If you're not sure how to figure the time, ask someone to help you, or dial 0 and ask an operator.

Al-Anon Family Groups/Alateen: 1-800-344-2666. Provides support group information for friends and families of alcoholics. You will be referred to a number in your home state. Open 9:00 A.M. to 4:30 P.M. Eastern Standard Time (you can leave a message on their tape at other times)

Girls and Boys Town National Hotline: 1-800-448-3000. For boys, girls, parents, and families. Offers help with any problem or serious concern (including physical and sexual abuse, drug abuse, alcoholism, family problems, parent/child conflicts, peer relationships, running away, school problems, depression, suicide). Open 24 hours a day, 7 days a week

CDC National AIDS Hotline: 1-800-342-2437. Offers information and referrals for HIV/AIDS and related issues. Referrals can be made on a local and national basis. English-speaking hotline open 24 hours a day, 7 days a week. Spanish-speaking hotline: 1-800-344-7432. Open 8:00 A.M. to 2:00 A.M. Eastern Standard time) Hotline for the Hearing Impaired or Deaf: 1-800-243-7889. Open Monday through Friday, 10:00 A.M. to 10:00 P.M. Eastern Standard Time

Crisis Hotline: 1-800-444-9999. Offers help with alcohol or any type of drug problem, addictions, depression, suicidal feelings, anorexia, and bulimia—and other serious personal problems; will provide assessment and referrals; will offer to talk to your family. Open 9:30 A.M. to 2:15 A.M. Eastern Standard Time

CHILDHELP I.O.F. National Child Abuse Hotline: 1-800-4-A-CHILD (1-800-422-4453). Offers crisis intervention, counseling, information and referrals for abused children (and adults); runaways (offers runaway shelter information); dealing with rape, teenage pregnancy, gay and lesbian issues; youth services (such as counseling and other referrals for kids); and childrens' legal rights. Can also give numbers for missing childrens' organizations around the U.S. Open 24 hours a day, 7 days a week

STD Hotline; CDC, Atlanta, Georgia: 1-800-227-8922. Can answer questions and talk with you about different sexually transmitted diseases. Offers referrals to free or low-cost clinics, support groups, and crisis lines. Open Monday through Friday, 8:00 A.M. to 11:00 P.M. Eastern Standard Time

If any of these numbers change, dial 1-800-555-1212 for new information. You can also dial your local area code plus 555-1212 for local information and information in your state.

Ellen Rosenberg's Growing Up Feeling Good elementary and secondary school student assembly programs and parent education, and her LIFE 101 programs for college and university audiences are nationally acclaimed. She has given presentations to more than a million students, staff and parents in forty-six states since 1976 and has established herself as one of the foremost authorities on the real issues facing today's kids.

The author of *Get A Clue! A Parents' Guide to Understanding and Communicating with Your Preteen*, Ellen has been an educator since 1965. She holds a master's degree in education, is certified as a sex educator and has taught Health and Human Sexuality at the junior high school, high school and college levels. Mother of a grown son and daughter, Ellen lives with her husband in Long Beach, New York.